FIX-IT and FORGET-IT®

SLOW COOKER

Champion Recipes

450 OF OUR VERY BEST RECIPES

PHYLLIS GOOD

Good Books
New York, New York

FIX-IT AND FORGET-IT® SLOW COOKER CHAMPION RECIPES

Copyright © 2016 by Good Books, an imprint of Skyhorse Publishing, Inc.

tographs for the following sections by Timothy W. Lawrence: Chicken and Turkey; Pastas, Grains, and Vegetarian; Soups, tews, and Chilis; Breakfasts and Brunches; Appetizers, Snacks, Spreads, and Beverages; Everyday From-Scratch Basics

tographs for the following sections by Dalila Tarhuni: Beef; Pork; Vegetables and Side Dishes; Breads; Sweets and Desserts

Photographs on pages 4, 7, and 598 by Jeremy Hess

Special thanks to Kitchen Sync in Brattleboro, VT, for use of many of the props photographed in these pages. Visit Kitchen Sync at www.facebook.com/kitchensyncvt

All rights reserved. No part of this book may be reproduced in any manner without the express written consent of the publisher, except in the case of brief excerpts in critical reviews or articles. All inquiries should be addressed to Good Books, 307 West 36th Street, 11th Floor, New York, NY 10018.

Good Books books may be purchased in bulk at special discounts for sales promotion, corporate gifts, fund-raising, or educational purposes. Special editions can also be created to specifications. For details, contact the Special Sales Department, Good Books, 307 West 36th Street, 11th Floor, New York, NY 10018 or info@skyhorsepublishing.com.

Good Books is an imprint of Skyhorse Publishing, Inc.®, a Delaware corporation.

Visit our website at www.goodbooks.com.

10 9 8 7 6 5 4 3 2

Library of Congress Cataloging-in-Publication Data is available on file.

ISBN: 978-1-68099-125-3
Ebook ISBN: 978-1-68099-136-9

Cover design by Laura Klynstra

Printed in China

Limit of Liability/Disclaimer of Warranty: The publisher and author have made their best effort in preparing this book with care and accuracy, and it is presented in good faith. But they make no representations or warranties with respect to the completeness or accuracy of the contents of this book. Sales representatives may not create or extend any warranty either verbally or in sales materials about this book. The advice and strategies contained in these materials may not be suitable for your situation. Consult with a professional where appropriate. Neither the author nor the publisher shall be liable for any commercial damages or loss of profit, including but not limited to special, consequential, or incidental damages.

Table of Contents

Welcome to *Fix-It and Forget-It Slow Cooker Champion Recipes!*   1

Hints for Cooking with a Slow Cooker   3

Your Slow Cooker Guidebook   5

Chicken and Turkey   9

Beef   85

Pork   153

Pastas, Grains, and Vegetarian   219

Soups, Stews, and Chilis   279

Vegetables and Side Dishes   341

Breads   415

Breakfasts and Brunches   439

Sweets and Desserts   465

Appetizers, Snacks, Spreads, and Beverages   529

Everyday From-Scratch Basics   559

Indexes

Complete Recipe and Ingredient Index   584

"Quick and Easy" Recipe Index   596

Metric Equivalent Measurements   597

About the Author   598

ker in stages. We've got those recipes
e, too.

So find the recipes that match your
od—or the time you have available to
p.

ake This Book Your Own

ite in it. Next to a recipe, note the
king time that worked for you. Star
recipes you—and the people at your
le—like. In the Index, give a grade to
h recipe you've made, so you can see
winners at a glance.

e Good Cooks' Pass-It-On
adition

od cooks love to share their recipes.
ey don't possess them; they pass them
.

This collection is rich because of all
e home cooks who generously offered
eir favorite recipes, so that all of us

could fix satisfyingly delicious food at
home.

Thanks to each of you who has shared
your gems. This book holds your precious
food traditions, and we are all grateful.

Thank you, too, to the cooks who
tested and evaluated these recipes. Your
comments, as well as those from the family and friends around your dinner tables,
were invaluable.

Welcome to the Community!

You'll love cooking, hosting, and eating
from this treasure of good food. *Fix-It
and Forget-It Slow Cooker Champion
Recipes* makes it possible for you to sit
at the table together with your family
and friends, around astonishingly tasty
food, no matter how wild and crazy
your day.

Sunday Roast Chicken

Ruth A. Feister
Narvon, PA

Makes 4–5 servings
Prep. Time: 30–35 minutes
Cooking Time: 3–4 hours
Ideal slow-cooker size: 6- or 7-qt. *oval*

Seasoning Mix:

1 Tbsp. salt

2 tsp. paprika

1½ tsp. onion powder

1½ tsp. garlic powder

1½ tsp. dried basil

1 tsp. dry mustard

1 tsp. cumin

2 tsp. pepper

½ tsp. dried thyme

½ tsp. savory

¼ stick (2 Tbsp.) butter

2 cups chopped onions

1 cup chopped green bell pepper

3-4-lb. roasting chicken

¼ cup flour

1-2 cups chicken stock

1. Combine Seasoning Mix ingredients in small bowl.

2. Melt butter over high heat in skillet. When butter starts to sizzle, add chopped onions and peppers, and 3 Tbsp. seasoning mix.

3. Cook until onions are golden brown. Cool.

4. Stuff cavity of chicken with cooled vegetables.

5. Sprinkle outside of chicken with 1 Tbsp. seasoning mix. Rub in well so it sticks.

6. Grease interior of slow cooker.

7. Place chicken in large slow-cooker crock.

8. Cover. Cook on Low 3–4 hours, or until instant-read thermometer registers 160°–165° when stuck in thigh, but not against bone.

9. Empty vegetable stuffing and juices into saucepan. Keep chicken warm on platter, covered with foil. Whisk in flour and 1 cup stock from slow cooker.

10. Cook over high heat until thickened. Add more stock if you prefer a thinner gravy.

Why I like this recipe—
The first time I served this dish was when we had family visiting us from Mississippi. We had a wonderful time sitting around a large table, sharing many laughs and catching up on the years since our last visit.

Garlic Lime Chicken

Loretta Krahn
Mountain Lake, MN

Makes 5 servings
Prep. Time: 10 minutes
Cooking Time: 4 hours
Ideal slow-cooker size: 5-qt.

skinless chicken thighs

½ cup soy sauce

¼–⅓ cup lime juice, according to your taste
   preference

Tbsp. Worcestershire sauce

garlic cloves, minced, *or* 1 tsp. garlic powder

½ tsp. dry mustard

½ tsp. ground pepper

Why I like this recipe—
This was the first recipe my son made in
the slow cooker. It's so easy, and he was so
proud of himself that evening at supper when
everyone enjoyed it.

1. Grease interior of slow-cooker crock.

2. Place chicken in slow cooker.

3. Combine remaining ingredients in a
bowl. Pour over chicken.

4. Cover. Cook on Low 4 hours, or until
instant-read thermometer registers 160°–165°
when stuck in thighs, but not against bone.

Garlic Mushroom Chicken Thighs

Elaine Vigoda
Rochester, NY

Makes 6 servings
Prep. Time: 15 minutes
Cooking Time: 4 hours
Ideal slow-cooker size: 5-qt.

boneless, skinless chicken thighs

Tbsp. flour

-10 garlic cloves, peeled and very lightly
crushed

Tbsp. oil

¼ lb. fresh mushrooms, any combination of
varieties, cut into bite-sized pieces or slices

⅓ cup balsamic vinegar

1¼ cups chicken broth

1-2 bay leaves

½ tsp. dried thyme, *or* 4 sprigs fresh thyme

2 tsp. apricot jam

1. Grease interior of slow-cooker crock.

2. Place flour in strong plastic bag without
any holes. One by one, put each thigh in bag,
hold the bag shut, and shake it to flour the
thighs fully.

3. Place thighs in crock. If you need to
make a second layer, stagger the pieces so
they don't directly overlap.

4. If you have time, sauté garlic in oil in
skillet just until it begins to brown.

5. Sprinkle garlic over thighs, including
those on the bottom layer.

6. Scatter cut-up mushrooms over thighs,
too, remembering those on the bottom layer.

7. Mix remaining ingredients together in a
bowl, stirring to break up the jam.

8. When well mixed, pour into the cooker
along the edges so you don't wash the
vegetables off the chicken pieces.

9. Cover. Cook on Low for 4 hours, or until
an instant-read meat thermometer registers
160°–165° when stuck into thighs.

10. Serve meat topped with vegetables,
with sauce spooned over.

Why I like this recipe—
My uncle owns a mushroom-growing
business, and he gave us this recipe with a
sack of mushrooms. We really like it and
we've made it often since then.

Chicken Dijon Dinner

Barbara Stutzman
Arcola, IL

Makes 4–6 servings
Prep. Time: 20 minutes
Cooking Time: 4 hours
Ideal slow-cooker size: 5-qt.

2 lbs. boneless, skinless chicken thighs

2 garlic cloves, minced

1 Tbsp. olive oil

6 Tbsp. white wine vinegar

4 Tbsp. soy sauce

4 Tbsp. Dijon mustard

1 lb. sliced mushrooms

Why I like this recipe—
This makes a delicious sauce. I always serve some mashed potatoes or noodles to catch it!

1. Grease interior of slow-cooker crock.

2. Place thighs in crock. If you need to add a second layer, stagger the pieces so they don't directly overlap each other.

3. Stir together garlic, oil, vinegar, soy sauce, and mustard until well mixed.

4. Gently stir in mushrooms.

5. Spoon sauce into crock, making sure to cover all thighs with some of the sauce.

6. Cover. Cook on Low for 4 hours, or until instant-read meat thermometer registers 160° when stuck in center of thighs.

7. Serve chicken topped with sauce.

Honey-Mustard Chicken (Deluxe Version)

Barbara Stutzman
Arcola, IL

Makes 6–8 servings
Prep. Time: 30 minutes
Cooking Time: 4 hours
Ideal slow-cooker size: 5-qt.

2–3 lbs. boneless, skinless chicken thighs

1 large onion, sliced, about ½ cup

3 garlic cloves, sliced

2 Tbsp. honey

¼ cup Dijon mustard

1 Tbsp. coarse-grain mustard

2 Tbsp. red wine vinegar

2 tsp. olive oil

1 tsp. coarsely ground black pepper

pinch cayenne pepper

½ cup water

2 green onions, sliced on an angle, for garnish, *optional*

1. Grease interior of slow-cooker crock.

2. Place chicken in crock. If you need to add a second layer, stagger the pieces so they don't directly overlap each other.

3. Mix onion and garlic slices, honey, mustards, vinegar, olive oil, peppers, and water together in a bowl.

4. Spoon sauce over chicken.

5. Cover. Cook on Low 4 hours, or until instant-read meat thermometer registers 160°–165° when stuck into center of thighs.

6. Serve chicken topped with sauce and garnished with green onions if you wish.

Why I like this recipe—

We love this chicken for family suppers, but it's popular with guests, too. That's when I use the green onion garnish, even though my family teases me.

Honey-Mustard Chicken (Quick & Easy Version)

Mary Kennell
Roanoke, IL

Makes 4 servings
Prep. Time: 15 minutes
Cooking Time: 4 hours
Ideal slow-cooker size: 4-qt.

4 boneless, skinless chicken thighs

¼ stick (2 Tbsp.) butter, melted

2 Tbsp. honey

2 tsp. prepared mustard

2 tsp. curry powder

salt and pepper, *optional*

1. Spray slow cooker with nonstick cooking spray and add chicken.

2. Mix butter, honey, mustard, and curry powder together in a small bowl. Pour sauce over chicken.

3. Cover and cook on Low 4 hours, or until instant-read meat thermometer registers 160°–165° when stuck into center of thighs.

Variations:
1. Use a small fryer chicken, quartered, instead of breasts or thighs.
—Frances Kruba, Dundalk, MD

2. Instead of curry powder, use ½ tsp. paprika.
—Jena Hammond, Traverse City, MI

Honey Garlic Chicken

Donna Treloar
Muncie, IN

Makes 4 servings
Prep. Time: 10 minutes
Cooking Time: 4 hours
Ideal slow-cooker size: 4-qt.

4 boneless, skinless chicken thighs

⅓ cup honey

1 cup ketchup

2 Tbsp. soy sauce

4 garlic cloves, minced

1. Grease interior of slow-cooker crock.

2. Place chicken thighs in crock.

3. In a bowl, mix together honey, ketchup, soy sauce, and minced garlic. Pour over chicken.

4. Cover. Cook on Low 4 hours or until instant-read meat thermometer registers 160°–165° when inserted into center of thighs.

5. Serve chicken and sauce together.

Variation:
Add sliced onions to the bottom of the crock before putting chicken in.

Good go-alongs with this recipe:
White, brown, or wild rice.

Lemony Greek Chicken

Ruth Shank
Monroe, GA

Makes 6 servings
Prep. Time: 15 minutes
Cooking Time: 4 hours
Ideal slow-cooker size: 4- or 5-qt.

6 boneless, skinless chicken thighs

2 medium onions, cut in quarters

¼ cup lemon juice

2 tsp. dried oregano

½ tsp. garlic powder

¼ tsp. black pepper

2 Tbsp. olive oil

Why I like this recipe—
We enjoy this chicken with pasta salad out on the deck in the summer. One of these years, I want to grow a whole variety of herbs. It would be fun to experiment with using them in this chicken (and other recipes).

1. Grease interior of slow-cooker crock.

2. Place thighs in cooker. If you need to make a second layer, stagger the pieces so they don't completely overlap each other.

3. Tuck onion quarters in around the chicken pieces.

4. In a small bowl, mix together lemon juice, oregano, garlic powder, and pepper. Pour over chicken and onions, making sure that all of the pieces are coated with the glaze.

5. Drizzle thighs and onions with olive oil.

6. Cover. Cook on Low 4 hours, or until an instant-read meat thermometer shows 160°–165° when inserted in thickest part of thighs.

QUICK
and
EASY

Tangy Chicken

Marilyn Kurtz
Willow Street, PA

Makes 6-8 servings
Prep. Time: 15 minutes
Cooking Time: 4-5 hours
Ideal slow-cooker size: 5-qt.

16-oz. jar chunky salsa, as hot or mild as you like

half an envelope dry taco seasoning mix

½ cup peach *or* apricot preserves

4 lbs. boneless, skinless chicken thighs

1. Grease interior of slow-cooker crock.

2. Pour salsa into cooker, and then stir in taco seasoning and preserves, mixing well.

3. Place chicken down into sauce, making sure all pieces are covered as much as possible.

4. Cover. Cook on Low 4–5 hours, or until instant-read meat thermometer registers 160°–165° when stuck in center of thighs.

5. Serve over cooked rice.

TIP

We like to serve this with a side of steamed broccoli.

Chicken Marengo

Bernadette Veenstra
Rockford, MI

Makes 6 servings
Prep. Time: 20 minutes
Cooking Time: 4 hours
Ideal slow-cooker size: 5-qt.

6 boneless, skinless chicken thighs
1 Tbsp. flour
¾ tsp. dried basil
¼ tsp. garlic powder
¾–1 tsp. salt, according to taste
¼ tsp. black pepper
½ cup white wine *or* chicken broth
2 Tbsp. tomato paste
2 14½ -oz. cans stewed tomatoes
1 onion, cut into 8 wedges
½ coarsely chopped green bell pepper
½ cup black olives slices

1. Grease interior of slow-cooker crock.

2. Arrange thighs in cooker. If you need to make a second layer, stagger the pieces so they don't directly overlap each other.

3. In a medium-sized bowl, mix together flour, basil, garlic powder, salt, pepper, wine, tomato paste, tomatoes, and onions. Pour over chicken.

4. Cover. Cook on Low for 4 hours, or until instant-read meat thermometer registers 160°–165° when stuck into the thighs.

5. Thirty minutes before end of cooking time, stir chopped bell pepper and olives into sauce.

6. Serve meat and vegetables over buttered noodles.

Why I like this recipe—
This is an unusual sauce for chicken, but always well received. The chicken comes out very tender and flavorful. I serve it with buttered noodles, but my neighbor who gave me the recipe serves it with French bread.

Maui Chicken

John D. Allen
Rye, CO

Makes 6 servings
Prep. Time: 20 minutes
Cooking Time: 4 hours
Ideal slow-cooker size: 5-qt.

6 boneless, skinless chicken thighs

2 Tbsp. oil

14½-oz. can chicken broth

20-oz. can pineapple chunks

¼ cup vinegar

2 Tbsp. brown sugar

2 tsp. soy sauce

1 garlic clove, minced

1 medium green bell pepper, chopped

3 Tbsp. cornstarch

¼ cup water

1. Grease interior of slow-cooker crock.

2. If you have time, brown chicken in oil in skillet until lightly browned. Transfer chicken to slow cooker. If you have to make two layers, stagger pieces so they don't directly overlap each other.

3. Combine remaining ingredients, except cornstarch and water, in bowl. Pour over chicken, remembering to spoon sauce over thighs on bottom layer.

4. Cover. Cook on Low 4 hours, or until instant-read meat thermometer registers 160°–165° when stuck in center of thighs.

TIP

Serve over rice.

5. Ten minutes before end of cooking time, dissolve cornstarch in water in a small bowl. When smooth, stir into slow cooker until dissolved. Continue cooking until sauce thickens.

Basil Chicken

**Sarah Niessen,
Akron, PA**

Makes 4–6 servings
Prep. Time: 15 minutes
Cooking Time: 4–5 hours
Ideal slow-cooker size: 5- or 6-qt.

1 lb. baby carrots

2 medium onions, sliced

1–2 cups celery slices and leaves

3-lb. chicken, cut up

½ cup chicken broth, *or* white cooking wine

2 tsp. salt

½ tsp. black pepper

1 tsp. dried basil

1. Grease interior of slow-cooker crock.

2. Place carrots, onions, and celery in bottom of slow cooker.

3. Add chicken.

4. Pour broth over chicken.

5. Sprinkle with salt, pepper, and basil.

6. Cover. Cook on Low 4–5 hours, or until instant-read meat thermometer registers 160°–165° when stuck in center of thighs (but not against bone) and vegetables are as tender as you like them.

Why I like this recipe—

This is a favorite busy-day supper. All I do when I get home is cook some pasta or slice some French bread, and dinner is served!

Chicken with Raspberry Jam

Pat Bechtel
Dillsburg, PA

Makes 5 servings
Prep. Time: 10 minutes
Cooking Time: 4¼ hours
Ideal slow-cooker size: 4- or 5-qt.

Tbsp. soy sauce

⅓ cup red raspberry fruit spread *or* jam

boneless, skinless chicken thighs

Tbsp. cornstarch

Tbsp. cold water

1. Grease interior of slow-cooker crock.

2. Mix soy sauce and raspberry spread or jam together in a small bowl until well blended.

3. Brush chicken with the sauce and place in slow cooker. Spoon remainder of the sauce over top.

4. Cook on Low 4 hours, or until instant-read meat thermometer registers 160°–165° when stuck in center of thighs.

5. Mix together cornstarch and cold water in a small bowl until smooth. Then remove chicken to a serving platter and keep warm. Turn slow cooker to High and stir in cornstarch and water to thicken.

6. When thickened and bubbly, after about 10–15 minutes, spoon sauce over chicken, then serve.

Why I like this recipe—
I let my kids eat these with their fingers when we don't have guests because the kids like to lick the sauce off their fingers! Messy, and so delicious.

Chicken with Fresh Fruit

Robin Schrock
Millersburg, OH

Makes 6 servings
Prep. Time: 20 minutes
Cooking Time: 4 hours
Ideal slow-cooker size: 5-qt.

2 Tbsp. olive oil

¾ tsp. salt

¾ tsp. black pepper

½ tsp. garlic powder

6 large boneless, skinless chicken thighs

12 oz. canned pineapple tidbits, drained,
    or 1½ cups fresh pineapple chunks

1½ cups fresh strawberries, quartered

2 small kiwi, peeled, quartered, and sliced

⅓ cup chopped red onions

4-oz. can chopped green chilies

1½ tsp. cornstarch

½ cup orange juice

1. Grease interior of slow-cooker crock.

2. In a small bowl, combine oil, salt, pepper, and garlic powder.

3. Rub the mixture on all sides of each thigh.

4. Lay thighs into crock. If you need to make a second layer, stagger the pieces so they don't directly overlap each other.

5. Cover. Cook on Low 4 hours, or until instant-read meat thermometer inserted in thighs registers 160°–165°.

6. While chicken is cooking place pineapple pieces, strawberries, kiwi, onions, and chilies in bowl. Stir together gently.

7. In a small bowl, mix cornstarch and orange juice until smooth. Stir mixture into small saucepan. Cook, stirring continuously until mixture thickens, about 2 minutes.

8. Stir sauce into fruit.

9. Place cooked chicken on platter. Spoon fruit mixture over each thigh, making sure not to brush off the rub, and serve.

Why I like this recipe—

I love fruit with meat, and this recipe caught my eye right away with its unusual combination. Turns out, it's delicious and very pretty on the plate since the fruit is added at the end.

Curried Chicken with Fruit

**Marlene Bogard
Newton, KS**

Makes 5 servings
Prep. Time: 20 minutes
Cooking Time: 4¼–5¼ hours
Ideal slow-cooker size: 5-qt.

½–3½-lb. fryer chicken, cut up

alt to taste

epper to taste

 Tbsp. curry powder

 garlic clove, crushed *or* minced

 Tbsp. melted butter

½ cup chicken broth, *or* 1 chicken bouillon
  cube dissolved in ½ cup water

 Tbsp. onion, chopped fine

 9-oz. can sliced peaches

½ cup pitted dried plums

 Tbsp. cornstarch

 Tbsp. cold water

TIPS

Serve over rice. Offer
peanuts, shredded coconut,
and fresh pineapple chunks
as condiments.

1. Grease interior of slow-cooker crock.

2. Sprinkle chicken with salt and pepper.
Arrange in slow cooker.

3. Combine curry, garlic, butter, broth, and
onions in bowl.

4. Drain peaches, reserving syrup. Add
½ cup syrup to curry mixture. Pour over
chicken. Lift top layer of meat and spoon
syrup over pieces on bottom layer.

5. Cover. Cook on Low 4–5 hours, or until
instant-read meat thermometer inserted
in thighs (but not against bone) registers
160°–165°.

6. Remove chicken pieces from cooker to
platter. Keep warm.

7. Turn cooker on High. Stir in dried
plums.

8. Dissolve cornstarch in cold water in
small bowl. Stir into hot sauce in cooker.

9. Cover. Cook on High 10 minutes, or until
thickened.

10. Stir in peaches.

11. To serve, place chicken on platter and
spoon fruit and sauce over top.

Dad's Spicy Chicken Curry

Tom & Sue Ruth
Lancaster, PA

Makes 8 servings
Prep. Time: 25 minutes
Cooking Time: 6–8 hours
Ideal slow-cooker size: 6- or 7-qt.

4 lbs. chicken pieces

2 onions, diced

2–3 diced red potatoes

3 tsp. salt

1 tsp. garlic powder

1 tsp. ground ginger

1 tsp. ground cumin

1 tsp. ground coriander

1 tsp. pepper

1 tsp. ground cloves

1 tsp. ground cardamom

1 tsp. ground cinnamon

½ tsp. chili powder

1 tsp. red pepper flakes

3 tsp. turmeric

10-oz. pkg. frozen chopped spinach, thawed and squeezed dry

1 cup plain yogurt

TIPS

Serve on rice. Accompany with fresh mango slices or mango chutney.

1. Grease interior of slow-cooker crock.

2. Place chicken in large slow cooker. Cover with water.

3. Cover cooker. Cook on High 2 hours, or until tender.

4. Drain chicken. Remove from slow cooker. Set aside to cool.

5. Meanwhile, add all remaining ingredients, except spinach and yogurt, to slow cooker to cook in broth.

6. Cover. Cook on Low 4–6 hours, or until potatoes are tender.

7. While potatoes are cooking, debone chicken and cut into small chunks or shred with two forks.

8. Twenty minutes before end of cooking time, stir spinach into slow cooker.

9. Ten minutes before end of cooking time, stir in chopped or shredded chicken and yogurt.

Variation:

Substitute 5 tsp. curry powder for the garlic powder, ginger, cumin, coriander, and pepper.

Salsa Chicken Curry

Joan Miller
Wayland, IA

Makes 10 servings
Prep. Time: 15–20 minutes
Cooking Time: 4 hours
Ideal slow-cooker size: 4- or 5-qt.

10 boneless, skinless chicken thighs

16-oz. jar salsa, mild, medium, *or* hot

1 medium-sized onion, chopped

2 Tbsp. curry powder

1 cup sour cream

1. Grease interior of slow-cooker crock.

2. Place half the chicken in the slow cooker.

3. Combine salsa, onion, and curry powder in a medium-sized bowl. Pour half the sauce over the meat in the cooker.

4. Repeat Steps 1 and 2.

5. Cover and cook on Low for 4 hours, or until instant-read meat thermometer inserted in thighs registers 160°–165°.

6. Remove chicken to serving platter and cover to keep warm.

7. Add sour cream to slow cooker and stir into salsa until well blended. Serve over the chicken.

Why I like this recipe—
My cousin got this recipe from a neighborhood group. When we tasted it at her house, I wanted the recipe. It's delicious.

Chicken Curry with Rice

Jennifer Yoder Sommers
Harrisonburg, VA

Makes 6 servings
Prep. Time: 10 minutes
Cooking Time: 3–4 hours
Ideal slow-cooker size: 3- or 4-qt.

1½ lbs. boneless, skinless chicken thighs, quartered

1 onion, chopped

1 apple, peeled and chopped

2 cups uncooked long-grain rice

2 Tbsp. curry powder

14½-oz. can chicken broth

2 cups frozen peas

1. Grease interior of slow-cooker crock.

2. Combine all ingredients in your slow cooker.

3. Cover and cook on Low 3–4 hours, or until instant-read meat thermometer inserted in thighs registers 160°–165°, and rice is tender.

Variation:

Wait to add the 2 cups of frozen peas until only thirty minutes before the end of the cooking time. They'll be less mushy this way!

Flaming Chicken Bombay

Irene Dewar
Pickerington, OH

Makes 8 servings
Prep. Time: 15 minutes
Cooking Time: 4 hours
Ideal slow-cooker size: 5-qt.

3 boneless, skinless chicken thighs

2 medium onions, chopped

1½ tsp. curry powder

1 tsp. salt

½ tsp. black pepper

¾ tsp. dried thyme

1 tsp. sugar

28-oz. can diced tomatoes, undrained

1 green bell pepper, diced

½ cup raisins

1½ cups uncooked instant rice

1 cup water

1. Grease interior of slow-cooker crock.

2. Lay thighs in cooker. If you need to create a second layer, stagger the pieces so they don't directly overlap each other.

3. In a bowl, mix together onions, curry powder, salt, pepper, thyme, sugar, and diced tomatoes with juice. Spoon over chicken, being sure to top each thigh with some of the sauce.

4. Cover. Cook on Low 3½ hours.

5. Remove thighs from cooker and place on platter. Cover to keep warm.

6. Stir diced green pepper, raisins, rice, and water into sauce in cooker.

7. Put thighs back into cooker.

8. Cover and continue cooking another 30 minutes on High.

9. Check to see that rice is fully cooked and that an instant-read meat thermometer registers 160°–165° when stuck in thighs. If more time is needed, cook an additional 30 minutes and check again.

10. When ready to serve, place thighs in a deep platter or bowl and surround with rice and vegetables.

Why I like this recipe—
We were first attracted to this recipe by its name, but its flavor kept it in my file! This is one dish that I always serve on a platter instead of from the slow cooker.

Chicken Tikka Masala

Susan Kasting
Jenks, OK

Makes 6 servings
Prep. Time: 20 minutes
Cooking Time: 4¼ hours
Ideal slow-cooker size: 6-qt.

2 lbs. boneless, skinless chicken thighs

1 medium onion, chopped

3 cloves garlic, minced

1½ Tbsp. grated ginger

29-oz. can puréed tomatoes

1 Tbsp. olive oil

1 Tbsp. garam masala

½ tsp cumin

½ tsp. paprika

1 cinnamon stick

1 tsp. salt

1–1½ tsp. cayenne pepper, depending on how
    much heat you like

2 bay leaves

¾ cup Greek yogurt

½ cup cream

1½ tsp. cornstarch

TIP

Serve over rice.

1. Grease interior of slow-cooker crock.

2. Lay thighs in crock. If you need to make
a second layer, stagger pieces so they don't
directly overlap each other.

3. In a good-sized bowl, mix together onion,
garlic, ginger, tomatoes, olive oil, garam
masala, cumin, paprika, cinnamon stick, salt,
cayenne pepper, and bay leaves.

4. Pour over thighs, making sure to top
each thigh with some of the sauce.

5. Cover. Cook 4 hours on Low, or until
instant-read meat thermometer registers
160°–165° when inserted in center of thigh.

6. Remove thighs and keep warm on platter
or bowl.

7. Mix Greek yogurt into sauce in cooker.

8. In a small bowl, combine cream and
cornstarch until smooth. Mix into sauce in
cooker.

9. Return chicken to cooker.

10. Cover. Cook an additional 15–20
minutes, or until sauce has thickened.

Good go-alongs with this recipe:
Naan bread.

Chicken Azteca

Katrine Rose
Woodbridge, VA

Makes 10–12 servings
Prep. Time: 15–20 minutes
Cooking Time: 4¼ hours
Ideal slow-cooker size: 6- or 7-qt.

2 15-oz. cans black beans, drained

4 cups frozen corn kernels

2 garlic cloves, minced

¾ tsp. ground cumin

2 cups chunky salsa, *divided*

10 boneless, skinless chicken thighs

2 8-oz. pkgs. cream cheese, cubed

1. Grease interior of slow-cooker crock.

2. Combine beans, corn, garlic, cumin, and half of salsa in slow cooker.

3. Arrange chicken thighs over top. Pour remaining salsa over top.

TIPS

Spoon chicken and sauce over cooked rice. Top with shredded cheese.

4. Cover. Cook on Low 4 hours, or until instant-read meat thermometer registers 160°–165° when inserted in center of thigh.

5. Remove chicken and cut into bite-sized pieces. Return to cooker.

6. Stir in cream cheese. Cook on High until cream cheese melts.

Chicken with Red Onions, Potatoes, and Rosemary

Kristine Stalter
Iowa City, IA

Makes 8 servings
Prep. Time: 15 minutes
Cooking Time: 4–5 hours
Ideal slow-cooker size: 6-qt.

2 red onions, each cut into 10 wedges

1¼ lbs. new potatoes, unpeeled and cut into small chunks

2 garlic bulbs, separated into cloves, unpeeled

1 tsp. salt

½ tsp. black pepper

4 Tbsp. olive oil

2 Tbsp. balsamic vinegar

5–6 sprigs rosemary

8 boneless, skinless chicken thighs

1. Grease interior of slow-cooker crock.

2. Spread onions, potatoes, and garlic cloves over bottom of crock.

3. Scatter salt and pepper over top.

4. Pour oil and vinegar over. Add rosemary, leaving some sprigs whole and stripping leaves off the rest.

5. Toss veggies and seasonings together.

6. Tuck chicken thighs among veggies. If you need to create a second layer, spoon some of the veggies and seasonings over the second layer, too.

7. Cover. Cook on Low 4 hours. Check if veggies are tender and if an instant-read meat thermometer registers 160°–165° when stuck in the thighs.

8. If the vegetables and chicken aren't done, cover and continue baking up to another hour on Low. Test again. Continue cooking until veggies are done to your liking and chicken has reached 160°–165°.

9. To serve, place thighs in a deep serving dish. Surround with veggies.

Why I like this recipe—

Yes, it seems like a lot of garlic, but the flavors soften and blend together in the cooking. We eat this dish as a complete dinner—bonus if I remembered to get some bread to mop up the delicious juices!

Chicken with Feta

Susan Tjon
Austin, TX

Makes 6 servings
Prep. Time: 15 minutes
Cooking Time: 4 hours
Ideal slow-cooker size: 4- or 5-qt.

boneless, skinless chicken thighs

Tbsp. lemon juice, *divided*

3-4 oz. feta cheese, crumbled

red or green bell pepper, chopped

1. Grease interior of slow-cooker crock.

2. Place thighs on bottom of crock. If you need to create a second layer, stagger the thighs so they don't completely overlap each other.

3. Sprinkle all thighs with 1 Tbsp. lemon juice.

4. Crumble feta cheese evenly over thighs. (If you've made 2 layers, lift up the top layer and sprinkle cheese over those underneath.)

5. Top with remaining lemon juice.

6. Cover. Cook on Low for 4 hours, or until instant-read meat thermometer registers 160°–165° when inserted in thighs.

7. While chicken is cooking, chop bell pepper. Sprinkle chicken with pepper just before serving.

Why I like this recipe—

This is so easy to put together and the flavor is delicious. I sometimes use a different chopped veggie at the end, depending on what I have on hand. The fresh flavor and color is really nice.

Butter Chicken

Pat Bishop
Bedminster, PA

Makes 8 servings
Prep. Time: 20 minutes
Cooking Time: 4¼ hours
Ideal slow-cooker size: 5- or 6-qt.

onions, diced

cloves garlic, minced

Tbsp. butter, softened to room temperature

Tbsp. grated fresh ginger

Tbsp. packed brown sugar

tsp. chili powder

¼ tsp. ground coriander

¼ tsp. turmeric

½ tsp. ground cinnamon

½ tsp. ground cumin

½ tsp. salt

¼ tsp. black pepper

28-oz. can diced tomatoes, undrained

cup chicken broth

¼ cup peanut butter, almond butter, or cashew
butter

3 lbs. boneless, skinless chicken thighs

1 cup sour cream

2 Tbsp. chopped fresh cilantro

1. Grease interior of slow-cooker crock.

2. In crock combine onions, garlic, butter, fresh ginger, brown sugar, chili powder, coriander, turmeric, cinnamon, cumin, salt, pepper, and tomatoes.

3. In a bowl, whisk broth with nut butter. Pour into crock. Stir everything together until well blended.

4. Settle chicken thighs into sauce, submerging as much as possible.

5. Cover. Cook on Low for 4 hours, or until instant-read meat thermometer registers 160°–165° when stuck in center of thigh pieces.

6. Remove chicken with slotted spoon and place in bowl. Cover and keep warm.

7. With immersion blender, purée sauce until smooth. Add chicken back into sauce.

8. Cover. Cook another 15 minutes, or until heated through.

9. Stir in sour cream.

10. Serve sprinkled with cilantro over basmati rice.

Why I like this recipe—
The sauce is so luxurious and delicious that sometimes I think I don't need the chicken (my husband says otherwise). This is a favorite dish to serve to guests.

Mexican Stuffed Chicken

Karen Waggoner
Joplin, MO

Makes 6 servings
Prep. Time: 20 minutes
Cooking Time: 4–4½ hours
Ideal slow-cooker size: 5-qt.

6 boneless, skinless chicken thighs

6-oz. piece of Monterey Jack cheese, cut into 2-inch-long, ½-inch-thick sticks

2 4-oz. cans chopped green chilies, drained

½ cup dry bread crumbs

¼ cup grated Parmesan cheese

1 Tbsp. chili powder

½ tsp. salt

¼ tsp. ground cumin

¾ cup flour

1 stick (½ cup) butter, melted

1. Grease interior of slow-cooker crock.

2. Spread out the thighs and flatten each one, either with the heel of your hand or a mallet, until they're about ⅛-inch thick.

3. Place a cheese stick in the middle of each thigh. Top with a mound of chilies. Roll up the thigh and tuck in ends. Secure with a toothpick. Set aside on a platter.

4. In a shallow bowl, mix bread crumbs, Parmesan cheese, chili powder, salt, and cumin.

5. In a second shallow bowl, coat chicken with flour.

6. Place melted butter in a third shallow bowl. Dip floured chicken into butter.

7. Then roll in crumb mixture.

8. Place chicken seam side down in crock. If you need to make a second layer, stagger the pieces so they don't overlap directly.

9. Cover. Cook on Low 4–4½ hours, or until an instant-read meat thermometer registers 160°–165° when stuck into the center of the meat.

10. Take the toothpicks out of the rolls before serving, or warn the people you're serving.

Why I like this recipe—
I consider this a company dish because it looks so attractive on a platter and it doesn't take any last-minute attention. That way, I can take care of other details just before the company comes.

Bacon Ranch Slow-Cooked Chicken

Lavina Hochstedler
Grand Blanc, MI

Makes 4 servings
Prep. Time: 10 minutes
Cooking Time: 4 hours
Ideal slow-cooker size: 4-qt.

¼ cup fried and crumbled bacon (do it yourself or buy it already crumbled)

1 garlic clove, minced

1 envelope dry ranch dressing mix

10¾-oz. can cream of chicken soup

1 cup sour cream

4 boneless, skinless chicken thighs

cooked noodles

Why I like this recipe—
This recipe is super easy. It tastes a little like an Alfredo sauce, and kids and adults alike enjoy it. I tend to use more bacon than it calls for!

Good go-alongs with this recipe:
Cole slaw, applesauce, and good dinner rolls.

1. Grease interior of slow-cooker crock.

2. Combine the bacon, garlic, dry dressing mix, soup, and sour cream. Mix together well.

3. Place chicken in crock.

4. Pour sauce over chicken.

5. Cover. Cook on Low 4 hours, or until instant-read meat thermometer registers 160°–165° when stuck in center of thighs.

6. Serve over hot noodles.

Cornbread Chicken

Kaye Taylor
Florissant, MO

Makes 6 servings
Prep. Time: 15–20 minutes
Cooking Time: 4 hours
Ideal slow-cooker size: 4- or 5-qt.

½-oz. pkg. cornbread mix

envelope dry ranch salad dressing mix

cup milk

boneless, skinless chicken thighs

-2 Tbsp. oil

1. Grease interior of slow-cooker crock.

2. In large resealable plastic bag, combine ornbread mix and salad dressing mix.

3. Pour milk into shallow bowl.

4. Dip thighs, one at a time, in milk, then lace in bag with dry mixes and shake to oat.

5. Place thighs in slow cooker. If you have o create a second layer, stagger them so they lon't completely overlap.

6. Drizzle each with a bit of oil, lifting the top layer to drizzle the first layer, too.

7. Cover. Cook on Low for 4 hours, or until instant-read meat thermometer registers 160°–165° when inserted in thighs.

8. If you wish, place the thighs on a rimmed baking sheet and run under the broiler to allow chicken to brown. Watch carefully so the thighs don't burn.

Why I like this recipe—
The cornbread mix gives a really nice flavor—and we love the extra crunch when I take the time to broil the finished chicken.

Old-Fashioned Stewed Chicken

Bonnie Goering
Bridgewater, VA

Makes 6–8 servings
Prep. Time: 20 minutes
Cooking Time: 3–4 hours
Ideal slow-cooker size: 5-qt.

-4-lb. chicken, cut up

small onion, cut into wedges

rib celery, sliced

carrot, sliced

Tbsp. chopped fresh parsley, *or* 1 tsp. dried parsley

Tbsp. chopped fresh thyme, *or* 1 tsp. dried thyme

1 Tbsp. chopped fresh rosemary, *or* 1 tsp. dried rosemary

3 tsp. salt

¼ tsp. pepper

3–4 cups hot water

⅓ cup flour

TIP

Serve with mashed potatoes or noodles and creamed peas.

1. Grease interior of slow-cooker crock.

2. Place chicken in slow cooker. Scatter vegetables, herbs, and seasonings around it and over top. Pour water down along interior wall of cooker so as not to disturb the other ingredients.

3. Cover. Cook on Low 3–4 hours, or until instant-read thermometer registers 160°–165° when stuck in thighs, but not against bone.

4. Remove chicken from cooker. When cool enough to handle, debone. Set aside and keep warm.

5. In small bowl, stir ⅓ cup flour into 1 cup chicken broth from slow cooker.

6. When smooth, stir back into slow cooker. Continue cooking on Low until broth thickens, stirring occasionally to prevent lumps from forming.

7. When gravy is bubbly and thickened, stir in chicken pieces.

Why I like this recipe—

I cook every Thursday afternoon for a 93-year-old woman who lives by herself. She taught me how to cook with fresh herbs from her garden. I've found they make food taste so much better that I've started an herb garden. And I dry some herbs to use during the winter.

Amish Wedding Chicken

Lydia A. Yoder
London, ON

Makes 20 servings
Prep. Time: 40–45 minutes
Cooking Time: 3–4 hours
Ideal slow-cooker size: 6-qt.

1½ sticks (12 Tbsp.) butter
1 cup chopped onions
2 cups chopped celery
2 Tbsp. parsley flakes
1½ tsp. salt
½ tsp. pepper
2 cups chicken broth
12–14 cups dried bread cubes
4 cups cut-up, cooked chicken*
2 eggs, beaten
1 tsp. baking powder

1. Grease interior of slow-cooker crock.

2. If you have time, sauté onion and celery in butter in skillet. Otherwise, use raw onions and celery.

3. Combine seasonings and broth in large bowl. Mix in bread cubes.

4. Fold in chicken and sautéed, or raw, onions and celery.

5. Add eggs and baking powder.

6. Lightly pack into large slow cooker.

7. Cover. Cook on Low 3–4 hours.

*See Old-Fashioned Stewed Chicken recipe on page 47 to make your own cooked chicken and broth.

TIP

1. The longer the dressing cooks, the drier it will become. Keep that in mind if you do not care for moist stuffing.
2. Serve with mashed potatoes, a vegetable, and lettuce salad.

Why I like this recipe—
This is the traditional main dish served at Amish weddings in the home of the bride in many communities across North America.

Our Favorite Chicken and Stuffing

Kim Stoll
Abbeville, SC

Makes 6 servings
Prep. Time: 10–15 minutes
Cooking Time: 3–4 hours
Ideal slow-cooker size: 5-qt.

6 boneless, skinless chicken thighs

6 slices Swiss cheese

¼ cup milk

10¾-oz. can cream of mushroom, or chicken, soup*

2 cups dry stuffing mix

1 stick (8 Tbsp.) butter, melted

1. Grease slow cooker with nonstick cooking spray.

2. Top each thigh with slice of cheese. Arrange cheese-covered chicken in slow cooker. If you have to stack the thighs, stagger them so they don't directly overlap each other.

3. In a mixing bowl, combine milk and soup until smooth. Pour over chicken. (If you've stacked the thighs, lift the ones on top to make sure the ones on the bottom are topped with sauce, too.)

4. Sprinkle stuffing mix evenly over sauced chicken, including those on the bottom.

5. Drizzle with melted butter.

6. Cover. Cook on Low 3–4 hours, or just until meat reaches 175° in the center.

Variation:
Use cornbread stuffing instead of regular stuffing mix.

—Betty Moore
Plano, IL

*To make your own Cream Soup, see recipes on pages 561 and 562.

Sunday Chicken Stew with Dumplings

Kathy Hertzler
Lancaster, PA

Makes 6 servings
Prep. Time: 1 hour
Cooking Time: 4½ hours
Ideal slow-cooker size: 5-qt. *oval*

½ cup flour

1 tsp. salt

½ tsp. white pepper

3-lb. broiler/fryer chicken, cut up and skin removed

2 Tbsp. olive oil

3 cups chicken broth

6 large carrots, cut in ½-inch-thick pieces

2 celery ribs, cut into ½-inch-thick slices

1 large sweet onion, chopped into ½-inch-thick slices

1–2 tsp. dried rosemary

1½ cups frozen peas

Dumplings:
1 cup flour

½ tsp. dried rosemary, crushed

2 tsp. baking powder

½ tsp. salt

1 egg, beaten

½ cup milk

TIP

The dumplings cook best if you use an oval, or wide, more shallow, slow cooker.

1. Grease interior of slow-cooker crock.

2. To prepare chicken, combine flour, salt, and pepper in a large resealable plastic bag.

3. Add chicken, one piece at a time. Shake to coat.

4. In a large skillet, brown chicken in olive oil, a few pieces at a time, being careful not to crowd the pan.

5. As the pieces brown, remove to a platter and keep warm.

6. When all the chicken is brown, gradually add broth to skillet while bringing to a boil. Stir up the browned, flavorful bits sticking to the skillet.

7. In a 5-quart slow cooker, layer in carrots, celery, and onion.

8. Sprinkle with rosemary.

9. Add chicken. Carefully add hot broth.

10. Cover. Cook 4 hours on Low, or until instant-read thermometer registers 160°–165° when stuck in thighs, but not against bone, vegetables are tender, and stew is bubbling.

11. Stir in peas.

12. When chicken is nearly finished cooking, make the dumplings by combining flour, crushed rosemary, baking powder, and salt in a small bowl.

13. In a separate bowl combine egg and milk.

14. Stir wet ingredients into dry ingredients until just combined.

15. Drop by spoonfuls into simmering chicken mixture. Do not stir.

16. Cover. Cook on High 25–30 minutes, or until a toothpick inserted in dumpling comes out clean. (Try this after 25 minutes; otherwise, do not lift the cover while dumplings are cooking.)

17. Serve each person a scoop of dumpling topped with vegetables and broth, with a piece of chicken on the side.

Creamy Herbed Chicken

LaVerne A. Olson
Lititz, PA

Makes 8 servings
Prep. Time: 10 minutes
Cooking Time: 4 hours
Ideal slow-cooker size: 6- or 7-qt.

8 boneless, skinless chicken thighs

10¾-oz. can cream of mushroom soup, *or* cream of chicken, soup*

¼ cup soy sauce

¼ cup oil

¼ cup wine vinegar

¾ cup water

½ tsp. minced garlic

1 tsp. ground ginger

½ tsp. dried oregano

1 Tbsp. brown sugar

TIP

Serve with rice.

Why I like this recipe—
This is a favorite with our whole family, even the grandchildren. The gravy is delicious!

1. Grease interior of slow-cooker crock.

2. Arrange chicken in slow cooker.

3. Combine remaining ingredients in bowl. Pour over chicken.

4. Cover. Cook on Low 3¾ hours, or until instant-read thermometer registers 160°–165° when stuck in thighs.

5. Uncover and cook 15 minutes more.

*To make your own Cream Soup, see recipes on pages 561 and 562.

Szechwan Chicken and Broccoli

Jane Meiser
Harrisonburg, VA

Makes 4 servings
Prep. Time: 20 minutes
Cooking Time: 3 hours
Ideal slow-cooker size: 4-qt.

4 boneless, skinless chicken thighs

2 Tbsp. oil

½ cup picante sauce

2 Tbsp. soy sauce

½ tsp. sugar

½ Tbsp. quick-cooking tapioca

1 medium onion, chopped

2 garlic cloves, minced

½ tsp. ground ginger

2 cups broccoli florets

1 medium red bell pepper, cut into pieces

1. Grease interior of slow-cooker crock.

2. Cut chicken into 1-inch cubes. If you have time, brown lightly in oil in skillet. Otherwise skip this step and place meat in slow cooker.

3. Stir in remaining ingredients.

4. Cover. Cook on Low 3 hours.

5. Serve over cooked rice.

Why I like this recipe—

I like to put this together just before I go to pick up my kids from school. That way, when we get home, I can be available for what they need with homework or talking instead of starting dinner.

Chicken Cacciatore with Mushrooms

**Phyllis Good
Lancaster, PA**

Makes 6–8 servings
Prep. Time: 15 minutes
Cooking Time: 4 hours
Ideal slow-cooker size: 6-qt.

2 large onions, sliced thin

3 lbs. boneless, skinless chicken thighs

2 garlic cloves, minced

28-oz. can stewed tomatoes

8-oz. can tomato sauce

1 tsp. salt

½ tsp. black pepper (coarsely ground is best)

2 tsp. dried oregano

1 tsp. dried basil

⅓ cup white wine

2 cups sliced fresh mushrooms

1. Grease interior of slow-cooker crock.

2. Place onions evenly over bottom of slow cooker.

3. Lay chicken thighs over onions. If you need to add a second layer, stagger the pieces so they don't directly overlap each other.

4. Combine remaining ingredients, except mushrooms, in a good-sized bowl. Pour over chicken.

5. Cover. Cook on Low 4 hours, or until instant-read meat thermometer registers 160°–165° when stuck in thighs.

6. Thirty minutes before end of cooking time, stir in sliced mushrooms. Cover and continue cooking.

7. Remove bay leaves before serving.

8. Serve over hot buttered linguine.

Why I like this recipe—
One of my friends served me a cacciatore, and I immediately requested the recipe. I altered it so I could use my slow cooker—the slow, moist heat makes the chicken succulent and flavorful.

Cheesy Buffalo Chicken Pasta

Christina Gerber
Apple Creek, OH

Makes 6–8 servings
Prep. Time: 15 minutes
Cooking Time: 4½–5 hours
Ideal slow-cooker size: 6-qt.

3 cups chicken broth

½ cup buffalo wing sauce, *divided*

1 Tbsp. dry ranch dressing mix

¼ teaspoon garlic powder

½ tsp. salt

⅛ tsp. black pepper

1½ lbs. boneless, skinless chicken thighs

8-oz. pkg. cream cheese, cubed

1 cup shredded sharp cheddar cheese

1 Tbsp. cornstarch

1 Tbsp. water

1 lb. linguine

chopped cilantro, *optional*

1. Grease interior of slow-cooker crock.

2. Mix broth, ¼ cup buffalo sauce, ranch dressing mix, and seasonings in crock.

3. Submerge chicken in sauce.

4. Scatter cubed cream cheese and shredded cheese over chicken.

5. Cover. Cook on Low 4 hours, or until instant-read thermometer registers 160°–165° when stuck in thighs.

6. When chicken is fully cooked, remove to bowl and shred with 2 forks. (Cover crock to keep sauce warm.)

7. Add remaining ¼ cup buffalo sauce to shredded chicken and toss to coat. Set aside but keep warm.

8. In a small bowl, stir cornstarch and water together until smooth. Stir into warm sauce in crock until sauce smooths out and thickens.

9. Break linguini in half and place in crock.

10. Top with shredded chicken and cover.

11. Cook on High 30–60 minutes, or just until linguini is fully cooked. Stir 3–4 times during cooking.

12. If you need more liquid for noodles to cook, add water ¼ cup at a time.

13. Garnish with cilantro if you wish, and serve immediately.

Why I like this recipe—
This is a great one-pot meal. No extra pan needed to cook the pasta!

Chicken, Sweet Chicken

Anne Townsend
Albuquerque, NM

Makes 6–8 servings
Prep. Time: 15 minutes
Cooking Time: 4 hours
Ideal slow-cooker size: 5-qt.

2 medium-sized raw sweet potatoes, peeled and cut into ¼-inch-thick slices

8 boneless, skinless chicken thighs

8-oz. jar orange marmalade

¼ cup water

¼–½ tsp. salt

½ tsp. pepper

1. Grease interior of slow-cooker crock.

2. Place sweet potato slices in slow cooker.

3. Arrange thighs on top of potatoes.

4. Spoon marmalade over the chicken and potatoes.

5. Pour water over all. Season with salt and pepper.

6. Cover. Cook on Low 4 hours, or until instant-read thermometer registers 160°–165° when stuck in thighs and potatoes are tender.

Why I like this recipe—
We enjoy this chicken as a change from more savory chicken dishes with the typical white potatoes.

Thai Chicken

**Joanne Good
Wheaton, IL**

Makes 6 servings
Prep. Time: 5 minutes
Cooking Time: 4 hours
Ideal slow-cooker size: 4-qt.

6 boneless, skinless chicken thighs

¾ cup salsa, your choice of mild, medium, *or* hot

¼ cup chunky peanut butter

1 Tbsp. low-sodium soy sauce

2 Tbsp. lime juice

Optional ingredients:

1 tsp. gingerroot, grated

2 Tbsp. cilantro, chopped

1 Tbsp. dry-roasted peanuts, chopped

TIP

Vegetarians can substitute 2 15-oz. cans of white beans, and some tempeh, for the chicken.

1. Grease interior of slow-cooker crock.

2. Put chicken in slow cooker.

3. In a bowl, mix remaining ingredients together (including gingerroot, if desired), except cilantro and chopped peanuts.

4. Cover. Cook on Low 4 hours, or until instant-read thermometer registers 160°–165° when stuck in thighs.

5. Skim off any fat. Remove chicken to a platter and serve topped with sauce. Sprinkle with peanuts and cilantro, if you wish.

6. Serve over cooked rice.

Teriyaki Chicken

Elaine Vigoda
Rochester, NY

Makes 6 servings
Prep. Time: 15 minutes
Cooking Time: 3–4 hours
Ideal slow-cooker size: 5-qt.

2 lbs. boneless, skinless chicken thighs, cut into large chunks

10-oz. bottle teriyaki sauce

½ lb. snow peas, *optional*

8-oz. can water chestnuts, drained, *optional*

1. Grease interior of slow-cooker crock.

2. Place chicken in slow cooker. Cover with sauce. Stir until sauce is well distributed.

3. Cover. Cook on Low 3 hours. If you want to include snow peas and water chestnuts, add them now. Cover and cook another hour on Low.

4. If you're skipping the vegetables, check to see if an instant-read thermometer registers 160°–165° when stuck in thighs. If it does, the chicken is done. If it doesn't, continue cooking another 30 minutes, taking the chicken's temperature at the end to see if it's done.

5. Serve over cooked white rice or Chinese rice noodles.

Why I like this recipe—
We haven't been tempted by Chinese takeout for a while since I got this recipe from my sister. It answers the Chinese craving quite nicely!

So-Simple Salsa Chicken

Leesa DeMartyn
Enola, PA

Makes 4–6 servings
Prep. Time: 5 minutes
Cooking Time: 4 hours
Ideal slow-cooker size: 4- or 5-qt.

4-6 boneless, skinless chicken breast halves

16-oz. jar chunky-style salsa, your choice of mild, medium, *or* hot

2 cups shredded cheese, your choice of flavor

1. Grease interior of slow-cooker crock.

2. Place chicken in slow cooker. Pour salsa over chicken.

3. Cover. Cook on Low 4 hours, or until instant-read thermometer registers 160°–165° when stuck in thighs.

4. Ten minutes before end of cooking time, top thighs with shredded cheese.

5. Serve over cooked rice. Or shred chicken, mix into sauce and cheese, and serve in a whole wheat or cheddar cheese wrap.

Why I like this recipe—

There are several variations of this recipe floating around the moms' group I attend. One mom adds cooked black beans. Another mom adds corn, and yet another mom turns this into soup. It's so handy for busy families!

Tex-Mex Chicken and Rice

Kelly Evenson
Pittsboro, NC

Makes 8 servings
Prep. Time: 25 minutes
Cooking Time: 3–4 hours
Ideal slow-cooker size: 5-qt.

1 cup uncooked converted white rice

28-oz. can diced peeled tomatoes

6-oz. can tomato paste

3 cups hot water

1 envelope dry taco seasoning mix

4 whole boneless, skinless chicken thighs, uncooked and cut into ½-inch cubes

2 medium onions, chopped

1 green bell pepper, chopped

4-oz. can diced green chilies

1 tsp. garlic powder

½ tsp. pepper

TIP

Serve with mixed green leafy salad and refried beans.

1. Grease interior of slow-cooker crock.

2. Combine all ingredients except chilies, garlic powder, and pepper in large slow cooker.

3. Cover. Cook on Low 3–4 hours, or until rice is tender and chicken is cooked.

4. Stir in green chilies and seasonings and serve.

Chicken Tacos

Susan Kasting
Jenks, OK

Makes 6–8 servings
Prep. Time: 10 minutes
Cooking Time: 4 hours
Ideal slow-cooker size: 4- or 5-qt.

4 large boneless, skinless chicken thighs

1 envelope dry taco seasoning

1 cup salsa, your choice of heat

10¾-oz. can cream of chicken soup*,
  or 8-oz. pkg. cream cheese, cubed

1. Grease interior of slow-cooker crock.

2. Holding thighs over crock, sprinkle each one, top and bottom, with taco seasoning.

3. Place seasoned thighs in crock.

4. In bowl, mix salsa and soup, or salsa and cubed cream cheese, together. Pour over chicken.

5. Cover. Cook on Low 4 hours, or until instant-read meat thermometer registers 160°–165° when stuck in center of thighs.

6. When chicken is done, lift into deep bowl and shred with 2 forks.

7. Stir shredded chicken back into sauce. Stir together well.

8. Serve with tortillas.

*To make your own Cream Soup, see recipes on pages 561 and 562.

TIPS

1. I top these with sour cream, grated cheese, and chopped cilantro.
2. You can also add a can of corn, drained, and/or black beans, drained, to the sauce in Step 4.

Mexican Chicken Bake

Gretchen H. Maust
Keezletown, VA

Makes 6–8 servings
Prep. Time: 15 minutes
Cooking Time: 4 hours
Ideal slow-cooker size: 6-qt.

½ cup raw brown rice

1⅓ cups water

2 14½-oz. cans diced tomatoes, undrained

15-oz. can black beans, drained

1 cup corn, fresh, frozen, *or* canned

1 Tbsp. cumin

1 Tbsp. chili powder

½ tsp. salt

¼ tsp. black pepper

4 garlic cloves, minced

4 boneless, skinless chicken thighs

1 cup red bell pepper, diced

1 cup green bell pepper, diced

2 cups shredded cheddar cheese

1. Grease interior of slow-cooker crock.

2. Pour rice and water into crock.

3. Stir in tomatoes, beans, corn, cumin, chili powder, salt, pepper, and minced garlic. Mix together well.

4. Submerge chicken thighs in mixture.

5. Cover. Cook on Low for 3 hours.

6. Stir in diced red and green peppers. Cover and continue cooking 1 more hour on Low, or until instant-read meat thermometer registers 160°–165° when stuck into thighs.

7. Remove chicken and cut into bite-sized pieces. Stir back into mixture.

8. Sprinkle cheese over top. Allow cheese to melt, then serve.

Why I like this recipe—

We enjoy Mexican Chicken Bake as a change from the more traditional chicken rice dishes. I add a green veg to the menu, and dinner is served!

African Chicken Treat

Anne Townsend
Albuquerque, NM

Makes 4 servings
Prep. Time: 10 minutes
Cooking Time: 4 hours
Ideal slow-cooker size: 5- or 6-qt.

1½ cups water

2 tsp. chicken bouillon granules

2 ribs celery, thinly sliced

2 onions, thinly sliced

1 red bell pepper, sliced

1 green bell pepper, sliced

½ cup extra crunchy peanut butter

8 boneless, skinless chicken thighs

crushed chili pepper of your choice

1. Grease interior of slow-cooker crock.

2. Combine water, chicken bouillon granules, celery, onions, and peppers in slow cooker.

3. Spread peanut butter over both sides of chicken pieces. Sprinkle with chili pepper. Place on top of ingredients in slow cooker.

4. Cover. Cook on Low 4 hours, or until instant-read meat thermometer registers 160°–165° when stuck in center of thighs.

Why I like this recipe—

I got this recipe from a friend after tasting it at a church potluck. The simple ingredients make a really tasty sauce.

Herby Barbecued Chicken

Lauren M. Eberhard
Seneca, IL

Makes 4–6 servings
Prep. Time: 10 minutes
Cooking Time: 4 hours
Ideal slow-cooker size: 4- or 5-qt.

1 whole chicken, cut up, *or* 8 boneless, skinless chicken thighs

1 onion, sliced thin

1 bottle your favorite barbecue sauce

1 tsp. dried oregano

1 tsp. dried basil

1. Grease interior of slow-cooker crock.

2. Place chicken in slow cooker.

3. Mix onion slices, sauce, oregano, and basil together in a bowl. Pour over chicken, covering as well as possible.

4. Cover and cook on Low 4 hours, or until instant-read meat thermometer registers 160°–165° when stuck in center of thighs.

Why I like this recipe—

We never get tired of this delicious chicken. One of my friends starts with cubed chicken and then adds a can of beans to Step 3.

Barbecued Chicken Sandwiches

Brittany Miller
Millersburg, OH

Makes 10 servings
Prep. Time: 25–30 minutes
Cooking Time: 5 hours
Ideal slow-cooker size: 5- or 6-qt.

3 lbs. boneless, skinless chicken thighs

1 cup ketchup

1 small onion, chopped

¼ cup water

¼ cup cider vinegar

2 Tbsp. Worcestershire sauce

1 Tbsp. brown sugar

1 garlic clove, minced

1 bay leaf

2 tsp. paprika

1 tsp. dried oregano

1 tsp. chili powder

½ tsp. salt

½ tsp. pepper

1. Grease interior of slow-cooker crock.

2. Place chicken in slow cooker.

3. In a medium-sized mixing bowl, combine ketchup, onion, water, vinegar, Worcestershire sauce, brown sugar, garlic, bay leaf, and seasonings. Pour over chicken.

TIP

This is enough chicken and sauce to fill up to 10 sandwich rolls.

4. Cover. Cook on Low 4 hours, or until instant-read meat thermometer registers 160°–165° when stuck in center of thighs.

5. Discard bay leaf.

6. Remove chicken to large bowl. Shred meat with 2 forks. Return chicken to slow cooker.

7. Stir shredded chicken and sauce together thoroughly.

8. Cover. Cook on Low 30 minutes.

9. Remove lid. Continue cooking 30 more minutes, allowing sauce to cook off and thicken.

Barbecued Chicken Pizza

Susan Roth
Salem, OR

Makes 4 to 6 servings
Prep. Time: 20–25 minutes
Cooking Time: 2 hours
Standing Time: 2 hours before you begin
Ideal slow-cooker size: 6-qt.

3- or 12-oz. pkg. prepared pizza dough, depending how thick you like your pizza crust

1 cup barbecue sauce, teriyaki-flavored, *or* your choice of flavor

2 cups cooked, chopped chicken (your own leftovers*, rotisserie chicken, or canned chicken)

20-oz. can pineapple tidbits, drained, *optional*

½ cup green bell pepper, chopped, *optional*

¼ cup red onion, diced or sliced, *optional*

2 cups shredded mozzarella cheese

1. If the dough's been refrigerated, allow it to stand at room temperature for 2 hours.

2. Grease interior of slow-cooker crock.

3. Stretch the dough into a large circle so that it fits into the crock, covering the bottom and reaching up the sides by an inch or so the whole way around. (If the dough is larger than the bottom of the cooker, fold it in half and stretch it to fit the bottom and an inch up the sides. This will make a thicker crust.)

4. Bake crust, uncovered, on High 1 hour.

*To make your own cooked chicken, see Old-Fashioned Stewed Chicken recipe on page 47.

5. Spread barbecue sauce over hot crust.

6. Drop chopped chicken evenly over sauce.

7. If you wish, spoon pineapple, chopped peppers, and onion over chicken.

8. Sprinkle evenly with cheese.

9. Cover. Cook on High for about 2 hours, or until the crust begins to brown around the edges.

10. Uncover, being careful not to let the condensation on the lid drip onto the pizza.

11. Let stand for 10 minutes. Cut into wedges and serve.

Why I like this recipe—
I refrigerated the leftovers, and they tasted great on the second day. We reheated it in the microwave at 60% power. —Gladys Voth

Barbecued Chicken Wings

Rosemarie Fitzgerald
Gibsonia, PA

Makes 10 full-sized servings
Prep. Time: 5 minutes
Cooking Time: 3–4 hours
Ideal slow-cooker size: 5-qt.

5 lbs. chicken wings, tips cut off

12-oz. bottle chili sauce

⅓ cup lemon juice

1 Tbsp. Worcestershire sauce

2 Tbsp. molasses

1 tsp. salt

2 tsp. chili powder

¼ tsp. hot pepper sauce

dash garlic powder

1. Grease interior of slow-cooker crock.

2. Use kitchen scissors or a sharp sturdy knife to cut through the 2 joints on each wing. Discard the wing tip.

3. Place the other 2 pieces of each wing into the crock. As you create layers, stagger the pieces so they don't directly overlap each other.

4. Combine remaining ingredients in a bowl. Spoon over chicken, lifting up pieces on top layers to sauce pieces on lower layers, too.

TIP

Take any leftover chicken off the bone and combine with leftover sauce. Serve over cooked pasta for a second meal.

5. Cover. Cook on Low 3–4 hours, or until instant-read meat thermometer registers 160°–165° when stuck in meaty part of wings (but not against bone).

Why I like this recipe—
These wings are also a great appetizer, yielding about 15 appetizer-size servings.

Herb-Roasted Turkey Breast

Kristi See
Weskan, KS

Makes 6 servings
Prep. Time: 15 minutes
Cooking Time: 5–7 hours
Ideal slow-cooker size: 6- or 7-qt. *oval*

5 tsp. lemon juice

1 Tbsp. olive oil

1–2 tsp. pepper

1 tsp. dried rosemary, crushed

1 tsp. dried thyme

1 tsp. garlic salt

6–7-lb. bone-in turkey breast

1 medium onion, cut into wedges

1 celery rib, cut into 2-inch-thick pieces

½ cup white wine *or* chicken broth

1. Grease interior of slow-cooker crock.

2. In a small bowl, combine lemon juice and olive oil. In another bowl, combine pepper, rosemary, thyme, and garlic salt.

3. With your fingers, carefully loosen skin from both sides of breast. Brush oil mixture under skin. Rub herb-seasoning mixture under and on top of skin.

4. Arrange onion and celery in slow cooker. Place turkey breast, skin-side up, on top of vegetables.

5. Pour wine around breast.

6. Cover. Cook on Low 5–7 hours, or until instant-read meat thermometer registers 160° when stuck in meaty part of breast (but not against bone).

Why I like this recipe—
I made this turkey recipe for our first Thanksgiving after we were married. We really enjoyed the taste. Cleanup was easy, and because I prepared the turkey in the slow cooker, I wasn't short on oven space.

Variations:
1. Add carrot chunks to Step 4 to add more flavor to the turkey broth.

2. Reserve broth for soups, or thicken with flour-water paste and serve as gravy over sliced turkey.

3. Freeze broth in pint-sized containers for future use.

4. Debone turkey and freeze in pint-sized containers for future use. Or freeze any leftover turkey.
                              —Liz Ann Yoder, Hartville, OH

Turkey Breast with Orange Sauce

Jean Butzer
Batavia, NY

Makes 4–6 servings
Prep. Time: 10 minutes
Cooking Time: 4–5 hours
Ideal slow-cooker size: 6-qt. *oval*

1 large onion, chopped

3 garlic cloves, minced

1 tsp. dried rosemary

½ tsp. pepper

2–3-lb. boneless, skinless turkey breast

1½ cups orange juice

Why I like this recipe—
This very easy, impressive-looking and -tasting recipe is perfect for guests. And carving is easy because there aren't bones to contend with.

1. Grease interior of slow-cooker crock.

2. Place onion in slow cooker.

3. Combine garlic, rosemary, and pepper in a small bowl.

4. Make gashes in turkey, about ¾ of the way through, at 2-inch intervals. Stuff with herb mixture. Place turkey in slow cooker.

5. Pour juice over turkey.

6. Cover. Cook on Low 4–5 hours, or until instant-read meat thermometer registers 160° when stuck in center of breast.

Stuffed Turkey Breast

Jean Butzer
Batavia, NY

Makes 8 servings
Prep. Time: 25 minutes
Cooking Time: 4–5 hours
Ideal slow-cooker size: 6- or 7-qt. *oval*

half a stick (¼ cup) butter, melted

1 small onion, finely chopped

½ cup finely chopped celery

2½-oz. pkg. croutons with real bacon bits

1 cup chicken broth

2 Tbsp. fresh minced parsley

½ tsp. poultry seasoning

1 whole uncooked turkey breast, *or* 2 halves,
    about 5 lbs. total

salt to taste

pepper to taste

24 x 26-inch piece of cheesecloth for each
    breast half

½ bottle dry white wine

1. Grease interior of slow-cooker crock.

2. Combine butter, onion, celery, croutons,
broth, parsley, and poultry seasoning in a
bowl.

3. Cut turkey breast in thick slices from
breastbone to rib cage, leaving slices attached
to bone (crosswise across breast).

4. Sprinkle turkey with salt and pepper.

5. Soak cheesecloth in wine. Place turkey
on cheesecloth. Stuff bread mixture into slits
between turkey slices.

6. Fold one end of cheesecloth over the
other to cover meat. Place in slow cooker.
Pour wine over turkey.

7. Cover. Cook on Low 4–5 hours or until
instant-read meat thermometer registers 160°
when stuck in center of breast but not against
bone.

8. Remove turkey from cooker and remove
cheesecloth immediately. (If you prefer a
browner result, remove from cooker, discard
cheesecloth, and brown turkey in 400° oven
for 15–20 minutes.)

9. Let turkey stand 10 minutes before
slicing through and serving.

10. Thicken the drippings, if you wish, for
gravy. Mix together 3 Tbsp. cornstarch and ¼
cup cold water in small bowl.

11. When smooth, stir into broth in cooker
(with turkey removed from cooker). Turn
cooker to High and stir until cornstarch paste
is dissolved. Allow to cook about 10 minutes,
until broth is thickened and smooth.

Why I like this recipe—
This is lovely for Thanksgiving, but I always
keep a breast or two in the freezer for other
occasions as well. We love the flavor of this
turkey and gravy.

Maple-Glazed Turkey Breast with Rice

Jeanette Oberholtzer
Manheim, PA

Makes 4 servings
Prep. Time: 10–15 minutes
Cooking Time: 4 hours
Ideal slow-cooker size: 4- or 5-qt.

6-oz. pkg. long-grain wild rice mix

1½ cups water

2-lb. boneless turkey breast, cut into 1½-2-inch chunks

¼ cup maple syrup

1 onion, chopped

¼ tsp. ground cinnamon

½ tsp. salt, *optional*

1. Grease interior of slow-cooker crock.

2. Combine all ingredients in the slow cooker.

3. Cook on Low 4 hours, or until turkey and rice are both tender, but not dry or mushy.

Why I like this recipe—
I love how pretty the wild rice looks in this turkey dish. It gives a nice hefty texture, too, with the tender turkey. You can substitute brown rice if you wish.

Indonesian Turkey

Elaine Sue Good
Tiskilwa, IL

Makes 4 servings
Prep. Time: 10 minutes
Cooking Time: 3–4 hours
Ideal slow-cooker size: 4-qt.

1½–2 lbs. turkey breast tenderloins

6 cloves garlic, pressed and chopped

1½ Tbsp. grated fresh ginger

1 Tbsp. sesame oil

3 Tbsp. soy sauce, *optional*

½ tsp. cayenne pepper, *optional*

⅓ cup peanut butter, your choice of chunky *or* smooth

TIPS

1. If you like spicier foods, be sure to include the cayenne pepper and add it as part of Step 3. And, if your diet allows, add the soy sauce during Step 3, also.
2. You may substitute 1½–2 lbs. boneless, skinless chicken thighs for the turkey breast tenderloins.

1. Grease interior of slow-cooker crock.

2. Place turkey in slow cooker.

3. Sprinkle with garlic, ginger, and sesame oil.

4. Cover and cook on Low 3–4 hours, or until meat thermometer registers 160°.

5. With a slotted spoon, remove turkey pieces from slow cooker. Stir peanut butter into remaining juices. If the sauce is thicker than you like, stir in ¼–⅓ cup water.

6. Spoon peanut butter sauce over turkey to serve.

Barbecued Turkey Cutlets

Maricarol Magill
Freehold, NJ

Makes 4 servings
Prep. Time: 10 minutes
Cooking Time: 3–4 hours
Ideal slow-cooker size: 4-qt.

1½–2 lbs. turkey cutlets

¼ cup molasses

¼ cup cider vinegar

¼ cup ketchup

3 Tbsp. Worcestershire sauce

1 tsp. garlic salt

3 Tbsp. chopped onion

2 Tbsp. brown sugar

¼ tsp. pepper

1. Grease interior of slow-cooker crock.

2. Place turkey cutlets in slow cooker.

3. Combine remaining ingredients in bowl. Pour over turkey.

4. Cover. Cook on Low 3–4 hours, or until meat thermometer registers 160°.

Parsley, Sage, and Ginger Turkey

Connie Butto
Lititz, PA

Makes 6 servings
Prep. Time: 20 minutes
Cooking Time: 4 hours
Ideal slow-cooker size: 5-qt.

2½–3 lbs. boneless, skinless turkey thighs

½ tsp. dried sage

1 tsp. dried parsley

¼–½ tsp. ground ginger, according to taste

⅔ cup chicken broth

½ cup white wine

¼ cup chopped onions

1. Grease interior of slow-cooker crock.

2. Cut thighs into 6–8 pieces. Place in slow cooker.

3. Mix all other ingredients together in a bowl.

4. Spoon over turkey.

5. Cover. Cook on Low 4 hours, or until instant-read meat thermometer registers 160° when stuck into meat.

6. Serve with broth.

Why I like this recipe—
I love the little kick of ginger in this turkey. It's a nice autumnal taste, although I keep making this turkey throughout the winter.

Turkey with Sweet Potatoes and Dried Fruit

Jean M. Butzer
Batavia, NY

Makes 4 servings
Prep. Time: 30–40 minutes
Cooking Time: 4–5 hours
Ideal slow-cooker size: 5-qt.

2 medium (2 cups) yams *or* sweet potatoes, cut crosswise into ½-inch-thick slices

2–3 lbs. (3–4) boneless, skinless turkey thighs, cut in half lengthwise

1 cup mixed chopped dried fruit

1 tsp. chopped garlic

½ tsp. salt

¼ tsp. pepper

¾ cup orange juice

¼ cup chopped fresh parsley

1. Grease interior of slow-cooker crock.

2. Place yam slices in slow cooker. Top with turkey thighs.

3. Sprinkle with dried fruit, garlic, salt, and pepper.

4. Gently pour orange juice into cooker down along the sides, being careful not to disturb fruit and seasonings.

5. Cover. Cook on Low 4–5 hours, or until instant-read meat thermometer registers 160°–165° when stuck in center of thigh.

6. Slice. Spoon juice and dried fruit over top. Then sprinkle with parsley just before serving.

Why I like this recipe—

I took this dish to a cousins' reunion last year, and it was so popular that I gave out six copies of the recipe. The turkey is pretty to look at and the flavor is amazing.

Slow-Cooked Turkey Dinner

Miriam Nolt
New Holland, PA

Makes 4–6 servings
Prep. Time: 15 minutes
Cooking Time: 4–5 hours
Ideal slow-cooker size: 4- or 5-qt.

1 onion, diced

6 small red potatoes, quartered

2 cups sliced carrots

1½–2 lbs. boneless, skinless turkey thighs, cut
  into good-sized chunks

¼ cup flour

2 Tbsp. dry onion soup mix

10¾-oz. can cream of mushroom soup*

⅔ cup chicken broth *or* water

1. Grease interior of slow-cooker crock.

2. Place vegetables in bottom of slow
cooker.

3. Place turkey thighs over vegetables.

4. Combine remaining ingredients in bowl.
Pour over turkey.

5. Cover. Cook on Low 4–5 hours, or until
instant-read meat thermometer registers
160°–165° when stuck in center of thighs and
vegetables are tender.

Variation:
Use 1 cup uncooked long-grain rice instead of
potatoes. Increase water to 1⅔ cups. Increase
dry onion soup to ¼ cup. Continue with Step
4 above.

*To make your own Cream Soup, see recipes
on pages 561 and 562.

Turkey Fajitas

Carol Ambrose
McMinnville, OR

Makes 8 servings
Prep. Time: 10–15 minutes
Cooking Time: 3–4 hours
Ideal slow-cooker size: 4-qt.

2¼ lbs. turkey tenderloins

1¼-oz. envelope taco seasoning mix

1 celery rib, chopped

1 onion, chopped

14½-oz. can mild diced tomatoes and green chilies, undrained

1 cup (4 oz.) shredded cheddar cheese

8 (7½-inch) flour tortillas

Toppings:
lettuce

sour cream

sliced olives

chopped tomatoes

1. Grease interior of slow-cooker crock.

2. Cut turkey into 2½-inch-long strips. Place in zip-top plastic bag.

3. Add taco seasoning to bag. Seal and shake to coat meat.

4. Empty seasoned turkey into slow cooker. Add celery, onion, and tomatoes. Stir together gently.

5. Cover. Cook on Low 3–4 hours, or just until turkey is cooked through and tender.

6. Stir in cheese.

7. Warm tortillas according to package directions. Spoon turkey mixture evenly into center of each tortilla, and roll up.

8. Serve with Toppings.

Why I like this recipe—
Put this recipe in your cooker. Then take your kids or grandkids out to play. When you're done, your meal is ready!

Powerhouse Beef Roast with Tomatoes, Onions, and Peppers

Donna Treloar
Gaston, IN

Makes 5–6 servings
Prep. Time: 15 minutes
Cooking Time: 6–8 hours
Ideal slow-cooker size: 4- or 5-qt.

3-lb. boneless beef chuck roast

1 garlic clove, minced

1 Tbsp. oil

2–3 onions, sliced

2–3 sweet green and red bell peppers, sliced

16-oz. jar salsa

2 14½-oz. cans Mexican-style stewed tomatoes

1. Grease interior of slow-cooker crock.

2. If you have time, brown roast and garlic in oil in skillet. Otherwise, place beef, garlic, and oil in slow cooker.

3. Add onions and peppers.

4. In a bowl, combine salsa and tomatoes. Pour over ingredients in slow cooker.

5. Cover. Cook on Low 6–8 hours, or until instant-read meat thermometer registers 145° when stuck into center of roast.

6. Remove meat from crock. Allow to stand for 10 minutes. Then slice and serve.

TIP

Make Beef Burritos with any leftovers. Shred the beef. Mix in remaining peppers, onions, and ½ cup of cooking juices. Add 1 Tbsp. chili powder, 2 tsp. cumin, and salt to taste. Heat thoroughly. Fill warm flour tortillas with mixture. Serve topped with sour cream, salsa, and guacamole.

Beef Roast with Mushroom Barley

Sue Hamilton
Minooka, IL

Makes 4–6 servings
Prep. Time: 5 minutes
Cooking Time: 5–7 hours
Ideal slow-cooker size: 6-qt.

1 cup pearl barley (not quick-cook)

½ cup onion, diced

6½-oz. can mushrooms, undrained

1 tsp. garlic, minced

1 tsp. Italian seasoning

¼ tsp. black pepper

2-3-lb. beef chuck roast

1¾ cups beef broth

chopped fresh parsley

1. Grease interior of slow-cooker crock.

2. Put barley, onion, mushrooms with liquid, and garlic in slow cooker.

3. Mix in seasoning and pepper.

4. Add roast. Pour broth over all.

Serve this with mashed potatoes. They'll benefit from the delicious broth in this dish.

5. Cover. Cook 5–7 hours on Low, or until instant-read meat thermometer registers 145° when stuck into center of roast, and barley is also tender.

6. Remove meat from crock. Allow to stand for 10 minutes. Then slice, pour broth over top, garnish with chopped fresh parsley, and serve.

Hearty New England Dinner

Joette Droz
Kalona, IA

Makes 6–8 servings
Prep. Time: 10 minutes
Cooking Time: 7–9 hours
Ideal slow-cooker size: 5-qt.

2 medium carrots, sliced

1 medium onion, sliced

1 celery rib, sliced

3-lb. boneless beef chuck roast

1 tsp. salt, divided

¼ tsp. pepper

1 envelope dry onion soup mix

2 cups water

1 Tbsp. vinegar

1 bay leaf

half a small head of cabbage, cut in wedges

3 Tbsp. melted butter

2 Tbsp. flour

1 Tbsp. dried, minced onion

2 Tbsp. prepared horseradish

1. Grease interior of slow-cooker crock.

2. Place carrots, onion, and celery in slow cooker. Place roast on top.

3. In a bowl, mix together ½ tsp. salt, pepper, dry onion soup mix, water, vinegar, and bay leaf.

4. Pour over roast and vegetables.

5. Cover. Cook on Low 6–8 hours, or until instant-read meat thermometer registers 145° when stuck into center of roast.

6. Remove beef and keep warm.

7. Discard bay leaf. Add cabbage to juice in slow cooker.

8. Cover. Cook on High 1 hour, or until cabbage is tender.

9. Melt butter in saucepan. Stir in flour and onion.

10. Add 1½ cups liquid from slow cooker, stirring until smooth. Stir in horseradish and ½ tsp. salt.

11. Bring to boil. Stirring continually, cook over low heat until thick and smooth, about 2 minutes. Return to cooker and blend with remaining sauce in cooker.

12. Slice beef. Top with vegetables and gravy. Pass any extra gravy in a separate bowl.

Why I like this recipe—

This is one of our favorite winter suppers. We have pickles on the side, and that's supper!

Peppery Roast

Lovina Baer
Conrath, WI

Makes 8–10 servings
Prep. Time: 10 minutes
Cooking Time: 6–8 hours
Ideal slow-cooker size: 5-qt.

4-lb. beef chuck roast *or* venison roast

1 tsp. garlic salt

1 tsp. onion salt

2 tsp. celery salt

1½ tsp. salt

2 tsp. Worcestershire sauce

2 tsp. pepper

½ cup ketchup

1 Tbsp. liquid smoke

3 Tbsp. brown sugar

1 Tbsp. dry mustard

dash of nutmeg

1 Tbsp. soy sauce

1 Tbsp. lemon juice

3 drops hot pepper sauce

1. Grease interior of slow-cooker crock.

2. Place roast in slow cooker.

3. Combine remaining ingredients and pour over roast.

4. Cover. Cook on Low 6–8 hours, or until instant-read meat thermometer registers 145° when stuck into center of roast.

5. Remove meat from crock. Allow to stand for 10 minutes. Then slice and serve.

Why I like this recipe—

We just love the blend of flavors in this roast. We've served it with mashed potatoes and a veg in the traditional way, but we've also served it as French dip on slices of toasted French bread.

Piquant Chuck Roast

Mary Jane Musser
Manheim, PA

Makes 6–8 servings
Prep. Time: 5 minutes
Cooking Time: 6–8 hours
Ideal slow-cooker size: 4- or 5-qt.

3-lb. beef chuck roast

½ cup orange juice

3 Tbsp. soy sauce

2 Tbsp. brown sugar

1 tsp. Worcestershire sauce

1. Grease interior of slow-cooker crock.

2. Place meat in slow cooker.

3. In a mixing bowl, combine remaining ingredients and pour over meat.

4. Cover. Cook on Low 6–8 hours, or until instant-read meat thermometer registers 145° when stuck into center of roast.

5. Shred meat with 2 forks. Mix well with sauce. Serve over cooked rice, noodles, or mashed potatoes.

Why I like this recipe—
Beef cooked in soy sauce is luscious and tender with excellent flavor.

Beef

Mexican Pot Roast

**Susan Segraves,
Lansdale, PA**

Makes 6–8 servings
Prep. Time: 5 minutes
Cooking Time: 6–8 hours
Ideal slow-cooker size: 4- or 5-qt.

1½ cups chunky salsa

6-oz. can tomato paste

1 envelope dry taco seasoning mix

1 cup water

3-lb. beef chuck roast

½ cup chopped cilantro

Why I like this recipe—
Our neighborhood gets together for Taco
Night once a month. This is always a hit, and
almost all my neighbors have asked for, and
gotten, the recipe by now!

1. Grease interior of slow-cooker crock.

2. In a mixing bowl, combine first four
ingredients.

3. Place roast in slow cooker and pour salsa
mixture over top.

4. Cover and cook on Low 6–8 hours, or
until instant-read meat thermometer registers
145° when stuck into center of roast.

5. Remove meat from crock. Allow to stand
for 10 minutes. Then slice and serve.

6. Stir cilantro into sauce before serving
with beef.

Spicy Beef Roast

Karen Ceneviva
Seymour, CT

Makes 6-8 servings
Prep. Time: 15-20 minutes
Cooking Time: 6-8 hours
Ideal slow-cooker size: 4- or 5-qt.

1-2 Tbsp. cracked black peppercorns

2 cloves garlic, minced

3 lbs. round tip roast *or* brisket, trimmed of fat

3 Tbsp. balsamic vinegar

¼ cup reduced-sodium soy sauce

2 Tbsp. Worcestershire sauce

2 tsp. dry mustard

1. Grease interior of slow-cooker crock.

2. Rub cracked pepper and garlic all over roast. Put roast in slow cooker.

3. Make several shallow slits in top of meat.

4. In a small bowl, combine remaining ingredients. Spoon over meat.

5. Cover. Cook on Low 6–8 hours, or until instant-read meat thermometer registers 145° when stuck into center of roast.

6. Remove meat from crock. Allow to stand for 10 minutes. Then slice and serve.

Why I like this recipe—
Once when I had made this roast for friends, my son said—in front of all the guests— "Mom, you always cook so well and you have a smile while you're doing it." That's the kind of compliment you don't forget. And this roast is that good!

QUICK and EASY

Wine Tender Roast

Rose Hankins
Stevensville, MD

Makes 5–6 servings
Prep. Time: 10 minutes
Cooking Time: 6–8 hours
Ideal slow-cooker size: 4- or 5-qt.

2½–3-lb. beef chuck roast

1 cup thinly sliced onions

½ cup chopped apple, peeled, *or* unpeeled

3 cloves garlic, chopped

1 cup red wine

salt and pepper

1. Grease interior of slow-cooker crock.

2. Put roast in slow cooker. Layer onions, apples, and garlic on top of roast.

3. Carefully pour wine over roast without disturbing its toppings.

4. Sprinkle with salt and pepper.

5. Cover. Cook on Low 6–8 hours, or until instant-read meat thermometer registers 145° when stuck into center of roast.

6. Remove meat from crock. Allow to stand for 10 minutes. Then slice and serve.

Why I like this recipe—
The sweetness of the apple is subtle and lovely in this roast. I like to thicken the juices left behind in the slow cooker and serve it as gravy.

Machaca Beef

Jeanne Allen
Rye, CO

Makes 4 servings
Prep. Time: 5–7 minutes
Cooking Time: 4 hours
Ideal slow-cooker size: 4-qt.

1½-lb. boneless beef chuck roast

1 large onion, sliced

4-oz. can chopped green chilies, undrained

2 beef bouillon cubes

1½ tsp. dry mustard

½ tsp. garlic powder

1 tsp. seasoning salt

½ tsp. pepper

1 cup salsa

1. Grease interior of slow-cooker crock.

2. Place beef in cooker.

3. Combine all remaining ingredients, except salsa, in bowl. Pour over roast. Add just enough water so that mixture covers meat.

4. Cover cooker. Cook on Low 4 hours, or until instant-read meat thermometer registers 145° when stuck into center of roast.

5. Remove roast to platter. Empty juices from cooker and reserve.

6. Shred beef using two forks to pull it apart.

7. Return shredded beef to cooker. Stir in salsa and enough of reserved juices to have the consistency you want.

8. Use as filling for burritos, chalupas, quesadillas, or tacos.

Why I like this recipe—
After living in New Mexico for the past 30 years, I get homesick for New Mexican cuisine now that I live in Colorado. I keep memories of New Mexico alive by cooking foods that remind me of home.

Plum Roast

Shirley Unternahrer
Wayland, IA

Makes 8 servings
Prep. Time: 10–15 minutes
Cooking Time: 6–8 hours
Ideal slow-cooker size: 6-qt.

3½–4-lb. beef chuck roast

12-oz. can cola

½–¾ tsp. salt

1 large onion, sliced

1 rib celery, sliced

1 whole clove garlic, sliced

2 cups fresh *or* canned plums, cut up

1. Grease interior of slow-cooker crock.

2. Layer first six ingredients into slow cooker in order.

3. Cover. Cook on Low 6–8 hours, or until instant-read meat thermometer registers 145° when stuck into center of roast.

4. One hour before end of cooking time, add plums (including juice if they're canned). Cover and continue cooking.

5. Remove meat from crock. Allow to stand for 10 minutes. Then slice. Top with broth and plums before serving.

Why I like this recipe—

It's a mystery to us why cola makes such a good meat sauce, but it does! We serve this over rice or potatoes to absorb the delicious sauce.

Bavarian Beef

Naomi E. Fast
Hesston, KS

Makes 6 servings
Prep. Time: 15 minutes
Cooking Time: 6–8 hours
Ideal slow-cooker size: 5- or 6-qt.

3–3½-lb. boneless beef chuck roast

oil

3 cups sliced carrots

3 cups sliced onions

2 large kosher dill pickles, chopped

1 cup sliced celery

½ cup dry red wine *or* beef broth

⅓ cup German-style mustard

2 tsp. coarsely ground black pepper

2 bay leaves

¼ tsp. ground cloves

⅓ cup flour

1 cup cold water

Serve over noodles or spaetzle.

1. Grease interior of slow-cooker crock.

2. If you have time, brown roast on both sides in oil in skillet. Place roast in slow cooker.

3. Distribute carrots, onions, pickles, and celery around roast in slow cooker.

4. Combine wine, mustard, pepper, bay leaves, and cloves in a bowl. Pour over ingredients in slow cooker.

5. Cover. Cook on Low 6–8 hours, or until instant-read meat thermometer registers 145° when stuck into center of roast.

6. Remove meat and vegetables to large platter. Cover to keep warm.

7. Mix flour with 1 cup cold water in bowl until smooth. Turn cooker to High. Stir in flour-water paste, stirring continually until broth is smooth and thickened.

8. Slice meat. Top with vegetables. Serve with broth alongside.

Melt-in-Your-Mouth Mexican Meat Dish

Marlene Bogard
Newton, KS

Makes 6 servings
Prep. Time: 15 minutes
Cooking Time: 6–8 hours
Ideal slow-cooker size: 6-qt.

4-lb. boneless beef chuck roast

1 tsp. salt

1 tsp. pepper

2 Tbsp. oil

1 onion, chopped

1 tsp. chili powder

1 tsp. garlic powder

1¼ cups diced green chili peppers

½ cup chipotle salsa

¼ cup hot pepper sauce

water

flour, *optional*

TIP

This highly seasoned meat is perfect for shredded beef Mexican tacos and burritos.

1. Grease interior of slow-cooker crock.

2. Season roast with salt and pepper. If you have time, sear on all sides in oil in skillet.

3. Place meat in slow cooker.

4. In a bowl, mix together remaining ingredients, except water and flour. Spoon over meat.

5. Pour water down along side of the cooker (so as not to wash off the topping) until roast is ⅓ covered.

6. Cover cooker. Cook on Low 6–8 hours, or until instant-read meat thermometer registers 145° when stuck into center of roast.

7. Thicken hot sauce with several Tbsp. flour, if you like, in the slow cooker.

8. Remove meat from crock. Allow to stand for 10 minutes. Then slice and serve.

Pot-Roast Complete

Naomi E. Fast
Hesston, KS

Makes 6–8 servings
Prep. Time: 15 minutes
Cooking Time: 6½–7½ hours
Ideal slow-cooker size: 5- or 6-qt.

3–3½ lb. boneless chuck roast

2 large onions, sliced

½ cup brown sugar

⅓ cup soy sauce

⅓ cup cider vinegar

2 bay leaves

2–3 garlic cloves, minced

1 tsp. grated fresh ginger *or* ¼ tsp. ground
ginger

1 cup julienned carrots, matchstick size,
or baby carrots

2 cups sliced button mushrooms

2–3 cups fresh spinach leaves, *or* 2 10-oz. pkgs.
frozen spinach, thawed and squeezed dry

2 Tbsp. cornstarch

1. Grease interior of slow-cooker crock.

2. Place meat in slow cooker. Top with
onions.

3. Combine brown sugar, soy sauce, and
vinegar in a small bowl. Spoon over beef.

TIP

Serve over rice.

4. Scatter bay leaves, garlic, and ginger over
roast.

5. Cover. Cook on Low 6–7 hours, or until
instant-read meat thermometer registers 145°
when stuck into center of roast.

6. Spread carrots, mushrooms, and spinach
over beef.

7. Cover. Cook on High 20 minutes.

8. In small bowl, mix cornstarch with ½
cup broth from slow cooker. Stir into broth in
slow cooker.

9. Cover. Cook 10 minutes more.

Why I like this recipe—
I can't count how many times I have used
this recipe over the last 15–20 years as a guest
meal.

Autumn Brisket

Karen Ceneviva
Seymour, CT

Makes 8 servings
Prep. Time: 20–30 minutes
Cooking Time: 6–8 hours
Ideal slow-cooker size: 6-qt.

3-lb. boneless beef brisket
salt to taste
pepper to taste
1-lb. cabbage, cut into wedges
1 large (¾ lb.) sweet potato, or several small
    ones, peeled and cut into 1-inch pieces
1 large onion, cut in wedges
salt to taste
pepper to taste
1 medium Granny Smith apple, cored and cut
    into 8 wedges
2 10 ¾-oz. cans cream of celery soup*
1 cup water
2 tsp. caraway seeds, *optional*

1. Grease interior of slow-cooker crock.
2. Place brisket in slow cooker.
3. Shake salt and pepper over meat to taste.
4. Top with cabbage, sweet potato, and onion.
5. Season to taste with salt and pepper.
6. Place apple wedges over vegetables.

*To make your own Cream Soup, see recipes on pages 563 and 564.

7. In a medium bowl combine soup, water, and caraway seeds if you wish.
8. Spoon mixture over brisket and vegetables.
9. Cover. Cook on Low 6–8 hours, or until instant-read meat thermometer registers 145° when stuck into center of roast, and vegetables are fork-tender.
10. Remove meat from cooker and allow to stand 10 minutes. Then slice and top with vegetables and broth before serving.

Why I like this recipe—
When I make this for the first time in chilly weather, my husband says he knows it's really autumn for sure. The scent alone makes the house feel warmer.

Cranberry Brisket

Roseann Wilson
Albuquerque, NM

Makes 5–6 servings
Prep. Time: 10–15 minutes
Cooking Time: 5–6 hours
Ideal slow-cooker size: 5-qt.

2½-lb. beef brisket

½ tsp. salt

¼ tsp. pepper

16-oz. can whole berry cranberry sauce

8-oz. can tomato sauce

½ cup chopped onion

1 Tbsp. prepared mustard

1. Grease interior of slow-cooker crock.

2. Rub brisket all over with salt and pepper. Place in slow cooker.

3. Combine cranberry sauce, tomato sauce, onion, and mustard in a mixing bowl. Spoon over brisket, being careful not to disturb seasoning on meat.

4. Cover. Cook on Low 5–6 hours, or until instant-read meat thermometer registers 145° when stuck into center of roast.

5. Remove brisket from cooker and allow to stand 10 minutes. Then cut into thin slices across grain. Skim fat from juices. Serve juices with brisket.

Why I like this recipe—

One time I was expressing my opinion that turkey is the best partner for cranberry sauce, and my friend didn't say anything, but sent me this recipe later that week. I have changed my mind! This is our favorite brisket recipe now.

Good-Time Beef Brisket

AmyMarlene Jensen
Fountain, CO

Makes 6-8 servings
Prep. Time: 10 minutes
Cooking Time: 6-8 hours
Ideal slow-cooker size: 5- or 6-qt.

3½–4-lb. beef brisket

1 can beer

2 cups tomato sauce

2 tsp. prepared mustard

2 Tbsp. balsamic vinegar

2 Tbsp. Worcestershire sauce

1 tsp. garlic powder

½ tsp. ground allspice

2 Tbsp. brown sugar

1 small green, or red, bell pepper, chopped

1 medium onion, chopped

1 tsp. salt

½ tsp. pepper

TIP

Serve on rolls or over couscous,
pasta, rice, or potatoes.

1. Grease interior of slow-cooker crock.

2. Place brisket in slow cooker.

3. Combine remaining ingredients in a bowl. Pour over meat.

4. Cover. Cook on Low 6–8 hours, or until instant-read meat thermometer registers 145° when stuck into center of roast.

5. Remove meat from cooker and allow to stand 10 minutes. Then cut across the grain into thin slices. Top with vegetables and broth before serving.

Smoked Beef Brisket

Joy Martin
Myerstown, PA

Makes 4–5 servings
Prep. Time: 5–10 minutes
Cooking Time: 5–6 hours
Ideal slow-cooker size: 4-qt.

Tbsp. liquid smoke

tsp. salt

₂ tsp. pepper

½-lb. beef brisket

½ cup chopped onion

½ cup ketchup

tsp. prepared Dijon mustard

½ tsp. celery seed

1. Grease interior of slow-cooker crock.

2. In a small bowl, mix together liquid smoke, salt, and pepper. Rub brisket with mixture.

3. Place meat in slow cooker. Top with onion.

4. In a small bowl, combine ketchup, mustard, and celery seed. Spread over meat.

5. Cover. Cook on Low 5–6 hours, or until instant-read meat thermometer registers 145° when stuck into center of roast.

6. Remove meat from cooker and allow to stand 10 minutes.

7. Meanwhile, transfer cooking juices to a blender. Cover and process until smooth. (Cover lid of blender with thick towel and hold it on tightly while using. Hot liquid expands when being processed.)

8. Cut brisket across the grain into thin slices. Top with cooking juices and pass any extra in a separate bowl.

Why I like this recipe—

I love to serve this from the slow cooker to guests—they are always impressed with the flavor I created without using a laborious smoking process outside!

Corned Beef and Cabbage

Carrie Darby
Wayland, IA

Esther Porter
Minneapolis, MN

Karen Ceneviva
New Haven, CT

Dorothy Lingerfe
Stonyford, C

Leona Yoder
Hartville, OH

Betty K. Drescher
Quakertown, PA

Bonita Ensenberger
Albuquerque, NM

Makes 8 servings
Prep. Time: 30 minutes
Cooking Time: 4½–5 hours
Ideal slow-cooker size: 5- or 6-qt.

3-4-lb. corned beef brisket (not in a brine), cut into 6–8 pieces

¾-1¼ cups water

5-6 carrots, cut in 2"-3" pieces

3 medium-sized onions, quartered

salt and pepper

half to a whole head of cabbage, cut into wedges

1. Grease interior of slow-cooker crock.

2. Place corned beef in slow cooker. Add water.

3. Place carrots and onions around the meat if possible, pushing the vegetables in so they're at least partly covered by the water. Sprinkle salt and pepper over all.

4. Cover and cook on Low 3 hours, or until instant-read meat thermometer registers 125° when stuck into center of brisket.

TIP

You can prepare the cabbage separately in a large soup pot. Place wedges in kettle and add 1 cup broth from cooker. Cook 20 to 30 minutes, covered, or until just tender. Stir into corned beef and vegetables right before serving.

5. Add cabbage to cooker, pushing down into liquid to moisten. Turn to High and cook an additional 1½–2 hours, or until meat registers 145° and vegetables are tender.

Variation

Add 3 medium-sized potatoes, peeled or unpeeled, cut into chunks, to Step 3.

—Sharon Timpe, Jackson, W

Apple Corned Beef and Cabbage

Donna Treloar
Hartford City, IN

Makes 8 servings
Prep. Time: 15 minutes
Cooking Time: 4–5 hours
Ideal slow-cooker size: 6-qt.

-4-lb. corned beef brisket (not in a brine), cut into 6–8 pieces

small head of cabbage, cut in thin wedges

-4 medium-sized potatoes, cut in chunks

-3 cups baby carrots, *or* sliced full-sized carrots, *optional*

qt. pure apple juice

cup brown sugar

Why I like this recipe—
The apple juice gives a lovely sweetness to this traditional dish. We like to emphasize the flavor by cutting a fresh red apple in thin horizontal slices to use as a garnish.

1. Grease interior of slow-cooker crock.

2. Place corned beef in slow cooker.

3. Place vegetables around and on top of meat.

4. Pour apple juice over everything. Sprinkle with brown sugar.

5. Cover and cook on Low 4–5 hours, or until instant-read meat thermometer registers 145° when stuck into center of brisket pieces and vegetables are tender but not overcooked.

Sauerbraten

Leona M. Slabaugh
Apple Creek, OH

Makes 8 servings
Prep. Time: 10–20 minutes
Marinating Time: 8 hours, or overnight
Cooking Time: 6–8 hours
Ideal slow-cooker size: 6-qt.

1 cup cider vinegar

¾ cup red wine vinegar

2 tsp. salt

½ tsp. black pepper

6 whole cloves

2 bay leaves

1 Tbsp. mustard seeds

3½-lb. boneless top round roast, tied

20 gingersnaps (about 5 oz.), crushed

1. Grease interior of slow-cooker crock.

2. Combine vinegars, salt, pepper, cloves, bay leaves, and mustard seeds in a large bowl.

3. Place roast in bowl. Spoon marinade over it.

4. Cover roast in marinade and refrigerate overnight, turning once.

5. Place roast and marinade in slow cooker.

6. Cover. Cook on Low 6–8 hours, or until instant-read meat thermometer registers 145° when stuck into center of roast.

7. Remove roast to platter and keep warm.

8. Strain liquid from slow cooker. Stir crushed gingersnaps into liquid until well blended.

9. Slice roast and serve with sauce alongside.

Why I like this recipe—

This is my version of the German "sour roast" that my husband's family ate when he was growing up. It's tangy, delicious, and very tender from that long marinade.

Layered Herby Stew

Elizabeth L. Richards
Rapid City, SD

Makes 6 servings
Prep. Time: 15 minutes
Cooking Time: 4–5 hours
Ideal slow-cooker size: 5-qt.

2½ lbs. boneless beef chuck roast, cut into 1½-inch pieces

1 medium to large onion, cut in 1-inch pieces

8–12 small red potatoes, or potato chunks

4–6 carrots, cut in 1-inch pieces

2 large ribs celery, cut in 1-inch pieces

2 Tbsp. Worcestershire sauce

¼ cup red wine or water

3 Tbsp. brown sugar

1 tsp. salt

½ tsp. pepper

⅛ tsp. allspice

¼ tsp. dried marjoram

¼ tsp. dried thyme

2 bay leaves

6 Tbsp. quick-cooking raw tapioca (use only 5 Tbsp. if using water instead of red wine)

28-oz. can diced tomatoes

parsley for garnish, optional

1. Grease interior of slow-cooker crock.

2. Layer all ingredients, except parsley, in slow cooker in order given.

3. Cover. Cook on Low 4–5 hours, or until meat is tender.

4. Garnish stew with parsley and serve with mashed potatoes or noodles.

Why I like this recipe—
This is my go-to dish for Sunday dinner, since I can quickly put it together before we leave for church and the house smells wonderful when we walk in the door at noon.

Classic Beef Stew

Wanda S. Curtin
Bradenton, FL

Miriam Nolt
New Holland, PA

Mary W. Stauffer
Ephrata, PA

Audrey Kneer
Willamsfield, IL

Paula King
Harrisonburg, VA

Jean Shaner
York, PA

Alma Z. Weaver
Ephrata, PA

Makes 6 servings
Prep. Time: 15 minutes
Cooking Time: 4–5 hours
Ideal slow-cooker size: 5-qt.

2 lbs. boneless beef chuck roast, cut into
½-inch pieces

¼–½ cup flour

1½ tsp. salt

½ tsp. black pepper

1 tsp. paprika

3½ Tbsp. quick-cooking raw tapioca

1 tsp. Worcestershire sauce

2 cups beef broth

half garlic clove, minced

1 bay leaf

4 carrots, sliced, *or* 1-lb. bag whole baby carrots

2 onions, chopped

1 rib celery, sliced

3 potatoes, diced

2 cups tomatoes, diced

1. Grease interior of slow-cooker crock.

2. Place meat in slow cooker.

3. Combine flour, salt, pepper, paprika, and tapioca in small bowl. Stir into meat until coated thoroughly.

4. Gently stir in remaining ingredients. Mix well.

5. Cover. Cook on Low 4–5 hours, or until meat is tender and vegetables are done to your liking.

6. Stir before serving.

Why I like this recipe—
So simple to make and such wonderful flavor! Stew is an old favorite from the slow cooker.

Beef

Tuscan Beef Stew

Karen Ceneviva
Seymour, CT

Makes 6 servings
Prep. Time: 5–10 minutes
Cooking Time: 4¼–5¼ hours
Ideal slow-cooker size: 5-qt.

10½-oz. can tomato soup

10½-oz. can beef broth

½ cup water

1 tsp. dry Italian seasoning

½ tsp. garlic powder

14½-oz. can Italian diced tomatoes

3 large carrots (¾ lb.), cut into 1-inch pieces

2 lbs. boneless beef chuck roast, cut into
    1½-inch pieces.

2 15½-oz. cans white kidney (cannellini) beans,
    rinsed and drained

1. Grease interior of slow-cooker crock.

2. Mix all ingredients together, except
beans, in slow cooker.

3. Cover. Cook on Low 4–5 hours, or until
vegetables and beef are tender.

4. Stir in beans. Cover. Cook on High for
final 10 minutes of cooking time.

Why I like this recipe—
We love the Italian flavors in this stew. My
daughter serves it over pasta for her hungry
teenagers.

Ready-When-You-Get-Home Dinner

Beatrice Orgish
Richardson, TX

Makes 6 servings
Prep. Time: 10–15 minutes
Cooking Time: 4–5 hours
Ideal slow-cooker size: 5-qt.

1 cup uncooked wild rice, rinsed and drained

1 cup chopped celery

1 cup chopped carrots

2 4-oz. cans mushrooms, drained

1 large onion, chopped

1 clove garlic, minced

½ cup slivered almonds

3 beef bouillon cubes

2½ tsp. seasoned salt

2-lb. boneless beef chuck roast, cut into
    1½-inch pieces

3 cups water

TIP

Add a bay leaf and 4-6 whole peppercorns to mixture before cooking. Remove before serving.

1. Grease interior of slow-cooker crock.

2. Place ingredients in order listed into slow cooker.

3. Cover. Cook on Low 4–5 hours or until beef and rice are tender. Stir before serving.

Santa Fe Stew

Jeanne Allen
Rye, CO

Makes 6 servings
Prep. Time: 20 minutes
Cooking Time: 4–5 hours
Ideal slow-cooker size: 5-qt.

2 lbs. boneless beef chuck roast, cut into 1½-inch pieces

1 large onion, diced

2 garlic cloves, minced

1½ cups water

1 Tbsp. dried parsley flakes

2 beef bouillon cubes

1 tsp. ground cumin

½ tsp. salt

3 carrots, sliced

14½-oz. can diced tomatoes

14½-oz. can green beans, drained, *or* 1 lb. frozen green beans

14½-oz. can corn, drained, *or* 1 lb. frozen corn

4-oz. can diced green chilies

3 zucchini squash, diced, *optional*

1. Grease interior of slow-cooker crock.

2. Place all ingredients, except zucchini, into slow cooker.

3. Cover. Cook on Low 4–5 hours, or until meat is tender and vegetables are as tender as you like them.

4. One hour before end of cooking time, stir in diced zucchini, if you want to include it.

Why I like this recipe—
I make this all year-round, although it's especially a hit at summer potlucks when I use veggies from my garden.

Easy Creamy Beef

Joyce B. Suiter
Garysburg, NC

Makes 8 servings
Prep. Time: 5 minutes
Cooking Time: 5–6 hours
Ideal slow-cooker size: 5-qt.

3 lbs. boneless beef chuck roast, cut into
   1½-inch pieces

10¾-oz. can cream of mushroom soup*

7-oz. jar mushrooms, undrained

½ cup red wine

1 envelope dry onion soup mix

1. Grease interior of slow-cooker crock.

2. Combine all ingredients in slow cooker.

3. Cover. Cook on Low 5–6 hours, or until meat is tender.

4. Serve over noodles, rice, or potatoes done your favorite way.

Why I like this recipe—

This is my family's favorite winter supper. I got the recipe from my sister-in-law when she served it to us in buns, years ago.

*To make your own Cream Soup, see recipes on pages 561 and 562.

Hungarian Goulash

Elaine Patton
West Middletown, PA

Makes 8 servings
Prep. Time: 15 minutes
Cooking Time: 4–5 hours
Ideal slow-cooker size: 5-qt.

2 lbs. round steak, cut into ¾-inch cubes

1 cup onion, chopped

1 clove garlic, pressed

2 Tbsp. flour

½ tsp. salt

½ tsp. pepper

1 tsp. paprika

¼ tsp. dried thyme, crushed

1 bay leaf

14½-oz. can stewed, *or* diced, tomatoes

1 cup low-fat sour cream

1. Grease interior of slow-cooker crock.

2. Place beef cubes, onion, and garlic in slow cooker.

3. Stir in flour and mix to coat steak cubes and vegetables.

TIP

After you've stirred in the sour cream, begin cooking noodles on stove-top. They're a great base for this flavorful stew.

4. Add salt, pepper, paprika, thyme, bay leaf, and tomatoes. Stir well.

5. Cover. Cook on Low 4–5 hours, or until meat is tender but not dry.

6. Add sour cream 30 minutes before end of cooking time. Stir in thoroughly.

Fruity Beef Tagine

Naomi E. Fast
Hesston, KS

Makes 6 servings
Prep. Time: 20 minutes
Cooking Time: 4–5 hours
Ideal slow-cooker size: 5-qt.

2 lbs. boneless beef chuck roast, cut into
   1½-inch cubes

4 cups sliced onions

2 tsp. ground coriander

1½ tsp. ground cinnamon

¾ tsp. ground ginger

14½-oz. can beef broth, plus enough water to
   equal 2 cups

16 oz. pitted dried plums

salt to taste

fresh ground pepper to taste

juice of one lemon

1. Grease interior of slow-cooker crock.

2. Place all ingredients except lemon juice
into cooker.

3. Cook on Low 4–5 hours, or until meat is
tender.

4. Stir in lemon juice during the last 10
minutes.

TIPS

1. Mix in a few very thin slices of lemon
   rind 10 minutes before end of cooking
   time to add flavor and eye appeal.
2. You can substitute lamb cubes for
   the beef.

Beef Burgundy

Joyce Kaut
Rochester, NY

Makes 6 servings
Prep. Time: 30 minutes
Cooking Time: 3–5 hours
Ideal slow-cooker size: 5-qt.

2 slices bacon, cut in squares

2 lbs. boneless beef chuck roast, cut into
   1½-inch pieces

¼ cup flour

½ tsp. salt

¼ tsp. seasoning salt

¼ tsp. dried marjoram

¼ tsp. dried thyme

¼ tsp. pepper

1 garlic clove, minced

1 beef bouillon cube, crushed

1 cup burgundy wine

¼ lb. fresh mushrooms, sliced

1–1½ cups ketchup

2 Tbsp. cornstarch

2 Tbsp. cold water

1. Grease interior of slow-cooker crock.

2. If you have time, cook bacon in skillet until crisp and browned. Remove bacon, reserving drippings. Or buy already cooked and crumbled bacon.

3. Again, if you have time, coat beef with flour and brown on all sides in bacon drippings. (Don't crowd the skillet so the beef browns rather than steams.) Or place pieces of beef and crumbled bacon straight into the crock.

4. Stir in seasonings and herbs, garlic, bouillon, and wine.

5. Cover. Cook on Low 4–5 hours (or 3–4 hours, if you've browned the beef well in Step 2), or until beef is just tender.

6. Stir in mushrooms and ketchup.

7. Dissolve cornstarch in water in a small bowl. Stir into slow cooker.

8. Cover. Cook on High 15 minutes, until sauce thickens.

Why I like this recipe—
I make this for guests because it's so delicious and looks fancy (but still is easy for me to pull off!). I serve it with French bread and a green salad. Easy!

Italian Beef Stew

Kathy Hertzler
Lancaster, PA

Makes 4-6 servings
Prep. Time: 30 minutes
Cooking Time: 4-5 hours
Ideal slow-cooker size: 5-qt.

Tbsp. flour

tsp. chopped fresh thyme

tsp. salt

¼–½ tsp. freshly ground pepper

¼-lb. boneless beef chuck roast, cut into 1½-inch pieces

Tbsp. olive oil

onion, chopped

cup tomato sauce

cup beef stock

cup red wine

garlic cloves, minced

2 Tbsp. tomato paste

2 cups frozen peas, thawed but not cooked

1 tsp. sugar

1. Grease interior of slow-cooker crock.

2. Spoon flour into small dish. Season with thyme, salt, and pepper. Add beef cubes and coat evenly.

3. Heat 3 Tbsp. oil in slow cooker on High. Add floured beef and brown on all sides.

4. Stir in remaining ingredients except peas and sugar.

5. Cover. Cook on Low 3½–4½ hours, or until beef is tender.

6. Add peas and sugar. Cook an additional 30 minutes, or until beef is tender and peas are warm.

Why I like this recipe—
I can keep a few herbs alive in pots on my windowsill in the winter, and this recipe is one of my favorite ways to use the thyme. When I'm feeling fancy, I garnish the finished stew with a few sprigs, too.

New Mexico Beef & Pork Stew

Helen Kenagy
Carlsbad, NM

Makes 8 servings
Prep. Time: 15 minutes
Cooking Time: 4–5 hours
Ideal slow-cooker size: 5-qt.

-lb. boneless beef chuck roast, cut into
1½-inch pieces, *divided*

alt to taste

epper to taste

-6 potatoes, cubed, *divided*

-8 carrots, diced, *divided*

ther vegetables of your choice, diced, *divided*

-2 4 ¼-oz. cans chopped green chilies,
undrained, *divided*

½ lbs. raw pork sausage, crumbled, *divided*

1. Grease interior of slow-cooker crock.

2. Place half the beef cubes in bottom of
slow cooker. Sprinkle with salt and pepper.

3. Layer half the vegetables and chilies
over beef. Sprinkle with salt and pepper.

4. Crumble half the sausage over top.
Sprinkle with salt and pepper.

TIP

With such a complete dish,
all you need to add is a green
salad and fresh bread if you
wish.

5. Repeat layering until all ingredients are
used.

6. Cover. Cook on Low 4–5 hours, or until
meat and veggies are as tender as you like
them.

Spanish Round Steak

Shari Jensen
Fountain, CO

Makes 4–6 servings
Prep. Time: 10 minutes
Cooking Time: 4–5 hours
Ideal slow-cooker size: 4- or 5-qt.

small onion, sliced, *divided*

green bell pepper, sliced in rings, *divided*

rib celery, chopped, *divided*

2-lb. boneless beef chuck roast, cut into
1½-inch pieces

2 Tbsp. chopped fresh parsley *or* 2 tsp. dried
parsley

1 Tbsp. Worcestershire sauce

1 Tbsp. dry mustard

1 Tbsp. chili powder

2 cups canned tomatoes

2 tsp. dry, minced garlic

½ tsp. salt

¼ tsp. pepper

1. Grease interior of slow-cooker crock.

2. Put half of onion, green pepper, and celery in slow cooker.

3. Layer in all of beef.

4. Put in remaining onion, green pepper, and celery.

5. Combine all remaining ingredients. Pour over meat.

6. Cover. Cook on Low 4–5 hours, or until meat is tender.

Why I like this recipe—

I remember getting this recipe from my mother-in-law when we got home from our honeymoon and I realized I didn't know how to make very many recipes. I was intimidated by trying to get supper on the table every day. This recipe has stuck with me over the years.

Zingy Short Ribs

Joan Terwilliger
Lebanon, PA

Makes 4–6 servings
Prep. Time: 30 minutes
Cooking Time: 9–10 hours
Ideal slow-cooker size: 6-qt.

3 bone-in beef short ribs

15-oz. can crushed tomatoes

3 Tbsp. tomato paste

2–3 Tbsp. hot pepper jam *or* horseradish jam

6 cloves garlic, peeled

¾ tsp. dried rosemary, crushed

1 Tbsp. dried minced onions

½ tsp. ground ginger

¼ cup dry red wine

1. Grease interior of slow-cooker crock.

2. Broil ribs 6 inches from heat until browned, 5–10 minutes per side.

3. Stack ribs into slow cooker. Stagger them so the top layer doesn't directly overlap the bottom layer.

4. Combine remaining ingredients in mixing bowl. Pour over ribs. (Lift the top layer and spoon sauce over bottom layer.)

5. Cover. Cook on Low 9–10 hours, or until meat is tender but not dry.

6. Spoon off fat. Then top ribs with sauce. Pass any remaining sauce in a bowl for individuals to add to their plates.

Why I like this recipe—
My husband always asks me to make these short ribs for his birthday. They're delicious.

Slow-Cooked Short Ribs

Jean A. Shaner
York, PA

Barbara L. McGinnis
Jupiter, FL

Makes 10–12 servings
Prep. Time: 35 minutes
Cooking Time: 9–10 hours
Ideal slow-cooker size: 6-qt.

⅔ cup flour

2 tsp. salt

½ tsp. pepper

4–4½ lbs. boneless beef short ribs
 or 6–7 lbs. bone-in beef short ribs

oil *or* butter

1 large onion, chopped

1½ cups beef broth

¾ cup wine *or* cider vinegar

½–¾ cup packed brown sugar, according to
 your taste preference

½ cup chili sauce

⅓ cup ketchup

⅓ cup Worcestershire sauce

5 garlic cloves, minced

1½ tsp. chili powder

1. Grease interior of slow-cooker crock.

2. Combine flour, salt, and pepper in plastic bag. Add ribs, a few at a time, and shake to coat.

3. If you have time, brown meat in small amount of oil or butter in batches in skillet.

TIPS

It is ideal to cook these ribs one day in advance of serving. Refrigerate for several hours or overnight. Remove layer of congealed fat before serving.

Transfer to slow cooker. Reserve drippings in skillet. If you don't have time, put the ribs straight into the cooker. As you layer them in, stagger them so they don't directly overlap each other.

4. Combine remaining ingredients in skillet. Cook, stirring up browned drippings, until mixture comes to a boil. Or mix all other ingredients together in a bowl. Pour over ribs.

5. Cover. Cook on Low 9–10 hours, or until meat is tender but not dry.

6. Debone and serve, topped with sauce.

Beef Ribs with Sauerkraut

Rosaria Strachan
Fairfield, CT

Makes 8–10 servings
Prep. Time: 10 minutes
Cooking Time: 8–10 hours
Ideal slow-cooker size: 6-qt.

3–4 lbs. beef short ribs

32-oz. bag, *or* 27-oz. can, sauerkraut, drained

2 Tbsp. caraway seeds

¼ cup water

1. Grease interior of slow-cooker crock.

2. Put ribs into slow cooker, staggering the layers so the ribs don't directly overlap each other.

3. Place sauerkraut and caraway seeds on top of ribs. Lift up top layer and spoon sauerkraut and seeds over bottom layer, too.

4. Pour in water.

5. Cover. Cook on Low 8–10 hours, or until meat is tender but not dry.

TIP

These need mashed potatoes to complete the meal!

TIP

If you really enjoy sauerkraut, double the amount of sauerkraut and divide the recipe between two 4- or 5-qt. cookers.

Stuffed Flank Steak

Renee Baum
Chambersburg, PA

Makes 6 servings
Prep. Time: 30 minutes
Cooking Time: 5–7 hours
Ideal slow-cooker size: 5- or 6-qt.

8-oz. pkg. crushed cornbread stuffing

1 cup chopped onion

1 cup chopped celery

¼ cup minced fresh parsley

2 eggs

1¼ cups beef broth

5⅓ Tbsp. (⅓ cup) butter, melted

½ tsp. seasoned salt, *optional*

½ tsp. pepper

1½-lb. flank steak

TIP

If you have a helpful butcher, ask him/her to pound the steak for you.

1. Grease interior of slow-cooker crock.

2. Combine stuffing, onion, celery, and parsley in large bowl.

3. In a small bowl, beat eggs. Stir in broth and butter. Pour over stuffing mixture. Sprinkle with seasoned salt if you wish, and pepper. Stir well.

4. Pound steak to ¼-inch thickness.

5. Spread 1½ cups stuffing mixture over steak. Roll up, starting with short side. Tie with string.

6. Place steak in slow cooker.

7. Wrap remaining stuffing tightly in foil and place on top of rolled steak.

8. Cover. Cook on Low 5–7 hours, or until instant-read meat thermometer reaches 145° when stuck into the center of the rolled steak.

9. Remove string before slicing.

Fruity Flank Steak

Ruth A. Feister
Narvon, PA

Makes 6 servings
Prep. Time: 10 minutes
Cooking Time: 5–7 hours
Ideal slow-cooker size: 4- or 5-qt.

1½–2-lb. flank steak

salt to taste

pepper to taste

14½-oz. can mixed fruit, *or* your choice of canned fruit

1 Tbsp. oil

1 Tbsp. lemon juice

¼ cup teriyaki sauce

1 tsp. cider vinegar

1 garlic clove, minced

1. Grease interior of slow-cooker crock.

2. Sprinkle steak with salt and pepper. Place in slow cooker.

3. Drain fruit, saving ¼ cup syrup. Set fruit aside.

4. In a small bowl, combine ¼ cup reserved syrup with remaining ingredients. Pour over steak.

5. Cover. Cook on Low 5–7 hours, or until instant-read meat thermometer reaches 145° when stuck into the center of the steak.

TIP

Top off this meal by serving the steak and fruit with baked rice.

6. Add drained fruit during last 15 minutes of cooking time.

7. Lift meat from cooker onto platter. Using sharp knife slice across the grain, making thin slices. Spoon fruit over meat.

Slow Cooker Beef with Mushrooms

Grace W. Yoder
Harrisonburg, VA

Makes 6 servings
Prep. Time: 10 minutes
Cooking Time: 4–5 hours
Ideal slow-cooker size: 4- or 5-qt.

2 medium onions, thinly sliced

½ lb. mushrooms, sliced, *or* 2 4-oz. cans sliced mushrooms, drained

2½-lb. beef flank *or* round steak

salt to taste

pepper to taste

1 Tbsp. Worcestershire sauce

1 Tbsp. oil

paprika to taste

1. Grease interior of slow-cooker crock.

2. Place sliced onions and mushrooms in slow cooker.

3. Score top of meat about ½-inch deep in diamond pattern.

4. Season with salt and pepper. Rub in Worcestershire sauce and oil. Sprinkle top with paprika.

5. Place meat on top of onions.

TIP

Add 1 Tbsp. lemon juice to Worcestershire sauce and oil in Step 4.
—Genelle Taylor, Perrysburg, OH

6. Cover. Cook on Low 4–5 hours, or until instant-read meat thermometer reaches 145° when stuck into the center of the steak.

7. To serve, cut beef across grain in thin slices. Top with mushrooms and onions.

Round Steak Roll-Ups

Linda Sluiter
Schererville, IN

Makes 4–6 servings
Prep. Time: 15 minutes
Cooking Time: 5–6 hours
Ideal slow-cooker size: 4-qt.

2-3-lb. round steak, about 1-inch thick, cut into strips

1 lb. bacon

1 cup ketchup

¾ cup brown sugar

1 cup water

half a yellow onion, chopped

1. Grease interior of slow-cooker crock.

2. Lay a bacon strip down, then a strip of beef on top of the bacon slice. Roll up and secure with toothpick. Place in slow cooker.

3. Combine remaining ingredients in a bowl. Pour over meat roll-ups.

4. Cover. Cook on Low 5–6 hours, or until instant-read meat thermometer reaches 145° when stuck into the center of a piece of steak.

Why I like this recipe—

I got this recipe from my aunt when she made these roll-ups for a family gathering. The steak gets very tender and the flavors are wonderful.

Three-Pepper Steak

Renee Hankins
Narvon, PA

Makes 10 servings
Prep. Time: 30 minutes
Cooking Time: 4–5 hours
Ideal slow-cooker size: 4- or 5-qt.

bell peppers (one red, one orange, and one yellow pepper—or any combination of colors), cut into ¼-inch-thick slices

garlic cloves, sliced

large onion, sliced

tsp. ground cumin

½ tsp. dried oregano

bay leaf

3½-lb. beef flank steak, cut across the grain in ¼–½-inch-thick slices

salt to taste

14½-oz. can diced tomatoes in juice

jalapeño chilies, sliced, *optional*

1. Grease interior of slow-cooker crock.

2. Place sliced peppers, garlic, onion, cumin, oregano, and bay leaf in slow cooker. Stir gently to mix.

TIP

We love this served over noodles, rice, or torn tortillas.

3. Put steak slices on top of vegetable mixture. Season with salt.

4. Spoon tomatoes with juice over top. Sprinkle with jalapeño pepper slices if you wish. Do not stir.

5. Cover. Cook on Low 4–5 hours, depending on your slow cooker. Check after 3½ hours to see if meat is tender. If not, continue cooking until tender but not dry.

Fajita Steak

Becky Harder
Monument, CO

Makes 6 servings
Prep. Time: 10 minutes
Cooking Time: 5–6 hours
Ideal slow-cooker size: 4-qt.

5-oz. can tomatoes with green chilies

¼ cup salsa, your choice of mild, medium, *or* hot

-oz. can tomato sauce

-lb. round steak, about 1-inch thick, cut in 2x4-inch strips

envelope dry fajita spice mix

cup water, *optional*

1. Grease interior of slow-cooker crock.

2. Combine all ingredients—except water—n your slow cooker.

3. Cover and cook on Low 5–6 hours, or ntil meat is tender but not overcooked.

4. Check meat occasionally to make sure it sn't cooking dry. If it begins to look dry, stir n water, up to 1 cup.

TIPS

Serve meat with fried onions and green peppers. Offer shredded cheese, avocado chunks, and sour cream as toppings. Let individual eaters wrap any or all of the ingredients in flour tortillas.

Variation:

Instead of the salsa, add 1 small onion, chopped, and 1 red bell pepper, cut in 1-inch pieces to Step 2. Mix ¼ cup flour and ¼ cup water in a jar with a tight-fitting lid. Shake until smooth. Fifteen to twenty minutes before end of cooking time, pour slowly into stew, stirring while you do so that it blends well. Cover and continue cooking until stew thickens.

—Audrey L. Kneer, Williamsfield, IL

Barbecued Roast Beef

Kim Stoltzfus
New Holland, PA

Makes 10–12 servings
Prep. Time: 10 minutes
Cooking Time: 6–8 hours
Ideal slow-cooker size: 6-qt. *oval*

4-lb. boneless beef chuck roast

1 cup ketchup

1 cup barbecue sauce

2 cups chopped celery

2 cups water

1 cup chopped onions

4 Tbsp. vinegar

2 Tbsp. brown sugar

2 Tbsp. Worcestershire sauce

1 tsp. chili powder

1 tsp. garlic powder

1 tsp. salt

TIP

Slice meat into thin slices, and serve in barbecue sauce over mashed potatoes or rice.

1. Grease interior of slow-cooker crock.

2. Place roast in crock.

3. Combine all other ingredients in large bowl. Spoon over roast.

4. Cover. Cook on Low 6–8 hours, or until instant-read meat thermometer reaches 145° when stuck into the center of the roast.

Ranch Hand Beef

Sharon Timpe
Mequon, WI

Makes 8–10 servings
Prep. Time: 10 minutes
Cooking Time: 5–6 hours
Ideal slow-cooker size: 5- or 6-qt.

3–3½-lb. boneless beef chuck roast

1 cup thinly sliced onions

10¾-oz. can cream of celery soup*

4-oz. can sliced mushrooms, drained

12-oz. can beer

½ cup ketchup

1 large bay leaf

½ tsp. salt

¼ tsp. lemon pepper

2 Tbsp. chopped fresh parsley, *or* 1½ tsp. dried parsley

TIPS

This works well two ways: served on buns as sandwiches, or over cooked noodles. Or, to give this dish a Mexican theme, serve the beef over tortilla chips or Fritos. Have bowls of shredded lettuce, diced avocado, sliced green onions, sliced ripe olives, sour cream, diced tomatoes, and shredded cheese available for garnishing the meat.

1. Grease interior of slow-cooker crock.

2. Place roast in slow cooker.

3. Combine remaining ingredients in large bowl. Pour over roast.

4. Cover. Cook on Low 5–6 hours, or until instant-read meat thermometer reaches 145° when stuck into the center of the roast.

5. Remove bay leaf.

6. Shred roast with two forks. Mix meat through sauce.

Variation:
If you prefer a thicker sauce, stir 2 Tbsp. cornstarch into ¼ cup water. When smooth, stir into hot sauce in cooker, 15 minutes before serving.

*To make your own Cream Soup, see recipes on pages 563 and 564.

Middle East Sandwiches (for a crowd)

**Esther Mast
East Petersburg, PA**

Makes 10–16 sandwiches
Prep. Time: 50 minutes
Cooking Time: 4¼–5¼ hours
Ideal slow-cooker size: 5- or 6-qt.

4 lbs. boneless beef chuck roast, *or* venison roast, cut in ½-inch cubes

4 Tbsp. cooking oil

2 cups chopped onions

2 garlic cloves, minced

1 cup dry red wine

6-oz. can tomato paste

1 tsp. dried oregano

1 tsp. dried basil

½ tsp. dried rosemary

2 tsp. salt

dash of pepper

¼ cup cornstarch

¼ cup cold water

10–16 pita breads

2 cups shredded lettuce

1 large tomato, seeded and diced

1 large cucumber, seeded and diced

8-oz. plain yogurt

TIP

All you need to top this off is salad or applesauce.

1. Grease interior of slow-cooker crock.

2. If you have time, brown meat, 1 lb. at a time, in skillet in 1 Tbsp. oil. As you finish one batch, place browned beef in slow cooker. Reserve drippings. If you don't have time, place meat cubes into crock.

3. Sauté onions and garlic in drippings until tender. Then add to meat in crock. Or stir into crock with meat without sautéing.

4. Stir in wine, tomato paste, oregano, basil, rosemary, salt, and pepper.

5. Cover. Cook on Low 4–5 hours, or until meat and onions are tender but not dry.

6. Turn cooker to High. Combine cornstarch and water in small bowl until smooth. Stir into meat mixture. Cook just until bubbly and thickened, stirring frequently.

7. Split pita breads to make pockets. Fill each with meat mixture, topped with lettuce, tomato, cucumber, and yogurt.

Flavorful Meat Loaf

Anne Townsend
Albuquerque, NM

Makes 8 servings
Prep. Time: 25 minutes
Cooking Time: 4–5 hours
Ideal slow-cooker size: 6-qt. *oval*

2 medium potatoes, peeled or unpeeled, cut in strips

Meat Loaf:
2 lbs. ground beef
½ lb. bulk sausage
1 onion, finely chopped
2–3 cloves garlic, minced, according to your taste preference
½ cup ketchup
¾ cup crushed saltines
2 eggs
2 tsp. Worcestershire sauce
2 tsp. seasoning salt
¼ tsp. pepper

Sauce:
½ cup ketchup
¼ cup brown sugar
1½ tsp. dry mustard
½ tsp. ground nutmeg

TIP

The potatoes take longer to cook than the meat so make sure the potatoes are tender before lifting them out.

1. Grease interior of slow-cooker crock.

2. Place potatoes in bottom of slow cooker.

3. Make a tinfoil sling for your slow cooker so you can lift the cooked Meat Loaf out easily. Begin by folding a strip of tin foil accordion-fashion so that it's about 1½–2 inches wide and long enough to fit from the top edge of the crock, down inside and up the other side, plus a 2-inch overhang on each side of the cooker. Make a second strip exactly like the first.

4. Place the one strip in the crock, running from end to end, over top the potatoes. Place the second strip in the crock, running from side to side, also over the potatoes. The 2 strips should form a cross in the bottom of the crock.

5. Combine Meat Loaf ingredients in a large bowl. Form into loaf.

6. Place loaf into crock, on top of the potatoes, and centering it where the 2 foil strips cross.

7. Combine Sauce ingredients in a separate bowl. Spoon over Meat Loaf.

8. Cover. Cook on Low 4–5 hours.

9. Remove Meat Loaf from crock. Let stand 10–15 minutes to allow meat to gather its juices before slicing to serve.

Why I like this recipe—
My husband has this at the top of his list of favorite Meat Loaf recipes.

Cheesy Meat Loaf

Mary Sommerfeld
Lancaster, PA

Makes 8 servings
Prep. Time: 15 minutes
Cooking Time: 3–4 hours
Ideal slow-cooker size: 6-qt. *oval*

2 lbs. ground chuck, *or* ground beef

2 cups shredded sharp cheddar *or* American
   cheese

1 tsp. salt

1 tsp. dry mustard

¼ tsp. pepper

½ cup chili sauce

2 cups crushed cornflakes

2 eggs

½ cup milk

TIP

Serve with your favorite
tomato sauce or ketchup.

1. Grease interior of slow-cooker crock.

2. Create a tinfoil sling for your crock
before mixing the meat loaf. (See directions
on page 146, Steps 3 and 4 in instructions, for
making Flavorful Meat Loaf.)

3. Combine all ingredients in a large bowl.
Shape into loaf. Place loaf in crock, centering
it where the 2 foil strips cross.

4. Cover. Cook on Low 3–4 hours.

5. Remove meat loaf from crock. Let stand
10–15 minutes to allow meat to gather its
juices before slicing to serve.

Beef

Festive Meatballs

Jean Butzer
Batavia, NY

Makes 5–7 servings
Prep. Time: 20 minutes
Cooking Time: 3¼–4¼ hours
Ideal slow-cooker size: 4-qt.

1½ lbs. ground beef

4¼-oz. can deviled ham

⅔ cup evaporated milk

2 eggs, beaten slightly

1 Tbsp. grated onion

2 cups soft bread crumbs

1 tsp. salt

¼ tsp. allspice

¼ tsp. pepper

¼ cup flour

¼ cup water

1 Tbsp. ketchup

2 tsp. dill weed

1 cup sour cream

TIP

Serve over rice or pasta.

1. Grease interior of slow-cooker crock.

2. Combine beef, ham, milk, eggs, onion, bread crumbs, salt, allspice, and pepper in large bowl. Shape into 2-inch meatballs. As you finish making a ball, place it in the slow cooker.

3. Cover. Cook on Low 3–4 hours. Turn to High.

4. In a bowl, dissolve flour in water until smooth. Stir in ketchup and dill weed. Add to meatballs, stirring gently.

5. Cook on High 15–20 minutes, or until slightly thickened.

6. Turn off heat. Stir in sour cream.

Lasagna Mexicana

Barbara Walker
Sturgis, SD

Makes 6 servings
Prep. Time: 20 minutes
Cooking Time: 3–4 hours
Ideal slow-cooker size: 5-qt.

1 lb. ground beef

16-oz. can refried beans

2 tsp. dried oregano

1 tsp. ground cumin

¾ tsp. garlic powder

9 uncooked lasagna noodles, *divided*

1 cup salsa, as hot or as mild as you like

1 cup water

2 cups sour cream

2¼ -oz. can sliced ripe olives, drained

1 cup Mexican-blend cheese, shredded

½ cup sliced green onions

1. Grease interior of slow-cooker crock.

2. If you have time, brown beef in a skillet. Using a slotted spoon, lift beef out of drippings and place in good-sized bowl. If you don't have time, place beef in bowl and use a sturdy spoon to break it up into small clumps.

3. Stir in beans and seasonings.

4. Place three uncooked noodles in bottom of crock, breaking and overlapping to fit.

5. Cover with half of meat/vegetable mixture.

6. Repeat layers of noodles and meat/vegetables.

7. Top with remaining noodles.

8. Combine salsa and water in a bowl. Pour over noodles.

9. Cover. Cook on Low 3–4 hours, or until noodles are tender but lasagna is not drying out around edges.

10. Spread lasagna with sour cream.

11. Sprinkle with olives, cheese, and green onions.

12. Let stand 10–15 minutes before serving to allow noodles and cheese to firm up.

Why I like this recipe—

This is a fun variation on traditional lasagna. It's always a hit as soon as people get past their surprise.

Enchilada Stack-Up

Sally Holzem
Schofield, WI

Makes 8 servings
Prep. Time: 30 minutes
Cooking Time: 4 hours
Ideal slow-cooker size: 5-qt.

1 lb. ground beef

1 cup chopped onion

½ cup chopped red, yellow, *or* orange bell
    peppers, *or* a mixture

1 tsp. olive oil

15-oz. can kidney beans, rinsed and drained

15-oz. can black beans, rinsed and drained

14½-oz. can diced tomatoes and green chilies

1½ tsp. cumin

¼ tsp. black pepper

6 8-inch tortillas

2 cups shredded cheddar cheese

1. Grease interior of slow-cooker crock.

2. Create a tinfoil sling for your crock before making the Enchilada Stack-Up. (See directions on page 146, Steps 3 and 4 in instructions for making Flavorful Meat Loaf.)

3. If you have time, brown ground beef, onions, and bell peppers in olive oil in skillet. Drain off drippings and discard. If you don't have time, place ground beef in good-sized bowl and break it up with a wooden spoon. Then stir in onions.

4. Stir kidney beans, black beans, tomatoes, cumin, and black pepper into beef-veggie mixture in bowl.

This is a great game-day meal. Good go-alongs with this recipe: Fresh fruit to cool the palate and sherbet for dessert.

5. Lay 1 tortilla in bottom of crock (and over top of the foil strips). Spoon ¾ cup beef and veggie mixture over top. Sprinkle with ¼ of cheese.

6. Repeat layers 5 times.

7. Cover and cook on Low 4 hours, until very hot in the middle.

8. Use foil strips as handles to remove stack from slow cooker to platter.

9. Gently ease foil strips out from underneath stack, or bend them over so they're out of the way.

10. Cover stack to keep warm. Allow to stand 10–15 minutes to firm up. Then cut into wedges and serve.

Beef

Spaghetti Sauce with a Kick

Andrea O'Neil
Fairfield, CT

Makes 4–6 servings
Prep. Time: 25 minutes
Cooking Time: 4 hours
Ideal slow-cooker size: 4- or 5-qt.

1 lb. ground beef

1 onion, chopped

2 28-oz. cans crushed tomatoes

16-oz. can tomato sauce

1-lb. bulk Italian sausage, crumbled

3 cloves garlic, crushed

1 Tbsp. Italian seasoning

2 tsp. dried basil

red pepper flakes to taste

1. Grease interior of slow-cooker crock.

2. If you have time, brown beef and onions in skillet. Stir frequently to break up clumps. When meat is no longer pink, drain off drippings and place in slow cooker. If you don't have time, crumble beef into cooker. Stir in onions and mix together well.

3. Stir remaining ingredients into slow cooker.

4. Cover. Cook on Low 4 hours.

TIP

Serve over your favorite pasta.

Variation:
Add 1–2 tsp. salt and 1–2 Tbsp. brown sugar or honey to Step 3, if you wish.

Honey Barbecue Pork Chops

Tamara McCarthy
Pennsburg, PA

Makes 8 servings
Prep. Time: 15 minutes
Cooking Time: 5-7 hours
Ideal slow-cooker size: 5- or 6-qt.

8 bone-in, ¾-inch-thick, blade-cut pork chops

1 large onion, sliced, *divided*

1 cup barbecue sauce

⅓ cup honey

Why I like this recipe—
Bone-in chops tend not to dry out as quickly, and this topping mixture helps to keep the meat succulent and irresistibly tasty.

1. Grease interior of slow-cooker crock.

2. Place one layer of pork chops in your slow cooker.

3. Arrange a proportionate amount of sliced onions over top.

4. Mix barbecue sauce and honey together in a small bowl. Spoon a proportionate amount of sauce over the chops.

5. Repeat the layers, staggering the chops so they don't directly overlap each other.

6. Cover and cook on Low 2½–3½ hours.

7. If the sauce barely covers the chops, flip them over at this point. If they're well covered, simply allow them to cook another 2½–3½ hours on Low, or until instant-read meat thermometer registers 140°–145° when stuck into center of chops (but not against bone).

Spicy Pork Chops

Cynthia Morris
Grottoes, VA

Makes 4 servings
Prep. Time: 5 minutes
Cooking Time: 4–5 hours
Ideal slow-cooker size: 5-qt.

bone-in, ¾-inch-thick, blade-cut pork chops

cup Italian salad dressing

½ cup brown sugar

⅓ cup prepared spicy mustard

1. Grease interior of slow-cooker crock.

2. Place pork chops in slow cooker.

3. Mix remaining 3 ingredients together in a bowl. Pour over chops.

4. Cover and cook on Low 4–5 hours, or until instant-read meat thermometer registers 140°–145° when stuck into center of chops (but not against bone).

TIP

Check the meat after cooking for 3 hours to make sure the meat is not overcooking.

Variation

You can substitute chicken thighs for pork chops.

Pork

Stuffed Pork Chops and Corn

Peggy Forsythe
Bartlett, TN

Makes 5–6 servings
Prep. Time: 15 minutes
Cooking Time: 4–5 hours
Ideal slow-cooker size: 4- or 5-qt.

5–6 bone-in, ¾-inch-thick, blade-cut pork chops

1 box stuffing mix for pork, prepared

14-oz. can whole corn, *optional*

10¾-oz. can cream of mushroom soup*

1. Grease interior of slow-cooker crock.

2. Place pork chops in slow cooker. If you need to create a second layer, stagger the chops so they don't directly overlap each other.

3. Spoon prepared stuffing mix over top of chops.

4. Spoon corn over stuffing. Pour soup over all—without adding water.

5. Cover and cook on Low 4–5 hours, or until instant-read meat thermometer registers 140°–145° when stuck into center of chops (but not against bone).

Why I like this recipe—
Corn and pork are simply strong partners flavor-wise.

*To make your own Cream Soup, see recipes on pages 561 and 562.

Pork

Pork and Sweet Potatoes

Vera F. Schmucker
Goshen, IN

Makes 4 servings
Prep. Time: 15 minutes
Cooking Time: 4–5 hours
Ideal slow-cooker size: 5-qt.

4 bone-in, ¾-inch-thick, blade-cut pork chops

salt and pepper to taste

4 sweet potatoes, cut in large chunks

2 onions, cut in quarters

½ cup apple cider

1. Grease interior of slow-cooker crock.

2. Place meat in bottom of slow cooker. Salt and pepper to taste.

3. Arrange sweet potatoes and onions over top of the pork.

4. Pour apple cider over all.

5. Cover and cook on Low 4–5 hours, or until instant-read meat thermometer registers 140°–145° when stuck into center of chops (but not against bone).

Why I like this recipe—
The sweet potatoes add a certain richness, but not heaviness, to this dish.

Pork Chops Pierre

Genelle Taylor
Perrysburg, OH

Makes 6 servings
Prep. Time: 30–40 minutes
Cooking Time: 4½–5½ hours
Ideal slow-cooker size: 5- or 6-qt.

6 bone-in, ¾-inch-thick, blade-cut pork chops

½ tsp. salt, *optional*

⅛ tsp. pepper

2 medium onions, chopped

2 ribs celery, chopped

1 large green bell pepper, sliced

14-oz. can stewed tomatoes

½ cup ketchup

2 Tbsp. cider vinegar

2 Tbsp. brown sugar

2 Tbsp. Worcestershire sauce

1 Tbsp. lemon juice

1 beef bouillon cube

2 Tbsp. cornstarch

2 Tbsp. water

1. Grease interior of slow-cooker crock.

2. Place chops in slow cooker. If you need to create a second layer, stagger the chops so they don't directly overlap each other.

3. Sprinkle with salt and pepper.

4. Spoon onions, celery, green pepper, and tomatoes over chops. Lift up chops on second layer and spoon veggies over chops on the bottom layer, too.

TIP

Serve over cooked
rice if you wish.

5. In a small bowl, combine ketchup, vinegar, sugar, Worcestershire sauce, lemon juice, and bouillon cube. Pour over vegetables, including those on the bottom layer.

6. Cover. Cook on Low 4–5 hours, or until instant-read meat thermometer registers 140°–145° when stuck into center of chops (but not against bone).

7. Remove chops to a platter and keep warm.

8. In a small bowl, mix together cornstarch and water until smooth. Stir into liquid in slow cooker.

9. Cover. Cook on High 30 minutes or until sauce thickens.

Baked Beans and Chops

John D. Allen
Rye, CO

Makes 6 servings
Prep. Time: 10 minutes
Cooking Time: 4–5 hours
Ideal slow-cooker size: 5- or 6-qt.

2 16½-oz. cans baked beans

6 bone-in, ¾-inch-thick, blade-cut pork chops, *divided*

1½ tsp. prepared mustard

1½ Tbsp. brown sugar

1½ Tbsp. ketchup

6 onion slices, ¼-inch thick

1. Grease interior of slow-cooker crock.

2. Pour baked beans into bottom of greased slow cooker.

3. Layer pork chops over beans. If you need to create a second layer, stagger the chops so they don't directly overlap each other.

4. Spread mustard over all pork chops. Sprinkle each with brown sugar and drizzle with ketchup.

5. Top each with onion slices.

6. Cover. Cook on Low 4–5 hours, or until instant-read meat thermometer registers 140°–145° when stuck into center of chops (but not against bone).

Why I like this recipe—
We know bacon and beans work together well in baked beans. This recipe just takes that combination a bit further and deeper by switching in chops.

Pork

Pork Chops in Orange Sauce

Kelly Evenson
Pittsboro, NC

Makes 4 servings
Prep. Time: 25 minutes
Cooking Time: 4-5 hours
Ideal slow-cooker size: 4- or 5-qt.

4 bone-in, ¾-inch-thick, blade-cut pork chops

salt to taste

pepper to taste

1 orange

¼ cup ketchup

¾ cup orange juice

1 Tbsp. orange marmalade

1 Tbsp. cornstarch

¼ cup water

1. Grease interior of slow-cooker crock.

2. Season pork chops on both sides with salt and pepper.

3. Grate ½ tsp. orange zest from top or bottom of orange (in order to preserve the orange segments for topping the cooked chops). Combine zest with ketchup, orange juice, and marmalade in a small bowl until well mixed.

4. Pour sauce over chops.

5. Cover. Cook on Low 4–5 hours, or until instant-read meat thermometer registers 140°–145° when stuck into center of chops (but not against bone).

6. Remove chops and keep warm on a platter.

7. In a small bowl, dissolve cornstarch in water. Stir into sauce in slow cooker until it becomes smooth. Cook on High 15 minutes, or until sauce thickens.

8. Serve chops with orange sauce on top, along with fresh orange segments.

Why I like this recipe—
Citrus and ketchup just do a knockout job together!

PORK

Oxford Canal Chops Deluxe

Willard E. Roth
Elkhart, IN

Makes 6 servings
Prep. Time: 25 minutes
Cooking Time: 4–5 hours
Ideal slow-cooker size: 5- or 6-qt.

6 bone-in, ¾-inch-thick, blade-cut pork chops

¼ cup flour

1 tsp. garlic powder

1 tsp. sea salt

1 tsp. black pepper

1 tsp. dried basil *and/or* dried oregano

2 medium onions, sliced

2 Tbsp. oil

1 cup burgundy wine

14½-oz. can beef broth

1 soup can of water

6-oz. can tomato sauce

8 oz. dried apricots

½ lb. fresh mushroom caps

1. Grease interior of slow-cooker crock.

2. Shake chops in bag with flour, garlic powder, salt, pepper, and basil or oregano.

3. Cook onions in oil in medium hot skillet until just softened. Remove onions to plate.

4. Add chops and brown on both sides.

5. Pour any remaining flour over chops in skillet.

TIP

This is a great dish to serve with the Celtic specialty Bubble and Squeak— Irish potatoes mashed with green cabbage or Brussels sprouts.

6. In large bowl mix together wine, broth, water, and tomato sauce. Pour over meat. Bring to boil.

7. Remove chops from skillet and place in cooker. If you need to create a second layer, stagger the chops so they don't directly overlap each other.

8. Layer in apricots and mushrooms, spreading them over both layers of chops. Pour heated broth over top.

9. Cover. Cook on Low 4–5 hours, or until instant-read meat thermometer registers 140°–145° when stuck into center of chops (but not against bone).

Why I like this recipe—
My favorite memory with this recipe was the time I prepared it in the tiny kitchen of a houseboat on the Oxford Canal and then shared it with five friends. It was a hit!

Apples, Sauerkraut, and Chops

Carol Sherwood
Batavia, NY

Makes 4 servings
Prep. Time: 25 minutes
Cooking Time: 4–5 hours
Ideal slow-cooker size: 5-qt.

1 onion, sliced and separated into rings, *divided*

⅛ tsp. garlic flakes *or* garlic powder, *divided*

3 cups sauerkraut, drained, *divided*

1 cup unpeeled apple slices, *divided*

1½ tsp. caraway seeds, *divided*

¼ tsp. salt, *divided*

¼ tsp. dried thyme, *divided*

¼ tsp. pepper, *divided*

4 bone-in, ¾-inch-thick, blade-cut pork chops

¾ cup apple juice

1. Grease interior of slow-cooker crock.

2. Place half of onion rings, garlic flakes, sauerkraut, apple slices, and caraway seeds in slow cooker.

3. Season with half the salt, thyme, and pepper.

4. Place pork chops on top of ingredients in slow cooker.

5. Layer remaining ingredients in order given.

6. Pour apple juice over all.

7. Cover. Cook on Low 4–5, or until instant-read meat thermometer registers 140°–145° when stuck into center of chops (but not against bone).

8. Serve chops topped with onion-sauerkraut-apple mixture.

Why I like this recipe—
This is a sturdy one-dish dinner. I often serve it with mashed potatoes.

PORK

Pork Chops with Mushroom Sauce

Jennifer J. Gehman
Harrisburg, PA

Makes 4–6 servings
Prep. Time: 5–10 minutes
Cooking Time: 4–5 hours
Ideal slow-cooker size: 4- or 5-qt.

4–6 bone-in, ¾-inch-thick, blade-cut pork chops

10¾-oz. can cream of mushroom soup*

¾ cup white wine

4-oz. can sliced mushrooms

2 Tbsp. quick-cooking tapioca

2 tsp. Worcestershire sauce

1 tsp. beef bouillon granules, *or* 1 beef bouillon cube

¼ tsp. minced garlic

¾ tsp. dried thyme, *optional*

TIP

Serve over rice.

1. Grease interior of slow-cooker crock.

2. Place pork chops in slow cooker.

3. Combine remaining ingredients in a good-sized bowl. Pour over pork chops.

4. Cook on Low 4–5 hours, or until instant-read meat thermometer registers 140°–145° when stuck into center of chops (but not against bone).

5. Serve chops topped with mushroom sauce.

*To make your own Cream Soup, see pages 561 and 562.

Lemon Sweet Pork Chops

Doris Slatten
Mt. Juliet, TN

Makes 8 servings
Prep. Time: 15 minutes
Cooking Time: 5–7 hours
Ideal slow-cooker size: *oval* 6- or 7-qt.

¼ tsp. salt

¼ tsp. coarsely ground black pepper

½ tsp. dried oregano

½ tsp. dried chives

⅛ tsp. dried dill

¼ tsp. minced garlic

8 bone-in, ¾-inch-thick, blade-cut pork chops

8 lemon slices

4 Tbsp. ketchup

4 Tbsp. brown sugar

1. Grease interior of slow-cooker crock.

2. In a small bowl, mix together salt, pepper, oregano, chives, dill, and garlic.

3. Sprinkle over both sides of each chop, then lay chop in crock. If you need to make a second layer, stagger the pieces so they don't directly overlap each other.

4. Place lemon slice on each chop.

5. In same small bowl, mix together ketchup and brown sugar. Drop a Tbsp. of mixture on top of each chop.

6. Cover. Cook on Low 5–7 hours, or until instant-read meat thermometer registers 140°–145° when stuck into center of chops (but not against bone).

Why I like this recipe—
We eat the lemon slices in this dish because they've been soaking up the flavors for 5–7 hours. They're not just a garnish here!

Pork

Pork Chops with a Hint of Asia

Shirley Unternahrer
Wayland, IA

Makes 4 servings
Prep. Time: 15 minutes
Marinating Time: 1 hour
Cooking Time: 4–5 hours
Ideal slow-cooker size: 4- or 5-qt.

½ cup orange juice

½ cup orange marmalade

2 cloves garlic, minced

3 Tbsp. soy sauce

2 Tbsp. brown sugar

2 Tbsp. rice vinegar, *or* 1 Tbsp. white vinegar

2 tsp. Asian-style chili paste

4 bone-in, ¾-inch-thick, blade-cut pork chops

8 oz. angel hair pasta

8 oz. snow peas, *or* broccoli

1. Grease interior of slow-cooker crock.

2. Mix orange juice, orange marmalade, minced garlic, soy sauce, brown sugar, vinegar, and chili paste in rectangular glass dish that will hold the pork chops in one layer.

3. Place chops in sauce to marinate for 1 hour. Place covered dish in fridge. Turn chops over once halfway through marinating time.

4. Place chops in slow cooker. Spoon marinade over top.

5. Cover. Cook 4–5 hours on Low, or until instant-read meat thermometer registers 140°–145° when stuck in center of chops (but not against bone).

6. Near end of cooking time for chops, cook pasta according to package directions.

7. Two minutes before end of pasta cooking time, stir snow peas into water with pasta. When done cooking, drain and keep warm.

8. Place chops on platter.

9. Toss pasta and snow peas with sauce in crock. Spoon onto serving platter next to chops. Serve.

Why I like this recipe—
Hadn't thought about pasta and snow peas as a go-along with Asian-tinged chops? Make this once, and it won't be the last, promise!

Pork

Pork Loin with Savory Fruit Sauce

Maricarol Magill
Freehold, NJ

Makes 4 servings
Prep. Time: 25–40 minutes
Cooking Time: 4–5 hours
Ideal slow-cooker size: 5- or 6-qt.

8-oz. pkg. dried mixed fruit (including plums and apricots), chopped
¼ cup golden raisins
2 tsp. minced fresh ginger
1 small onion, chopped
⅓ cup brown sugar
2 Tbsp. cider vinegar
¾ cup water
¼ tsp. ground cinnamon
¼ tsp. curry powder
½ tsp. salt, *divided*
½ tsp. pepper, *divided*
2¼-lb. boneless pork loin roast, wide and short (not skinny and long)
¾ lb. fresh green beans, ends nipped off
1 Tbsp. Dijon mustard
1 Tbsp. cornstarch
1 Tbsp. cold water

1. Grease interior of slow-cooker crock.

2. In slow cooker, combine dried fruit, raisins, ginger, onion, sugar, vinegar, water, cinnamon, curry powder, and ¼ tsp. each of salt and pepper. Stir.

3. Season pork with remaining ¼ tsp. salt and pepper. Place pork on top of fruit mixture in slow cooker. Cover. Cook on Low 2 hours.

4. Layer green beans over pork. Cover.

5. Cook for 2 more hours on Low, or until instant-read meat thermometer registers 140°–145° when stuck into center of loin, and beans are done to your liking.

6. When meat and beans are tender, remove to separate plates. Cover and keep warm.

7. Stir mustard into sauce in cooker.

8. In a small bowl, mix cornstarch with 1 Tbsp. cold water until smooth. Stir into sauce.

9. Cover. Turn cooker to High and let sauce cook a few minutes until thickened.

10. Slice pork and serve topped with sauce and surrounded with green beans.

Why I like this recipe—
We discovered this to be a great Christmas dinner one year when we were remodeling and had limited kitchen facilities. I put the ingredients in the slow cooker, and we played Scrabble all day while it cooked. I served it with microwaved rice pilaf. It was my most stress-free Christmas ever!

Autumn Harvest Pork Loin

Stacy Schmucker Stoltzfus
Enola, PA

Makes 4–6 servings
Prep. Time: 30 minutes
Cooking Time: 3–4 hours
Ideal slow-cooker size: 5- or 6-qt.

1 cup cider *or* apple juice

2-lb. boneless pork loin roast, wide and short (not skinny and long)

salt

pepper

2 large Granny Smith apples, peeled and sliced

1½ whole butternut squashes, peeled, seeded, and cubed

½ cup brown sugar

¼ tsp. cinnamon

¼ tsp. dried thyme

¼ tsp. dried sage

1. Heat cider in hot skillet. Sear pork loin on all sides in cider.

2. Grease interior of slow-cooker crock.

3. Sprinkle meat with salt and pepper on all sides. Place in slow cooker, along with pan juices.

4. In a good-sized bowl, combine apples and squash. Sprinkle with sugar and herbs. Stir. Spoon around pork loin in cooker.

5. Cover. Cook on Low 3–4 hours, or until instant-read meat thermometer registers 140°–145° when stuck into center of loin, and squash is done to your liking.

6. Remove pork from cooker. Let stand 10–15 minutes. Slice into ½-inch-thick slices.

7. Serve topped with apples and squash.

Why I like this recipe—
Things just work together well here!

Savory Slow Cooker Pork Tenderloin

Kathy Hertzler
Lancaster, PA

Makes 6 servings
Prep. Time: 5–15 minutes
Cooking Time: 3–4 hours
Ideal slow-cooker size: 4-qt.

2-lb. pork loin roast, wide and short (not skinny and long)

1 cup water

¾ cup red wine

3 Tbsp. light soy sauce

1-oz. envelope dry onion soup mix

6 cloves garlic, peeled and chopped

freshly ground pepper

1. Grease interior of slow-cooker crock.

2. Place pork tenderloin in slow cooker. Pour water, wine, and soy sauce over pork.

3. Turn pork over in liquid several times to completely moisten.

4. Sprinkle with dry onion soup mix. Top with chopped garlic and pepper.

5. Cover. Cook on Low 3–4 hours, or until instant-read meat thermometer registers 145° when stuck into center of loin.

TIPS

Here's a good go-along: mix ½ cup uncooked long grain white rice and ½ cup uncooked brown rice in a microwavable bowl. Stir in 2½ cups water and ¾ tsp. salt. Cover. Microwave 5 minutes on High, and then 20 minutes on 50%. Place finished pork on a large platter and the finished rice alongside, topped with the juice from the meat. A green salad goes well with this to make a meal.

PORK

Tomato-Glazed Pork with Grilled Corn Salsa

Janet Melvin
Cincinnati, OH

Makes 6-8 servings
Prep. Time: 45 minutes
Cooking Time: 3-4 hours
Ideal slow-cooker size: 5 qt.

Tomato Glaze:
2 Tbsp. dry mustard

1 Tbsp. ground ginger

1 Tbsp. ground fennel

1 Tbsp. minced garlic

¼ cup mayonnaise

1 cup tomato ketchup

¼ cup honey

1 Tbsp. Worcestershire sauce

¼ cup grated fresh horseradish

3 Tbsp. white wine mustard

2 Tbsp. minced capers

1 Tbsp. Tabasco sauce

2½-3-lb. boneless pork loin roast, short and
wide in shape

Salsa:
3 ears sweet corn, husked and silked, *or* 4 cups
frozen or canned corn

½ cup olive oil

¼ cup chopped sun-dried tomatoes

1 clove garlic, minced

½ cup wild mushrooms, sliced

2 Tbsp. chopped fresh cilantro

2 Tbsp. fresh lime juice

1 chipotle pepper in adobo sauce, finely
chopped

½ tsp. salt

1. Grease interior of slow-cooker crock.

2. Prepare glaze by mixing together dry mustard, ginger, fennel, garlic, and mayonnaise.

3. When well blended, stir in remaining glaze ingredients.

4. Place pork in slow cooker, fat side up. Cover with glaze.

5. Cover. Cook on Low 3–4 hours, or until instant-read meat thermometer registers 140°–145° when stuck into center of roast.

6. If you're using corn-on-the cob, brush ears of corn with olive oil while roast is cooking. Wrap in foil. If you're using canned or frozen corn, skip to Step 9.

7. Bake corn at 350° for 15 minutes. Unwrap and grill or broil until evenly browned.

8. Cool. Cut kernels from cob.

9. Combine corn with rest of salsa ingredients.

10. Cover and refrigerate until ready to use.

11. When pork is finished cooking, remove from cooker to cutting board. Cover with foil and let stand for 10 minutes.

12. Slice and serve on top of grilled corn salsa.

Why I like this recipe—
Guest-worthy, tasty, and beautiful. Don't be put off by the long list of ingredients; there's no fancy footwork in this recipe. Just bringing together a bunch of great flavors.

Spicy Pork Olé

Mary Kennell
Roanoke, IL

Makes 5 servings
Prep. Time: 10–15 minutes
Cooking Time: 2¾–3¼ hours
Ideal slow-cooker size: 4-qt.

1½ lbs. pork loin roast, cut into bite-sized
   pieces

2 Tbsp. taco seasoning

2 cups mild salsa

⅓ cup peach jam

2 Tbsp. cornstarch

¼ cup water

1. Spray slow-cooker with nonstick cooking spray.

2. Place pork in slow cooker. Sprinkle with taco seasoning and stir to coat.

3. Add salsa and jam. Stir.

4. Cook on Low 2½–3 hours, or until meat is tender. Remove meat to serving dish and keep warm.

5. In a bowl, blend cornstarch and water. Turn cooker to High. When sauce simmers, stir in cornstarch-water mixture. Continue stirring until fully absorbed. Continue cooking, stirring occasionally, until sauce thickens.

6. Serve over or alongside pork.

Why I like this recipe—
Because I like what happens when salsa, taco seasoning, and peach jam meet.

North Carolina Barbecue

J. B. Miller
Indianapolis, IN

Makes 8–12 servings
Prep. Time: 15 minutes
Cooking Time: 4–7 hours
Ideal slow-cooker size: 4- or 5-qt.

3-4-lb. pork butt roast

1 cup apple cider vinegar

¼ cup + 1 Tbsp. prepared mustard

¼ cup + 1 Tbsp. Worcestershire sauce

2 tsp. red pepper flakes

1. Grease interior of slow-cooker crock.

2. Trim fat from pork. Place in slow cooker.

3. In a bowl, mix remaining ingredients together. Spoon over meat.

4. Cover and cook on High 4 hours, or Low 7 hours, or until instant-read meat thermometer registers 150°–160° when stuck into center of roast.

5. Slice, or break meat apart, and serve drizzled with the cooking juices. If you use the meat for sandwiches, you'll have enough for 8–12 sandwiches.

Why I like this recipe—
Don't leave any of the good cooking juices behind in the cooker. A spoonful of the broth over each pork sandwich makes them memorable.

Barbecued Pork and Beef Sandwiches

Nanci Keatley
Salem, OR

Makes 12 servings
Prep. Time: 15–30 minutes
Cooking Time: 6 hours
Ideal slow-cooker size: 6- or 7-qt.

1 cup onion, finely chopped

2 cups green bell pepper, finely chopped

6-oz. can tomato paste

½ cup brown sugar

¼ cup cider vinegar

1 Tbsp. chili powder

1 tsp. salt

2 tsp. Worcestershire sauce

1 tsp. dry mustard

1 tsp. hot sauce

1½ lbs. lean stewing beef

1½ lbs. lean pork cubes

1. Grease interior of slow-cooker crock.

2. Blend all ingredients—except beef and pork—in slow cooker.

3. When thoroughly mixed, stir in beef and pork pieces.

4. Cover. Cook 6 hours on Low, or until meat is tender.

5. Stir to shred meat before serving.

TIP

Serve in sandwich buns or pita bread, or over rice. Garnish with scallions, if desired.

Why I like this recipe—

Why hadn't anyone thought of putting beef and pork together in a barbecue sauce before this?!

Pulled Pork BBQ

Marsha Sabus
Fallbrook, CA

Makes 4–6 servings
Prep. Time: 20 minutes
Cooking Time: 6 hours
Ideal slow-cooker size: 3- or 4-qt.

2 tsp. salt

2 tsp. pepper

1 Tbsp. paprika

2-lb. pork butt roast

2 Tbsp. olive oil

1 large onion, chopped

12-oz. can beer

1 bottle Sweet Baby Ray's Hickory and Brown
   Sugar Barbecue Sauce

½ cup ketchup

3-4 drops hot pepper sauce

1. Grease interior of slow-cooker crock.

2. Rub or pat salt, pepper, and paprika on pork butt.

3. If you have time, brown each side of meat in olive oil in good-sized skillet. Place browned butt in slow cooker.

4. Again, if you have time, add onion to skillet. Sauté just until tender. Add to slow cooker.

5. Mix remaining ingredients in a good-sized bowl. Pour over pork in slow cooker.

TIP

Serve the meat on toasted buns with coleslaw—either inside the rolls, or alongside.

6. Cover. Cook on Low and cook 6 hours, or until instant-read meat thermometer registers 150°–160° when stuck into center of roast.

7. Remove pork from slow cooker to platter. Shred meat with 2 forks.

8. Return pulled pork to slow cooker. Mix thoroughly with sauce.

Why I like this recipe—
This recipe can easily be doubled for a large group.

Pulled Pork with Dr Pepper

Christina Gerber
Apple Creek, OH

Makes 6-8 sandwiches
Prep. Time: 20-25 minutes
Cooking Time: 4-8 hours
Ideal slow-cooker size: 6-qt.

1 medium onion, cut in eighths

2½-3-lb. pork butt roast

2 12-oz. cans Dr Pepper

1 garlic clove, minced

1½ tsp. dry mustard

¼-½ tsp. cayenne pepper, according to taste

1 tsp. salt

1 tsp. ground black pepper

¼ cup apple cider vinegar

3 Tbsp. Worcestershire sauce

your favorite barbecue sauce

your favorite rolls or buns

1. Grease interior of slow-cooker crock.

2. Place cut-up onions on bottom of crock.

3. Place pork roast on top of onions.

4. Pour Dr Pepper over top.

5. In a bowl, mix together garlic, dry mustard, cayenne pepper, salt, black pepper, vinegar, and Worcestershire sauce.

6. Spoon sauce over roast, patting it on with your hands to help it stick.

7. Cover. Cook on Low 6–7 hours, or on High 3–4 hours, or until instant-read meat thermometer registers 145°–150° when stuck into center of roast.

8. Using 2 sturdy metal spatulas, remove meat from crock and place on large cutting board. Using 2 forks, shred pork.

9. Place shredded pork back into crock. Mix well with sauce.

10. Cover. Cook 1 more hour on Low.

11. Using a slotted spoon, lift shredded meat and onions out of crock and into large bowl.

12. Stir barbecue sauce into meat and onions, ¼ cup at a time, until you get the sauciness you like.

13. Serve in rolls or buns.

Good go-alongs with this recipe:
Coleslaw and oven fries.

Pork and Apricots with Mashed Sweet Potatoes

Carolyn Baer
Conrath, WI

Makes 8 servings
Prep. Time: 35–40 minutes
Cooking Time: 4–8 hours
Ideal slow-cooker size: 6-qt.

2½ lbs. sweet potatoes, peeled and cut into 1-inch-thick chunks

3½–4-lb. boneless pork picnic shoulder roast

1 tsp. dried tarragon, crushed

1½ tsp. fennel seed, crushed

3 cloves garlic, minced

1½ tsp. salt

1 tsp. pepper

2 Tbsp. cooking oil

12–16 oz. kielbasa, *or* other smoked sausage links, cut in half lengthwise, then in 2-inch pieces

14-oz. can chicken broth

¾ cup apricot nectar, *divided*

½ cup dried apricots

4 tsp. cornstarch

1. Grease interior of slow-cooker crock.

2. Place sweet potato slices in bottom of slow cooker.

3. Trim fat from pork roast.

4. Combine tarragon, fennel seed, minced garlic, salt, and pepper in small bowl.

5. Rub spice mix all over pork roast.

6. If you have time, brown roast on all sides in hot oil in large skillet. (Or skip to Step 8.)

7. Drain off drippings.

8. Place roast on top of sweet potatoes.

9. Place sausage pieces around roast in cooker.

10. Pour broth and ½ cup apricot nectar over all.

11. Cover and cook for 3½ hours on High, or 7½ hours on Low, or until instant-read meat thermometer registers 145°–150° when stuck into center of roast.

12. Add dried apricots to cooker. Cover and continue cooking on High 30 more minutes.

13. With slotted spoon, transfer pork, sausage, and apricots to serving platter. Cover and keep warm.

14. Transfer sweet potatoes to a large bowl.

15. Mash with potato masher.

16. Strain cooking liquid from cooker into a glass measuring cup.

17. Skim and discard fat.

18. Reserve 2 cups liquid, adding chicken broth if necessary to make 2 cups.

19. In a small bowl, whisk together ¼ cup apricot nectar and cornstarch until smooth.

20. In a medium saucepan, combine cooking liquid and cornstarch mixture.

21. Cook and stir over medium heat until thick and bubbly. Cook two minutes longer.

22. Cut pork into chunks. Mix with sausage pieces and apricots. Place around edges of platter. Pile mashed sweet potatoes into center of platter. Spoon sauce over top. Place remaining sauce in bowl and pass after platter.

Why I like this recipe—

I like the taste of this whole amazing combination so much that I go into great detail (Steps 16–21) about how to make an amazing gravy to top it all off. That's so you don't worry that you can't. All those words make it long and involved—but it's not a bit hard, and the cheers you'll get from the people at your table will be worth the 15 minutes or so you spent with the whisk in your hand!

Cranberry Orange Pork Roast

**Barbara Aston
Ashdown, AR**

Makes 6–8 servings
Prep. Time: 10 minutes
Cooking Time: 7–8 hours
Ideal slow-cooker size: 5-qt.

3-4-lb. pork butt roast
salt to taste
pepper to taste
1 cup ground, *or* finely chopped, cranberries
¼ cup honey
1 tsp. grated orange peel
⅛ tsp. ground cloves
⅛ tsp. ground nutmeg

1. Grease interior of slow-cooker crock.

2. Sprinkle roast with salt and pepper. Place in slow cooker.

3. Combine remaining ingredients. Pour over roast.

4. Cover. Cook on Low 7–8 hours, or until instant-read meat thermometer registers 145°–150° when stuck into center of roast.

5. To serve, cut into slices or chunks and top with sauce.

Why I like this recipe—

If I'm making this pork for guests, I like to garnish it with a few twisted orange slices and some ruffles of kale.

Pork Roast with Sauerkraut

Gail Bush
Landenberg, PA

Barbara Hershey
Lititz, PA

Makes 8 servings
Prep. Time: 5–10 minutes
Cooking Time: 7 hours
Ideal slow-cooker size: 6- or 7-qt.

2 3-lb. pork picnic shoulder roasts

2 large cans sweet Bavarian sauerkraut with caraway seeds

¼ cup brown sugar

1 envelope dry onion soup mix

½–1 cup water

1. Grease interior of slow-cooker crock.

2. Place roasts in slow cooker.

3. Combine sauerkraut, brown sugar, and onion soup mix. Layer over roasts.

4. Cover. Cook on Low 7 hours, or until instant-read meat thermometer registers 145°–150° when stuck into center of roast.

TIP

If you can't find Bavarian sauerkraut with caraway seeds, substitute with 2 large cans regular sauerkraut and 1 tsp. caraway seeds.

Saucy Spareribs

Phyllis Good
Lancaster, PA

Makes 4 servings
Prep. Time: 15 minutes
Cooking Time: 4–6 hours
Ideal slow-cooker size: 6-qt.

3–4 lbs. country-style pork spareribs, cut into serving-sized pieces

¾ cup ketchup

1–2 Tbsp. sriracha sauce, depending how much heat you like, *optional*

3 Tbsp. packed brown sugar

¼ cup honey

¼ cup lemon juice

2 Tbsp. soy sauce

¾ tsp. ground ginger

¼ tsp. chili powder

¼ tsp. ground mustard

¼ tsp. garlic powder

¼ tsp. black pepper (coarsely ground is best)

1. Grease interior of slow-cooker crock.

2. Place cut-up ribs into slow cooker.

3. Mix all remaining ingredients together in a bowl until well combined.

4. Pour over ribs.

5. Cover. Cook on Low 4–6 hours, or until the meat begins to fall off the bones.

Variations:

Double the amount of sauce if you like a lot to eat with the ribs, or if you're serving them with pasta, rice, or potatoes and want to spoon sauce over top.

Just Peachy Ribs

Amymarlene Jensen
Fountain, CO

Makes 4–6 servings
Prep. Time: 10 minutes
Cooking Time: 5–6 hours
Ideal slow-cooker size: 6-qt.

4-lb. boneless pork spareribs

½ cup brown sugar

¼ cup ketchup

¼ cup white vinegar

1 garlic clove, minced

1 tsp. salt

1 tsp. pepper

2 Tbsp. soy sauce

15-oz. can spiced cling peaches, cubed, with juice

1. Grease interior of slow-cooker crock.

2. Cut ribs in serving-size pieces and brown in broiler or in saucepan in oil if you have time.

3. Drain. Place in slow cooker.

4. Combine remaining ingredients in bowl. Pour over ribs.

5. Cover. Cook on Low 5–6 hours, or until instant-read meat thermometer registers 150° when stuck into center of ribs.

6. Serve topped with peach sauce.

Why I like this recipe—
We love the flavor of these ribs. We usually make a party out of them with one of our sons and his wife.

Barbecued Ribs

Moreen Weaver
Bath, NY

Makes 4–6 servings
Prep. Time: 10–15 minutes
Cooking Time: 6–8 hours
Ideal slow-cooker size: 5- or 6-qt., *oval*

4–4½ lbs. spare ribs *or* country-style ribs

2½ cups barbecue sauce

¾ cup cherry preserves *or* jam

1 Tbsp. Dijon mustard

1 garlic clove, minced

1½ tsp. pepper

1. Grease interior of slow-cooker crock.

2. Cut ribs into serving-sized pieces. Place rib pieces in slow cooker.

3. Combine all other ingredients in a mixing bowl.

4. Pour sauce over ribs. If you've stacked the ribs, be sure that all are topped with sauce.

5. Cover. Cook 6–8 hours on Low, or until the meat begins to fall off the bones.

Why I like this recipe—
In our family, these ribs are often requested on birthdays—all that changes are the side dishes the birthday person picks!

Sesame Pork Ribs

Joette Droz
Kalona, IA

Makes 6 servings
Prep. Time: 10 minutes
Cooking Time: 5–6 hours
Ideal slow-cooker size: 5-qt.

1 medium onion, sliced

¾ cup packed brown sugar

¼ cup soy sauce

½ cup ketchup

¼ cup honey

2 Tbsp. cider *or* white vinegar

3 garlic cloves, minced

1 tsp. ground ginger

¼–½ tsp. crushed red pepper flakes

2 Tbsp. sesame seeds

5 lbs. country-style pork ribs

2 Tbsp. sesame seeds

4–5 spring onions, sliced thin

1. Grease interior of slow-cooker crock.

2. Place onion slices in bottom of slow cooker.

3. Combine brown sugar, soy sauce, ketchup, honey, vinegar, garlic, ginger, and red pepper flakes in large bowl. Add ribs and turn to coat.

4. Place ribs on top of onions in slow cooker. Pour sauce over meat.

5. Cover. Cook on Low 5–6 hours, or until the meat begins to fall off the bones.

TIPS

Place ribs on serving platter. Sprinkle with sesame seeds and sliced green onions. Serve sauce on the side.

BBQ Pork Ribs

Virginia Bender
Dover, DE

Makes 6 servings
Prep. Time: 10 minutes
Cooking Time: 4–6 hours
Ideal slow-cooker size: 6-qt.

4 lbs. pork ribs

½ cup brown sugar

12-oz. jar chili sauce

¼ cup balsamic vinegar

2 Tbsp. Worcestershire sauce

2 Tbsp. Dijon mustard

1 tsp. hot sauce

1. Grease interior of slow-cooker crock.

2. Place ribs in slow cooker.

3. Combine remaining ingredients in a good-sized bowl.

4. Pour half of sauce over ribs.

5. Cover. Cook on Low 4–6 hours, or until meat is falling off the bones.

6. Serve with remaining sauce.

Why I like this recipe—
I have used the wonderful sauce from this recipe for beans and beef, also.

Apple Raisin Ham

Betty B. Dennison
Grove City, PA

Makes 6 servings
Prep. Time: 10–15 minutes
Cooking Time: 3–4 hours
Ideal slow-cooker size: 4- or 5-qt.

1½ lbs. fully cooked ham slices

21-oz. can apple pie filling

⅓ cup golden raisins

⅓ cup orange juice

¼ tsp. ground cinnamon

2 Tbsp. water

TIP

This is a great way to use leftovers, and you can use any leftovers from this dish to make wonderful sandwiches.

1. Grease interior of slow-cooker crock.

2. Cut ham slices into six equal pieces and place in slow cooker. If you have to make a second layer, stagger the pieces so they aren't directly on top of each other.

3. In a mixing bowl, combine pie filling, raisins, orange juice, cinnamon, and water.

4. Spread ⅙ of the apple mixture on top of each slice.

5. Cover and cook on Low 3–4 hours.

Pork

Honey-Dijon Holiday Ham

Robin Schrock
Millersburg, OH

Makes 10 servings
Prep. Time: 15 minutes
Cooking Time: 4–5 hours
Ideal slow-cooker size: 6-qt.

5-lb. bone-in, fully cooked ham

⅓ cup apple juice

¼ cup packed brown sugar

1 Tbsp. honey

1 Tbsp. Dijon mustard

1. Grease interior of slow-cooker crock.

2. Place ham in slow cooker.

3. In a small bowl, mix juice, brown sugar, honey, and mustard together. Spread over ham.

4. Cover. Cook on Low 4–5 hours, or until instant-read meat thermometer registers 100° when stuck into center of ham (but not against bone).

5. Slice ham and serve.

6. Pass sauce to top ham slices.

Why I like this recipe—
Well, the name says it all! It wouldn't be Christmas at our house without this ham. I got the recipe years ago from my friend Betsy.

Ham with Sweet Potatoes and Oranges

Esther Becker
Gordonville, PA

Makes 4 servings
Prep. Time: 15 minutes
Cooking Time: 3–4 hours
Ideal slow-cooker size: 5- or 6-qt.

2-3 sweet potatoes, peeled and sliced ¼-inch thick

1½–2-lb. ham slice

3 seedless oranges, peeled and sliced

3 Tbsp. orange juice concentrate

3 Tbsp. honey

½ cup brown sugar

2 Tbsp. cornstarch

1. Grease interior of slow-cooker crock.

2. Place sweet potato slices in slow cooker.

3. Arrange ham and orange slices on top of potatoes.

4. Combine remaining ingredients in a small bowl. Drizzle over ham and oranges.

5. Cover. Cook on Low 3–4 hours.

TIP

Delicious served with a fruit salad.

Barbecued Ham Steaks

Phyllis Good
Lancaster, PA

Makes 4 servings
Prep. Time: 15 minutes
Cooking Time: 3–4 hours
Ideal slow-cooker size: 6- or 7-qt, *oval*

1 small onion, chopped

7-oz. bottle 7-Up, Sprite, *or* ginger ale

¼ cup ketchup

1 tsp. dry mustard

1 tsp. salt

⅛ tsp. black pepper

4 whole cloves

2 lbs. ham slices

1. Grease interior of slow-cooker crock.

2. Mix together chopped onion, soda, ketchup, mustard, salt, pepper, and whole cloves in crock.

3. Submerge slices in sauce. Overlap slices if you must, but as little as possible.

4. Cover. Cook on Low 3–4 hours, or until meat is heated through but not dry.

5. Fish out cloves and discard.

6. If needed, cut each steak into serving-size pieces and serve topped with barbecue sauce.

Why I like this recipe—
This is a favorite for Sunday dinner. I usually put some kind of potatoes in another crock and have a green salad waiting in the fridge.

Ham in Cider

Dorothy M. Van Deest
Memphis, TN

Makes 6–8 servings
Prep. Time: 5 minutes
Cooking Time: 4½–5½ hours
Ideal slow-cooker size: 5- or 6-qt.

3-4-lb. smoked ham

4 cups sweet cider, *or* apple juice

1 cup brown sugar

2 tsp. dry mustard

1 tsp. ground cloves

2 cups white seedless raisins

1. Grease interior of slow-cooker crock.

2. Place ham and cider in slow cooker.

3. Cover. Cook on Low 4–5 hours, or until instant-read meat thermometer registers 100° when stuck into center of ham (but not against bone).

4. Remove ham from cider and place in baking pan.

5. Make a paste of sugar, mustard, cloves, and a little hot cider. Brush over ham. Pour a cup of juice from slow cooker into baking pan. Stir in raisins.

6. Bake at 375° for 30 minutes, until the paste has turned into a glaze.

7. Slice and serve.

Why I like this recipe—
My family loves this ham, so I make it for Easter and often for other special family feasts. I like having a few packages of ham leftovers in the freezer, too, which makes casseroles and sandwiches nicer.

Black Beans with Ham

Colleen Heatwole
Burton, MI

Makes 8–10 servings
Prep. Time: 20 minutes
Soaking Time: 8 hours or overnight
Cooking Time: 3–6 hours
Ideal slow-cooker size: 6-qt.

4 cups dry black beans

1-2 cups diced ham

1 tsp. salt, *optional*

1 tsp. cumin

½–1 cup minced onion

2 garlic cloves, minced

3 bay leaves

1 qt. diced tomatoes

1 Tbsp. brown sugar

1. Cover black beans with water and soak 8 hours, or overnight, in slow cooker.

2. Drain. Grease interior of slow-cooker crock. Pour beans into slow-cooker crock.

3. Add all remaining ingredients. Stir well. Cover with water.

4. Cover cooker. Cook on Low 3–6 hours, or until beans are as tender as you like them.

Why I like this recipe—

This is our favorite black bean recipe. We usually serve this dish over rice. It's good any time of the year, but we make it especially frequently in the winter.

Potatoes and Green Beans with Ham

Mary B. Sensenig
New Holland, PA

Makes 4 servings
Prep. Time: 5 minutes
Cooking Time: 3–8 hours
Ideal slow-cooker size: 4- or 5-qt.

1-lb. ham slice, cut in chunks

2 cups green beans, frozen *or* fresh

2 cups red-skinned potatoes, quartered but not peeled

½ cup water

½ cup chopped onion

4 slices American cheese

1. Grease interior of slow-cooker crock.

2. Place all ingredients, except cheese, in slow cooker. Gently mix together.

3. Cover and cook on High 3–4 hours, or on Low 6–8 hours, or until vegetables are tender.

4. One hour before the end of the cooking time, lay cheese slices over top. Cover and continue cooking.

Why I like this recipe—
This is an old-fashioned favorite I remember from my childhood. I always serve it with applesauce and bread and butter.

Scalloped Potatoes and Ham

Carol Sherwood
Batavia, NY

Mary Stauffer
Ephrata, PA

Sharon Anders
Alburtis, PA

Esther Hartzler
Carlsbad, NM

Dawn Hahn
Lititz, PA

Diann J. Dunham
State College, PA

Makes 4-6 servings
Prep. Time: 20 minutes
Cooking Time: 6-8 hours
Ideal slow-cooker size: 5-qt.

2-3 lbs. potatoes, peeled, sliced, and *divided*

1 lb. cooked ham, cubed and *divided*

1 small onion, chopped and *divided*

2 cups shredded cheddar cheese, *divided*

10¾-oz. can cream of celery, *or* mushroom, soup*

1. Spray the interior of the cooker with nonstick cooking spray.

2. Layer ⅓ each of the potatoes, ham, onion, and cheese into the cooker.

3. Repeat twice.

4. Spread soup on top.

5. Cover and cook on Low 6–8 hours, or until potatoes are tender.

*To make your own Cream Soup, see recipes on pages 561–564.

TIP

For a creamier sauce, combine a can of creamed soup with ½ cup water in a bowl before pouring over contents of cooker in Step 4.
—Jeannine Janzen, Elbing, KS

Creamy Ham and Red Beans over Rice

Phyllis Good
Lancaster, PA

Makes 6 servings
Prep. Time: 20 minutes
Cooking Time: 4½–10½ hours
Ideal slow-cooker size: 6 qt.

1 lb. dried red-skinned kidney beans

2 Tbsp. oil

2 cups diced onions

1½–2 cups diced celery

1 cup diced green bell pepper

4 large garlic cloves, minced

1 Tbsp. Creole seasoning

4 bay leaves

1 tsp. dried thyme

2 quarts water

2½ lbs. meaty ham hocks

salt and pepper, *optional*

6 cups cooked rice

1. Rinse the dried beans and pick out any stones or debris.

2. Grease interior of slow-cooker crock.

3. Place dried beans in slow cooker. Stir in all remaining ingredients except cooked rice, submerging ham hocks in liquid.

4. Cover. Cook on Low 8–10 hours or on High 4–6 hours, or until beans are tender and meat is falling off the bone.

5. Using tongs or a slotted spoon, remove ham hocks from cooker. Fish out bay leaves, too.

6. Allow meat to cool enough to pull or cut into bite-sized pieces.

7. Stir meat chunks back into bean mixture. Heat 15 minutes.

8. Place 1 cup or so cooked rice in each individual serving bowl. Top with creamy ham and beans.

Variations:

1. Instead of using dried kidney beans, use 3 14½-oz. cans kidney beans. Skip Step 1 and cook 4 hours on High, or 8 hours on Low, or until meat is falling-off-the-bone tender. Add canned beans halfway through cooking time.

2. Instead of using store-bought Creole seasoning, make your own: ⅔ tsp. paprika, 1 tsp. salt, 1 tsp. garlic powder, ½ tsp. black pepper, ½ tsp. onion powder, ½ tsp. cayenne pepper, ½ tsp. dried oregano, ½ tsp. dried thyme. Stir together well. Store any leftovers in a dry, tightly covered container.

Melt-in-Your-Mouth Sausages

Ruth Ann Gingrich
New Holland, PA

Ruth Hershey
Paradise, PA

Carol Sherwood
Batavia, NY

Nancy Zimmerman
Loysville, PA

Makes 6–8 servings
Prep. Time: 15 minutes
Cooking Time: 4–6 hours
Ideal slow-cooker size: 4-qt.

2 lbs. sweet Italian sausage, cut into 5-inch lengths

48-oz. jar spaghetti sauce

6-oz. can tomato paste

1 large green bell pepper, thinly sliced

1 large onion, thinly sliced

1 Tbsp. grated Parmesan cheese

1 tsp. dried parsley *or* 1 Tbsp. chopped fresh parsley

1 cup water

TIPS

Serve in buns, or cut sausage into bite-sized pieces and serve over cooked pasta. Sprinkle with more Parmesan cheese.

1. Grease interior of slow-cooker crock.

2. If you have time, place sausage in skillet. Cover with water. Simmer 10 minutes. Drain. (You do this to cook off the fat.)

3. Combine remaining ingredients in slow cooker. Add sausage.

4. Cover. Cook on Low 4–6 hours, or until the veggies are as tender as you like them.

Pork

Italian Sausage Spaghetti

Eleanor Larson
Glen Lyons, PA

Makes 12 servings
Prep. Time: 20 minutes
Cooking Time: 4 hours
Ideal slow-cooker size: 5- or 6-qt.

1½ lbs. Italian sausage, hot *or* sweet, cut into ½–¾-inch-thick slices

1 cup diced onions

3 Tbsp. sugar

1 tsp. dried oregano

½ tsp. salt

2 garlic cloves, minced

28-oz. can crushed tomatoes, undrained, *or* your favorite spaghetti sauce

15-oz. can tomato sauce

12-oz. can tomato paste

1½ lbs. uncooked spaghetti

1. Grease interior of slow-cooker crock.

2. Combine all ingredients except spaghetti in slow cooker.

3. Cover. Cook on Low 4 hours.

4. About 30 minutes before end of the sauce's cooking time, cook spaghetti in large soup pot according to package directions.

5. Drain spaghetti and top with sauce.

Why I like this recipe—

I grew up with hamburger in the spaghetti sauce, but when I found this recipe as a new homemaker, I loved it. This is our favorite spaghetti sauce. In fact, there's a fun little story about this recipe: This recipe appeared in the very first *Fix-It and Forget-It Cookbook*. When we revised and updated that book, I dropped this recipe for some reason. One day, a woman and her son showed up at our Good Cooking Store to protest. They said it was their very favorite recipe in that original book, and they wanted to know why it got eliminated in the next edition. I promptly went home and made the recipe—and I completely agreed with them. Leaving it out was a big mistake. So here it is again, for all of us to enjoy!

Pork

Old World Sauerkraut Supper

Josie Bollman
Maumee, OH

Joyce Bowman
Lady Lake, FL

Vera Schmucker
Goshen, IN

Makes 8 servings
Prep. Time: 15 minutes
Cooking Time: 2–5 hours
Ideal slow-cooker size: 5-qt.

3 strips bacon, cut into small pieces

2 Tbsp. flour

2 15-oz. cans sauerkraut

2 small potatoes, cubed

2 small apples, cubed

3 Tbsp. brown sugar

1½ tsp. caraway seeds

3 lbs. Polish sausage, cut into 3-inch pieces

½ cup water

1. Grease interior of slow-cooker crock. If you have time, fry bacon until crisp. Drain, reserving drippings. Or pick up a pack of already-crumbled bacon at your grocery store.

2. If you have bacon drippings, stir in flour, blending well. Stir in sauerkraut and bacon. If you don't have drippings, stir flour, sauerkraut, and bacon into slow cooker.

3. Stir in remaining ingredients.

4. Cover. Cook on Low 4–5 hours, or on High 2–3 hours.

Why I like this recipe—

I'm not sure that this recipe is really old, but the flavors are wonderful and make a nice change from the traditional pork and sauerkraut I make otherwise. I like to make this dish for guests since it's a little different but still so simple to put together.

POrK

Creamy Sausage and Potatoes

Janet Oberholtzer
Ephrata, PA

Makes 6 servings
Prep. Time: 15 minutes
Cooking Time: 6–8 hours
Ideal slow-cooker size: 3½-qt.

3 lbs. small potatoes, peeled and quartered

1 lb. smoked sausage, cut into ¼-inch slices

8-oz. pkg. cream cheese, softened

10¾-oz. can cream of celery soup*

1 envelope dry ranch salad dressing mix

1. Grease interior of slow-cooker crock.

2. Place potatoes in slow-cooker. Add sausage.

3. In a bowl, beat together cream cheese, soup, and salad dressing mix until smooth. Pour over potatoes and sausage.

4. Cover and cook on Low 6–8 hours, or until the potatoes are tender, stirring halfway through cooking time if you're home. Stir again before serving.

*To make your own Cream Soup, see recipes on pages 563 and 564.

TIPS

1. Small red potatoes are great in this dish. If you use them, don't peel them.
2. You may substitute smoked turkey sausage for the smoked pork sausage.

Sausage and Sweet Potatoes

Ruth Hershey
Paradise, PA

Makes 4–6 servings
Prep. Time: 15–20 minutes
Cooking Time: 3–8 hours
Ideal slow-cooker size: 3-qt.

1 lb. bulk sausage

2 sweet potatoes, peeled and sliced

3 apples, peeled and sliced

2 Tbsp. brown sugar

1 Tbsp. flour

¼ cup water

1. Grease interior of slow-cooker crock.

2. Brown loose sausage in skillet, breaking up chunks of meat with a wooden spoon. Drain.

3. Layer sausage, sweet potatoes, and apples in slow cooker.

4. Combine remaining ingredients and pour over ingredients in slow cooker.

5. Cover. Cook on Low 6–8 hours, or on High 3–4 hours.

Why I like this recipe—
This dish smells like autumn to me! We love to eat this with cornbread.

Green Beans and Sausage

Mary B. Sensenig
New Holland, PA

Makes 4–5 servings
Prep. Time: 5 minutes
Cooking Time: 3–8 hours
Ideal slow-cooker size: 4-qt.

1 lb. smoked sausage, cut into ½-inch slices

1 qt. fresh *or* frozen green beans

1 small onion, chopped

½ cup brown sugar

¼ cup ketchup

1. Grease interior of slow-cooker crock.

2. Place sausage in slow-cooker. Top with beans and then onion.

3. In a bowl, stir together sugar and ketchup. Spoon over top.

4. Cover and cook on Low 6–8 hours, or on High 3–4 hours, or until beans are as tender as you like them.

Why I like this recipe—

If I have leftovers (depends if my kids are at home), I turn them into soup by adding beef broth and some cooked rice or noodles.

Golden Autumn Stew

Naomi E. Fast
Hesston, KS

Makes 8–10 servings
Prep. Time: 30–40 minutes
Cooking Time: 6 hours
Ideal slow-cooker size: 5-qt.

2 cups cubed Yukon gold potatoes

2 cups cubed, peeled sweet potatoes

2 cups cubed, peeled butternut squash

1 cup cubed, peeled rutabaga

1 cup diced carrots

1 cup sliced celery

1 lb. smoked sausage

2 cups apple juice *or* cider

1 tart apple, thinly sliced

salt to taste

pepper to taste

1 Tbsp. sugar *or* honey

1. Grease interior of slow-cooker crock.

2. Combine vegetables in slow cooker.

3. Place ring of sausage on top. Or arrange sausage links or pieces over top of vegetables.

4. Pour in apple juice. Place apple slices over top.

5. Cover. Cook on High 2 hours, and then on Low 4 hours, or until vegetables are tender. Do not stir.

6. To prepare to serve, remove sausage and keep warm. Season vegetables with salt, pepper, and sugar as desired. Place vegetables in bowl. Slice meat into ½-inch slices and place on top.

TIP

Don't omit the rutabaga! Get acquainted with its rich uniqueness. It will surprise and please your taste buds.

Serving suggestion: I like to serve the stew with hot baking-powder biscuits and honey, and a green salad or coleslaw.

Pork

Sausage Town

Kathy Hertzler
Lancaster, PA

Makes 4-6 servings
Prep. Time: 15 minutes
Cooking Time: 9-10 hours
Ideal slow-cooker size: 5-qt.

1 cup chopped onions

¾ cup dry lentils, rinsed well and picked clean

¾ cup shredded cheddar cheese

2 cloves garlic, crushed

½ tsp. dried thyme

½ tsp. dried basil

½ tsp. dried oregano

⅛ tsp. dried sage

¼ tsp. salt

freshly ground black pepper to taste

1-2 lbs. sausage of your choice, bulk *or* squeezed out of casing and broken into small chunks

4 14½-oz. cans chicken broth

¾ cup uncooked long grain brown rice

1. Grease interior of slow-cooker crock.

2. Place onions, lentils, cheese, garlic, thyme, basil, oregano, sage, salt, black pepper, sausage, and chicken broth into crock. Stir together well.

3. Cover. Cook on Low 6–7 hours.

4. Stir in uncooked rice.

5. Cover. Continue cooking on Low another 3 hours, or until both rice and lentils are as tender as you like them.

6. If dish is juicier than you want, uncover during last 30 minutes of cooking and turn cooker to High.

7. Stir well and serve.

Why I like this recipe—
I first got this recipe when we had a potluck at work and my co-worker cooked this dish all day in the office. We were hungry all day, smelling it!

Sausage Tortellini

Christie Detamore-Hunsberger
Harrisonburg, VA

Makes 8 servings
Prep. Time: 25–30 minutes
Cooking Time: 1½–2½ hours
Ideal slow-cooker size: 6-qt.

1 lb. sausage of your choice, cut into
½-inch-thick slices

1 cup chopped onions

2 cloves garlic, minced

5 cups beef *or* chicken broth

¾ cup water

¾ cup red wine

2 14¾-oz. cans diced tomatoes, undrained

1 cup thinly sliced carrots

¾ tsp. dried basil

¾ tsp. dried oregano

16-oz. can tomato sauce

¾ cup sliced zucchini, *optional*

16-oz. pkg. tortellini

3 Tbsp. chopped fresh parsley

1. Grease interior of slow-cooker crock.

2. If you have time, brown sausage in its own drippings in a skillet. When lightly browned, stir in onions and garlic and cook just until softened.

3. Using a slotted spoon, lift meat and veggies out of drippings (to be discarded) and put into crock.

4. Add broth, water, wine, tomatoes, carrots, basil, oregano, and tomato sauce to crock. Stir together well.

5. Add zucchini if you wish, and tortellini.

6. Cover. Cook on High 1½–2½ hours, or until pasta is as tender as you like it, but not mushy.

7. Stir in parsley and serve.

Why I like this recipe—

This is my go-to recipe for our monthly church potluck. I know exactly how long my slow cooker needs with this recipe (2 hours), and I always take home an empty crock!

Fresh Vegetables Pasta Sauce

Dorothy Lingerfelt
Stonyford, CA

Makes 8–10 servings
Prep. Time: 35–45 minutes
Cooking Time: 5 hours
Ideal slow-cooker size: 6- or 7-qt.

3 medium onions, chopped

1 medium green bell pepper, chopped

1 medium red bell pepper, chopped

5 garlic cloves, minced

3 medium yellow summer squash, peeled or unpeeled and chopped

3 medium tomatoes, chopped

½ tsp. salt

½ tsp. coarsely ground black pepper

½ lb. fresh mushrooms, sliced

2 28-oz. cans crushed tomatoes

6-oz. can tomato paste

2 2¼ -oz. cans sliced ripe olives, drained

2 Tbsp. dried rosemary

1 tsp. dried oregano

1 tsp. dried basil

3 Tbsp. chopped fresh oregano

¼ cup chopped fresh basil

cooked pasta

1. Grease interior of slow-cooker crock.

2. Place all ingredients in crock, except fresh oregano, fresh basil, and cooked pasta.

3. Stir together gently until well mixed.

4. Cover. Cook on Low 4 hours.

5. Remove lid and continue cooking 1 more hour to thicken sauce.

6. Ten minutes before end of cooking time, stir in fresh oregano and fresh basil.

7. Serve over just-cooked pasta.

Why I like this recipe—

All the veggies make a delicious sauce—my daughter is impressed that her kids don't make a fuss about eating veggies at all when I serve this sauce over pasta.

Pasta with Tomatoes, Olives, and Two Cheeses

Diane Clement
Rogers, AR

Makes 6–8 servings
Prep. Time: 30 minutes
Cooking Time: 3 hours
Ideal slow-cooker size: 5- or 6-qt.

1½ cups chopped onion

1 tsp. minced garlic

3 28-oz. cans Italian plum tomatoes, drained

2 tsp. dried basil

¼–½ tsp. red pepper flakes, according to the amount of heat you like

2 cups chicken broth

salt and black pepper to taste

1 lb. uncooked penne or rigatoni

3 Tbsp. olive oil

2½ cups Havarti cheese

⅓ cup sliced, pitted, brine-cured olives (such as Kalamata)

⅓ cup grated Parmesan cheese

¼ cup finely chopped fresh basil

1. Grease interior of slow-cooker crock.

2. Place onion, garlic, tomatoes, dried basil, and red pepper flakes in crock. Stir together well, breaking up tomatoes with back of spoon.

3. Stir in chicken broth.

4. Season with salt and pepper.

5. Cover. Cook on High 2 hours.

6. Uncover. Continue cooking on High 1 hour, or until sauce is reduced to the consistency you like.

7. During last 30 minutes of cooking, prepare pasta according to package directions in a large stockpot until al dente.

8. Drain pasta and stir in olive oil. Cover and keep warm.

9. When sauce is done cooking, pour over pasta and toss to blend.

10. Stir in Havarti cheese and allow to melt.

11. Spoon into serving bowl. Top with olives and Parmesan cheese.

12. Sprinkle with fresh basil, then serve immediately.

Why I like this recipe—

This is one of my never-fail guest-pleaser recipes. I make it over and over again for guests because we love to get together with our friends and I don't want to be stuck in the kitchen or stressed about preparing a new dish every time.

Pastas, Grains & Vegetarian

Lotsa Veggies Spaghetti

Jean M. Butzer
Batavia, NY

Makes 4–5 servings
Prep. Time: 15 minutes
Cooking Time: 2–3 hours
Ideal slow-cooker size: 5-qt.

1 cup chopped onions

½ cup chopped celery

1 garlic clove, minced

24-oz. jar meatless pasta sauce

15-oz. can garbanzo beans, rinsed and drained

14½-oz. can diced tomatoes with garlic and onions, undrained

1 tsp. sugar

½–¾ tsp. salt, according to taste

½ tsp. dried oregano

1 bay leaf

1 lb. spaghetti

¼ cup grated Parmesan cheese

1. Grease interior of slow-cooker crock.

2. Place all ingredients, except spaghetti and cheese, into slow cooker. Stir together until well mixed.

3. Cover. Cook on Low 2–3 hours, or until vegetables are as tender as you like them and the flavors are well blended.

4. Remove the bay leaf. Serve sauce over cooked spaghetti.

5. Top individual servings with grated cheese.

Why I like this recipe—
It's amazing how the aroma of spaghetti sauce cooking makes the house feel good. And the flavor of slow-cooked sauce is hard to beat.

Mushroom Spaghetti Sauce

Natalia Showalter
Mt. Solon, VA

Makes 10 servings
Prep. Time: 30–45 minutes
Cooking Time: 2–4 hours
Ideal slow-cooker size: 5-qt.

4 medium onions, chopped

6 garlic cloves, minced

4 large bell peppers, chopped, your choice of colors

¾–1 lb. fresh mushrooms, sliced

4 cups tomato sauce

8 cups chunky tomatoes, fresh or canned

1½ tsp. salt

¼ cup evaporated cane juice *or* sugar

2 Tbsp. honey

6 bay leaves

1 tsp. garlic powder

1 tsp. dried thyme

1 tsp. dried oregano

1 tsp. dried basil

1 tsp. black pepper

1 tsp. chili powder

½ tsp. ground cumin

½ tsp. cayenne pepper or to taste

2 Tbsp. dried parsley flakes

cooked spaghetti

freshly grated Parmesan cheese, *optional*

1. Grease interior of slow-cooker crock.

2. Place all ingredients except spaghetti and Parmesan cheese in crock. Mix together well.

3. Cover. Cook on Low 2–4 hours, or until vegetables are as tender as you like them.

4. Serve over cooked spaghetti. Sprinkle with cheese if you wish.

Why I like this recipe—

My kids love mushrooms because of this sauce. I now keep mushrooms on hand in my pantry and fridge; we use them as a pizza topping as well.

Cherry Tomato Spaghetti Sauce

Beverly Hummel
Fleetwood, PA

Makes 8–10 servings
Prep. Time: 20 minutes
Cooking Time: 4–5 hours
Ideal slow-cooker size: 6-qt.

4 quarts cherry tomatoes

1 onion, chopped

2 cloves garlic, minced

3 tsp. sugar

1 tsp. dried rosemary

2 tsp. dried thyme

1 tsp. dried oregano

1 tsp. dried basil

1 tsp. salt

½ tsp. coarsely ground black pepper

cooked spaghetti

1. Grease interior of slow-cooker crock.

2. Stem tomatoes and cut them in half. Place in slow cooker.

3. Add chopped onions and garlic to cooker.

4. Stir in sugar, herbs, and seasonings, mixing well.

5. Cover. Cook on Low 4–5 hours, or until the veggies are as tender as you like them.

6. For a thicker sauce, uncover the cooker for the last 30–60 minutes of cooking time.

7. Serve over just-cooked spaghetti.

Why I like this recipe—
We have a very prolific cherry-tomato plant that reseeds itself every year. When we're tired of popping them straight in our mouths, I make this sauce and freeze it.

Pastas, Grains & Vegetarian

Southern Italy Sauce

Monica Wagner
Quarryville, PA

Makes 8–10 servings
Prep. Time: 30 minutes
Cooking Time: 4–5 hours
Ideal slow-cooker size: 6-qt.

½ cup pitted Kalamata olives, *divided*

3 28-oz. cans stewed tomatoes, undrained

6-oz. can tomato paste

1 large onion, chopped

4 cloves garlic, minced

1 Tbsp., plus 1 tsp., dried parsley

2 Tbsp. capers, drained

2 tsp. dried basil

¼ tsp. cayenne pepper

¼ tsp. salt

¼ tsp. coarsely ground black pepper

cooked pasta *or* rice

Parmesan cheese, *optional*

1. Grease interior of slow-cooker crock.

2. Chop ¼ cup olives. Place in slow cooker.

3. Halve remaining olives. Set aside.

4. Cut up stewed tomatoes so they're in small chunks. Add, along with their juice, to the cooker.

5. Add all remaining ingredients to slow cooker, except halved olives, cooked pasta or rice, and cheese. Mix together well.

6. Cover. Cook on Low 4–5 hours.

7. Stir in halved olives.

8. Serve over just-cooked pasta or rice. If you wish, shave or grate Parmesan cheese over individual servings.

Why I like this recipe—

My husband says our house smells like an Italian restaurant in a good way when I make this sauce. We think the end results are just as tasty as the restaurant version, too!

Classic Spinach Lasagna

Bernice Esau
North Newton, KS

Makes 10 servings
Prep. Time: 30 minutes
Cooking Time: 4–5 hours
Ideal slow-cooker size: 6- or 7-qt.

1 small onion, chopped

1 medium garlic clove, minced

3 14½-oz. cans diced *or* stewed tomatoes, undrained

2 6-oz. cans tomato paste

¾ cup dry red wine

1 tsp. dried basil

½ tsp. salt

½ tsp. dried oregano

½ tsp. coarsely ground black pepper

2 16-oz. containers ricotta cheese

3 large eggs, *divided*

2 10-oz. pkgs. frozen chopped spinach, thawed and squeezed dry

8 oz. uncooked lasagna noodles, *divided*

16 oz. mozzarella cheese, sliced or shredded, *divided*

¼ cup grated Parmesan cheese

1. Grease interior of slow-cooker crock.

2. In a large bowl, gently mix together onion, garlic, tomatoes, tomato paste, red wine, basil, salt, oregano, and black pepper.

3. In a separate bowl, mix ricotta with 2 eggs.

4. In another bowl, mix spinach with 1 egg.

5. Spoon 2 cups tomato mixture into crock.

6. Arrange half the noodles over sauce, overlapping and breaking to fit.

7. Spoon half of ricotta mixture over noodles.

8. Top with half the mozzarella, half the spinach mixture, and half the remaining tomato sauce.

9. Repeat layers, ending with sauce.

10. Sprinkle with Parmesan cheese.

11. Cover. Cook on Low 4–5 hours, or until noodles are fully cooked.

12. Let stand 10–15 minutes so lasagna can firm up before serving.

Why I like this recipe—

I received my first slow cooker at my bridal shower. My friends and aunts had also given their favorite recipes to use with it. This lasagna recipe, from my Aunt Linda, is the one I use the most.

Easy Black Bean Lasagna

Kristen Leichty
Ames, IA

Makes 10–12 servings
Prep. Time: 30 minutes
Cooking Time: 5 hours
Ideal slow-cooker size: 6- or 7-qt

15-oz. can black beans, rinsed and drained

2 29-oz. can crushed tomatoes

15-oz. can refried beans

¾ cup chopped onions

½ cup chopped green bell pepper

¾ cup medium salsa

1 tsp. chili powder

½ tsp. ground cumin

8 oz. cottage cheese

½ tsp. garlic powder

2 eggs

¾ tsp. salt

½ tsp. black pepper

10 uncooked lasagna noodles, *divided*

1½ cups shredded cheddar cheese, *divided*

1½ cups shredded mozzarella cheese, *divided*

1. Grease interior of slow-cooker crock.

2. In a large bowl, combine black beans, tomatoes, refried beans, onions, green peppers, salsa, chili powder, and cumin. Mix together well.

3. In a small bowl, combine cottage cheese, garlic powder, eggs, salt, and pepper.

4. Spread 2 cups tomato mixture in bottom of crock.

5. Top with half the noodles, overlapping and breaking to fit.

6. Top with half the remaining tomato mixture.

7. Spoon cottage cheese mixture over top.

8. Top with half the shredded cheeses.

9. Put in remaining noodles, again overlapping and breaking to fit.

10. Spoon remaining tomato mixture over noodles.

11. Top with rest of shredded cheeses.

12. Cover. Cook on Low 5 hours, or until noodles are fully cooked.

13. Let stand 15 minutes so lasagna can firm up before serving.

Why I like this recipe—
We love this Mexican-flavored variation on lasagna. I sometimes add some fried ground beef instead of the black beans although I don't change the name!

Pastas, Grains & Vegetarian

Summer Squash Lasagna

Natalia Showalter
Mt. Solon, VA

Makes 12 servings
Prep. Time: 30–45 minutes
Cooking Time: 4–5 hours
Ideal slow-cooker size: 6- or 7-qt.

2 medium zucchini squash, unpeeled and
   sliced thinly
2 medium yellow squash, unpeeled and sliced
   thinly
8 oz. portobello mushrooms, sliced
1 large onion, diced
1 red sweet bell pepper, chopped
4 cups fresh tomatoes, chopped
6-oz. can tomato paste
1 Tbsp. minced garlic
½ tsp. dried basil
1 Tbsp. brown sugar
½ tsp. salt
½ tsp. dried oregano
½ tsp. coarsely ground black pepper
15 oz. ricotta cheese *or* 12 oz. cottage cheese
8-oz. pkg. cream cheese, softened
2 large eggs, beaten
1 tsp. dried parsley
6-8 uncooked lasagna noodles, *divided*
2-4 cups shredded mozzarella cheese, *divided*
2 cups shredded Colby cheese, *or* Italian
   cheese blend, *divided*

1. Grease interior of slow-cooker crock.

2. Place green and yellow squash,
mushrooms, onion, sweet pepper, tomatoes,
tomato paste, garlic, basil, brown sugar, salt,
oregano, and pepper into large bowl. Mix
together gently but well.

3. In a separate bowl, combine ricotta,
cream cheese, eggs, and parsley until well
blended. Set aside.

4. Spread half of vegetable mixture in
bottom of crock.

5. Top with 3 or 4 noodles, breaking them
to fit and cover the vegetables.

6. Spread with half the ricotta mixture.

7. Sprinkle with half the mozzarella and
Colby cheeses.

8. Repeat layers.

9. Cover. Cook on Low 4–5 hours, or until
vegetables are as tender as you like them and
noodles are fully cooked.

10. Let stand 10–15 minutes to allow
lasagna to firm up before serving.

Why I like this recipe—
This is a favorite summer dish when the
garden is in full swing. I love that I don't have
to turn on the oven to make it!

Vegetarian Lasagna

Margaret W. High
Lancaster, PA

Makes 8–10 servings
Prep. Time: 25 minutes
Cooking Time: 3–4 hours, or
when noodles are al dente
Ideal slow-cooker size: 6-qt., *oval*

3 cups grated mozzarella

1½ cups ricotta cheese *or* cottage cheese

5 cups spaghetti sauce (the more herbs, the better), *divided*

½ lb. sliced fresh mushrooms, *divided*

12 lasagna noodles, uncooked, *divided*

½ lb. chopped fresh spinach, *divided*

6 oz. sliced black olives, *divided, optional*

¼ cup freshly grated Parmesan

¼ cup water (if your sauce is on the thin side, skip the water)

1. Grease interior of slow-cooker crock.

2. In a bowl, mix together grated mozzarella and ricotta cheeses. Set aside.

3. Put 1 cup spaghetti sauce in crock.

4. Scatter ⅓ of mushrooms over top.

5. Add ⅓ of noodles on top, breaking as necessary to fit them in, and covering the mushrooms as completely as possible.

6. Spread ⅓ of cheese mixture over noodles.

7. Top with half the spinach and half the black olives, then ⅓ of remaining sauce, half the remaining mushrooms, half the noodles, and half the cheese.

8. Make another whole set of layers, ending with a layer of sauce on top.

9. Sprinkle with Parmesan. Pour water down the side of crock if your sauce is really thick.

10. Cover. Cook on Low 3–4 hours, or until noodles are al dente.

11. Let stand 10–15 minutes before serving to allow cheeses to firm up.

TIP

Use a metal serving spoon to cut out servings, but be careful not to scrape/scratch the ceramic crock. I never try to fuss with squares of lasagna with this recipe.

Variations:
Add other veggies if you wish, reducing the amount of spinach and mushrooms—broccoli, zucchini, Swiss chard. Cut-up artichokes instead of, or in addition to, black olives are also good.

Good go-alongs with this recipe:
Green salad and French bread dipped in olive oil with salt and pepper.

Pastas, Grains & Vegetarian

Creamy Ziti in the Crock

Judi Manos
West Islip, NY

Makes 8 servings
Prep. Time: 20 minutes
Cooking Time: 2–3 hours
Ideal slow-cooker size: 5- or 6-qt.

5 cups spaghetti *or* marinara sauce, *divided*

8-oz. pkg. cream cheese, cubed, room temperature

1 tsp. dried basil

⅛ tsp. pepper

14½-oz. can diced tomatoes, undrained

4 cups uncooked ziti pasta, *divided*

1 cup mozzarella cheese, *divided*

⅓ cup grated Parmesan cheese

1. Grease interior of slow-cooker crock.

2. Heat 1–2 cups spaghetti sauce in saucepan or microwave. Add cream cheese cubes and stir until melted.

3. Add remaining spaghetti sauce, basil, pepper, and diced tomatoes to warmed creamy sauce.

4. Put ⅓ of tomato sauce mixture in bottom of crock.

5. Add 2 cups ziti, topped with ½ cup mozzarella.

6. Add half of remaining tomato mixture.

7. Layer in final 2 cups of ziti and ½ cup mozzarella.

8. Spoon on remaining tomato mixture. Sprinkle with Parmesan.

9. Cover. Cook on High for 2–3 hours, until pasta is al dente and sauce is bubbling at edges.

Variations:

Add some spinach leaves, sliced black olives, chopped kielbasa, or sliced mushrooms as you make layers. Just keep the sauce and pasta proportions the same so there is enough liquid for the pasta.

Good go-alongs with this recipe:

Green salad and Italian bread.

Pastas, Grains & Vegetarian

Veggie Mac and Cheese

Dorothy Lingerfelt
Stonyford, CA

Makes 8–10 servings
Prep. Time: 15 minutes
Cooking Time: 4–4½ hours
Ideal slow-cooker size: 6-qt.

8 oz. uncooked elbow macaroni

3½ cups milk

3 cups chopped broccoli, fresh *or* frozen (and thawed)

2 cups chopped cauliflower, fresh *or* frozen (and thawed)

3 carrots, sliced thinly

1 medium onion, chopped

¼ tsp. black pepper

¾ tsp. salt

¼ tsp. paprika

1 Tbsp. Dijon mustard

4 cups shredded cheddar cheese

1. Grease interior of slow-cooker crock.

2. Gently mix all ingredients together in crock, making sure that everything gets distributed well.

3. Cover. Cook on Low 4 hours, or until vegetables and macs are as tender as you like them.

4. If you find water around the edges of the dish at end of cooking time, cook on High, uncovered, for 20 minutes. That will also make the top slightly crusty and crunchy.

Why I like this recipe—
This really is a one-pot dinner. I love the convenience of such meals on the days I'm at the office.

Pastas, Grains & Vegetarian

Horseradish Mac and Cheese

Phyllis Good
Lancaster, PA

Makes 4–6 servings
Prep. Time: 10–15 minutes
Cooking Time: 4–4½ hours
Ideal slow-cooker size: 4- or 5-qt.

8 oz. uncooked elbow macaroni

12-oz. can evaporated milk

1½ cups milk, your choice of whole, skim, or in between

1 Tbsp., plus 1 tsp., horseradish mustard

¾ tsp. salt

¼ tsp. black pepper

1½ cups shredded Swiss cheese

1½ cups shredded horseradish cheese *or* cheddar cheese, *divided*

1. Grease interior of slow-cooker crock.

2. Combine all ingredients in crock except ¾ cup shredded horseradish or cheddar cheese.

3. Sprinkle top with remaining ¾ cup grated cheese.

4. Cover. Cook on Low 4 hours, or until macs are tender but not overcooked.

5. If there's water around the edges at end of cooking time, turn cooker to High for 20 minutes and continue cooking, uncovered.

Why I like this recipe—

This is a family favorite and we often eat it at home, but we also make it to take to potlucks, too. We always have an empty crock to take home!

Creamy Mac and Cheese

Renee Hankins
Narvon, PA

Makes 6 servings
Prep. Time: 5 minutes
Cooking Time: 3–4 hours
Ideal slow-cooker size: 5-qt.

12 oz. uncooked elbow macaroni

2 cups milk

12-oz. can evaporated milk

1 small onion, chopped

½ tsp. salt

¼ tsp. black pepper

1 cup grated Gouda cheese

1½ cups grated cheddar cheese

1. Grease interior of slow-cooker crock.

2. Mix all ingredients, except Gouda and cheddar cheeses, in crock.

3. Cover. Cook on Low 3–4 hours, or until macaronis are as soft as you like them.

4. Thirty minutes before end of cooking time, stir in cheeses. Cover and continue cooking.

5. If you want a crispy top, or if water has gathered around the edges, uncover during last 30 minutes of cooking time.

Why I like this recipe—

When my daughter was 8, she ate this mac and cheese at a friend's house and liked it so much she asked for the recipe! The moms had a good laugh about that over the phone—I was amused to see how my daughter takes after me!

Red Beans and Pasta

Naomi E. Fast
Hesston, KS

Makes 6–8 servings
Prep. Time: 10–15 minutes
Cooking Time: 3–4 hours
Ideal slow-cooker size: 5-qt.

3 15-oz. cans chicken *or* vegetable broth

½ tsp. ground cumin

1 Tbsp. chili powder

1 garlic clove, minced

8 oz. uncooked spiral pasta

half a large green bell pepper, diced

half a large red bell pepper, diced

1 medium onion, diced

15-oz. can red beans, rinsed and drained

chopped fresh parsley

chopped fresh cilantro

Why I like this recipe—
I love how simple this recipe is, yet it cooks up with some special flavor.

1. Grease interior of slow-cooker crock.

2. Combine broth, cumin, chili powder, and garlic in slow cooker.

3. Cover. Cook on High until mixture comes to boil.

4. Add pasta, vegetables, and beans. Stir together well.

5. Cover. Cook on Low 3–4 hours, or until macaronis are as tender as you like them.

6. Add parsley and cilantro just before serving.

Pasta Bean Pot

Donna Conto
Saylorsburg, PA

Makes 8 servings
Prep. Time: 10–15 minutes
Cooking Time: 4–5 hours
Ideal slow-cooker size: 4-qt.

1 Tbsp. olive oil

1 medium onion, chopped

1 garlic clove, minced

½ tsp. vinegar

8 oz. uncooked elbow macaroni

28-oz. can stewed *or* diced tomatoes

15-oz. can cannellini beans, undrained

15-oz. can kidney beans, undrained

12-oz. can chicken broth

1 tsp. dried oregano

1 tsp. parsley

dash red pepper

1. Grease interior of slow-cooker crock.

2. Put all ingredients in slow cooker. Mix well.

3. Cover. Cook on Low 4–5 hours, or until macaronis are tender but not mushy.

Why I like this recipe—
I like to have Pasta Bean Pot cooking as my granddaughter and I bake cookies. That frees us from worrying about making dinner.

Minestra Di Ceci

Jeanette Oberholtzer
Manheim, PA

Makes 4–6 servings
Prep. Time: 25 minutes
Soaking Time: 8 hours, or overnight
Cooking Time: 5½–6 hours
Ideal slow-cooker size: 4-qt.

1 lb. dry garbanzo beans
1 sprig fresh rosemary
10 leaves fresh sage
2 Tbsp. salt
1–2 large garlic cloves, minced
olive oil
1 cup uncooked small pasta, your choice of
    shape, or uncooked penne

1. Grease interior of slow-cooker crock.

2. Wash garbanzo beans. Place in slow cooker. Cover with water. Stir in rosemary, sage, and salt. Soak 8 hours, or overnight.

3. Drain water. Remove herbs.

4. Refill slow cooker with peas and fresh water to 1 inch above peas.

5. Cover. Cook on Low 5 hours.

6. Sauté garlic in olive oil in skillet until clear.

7. Purée half of the garbanzo beans, along with several cups of broth from cooker, in blender. Return purée to slow cooker.

8. Add garlic and oil.

9. Boil pasta in saucepan until al dente, about 5 minutes. Drain. Add to beans.

10. Cover. Cook on High 30–60 minutes, or until pasta is tender and heated through, but not mushy.

Variation:
Add ½ tsp. black pepper in Step 1, if you like.

Pastas, Grains & Vegetarian

Tortellini with Broccoli

Susan Kasting
Jenks, OK

Makes 4 servings
Prep. Time: 10 minutes
Cooking Time: 2½–3 hours
Ideal slow-cooker size: 4-qt.

½ cup water

26-oz. jar pasta sauce (your favorite)

1 Tbsp. Italian seasoning

9-oz. pkg. frozen spinach and cheese tortellini

16-oz. pkg. frozen broccoli florets

1. Grease interior of slow-cooker crock.

2. In a bowl, mix water, pasta sauce, and seasoning together.

3. Pour ⅓ of sauce into bottom of slow cooker. Top with all the tortellini.

4. Pour ⅓ of sauce over tortellini. Top with broccoli.

5. Pour remaining sauce over broccoli.

6. Cook on High 2½–3 hours, or until broccoli and pasta are tender but not mushy.

Why I like this recipe—
My son made this tortellini by himself when I needed to be out of town for the better part of a week. He was so proud of himself for making a delicious dinner and doing a truly helpful job!

Pastas, Grains & Vegetarian

Tastes-Like-Chili-Rellenos

**Roseann Wilson
Albuquerque, NM**

Makes 6 servings
Prep. Time: 10 minutes
Cooking Time: 2–3 hours
Ideal slow-cooker size: 3-qt.

2 tsp. butter

2 4-oz. cans whole green chilies

½ lb. grated cheddar cheese

½ lb. grated Monterey Jack cheese

14½-oz. can stewed tomatoes

4 eggs

2 Tbsp. flour

¾ cup evaporated milk

1. Grease sides and bottom of slow cooker with butter.

2. Cut chilies into strips. Layer chilies and cheeses in slow cooker. Pour in stewed tomatoes.

3. Combine eggs, flour, and milk. Pour into slow cooker.

4. Cover. Cook on High 2–3 hours.

Why I like this recipe—
My family always loved to order chiles rellenos at restaurants. They are peppers stuffed with cheese and dipped in batter and fried. I was thrilled to find this easy slow-cooker version that didn't involve frying!

Arroz con Queso

Nadine L. Martinitz
Salina, KS

Makes 6–8 servings
Prep. Time: 15 minutes
Cooking Time: 6–9 hours
Ideal slow-cooker size: 4-qt.

14½-oz. can whole tomatoes, mashed

15-oz. can Mexican-style beans, undrained

1½ cups uncooked long grain rice

1 cup grated Monterey Jack cheese

1 large onion, finely chopped

1 cup cottage cheese

4½-oz. can chopped green chili peppers, drained

1 Tbsp. oil

3 garlic cloves, minced

1 tsp. salt

1 cup grated Monterey Jack cheese

TIP

We eat this with salsa on the side.

1. Grease interior of slow-cooker crock.

2. Combine all ingredients except final cup of cheese in well-greased slow cooker.

3. Cover. Cook on Low 6–9 hours, or until rice is fully cooked but dish is not dry.

4. Sprinkle with remaining cheese before serving.

Pastas, Grains
& Vegetarian

Double Corn Tortilla Bake

Kathy Keener Shantz
Lancaster, PA

Makes 4 servings
Prep. Time: 15 minutes
Cooking Time: 2–3 hours
Ideal slow-cooker size: 3- or 4-qt.

8 corn tortillas, divided

1½ cups shredded Monterey Jack cheese, *divided*

1 cup corn, fresh, frozen, *or* canned (drained of juice), *divided*

4 green onions, sliced, about ½ cup, *divided*

2 eggs, beaten

1 cup buttermilk

4-oz. can diced green chilies

1. Grease interior of slow-cooker crock.

2. Tear 4 tortillas into bite-sized pieces. Scatter evenly over bottom of crock.

3. Top with half the cheese, half the corn, and half the green onions.

4. Repeat layers.

5. In a mixing bowl, stir together eggs, buttermilk, and chilies. Gently pour over tortilla mixture.

6. Cover. Cook on Low 2–3 hours, or until knife inserted in center comes out clean.

Why I like this recipe—

This is a potluck favorite because it's easy and uses common ingredients, but the flavor is amazing. I get requests for this recipe often.

Black Bean Burritos

Esther Nafziger
La Junta, CO

Makes 6-8 servings
Prep. Time: 20 minutes
Cooking Time: 6-10 hours
Ideal slow-cooker size: 5-qt.

2 cups dried black beans
7 cups water
hot chilies, diced, to taste
½ cup chopped onion
⅓ cup salsa, as hot or mild as you like
3 cloves garlic, minced
1 tsp. dried oregano
1 tsp. chili powder
2 tsp. salt
½ tsp. black pepper
6-8 flour tortillas
chopped lettuce
fresh tomatoes, chopped, *or* salsa
1½ cups shredded cheese of your choice

1. Grease interior of slow-cooker crock.

2. Sort and rinse dried beans.

3. Place in crock. Add water.

4. Cover. Cook on Low 9–10 hours, or on High 6–7 hours, or until beans are as tender as you like them.

5. Drain off any cooking liquid.

6. Stir hot chilies, onion, salsa, garlic, oregano, chili powder, salt, and pepper into cooked beans in crock.

TIP

Leftover filling freezes well.

7. Cover. Cook on High 1 hour, or on Low 2 hours, or until veggies are as tender as you want.

8. Spoon filling down center of each tortilla. Top with lettuce, tomatoes or salsa, and cheese.

9. Fold top and bottom of each tortilla over filling. Roll up to serve.

Good go-alongs with this recipe:
Spanish rice.

Sweet Pepper Burritos

Anita King
Bellefontaine, OH

Makes 6 servings
Prep. Time: 35 minutes
Cooking Time: 2–2¼ hours
Baking Time: 10–15 minutes
Ideal slow-cooker size: 5-qt.

¾ cup raw brown rice

1¼ cups water

1 medium onion, chopped

2 tsp. ground cumin

½ tsp. black pepper

2 medium sweet red bell peppers, diced

1 medium sweet yellow bell pepper, diced

1 medium sweet green bell pepper, diced

1½ cups cheddar cheese, shredded

3-oz. pkg. cream cheese, cubed

6 whole wheat tortillas, about 6-inch in
diameter

salsa, as mild or hot as you like, *optional*

1. Grease interior of slow-cooker crock.

2. Place raw brown rice, water, onion,
cumin, and black pepper in crock. Stir until
well mixed.

3. Cover. Cook on High for 1¾ hours, or
until rice is nearly tender.

4. While rice is cooking, dice sweet bell
peppers.

5. Stir in at end of cooking time, along with
cheddar and cream cheeses.

6. Cover. Continue cooking on High 30
more minutes, or until rice and peppers are as
tender as you like them.

7. Spoon ⅔ cup rice-pepper-cheese mixture
onto lower half of each tortilla. Fold in the
sides. Then bring up the bottom and roll up.

8. Place each burrito, seam side down, in
greased 9x13-inch baking pan.

9. Cover. Bake at 425° 10–15 minutes.

10. Let stand 4 minutes. Serve with salsa if
you wish.

Why I like this recipe—
We love the Mexican flavors of this dish and
its pretty colors. Sometimes I hold back a few
slices of the bell pepper to sprinkle on top at
the end.

Pastas, Grains
& Vegetarian

Cornbread-Topped Frijoles

Andy Wagner
Quarryville, PA

Makes 8–10 servings
Prep. Time: 20–30 minutes
Cooking Time: 3 hours
Ideal slow-cooker size: 5-qt.

1 medium onion, chopped

1 medium green bell pepper, chopped

2 garlic cloves, minced

16-oz. can kidney beans, rinsed and drained

15-oz. can pinto beans, rinsed and drained

14½-oz. can diced tomatoes, undrained

8-oz. can tomato sauce

1 tsp. chili powder

½ tsp. coarsely ground black pepper

¼ tsp. hot pepper sauce

Cornbread Topping:

½ cup flour

½ cup yellow cornmeal

2 tsp. sugar

1 tsp. baking powder

¼ tsp. salt

1 egg, lightly beaten

¾ cup skim milk

½ cup cream-style corn

1½ Tbsp. canola oil

1. Grease interior of slow-cooker crock.

2. Stir onion, green pepper, garlic, both beans, tomatoes, tomato sauce, chili powder, black pepper, and hot sauce together in crock.

3. Cover. Cook on High 1 hour.

4. While frijoles are cooking, in a large bowl, mix together flour, cornmeal, sugar, baking powder, and salt.

5. In another bowl, combine egg, milk, corn, and oil.

6. Add wet ingredients to dry, mixing well.

7. Spoon evenly over frijoles in crock. Do not stir.

8. Cover. Cook on High 2 more hours, or until a toothpick inserted in center of cornbread comes out clean.

Why I like this recipe—
"Frijoles" are just beans in Mexican cooking. Here, they get a tasty cornbread lid that soaks up some of the beans' juice as they bake. We serve this with a green tossed salad.

QUICK and EASY

Mexican Rice and Beans

Helen Schlabach
Winesburg, OH

Makes 6–8 servings
Prep. Time: 10 minutes
Cooking Time: 2–3 hours
Ideal slow-cooker size: 4-qt.

15-oz. can black beans, rinsed and drained

10-oz. pkg. frozen whole-kernel corn

1 cup raw long-grain brown rice

16-oz. jar thick and chunky mild or medium salsa

1½ cups vegetable, cocktail, or tomato juice

½ tsp. ground cumin

½ tsp. dried oregano

½ tsp. salt

¼ tsp. black pepper

¾ cup shredded cheddar cheese

1. Grease interior of slow-cooker crock.

2. Combine all ingredients, except cheese, in crock.

3. Cover. Cook on High 2–3 hours, until rice is tender, stirring once halfway through.

4. Scatter cheese over rice and beans.

5. Allow to stand, uncovered, until cheese melts.

Why I like this recipe—
My niece is a vegetarian. When she moved into her first apartment, she asked me if I had any easy slow-cooker vegetarian recipes. I gave her this one, and she loves it.

Jamaican Rice and Beans

**Lorraine Pflederer
Goshen, IN**

Makes 4 servings
Prep. Time: 10 minutes
Cooking Time: 2 hours
Ideal slow-cooker size: 3-qt.

14-oz. can light coconut milk

½ cup water

scant ½ tsp. allspice

½ tsp. salt

3 fresh thyme sprigs, *or* 1 tsp. dried thyme

1 garlic clove, crushed

15-oz. can dark red kidney beans, drained and rinsed

1 cup uncooked instant rice

1. Grease interior of slow-cooker crock.

2. Stir all ingredients into the crock except uncooked rice.

3. Cover. Cook on Low 1½ hours.

4. Stir rice into cooker.

5. Cover. Cook on High 20–30 minutes, or until rice is tender but not dry.

6. Stir and serve.

Why I like this recipe—

We enjoy these flavors because they are different from most bean recipes. I often serve these with grilled sausages and sliced tomatoes.

Crock-O-Beans

Nanci Keatley
Salem, OR

Makes 6 servings
Prep. Time: 10–15 minutes
Cooking Time: 6 hours
Ideal slow-cooker size: 6-qt.

15-oz. can tomato purée

1 medium onion, chopped

2 cloves garlic, chopped

1 Tbsp. chili powder

1 Tbsp. oregano

1 Tbsp. cumin

1 Tbsp. parsley

1–2 tsp. hot sauce, depending upon your
   preference for heat

15-oz. can black beans, drained and rinsed

15-oz. can kidney beans, drained and rinsed

15-oz. can garbanzo beans, drained and rinsed

2 15-oz. cans baked beans

15-oz. can whole-kernel corn

4 cups cooked rice

1. Grease interior of slow-cooker crock.

2. Place tomato purée, onion, garlic, and
seasonings in slow cooker. Stir together well.

3. Add each can of beans, stirring well
after each addition. Stir in corn.

4. Cover and cook on Low 6 hours.

5. Serve beans over cooked rice.

Why I like this recipe—
I first tasted these beans at a housewarming.
I watched carefully at the end of the party to
see who would take the empty slow cooker
so I could ask for the recipe. I've made them
many times since!

Brown Rice Vegetable Dinner

Judy Buller
Bluffton, OH

Makes 6–8 servings
Prep. Time: 20–30 minutes
Cooking Time: 3–6 hours
Ideal slow-cooker size: 5 qt.

3 cups vegetable broth

3 Tbsp. soy sauce

1½ cups uncooked brown rice

2 cups chopped onions, *divided*

2 garlic cloves, minced

½ tsp. dried thyme

1 medium carrot, cut in thin sticks

1 cup broccoli florets

1 cup cauliflower florets

1 cup sliced zucchini, peeled or not

1 cup sliced yellow squash, peeled or not

1 medium red bell pepper, cut in strips

1 cup cashews

2 cups shredded cheddar cheese

1. Grease interior of slow-cooker crock.

2. Place broth, soy sauce, uncooked rice, onions, garlic, thyme, carrot, broccoli, and cauliflower in crock.

3. Cover. Cook on High 2 hours or on Low 3–4 hours, or until vegetables are nearly tender.

4. Stir in zucchini, yellow squash, and pepper strips.

5. Cover. Cook on High 1 more hour or on Low 2 more hours, or until all vegetables are as tender as you like them.

6. Just before serving, sprinkle dish with cashews and cheese. When cheese has melted, serve.

Variations:

Use any vegetable in season. Remember that denser veggies need to cook longer than more delicate ones.

Pastas, Grains & Vegetarian

Sunshine Dish

**Abigail Zuck
Manheim, PA**

Makes 4 main-dish, or 6–8
 side-dish, servings
Prep. Time: 10–30 minutes
Cooking Time: 2½–3½ hours
Ideal slow-cooker size: 4-qt.

2 cups shredded carrots (shred your own, or pick up a pkg. of already shredded carrots in your grocery store)

2 cups cream-style, or whole kernel, corn

2 eggs

1½ cups sharp cheese, cubed

¼ cup milk

1 Tbsp. butter, melted

¼ tsp. ground mustard, optional

¼ cup finely chopped onion

½ tsp. salt

¼ tsp. black pepper

⅔ cup uncooked instant rice

1⅓ cups water

1. Grease interior of slow-cooker crock.

2. Mix all ingredients, except rice and water, in crock.

3. Cover. Cook on Low 2–3 hours, or until veggies are as tender as you like them.

4. Stir in uncooked rice and water.

5. Cover. Cook on High 20–30 minutes, or until rice is fully cooked.

Why I like this recipe—
I make this casserole a lot! It's a favorite for winter holidays, but it's also comfort food for my family, so they request it often.

Pastas, Grains & Vegetarian

Creamy Black-Eyed Peas

Margaret W. High
Lancaster, PA

Makes 6–8 servings
Prep. Time: 20 minutes
Cooking Time: 4½–6¾ hours
Ideal slow-cooker size: 4-qt.

2 cups dry black-eyed peas

5 cups water

1 onion, chopped

2 bay leaves

½ tsp. dried thyme

1 Tbsp. brown sugar

2 Tbsp. butter

1 tsp. salt

2 Tbsp. flour

½–1 cup whole milk, room temperature

hot cornbread, for serving

1. Grease interior of slow-cooker crock.

2. Combine black-eyed peas, water, onion, bay leaves, thyme, brown sugar, and butter in slow cooker.

3. Cover and cook on Low for 4–6 hours, until peas are tender.

4. Remove bay leaves. Add salt.

5. Separately, whisk flour and milk together. Decide how much milk to use depending on how soupy your peas are or how saucy you want them.

6. Whisk milk mixture into beans. Cover and cook again on Low for 30–45 minutes, until creamy and thickened. Taste and adjust salt.

7. Serve over cornbread.

Variations:
Serve over rice or biscuits.

Good go-alongs with this recipe:
Great with Southern food like cooked collard greens, fried fish, biscuits and jam, and peach cobbler. I usually include something spicy, too, since the black-eyed peas are creamy and mild.

Pastas, Grains & Vegetarian

Herbed Rice and Lentil Bake

Peg Zannotti
Tulsa, OK

Makes 4 servings
Prep. Time: 15 minutes
Cooking Time: 2–4 hours
Ideal slow-cooker size: 4-qt.

2²/₃ cups vegetable broth or water

¾ cup dried green lentils, picked over for any stones and rinsed

¾ cup chopped onions

½ cup uncooked brown rice

¼ cup dry white wine or water

½ tsp. dried basil

¼ tsp. dried oregano

¼ tsp. dried thyme

⅛ tsp. garlic powder

½ cup shredded Italian-mix cheese *or* cheddar cheese

1. Grease interior of slow-cooker crock.

2. Place everything in the crock, except cheese. Stir together until well mixed.

3. Cover. Cook on Low 3–4 hours, or on High 2–3 hours, or until lentils and rice are both as tender as you like them.

4. Just before serving, sprinkle top with cheese. Allow to melt, and then serve.

Variations:

1. Add ½ tsp. salt in Step 2 if you wish.
2. Before adding cheese, top mixture with ½ cup Italian-flavored panko bread crumbs. Cook, uncovered, 5–10 minutes. Sprinkle with cheese. Allow cheese to melt, and then serve.

Pastas, Grains & Vegetarian

Thai Veggie Curry

Christen Chew
Lancaster, PA

Makes 4–5 servings
Prep. Time: 30 minutes
Cooking Time: 5–6 hours
Ideal slow-cooker size: 4- or 5-qt.

2 large carrots, thinly sliced

1 medium onion, chopped

3 cloves garlic, chopped

2 large potatoes, peeled or not, and diced

15½-oz. can garbanzo beans, rinsed and drained

14½-oz. can diced tomatoes, undrained

2 Tbsp. curry powder

1 tsp. ground coriander

1 tsp. cayenne pepper

2 cups vegetable stock

½ cup frozen green peas

½ cup coconut milk

salt to taste

cooked rice

Why I like this recipe—
I got this delicious curry recipe from my friend Lisa. Her family adds chopped cilantro and flaked coconut at the table, but my husband says it's just fine without.

1. Grease interior of slow-cooker crock.

2. Stir all ingredients except peas, coconut milk, salt, and cooked rice into crock. Mix together well, making sure seasonings are distributed throughout.

3. Cover. Cook on Low 5–6 hours, or until vegetables are as tender as you like them.

4. Just before serving, stir in peas and coconut milk. Season with salt to taste.

5. Serve over cooked rice.

Spinach Rice Bake

Esther Porter
Minneapolis MN

Makes 4 servings
Prep. Time: 10–15 minutes
Cooking Time: 1–2 hours
Ideal slow-cooker size: 3-qt.

10-oz. pkg. frozen chopped spinach

¾ cup grated cheese of your choice

½ tsp. garlic salt

1 Tbsp. diced onion

⅓ cup uncooked instant rice

1 egg, beaten

1 cup milk

1. Grease interior of slow-cooker crock.

2. Thaw spinach. Squeeze it as dry as you can. Place in crock.

3. Stir grated cheese, garlic salt, onion, and rice into spinach, mixing well.

4. Mix in egg and milk.

5. Cook on Low 1–2 hours, or until set in the middle. (Stick the blade of a knife into the center. If it comes out clean, the bake is done. If it doesn't, cover and continue cooking another 15 minutes.)

Good go-alongs with this recipe:
Baked sweet potatoes or baked squash.

Salsa Lentils

Karen Stanley
Amherst, VA

Makes 4 servings
Prep. Time: 15 minutes
Cooking Time: 2–4 hours
Ideal slow-cooker size: 4- or 5-qt.

2 cups dry green lentils, picked over for any stones and rinsed

4 cups water

2 cups chopped onions

¼ cup chopped garlic

2 cups salsa, mild, medium, *or* hot

1–3 jalapeño peppers, seeded and chopped

1¼ -oz. pkg. dry taco seasoning

½ tsp. salt

1 cup chopped fresh cilantro

cooked rice *or* corn chips

chopped lettuce

diced fresh tomatoes

grated cheese of your choice

sour cream

1. Grease interior of slow-cooker crock.

2. Place lentils, water, chopped onions and garlic, salsa, jalapeño peppers, taco seasoning, and salt in crock. Stir together until well mixed.

3. Cover. Cook on Low 3–4 hours or on High 2–3 hours, or until lentils are tender.

4. Just before serving, stir in chopped cilantro.

5. Serve over rice or corn chips.

6. Top with remaining ingredients.

Why I like this recipe—
This is my go-to dish when I want to make a vegetarian dish. It's flexible because of the garnishes, and the flavor is always popular.

Lentils Swiss-Style

Lenore Waltner
North Newton, KS

Makes 6 servings
Prep. Time: 20–30 minutes
Cooking Time: 2–6 hours
Ideal slow-cooker size: 5-qt.

1¾ cups dry lentils, picked over for any stones and rinsed

2 cups water

1 whole bay leaf

2 tsp. salt

¼ tsp. coarsely ground black pepper

½ tsp. dried marjoram

½ tsp. dried sage

½ tsp. dried thyme

2 large onions, chopped

2-4 cloves garlic, minced

2 cups home-canned tomatoes, *or* 14½-oz. can diced *or* stewed tomatoes

2 large carrots, sliced thinly

½ cup celery, sliced thinly

1 green bell pepper, chopped, *optional*

¼ cup chopped fresh parsley

¼ cup sherry

3 cups shredded Swiss *or* cheddar cheese

1. Grease interior of slow-cooker crock.

2. Place lentils, water, bay leaf, salt, black pepper, marjoram, sage, thyme, onions, garlic, tomatoes, carrots, and celery in slow cooker. Stir together until well mixed.

3. Cover. Cook on Low 4–6 hours, or on High 2–3 hours, or until lentils and raw vegetables are as tender as you like them.

4. Twenty minutes before end of cooking time, stir in chopped green pepper, if you wish.

5. Just before serving, stir in parsley and sherry. Sprinkle with cheese. When cheese has melted, serve.

Variations:
Start thawing a 10-oz. pkg. of frozen spinach. Break the block in half when it's thawed enough to do that. Place half back in the freezer. Allow the other half to thaw completely. Squeeze it dry and then stir spinach into lentil mixture in Step 4.
—Zoë Rohrer

Good go-alongs with this recipe:
Fresh fruit and rolls.

Pastas, Grains & Vegetarian

Curried Lentils

Susan Kasting
Jenks, OK

Makes 4–6 servings
Prep. Time: 15 minutes
Cooking Time: 3½–5½ hours
Ideal slow-cooker size: 4- or 5-qt.

1 large onion, chopped

5 tsp. curry powder

¼ tsp. cayenne pepper

5½ cups vegetable broth

1 lb. dried lentils, picked over for any stones
and rinsed

15-oz. can garbanzo beans, rinsed and drained

10-oz. pkg. frozen chopped spinach, thawed
and squeezed dry

½ cup plain yogurt

Good go-alongs with this recipe:
Pita bread.

1. Grease interior of slow-cooker crock.

2. Add chopped onion, curry powder,
cayenne, broth, and lentils to crock. Mix
together well.

3. Cover. Cook on Low 4–5 hours, or on
High 3–4 hours, or until onions and lentils
are as tender as you like them.

4. Stir in beans and spinach. Cover.
Continue cooking on either Low or High
another 30 minutes, or until dish is thoroughly
hot.

5. Serve, adding a dollop of yogurt to each
individual dish.

Baked Lentils with Cheese

Kay Nussbaum
Salem, OR

Makes 4 main-dish, or 8 side-dish, servings
Prep. Time: 25–30 minutes
Cooking Time: 3–8 hours
Ideal slow-cooker size: 4-qt.

1¾ cups raw lentils, rinsed and picked clean

2 cups water

1 whole bay leaf

½ tsp. salt

¼ tsp. black pepper

⅛ tsp. dried marjoram

⅛ tsp. dried sage

⅛ tsp. dried thyme

2 large onions, chopped

2 cloves garlic, minced

2 cups, *or* 14½ -oz. can, stewed tomatoes

2 large carrots, sliced thinly

½ cup celery, sliced thinly

1 sweet bell pepper, chopped, *optional*

2 Tbsp. dried parsley

1 cup cheddar cheese, grated

1. Grease interior of slow-cooker crock.

2. Mix all ingredients together in crock, except sweet pepper, parsley, and grated cheese.

3. Cover. Cook on Low 6–8 hours, or on High 3–5 hours, or until lentils and vegetables are as tender as you like them.

4. Twenty minutes before end of cooking time, stir in chopped peppers if you wish, and parsley.

5. Just before serving, uncover crock and scatter grated cheese over top. Serve when it's melted.

Why I like this recipe—
I like to mix this dish up before I leave for the day. It smells great when I come in the door at suppertime, and it's a treat to have supper ready.

Quinoa and Black Beans

Gloria Frey
Lebanon, PA

Makes 6–8 servings
Prep. Time: 15–20 minutes
Cooking Time: 2½–3 hours
Ideal slow-cooker size: 4-qt.

1 medium onion, chopped

3 cloves garlic, chopped

1 red bell pepper, chopped

1½ cups vegetable broth

1 tsp. ground cumin

¼ tsp. cayenne pepper

½ tsp. salt

¼ tsp. coarsely ground black pepper

1 cup fresh, frozen, or canned corn, drained

2 15-oz. cans black beans, rinsed and drained

¾ cup uncooked quinoa

½ cup fresh cilantro, chopped

Why I like this recipe—
My daughter introduced us to quinoa, and we really like it. This is a delicious supper and also packs well the next day in a lunch box.

1. Grease interior of slow-cooker crock.

2. Mix all ingredients together, except quinoa and cilantro, in crock.

3. Cover. Cook on Low 2 hours, or until veggies are as tender as you like.

4. Stir in quinoa. Cover and continue cooking on Low 20–30 more minutes, or until quinoa is tender.

5. Just before serving, stir in cilantro.

Pastas, Grains & Vegetarian

Vegetables with Red Quinoa

Gladys Voth
Hesston, KS

Makes 6–8 servings
Prep. Time: 20 minutes
Cooking Time: 1½–4 hours
Ideal slow-cooker size: 4-qt.

4 cups cubed, peeled and deseeded butternut squash (¾-inch in size)

2 cups cubed and peeled beets (¾-inch in size)

2 cups sliced celery (½-inch thick), about 2 stalks

6 cloves garlic, coarsely chopped

1½ cups vegetable broth

3 Tbsp. dried basil

1 cup uncooked red quinoa, rinsed

Mixed-berry almond nondairy yogurt, for topping

½ cup cashew nuts, for topping

1. Grease interior of slow-cooker crock.

2. Place peeled and cubed butternut squash and beets in crock. Add celery and garlic.

3. Pour vegetable broth over ingredients in slow cooker.

4. Crush dried basil between fingers while adding to slow cooker.

5. Stir everything together well.

6. Cover. Cook on High 1½–2 hours or on Low 3–4 hours.

7. Thoroughly rinse quinoa in a colander in cold water to remove bitterness. Drain. Set aside.

8. Twenty to thirty minutes before end of cooking time, stir quinoa into crock. Cover and cook on High 20–30 minutes.

9. Serve hot or at room temperature.

10. Top each serving with nondairy yogurt and a sprinkling of cashews.

Why I like this recipe—

This red dish is fun to include on a Valentine's Day or Christmas menu.

NOTE

Quinoa, an ancient seed food, has gained popularity in North America. It is chewy, mildly nutty, and high in protein. It is gluten free and cholesterol free.

Good go-alongs with this recipe:

A fresh fruit, pineapple, and banana salad lends eye appeal to the plate while adding a contrast in flavors.

Barley with Mushrooms

Rosemary Martin
Bridgewater, VA

Makes 4 servings
Prep. Time: 10–15 minutes
Cooking Time: 3–6 hours
Ideal slow-cooker size: 3-qt.

¾ cup uncooked pearl barley

½ cup diced onions

1 clove garlic, minced

14½-oz. can vegetable broth

3 cups chopped fresh mushrooms, *or* 4-oz. can
mushrooms, with liquid

½ cup slivered almonds, *optional*

pinch cayenne pepper *or* black pepper to taste

⅓ cup shredded sharp cheddar cheese,
optional

1. Grease interior of slow-cooker crock.

2. Place all ingredients in slow cooker
except cheese.

3. Cover. Cook on Low 5–6 hours, or on
High 3–4 hours, or until barley and onions
are as tender as you like them.

4. Just before serving, uncover and sprinkle
with cheese. Allow cheese to melt, and then
serve.

Why I like this recipe—
We love the earthy flavor of this dish. I serve
it as a side dish with thinly sliced roast beef.

Pastas, Grains
& Vegetarian

Moroccan Sweet Potato Medley

Pat Bishop
Bedminster, PA

Makes 6 servings
Prep. Time: 20 minutes
Cooking Time: 2¼–4¼ hours
Ideal slow-cooker size: 5-qt.

1 medium onion, sliced

2 cloves garlic, minced

1½ tsp. ground coriander

1½ tsp. cumin

¼–½ tsp. black pepper, coarsely ground,
   according to taste

2 medium sweet potatoes, peeled and cubed,
   or 1-lb. can sweet potatoes, cubed and
   drained

14½-oz. can stewed tomatoes, undrained

¾ cup uncooked bulgur

2¼ cups water

15-oz. can garbanzo beans, rinsed and drained

½ cup raisins

1 cup cilantro leaves, chopped

1. Grease interior of slow-cooker crock.

2. Place sliced onion, garlic, coriander,
cumin, pepper, sweet potatoes, tomatoes,
bulgur, and water in slow cooker.

3. Cover. Cook on Low 2 hours if you're
using canned sweet potatoes, or 4 hours if
you're using raw sweet potatoes, or until
vegetables are done to your liking and bulgur
is tender.

4. Stir in beans and raisins.

5. Cover. Cook 15 more minutes.

6. Serve, topping each individual plate or
bowl with a scattering of chopped cilantro
leaves.

Why I like this recipe—
We have fond memories of serving this to the
adults at our son's first birthday party. He
is grown now, and asked me for this recipe
when he moved out. I love that connection
across the years!

Filled Acorn Squash

Teresa Martin
New Holland, PA.

Makes 4 servings
Prep. Time: 20–30 minutes
Cooking Time: 5–11 hours
Ideal slow-cooker size: 7-qt. *oval*

2 medium acorn squash, about 1¼ lbs. each

2 Tbsp. water

15-oz. can black beans, rinsed and drained

½ cup pine nuts, raw, *or* toasted if you have time

1 large tomato, coarsely chopped

2 scallions, sliced thinly

1 tsp. ground cumin

½ tsp. coarsely ground black pepper, *divided*

2 tsp. olive oil

½–¾ cup shredded Monterey Jack cheese

1. Grease interior of slow-cooker crock.

2. Place washed whole squash in slow cooker.

3. Spoon in water.

4. Cover. Cook on High for 4–6 hours or on Low for 7–9 hours, or until squash are tender when you pierce them with a fork.

5. While squash are cooking, mix together beans, pine nuts, tomato, scallions, cumin, and ¼ tsp. black pepper. Set aside.

6. Use sturdy tongs, or wear oven mitts, to lift squash out of cooker. Let cool until you can cut them in half.

7. Scoop out seeds.

TIPS

1. I enjoy serving this recipe in the fall when I can buy squash at our local farmers market or at roadside stands, where they are plentiful and inexpensive.
2. This dish is high in protein and fiber and low in fat.

8. Brush cut sides and cavity of each squash half with olive oil.

9. Sprinkle all 4 cut sides with remaining black pepper.

10. Spoon heaping ½ cup of bean mixture into each halved squash, pressing down gently to fill cavity.

11. Return halves to slow cooker. Cover. Cook on High another hour, or on Low another hour or 2, until vegetables are as tender as you like them and thoroughly hot.

12. Uncover and sprinkle with cheese just before serving. When cheese has melted, put a filled half squash on each diner's plate.

Pastas, Grains & Vegetarian

Crustless Spinach Quiche

Barbara Hoover
Landisville, PA

Makes 8 servings
Prep. Time: 15 minutes
Cooking Time: 2–4 hours
Ideal slow-cooker size: 3- or 4-qt.

2 10-oz. pkgs. frozen chopped spinach

2 cups cottage cheese

½ stick (¼ cup) butter, cut into pieces

1½ cups sharp cheese, cubed

3 eggs, beaten

¼ cup flour

1 tsp. salt

1. Grease interior of slow-cooker crock.

2. Thaw spinach completely. Squeeze as dry as you can. Then place in crock.

3. Stir in all other ingredients and combine well.

4. Cover. Cook on Low 2–4 hours, or until quiche is set. Stick blade of knife into center of quiche. If blade comes out clean, quiche is set. If it doesn't, cover and cook another 15 minutes or so.

5. When cooked, allow to stand 10–15 minutes so mixture can firm up. Then serve.

Variations:
1. Double the recipe if you wish. Cook it in a 5-quart slow cooker.
2. Omit cottage cheese. Add 1 cup milk, 1 tsp. baking powder, and increase flour to 1 cup instead.
3. Reserve sharp cheese and sprinkle on top. Allow to melt before serving.

—Barbara Jean Fabel

Zucchini Torte

Mary Clair Wenger
Kimmswick, MO

Makes 8 servings
Prep. Time: 25 minutes
Cooking Time: 4–5 hours
Ideal slow-cooker size: 4-qt.

5 cups diced zucchini

1 cup grated carrots

1 small onion, diced finely

1½ cups biscuit baking mix

½ cup grated Parmesan cheese

4 eggs, beaten

¼ cup olive oil

2 tsp. dried marjoram

½ tsp. salt

pepper to taste

1. Grease interior of slow-cooker crock.

2. Mix together all ingredients. Pour into greased slow cooker.

3. Cover and cook on Low for 4–5 hours, until set. Remove lid last 30 minutes to allow excess moisture to evaporate.

4. Serve hot or at room temperature.

Why I like this recipe—
This is my family's favorite way to eat zucchini. We found that leftovers are delicious at room temperature, which makes it good for a picnic or potluck.

Summer Veggie Bake

Eone Riales Nesbit, MS

Makes 8–10 servings
Prep. Time: 30 minutes
Cooking Time: 4½ hours
Ideal slow-cooker size: 4-qt.

3 medium-sized green zucchini, sliced in thin coins, *divided*

3 ears of yellow sweet corn, kernels sliced off, *divided*

3 large red tomatoes, diced, *divided*

1 small onion, sliced in rings, *divided*

½ red bell pepper, sliced thinly, *divided*

¼ cup fresh basil leaves, *divided*

3 Tbsp. olive oil, *divided*

salt and pepper to taste

1 cup small-curd cottage cheese

1½ cups saltine cracker crumbs

¾ cup shredded sharp cheddar cheese, *divided*

1. In lightly greased crock, layer ⅓ of each vegetable: zucchini, corn, tomatoes, onion, bell pepper, and basil leaves. Drizzle with 1 Tbsp. olive oil. Sprinkle lightly with salt and pepper.

2. Separately, combine cottage cheese, cracker crumbs, and ½ cup cheddar.

3. Dollop ⅓ of mixture over vegetables.

4. Make another layer of vegetables the same way, another layer of cheese mixture, and a final layer of vegetables.

TIP

Serve with crusty bread and olive oil for dipping.

5. Sprinkle remaining ¼ cup cheddar over top.

6. Cover and cook on Low 4 hours. Remove lid and cook another 30 minutes to allow excess moisture to evaporate.

Baked Tomato Rarebit

Edwina Stoltzfus
Lebanon, PA

Makes 6 servings
Prep. Time: 25 minutes
Cooking Time: 4–5 hours
Ideal slow-cooker size: 3-qt.

4 cups fresh bread cubes

1½ cups grated sharp cheddar cheese

3 eggs, beaten

½ tsp. dry mustard

1½ tsp. salt

pinch pepper

3 cups stewed tomatoes with peppers and
onions

Why I like this recipe—
I got this recipe from British friends when
we were visiting them in Cornwall, but I
modified it to make in the slow cooker. It's
convenient and easy to take to a potluck.

1. In lightly greased slow cooker, lay in half
the bread cubes followed by half the cheese.

2. Repeat layers.

3. Separately, whisk together eggs, mustard,
salt, and pepper.

4. Pour egg mixture over bread and cheese
layers.

5. Pour stewed tomatoes evenly over all.

6. Cover and cook on Low for 4–5 hours,
until bubbling and browning around the
edges.

Herbal Apple Cheese Dish

Jane D. Look
Mapleton, IL

Makes 4 servings
Prep. Time: 20 minutes
Cooking Time: 2 hours
Ideal slow-cooker size: 6-qt.

3 Tbsp. butter

2 cups chopped tart apples, peeled or not

½ cup chopped onion

¼ tsp. garlic powder

¼ tsp. dried thyme *or* ¾ tsp. chopped fresh thyme

¼ tsp. dried marjoram *or* ¾ tsp. chopped fresh marjoram

4 Tbsp. flour

1 tsp. salt

1 cup milk

1 cup grated cheddar cheese

¼ cup chopped walnuts

4 egg yolks

6 egg whites

¼ tsp. cream of tartar

1. Melt butter in a saucepan.

2. Sauté apples, onion, garlic powder, thyme, and marjoram in butter for 3 minutes.

3. Gradually stir in flour, salt, and milk over low heat. Continue stirring until sauce thickens and bubbles.

4. Stir in cheese and nuts.

5. Beat egg yolks well and stir in.

6. Beat whites with cream of tartar until stiff. Fold into mixture.

7. Lightly grease interior of baking dish that will fit into your slow cooker.

8. Pour mixture into baking dish, and set dish on a small trivet or jar rings in the crock.

9. Cover cooker and cook on High for 2 hours, or until eggs are set.

10. Using sturdy tongs, or a metal spatula in one hand and a spoon in the other, lift out the baking dish.

11. Allow to stand for 10 minutes before cutting into wedges and serving.

Why I like this recipe—
The bit of fuss is totally worth the exclamations when I bring this dish to the table with guests. The flavor is wonderful, too. We used this recipe as part of a buffet we put together for my parents' fiftieth wedding anniversary. It was the first pan to be emptied!

Beefy Vegetable Soup

Nancy Graves
Manhattan, KS

Makes 6-8 servings
Prep. Time: 10 minutes
Cooking Time: 6-8 hours
Ideal slow-cooker size: 5-qt.

2-lb. boneless beef chuck roast, cut into
   1½-inch pieces

15-oz. can corn, whole-grain *or* cream-style

1 lb. fresh *or* frozen green beans

1-lb. bag frozen peas

40-oz. can stewed tomatoes

5 beef bouillon cubes

Tabasco to taste

2 tsp. salt

1. Grease interior of slow-cooker crock.

2. Combine all ingredients in slow cooker.
Do not drain vegetables.

3. Add water to fill slow cooker to within 3 inches of top.

4. Cover. Cook on Low 6–8 hours, or until meat is tender and vegetables are as soft as you like them.

Variation:
Add 1 large onion and sliced 2 cups sliced carrots to Step 2.

Soups, Stews & Chilis

Vegetable Beef Borscht

Jeanne Heyerly
Chenoa, IL

Makes 6–8 servings
Prep. Time: 20 minutes
Cooking Time: 6–8 hours
Ideal slow-cooker size: 5-qt.

1½-lb. boneless beef chuck roast, cut into
    1½-inch pieces
half a head of cabbage, sliced thin
3 medium potatoes, diced
4 carrots, sliced
1 large onion, diced
1 cup tomatoes, diced
1 cup corn
1 cup green beans
2 cups beef broth
2 cups tomato juice
¼ tsp. garlic powder
¼ tsp. dill seed
2 tsp. salt
½ tsp. pepper
water
sour cream, *optional*

1. Grease interior of slow-cooker crock.

2. Mix together all ingredients except water
and sour cream. Add water to fill slow cooker
three-quarters full.

3. Cover. Cook on Low 6–8 hours, or until
meat is tender and vegetables are as soft as
you like them.

4. Pass sour cream around the table so
individuals can add a dollop to their bowls if
they wish.

Variation:
Add 1 cup diced, cooked red beets during the
last half hour of cooking.

Why I like this recipe—
The cabbage fits right in here. It can be bold,
but it's a teamplayer in this borscht.

Winter's Night Beef Stew

Kimberly Jensen
Bailey, CO

Makes 6–8 servings
Prep. Time: 25 minutes
Cooking Time: 6½ hours
Ideal slow-cooker size: 5-qt.

2-lb. boneless beef chuck roast, cut in
1½-inch pieces

28-oz. can tomatoes

2 carrots, sliced

2 ribs celery, sliced

1 small onion, coarsely chopped

4 cups water

½ cup red wine

4 beef bouillon cubes

2 tsp. garlic powder

1 tsp. pepper

1 tsp. dry oregano

½ tsp. dry thyme

1 bay leaf

¼–½ cup couscous

1. Grease interior of slow-cooker crock.

2. Place meat and vegetables into slow cooker.

3. Combine all other ingredients in separate bowl except couscous.

4. Pour over ingredients in slow cooker. Mix together well.

5. Cover. Cook on Low 6 hours.

6. Stir in couscous. Cover and cook 30 minutes.

Variation:
Add 1½ cups sliced zucchini and/or 1 cup sliced mushrooms to the stew 1 hour before end of cooking time.

Why I like this recipe—
Hey, I make this any time of the year, especially when I can find fresh zucchini and mushrooms.

Can't Beet Beef Stew!

Bob Coffey
New Windsor, NY

Makes 6–8 servings
Prep. Time: 30 minutes
Cooking Time: 6 hours
Ideal slow-cooker size: 5- or 6-qt.

4 large beets, roasted in the oven at 425° until tender, then cooled, peeled, and diced, *or if* you don't have time for that much food prep, 2 15½-oz. jars prepared beets, drained

2 large onions, diced

3 garlic cloves, diced

2 large carrots, peeled and diced

2 large parsnips, peeled and diced

2 ribs celery, diced

15½-oz. can petite diced tomatoes, undrained

1 bay leaf

2 lbs. boneless beef chuck roast, cut into 1½-inch pieces

4 cups beef broth

¼ cup finely chopped fresh dill

coarse salt and pepper to taste

TIPS

1. When making recipes with bay leaves, I keep an index card next to my slow cooker and make a note on it, saying how many I used. Then I know how many to fish out later on.
2. The same beet pigment that will turn this stew a beautiful deep ruby color will turn your fingertips pink for days when handling them. Plan ahead and have disposable gloves ready so you won't be caught red-handed!
3. From the tester: This is a great recipe. If you're wary about red beets, you barely taste them, if at all. But they help to make the stew a wonderful rich color.
—A. Catherine Boshart

1. Grease interior of slow-cooker crock.

2. If roasting beets yourself, halve them. Place face down in single layer in greased baking pan. Cover and bake at 425° until tender, about 20 minutes. Uncover and allow to cool until you can handle them. Peel. Dice.

3. Place onion and garlic in crock. Stir in beets.

4. Add rest of ingredients, except dill, salt, and pepper to crock.

5. Cover. Cook on Low 6 hours, or until meat and vegetables are tender.

6. Stir in dill. Season to taste with salt and pepper.

7. Fish out bay leaf before serving.

Soups, Stews & Chilis

Moroccan Beef Stew

Joyce Cox
Port Angeles, WA

Makes 6–8 servings
Prep. Time: 30 minutes
Cooking Time: 6–8 hours
Ideal slow-cooker size: 4-qt.

5 garlic cloves, minced

2 cups thinly sliced onion

2-lb. boneless beef chuck roast, cut into 1½-inch cubes

15-oz. can diced tomatoes with juice

1 cup beef broth

1 Tbsp. honey

2 tsp. ground cumin

2 tsp. ground coriander

1 tsp. ground ginger

1 tsp. ground turmeric

1 cinnamon stick

1 bay leaf

1 cup pitted, chopped prunes

2 tsp. salt

½ tsp. pepper

TIPS

1. Serve over hot cooked couscous or brown rice.
2. Sprinkle individual servings with chopped parsley and some grated lemon or orange zest.

1. Grease interior of slow-cooker crock.

2. Place all ingredients in slow cooker. Stir well.

3. Cover and cook on Low 6–8 hours, or until meat and vegetables are as tender as you like them.

4. Remove cinnamon stick and bay leaf before serving.

Old-Fashioned Vegetable Beef Soup

Pam Hochstedler
Kalona, IA

Makes 6–8 servings
Prep. Time: 25 minutes
Cooking Time: 6–8 hours
Ideal slow-cooker size: 5-qt.

2 lbs. beef short ribs

2 qts. water

1 tsp. salt

1 tsp. celery salt

1 small onion, chopped

1 cup diced carrots

½ cup diced celery

2 cups diced potatoes

1-lb. can whole kernel corn, undrained

1-lb. can diced tomatoes and juice

1. Grease interior of slow-cooker crock.

2. Combine meat, water, salt, celery salt, onion, carrots, celery, and potatoes in slow cooker.

3. Cover. Cook on Low 4–6 hours, or until meat is tender and falling off the bone.

4. Debone meat, cut into bite-sized pieces, and return to pot.

5. Add corn and tomatoes.

6. Cover and cook on Low 1 hour, or until soup is hot in the center.

Why I like this recipe—
I love the deep beefy flavor of short ribs. They develop a powerful broth here.

Beef Barley Soup

Stacie Skelly
Millersville, PA

Makes 8–10 servings
Prep. Time: 15 minutes
Cooking Time: 7¼–9½ hours
Ideal slow-cooker size: 6-qt. *oval*

3-4-lb. boneless beef chuck roast

2 cups carrots, chopped

6 cups vegetable *or* tomato juice, *divided*

2 cups quick-cook barley

water, to desired consistency

salt and pepper to taste

1. Grease interior of slow-cooker crock.

2. Place roast, carrots, and 4 cups juice in slow cooker.

3. Cover and cook on Low 6–8 hours, or until meat is tender.

4. Remove roast. Place on platter and cover with foil to keep warm.

5. Meanwhile, add barley to slow cooker. Stir well. Turn heat to High and cook 45 minutes to 1 hour, or until barley is tender.

6. While barley is cooking, cut meat into bite-sized pieces.

7. When barley is tender, return chopped beef to slow cooker.

8. Add 2 cups juice, water if you wish, and salt and pepper, if needed.

9. Cover. Cook 30 minutes on High, or until soup is heated through.

Why I like this recipe—
The barley adds sturdiness and great texture here.

Soups, Stews & Chilis

Easy Veggie-Beef Soup

Rebecca Plank Leichty
Harrisonburg, VA

Makes 6–8 servings
Prep. Time: 20 minutes
Cooking Time: 3–6 hours
Ideal slow-cooker size: 5-qt.

1 lb. ground beef, *or* 2 cups boneless beef chuck roast cut into 1-inch pieces

2 cups sliced carrots

1 lb. frozen green beans, thawed

14½-oz. can corn, drained, *or* 16-oz. bag frozen corn, thawed

28-oz. can diced tomatoes

3 cups beef, *or* veggie, broth

3 tsp. instant beef bouillon

2 tsp. Worcestershire sauce

1 Tbsp. sugar

1 Tbsp. minced onion

10¾-oz. can cream of celery soup*

1. Grease interior of slow-cooker crock.

2. If you have time, brown ground beef in skillet over medium heat. Break up clumps with a wooden spoon. Or skip this step and go straight to Step 3.

3. Place meat in slow cooker.

*To make your own Cream Soup, see recipes on pages 563 and 564.

TIP

Serve with freshly baked bread and homemade jam.

4. Add all remaining ingredients except celery soup. Mix well.

5. Stir in soup.

6. Cover. Cook on Low 6 hours or on High 3–4 hours, or until veggies are as tender as you like them.

Why I like this recipe—

Two modern-day conveniences—the slow cooker and bread machine—allow me to prepare tasty meals without too much last-minute dashing around. Utilizing both gives me time to plan table settings and decorations, too.

Tasty Meatball Stew

Barbara Hershey
Lititz, PA

Makes 8 servings
Prep. Time: 1 hour (includes preparing
   and baking meatballs)
Cooking Time: 4–5 hours
Ideal slow-cooker size: 4-, 5-, or 6-qt."

Meatballs:
2 lbs. lean ground beef
2 eggs, beaten
2 Tbsp. dried onion
⅔ cup dried bread crumbs
½ cup milk
1 tsp. salt
¼ tsp. pepper
1 tsp. Dijon mustard
2 tsp. Worcestershire sauce

Stew:
6 medium potatoes, unpeeled if you wish, and
   diced fine
1 large onion, sliced
8 medium carrots, sliced
4 cups vegetable juice
1 tsp. basil
1 tsp. dried oregano
½ tsp. salt
½ tsp. pepper

1. In a bowl, thoroughly mix meatball ingredients together. Form into 1-inch balls.

2. Place meatballs on a lightly greased jelly-roll pan. Bake at 400° for 20 minutes.

3. Grease interior of slow-cooker crock.

4. Meanwhile, to make stew, prepare potatoes, onion, and carrots. Place in slow cooker.

TIPS

1. You can speed up the preparation of this dish by using frozen meatballs, either your own or store-bought ones.
2. If you will be gone more hours than the time required to cook the slow-cooker dish that you want to make, you can cook that recipe in your slow-cooker overnight on Low. I've done this many times. In the morning I put the slow-cooker insert, now full of the cooked food, into the refrigerator. When I get home, I reheat the food in the microwave.

5. When meatballs finish baking, remove them from pan. Blot dry with paper towels to remove excess fat.

6. Place meatballs on top of vegetables in slow cooker.

7. In a large bowl, combine vegetable juice and seasonings. Pour over meatballs and vegetables in slow cooker.

8. Cover cooker. Cook on Low 4–5 hours, or until vegetables are as tender as you like them.

Fix-It and Forget-It Slow Cooker Champion Recipes   **293**

Soups, Stews & Chilis

Chili-Taco Soup

Frances L. Kruba
Dundalk, MD

Makes 8 servings
Prep. Time: 25–30 minutes
Cooking Time: 5–7 hours
Ideal slow-cooker size: 4- or 5-qt.

2 lbs. boneless beef chuck roast, cut into
   1½-inch pieces

2 15-oz. cans stewed tomatoes, Mexican *or*
   regular, undrained

1 envelope dry taco seasoning mix

2 15-oz. cans pinto beans, undrained

15-oz. can whole-kernel corn, undrained

1. Grease interior of slow-cooker crock.

2. Combine all ingredients in slow cooker.

3. Cover and cook on Low 5–7 hours, or
until meat is tender but not dry.

Why I like this recipe—

Most taco soups are built around ground beef.
The chuck roast cubes add unusually great
flavor to this Taco Soup.

Trail Chili

Jeanne Allen
Rye, CO

Makes 6–8 servings
Prep. Time: 15 minutes
Cooking Time: 4 hours
Ideal slow-cooker size: 4- or 5-qt.

2 lbs. ground beef

1 large onion, diced

1 Tbsp. oil

28-oz. can diced tomatoes

2 8-oz. cans tomato purée

1 or 2 16-oz. cans kidney beans, undrained

4-oz. can diced green chilies

1 cup water

2 garlic cloves, minced

2 Tbsp. mild chili powder

2 tsp. salt

2 tsp. ground cumin

1 tsp. pepper

TIPS

Top individual servings with shredded cheese. Serve with taco chips.

Why I like this recipe—
Lotsa beans, or a little bit of beans—it's totally up to you.

1. Grease interior of slow-cooker crock.

2. If you have time, brown beef and onion in oil in skillet. Drain. Place in slow cooker. Or if you don't have time, place ground beef in cooker. Break it up into small clumps using a wooden spoon.

3. Stir in remaining ingredients.

4. Cover. Cook on Low 4 hours.

Best Bean Chili

Carolyn Baer
Conrath, WI

Makes 6 servings
Prep. Time: 20–30 minutes
Cooking Time: 4 hours
Ideal slow-cooker size: 4- or 5-qt.

1 lb. lean ground beef

1½ cups chopped onion

1 cup chopped green bell pepper

1 tsp. minced garlic

1–3 Tbsp. chili powder, according to your taste preference

1–2 tsp. ground cumin, also according to your taste preference

15-oz. can red kidney beans, rinsed and drained

15-oz. can pinto beans, rinsed and drained

3 14½-oz. cans diced Italian- *or* Mexican-seasoned tomatoes

2 Tbsp. brown sugar

1 tsp. unsweetened cocoa powder

1. Grease interior of slow-cooker crock.

2. If you have time, spray large skillet with cooking spray. Brown beef in skillet over medium heat. If you don't have time, place ground beef in cooker. Break it up into small clumps using a wooden spoon.

3. Transfer contents of skillet to slow cooker.

TIP

Offer a sprinkle of soy sauce and/or ground ginger with individual servings to enhance the flavor of the chili.

4. Add onion, peppers, and garlic, seasonings, beans, tomatoes, sugar, and cocoa powder to cooker. Mix together well.

5. Cover. Cook on Low 4 hours.

Why I like this recipe—
Some subtle flavor surprises here—cumin and cocoa powder—and if you want a little more adventure—soy sauce and ground ginger!

Soups, Stews & Chilis

Ohio Chili

Bob Coffey
New Windsor, NY

Makes 10–12 servings
Prep. Time: 25 minutes
Cooking Time: 4–5 hours
Ideal slow-cooker size: 5½- or 6-qt.

2 large onions, chopped

3 garlic cloves, smashed and chopped

2 large green bell peppers, chopped

2 ribs celery, chopped

2 15-oz. cans dark red kidney beans, rinsed and drained

15-oz. can pinto beans, rinsed and drained

15-oz. can ranch beans, undrained

2 15-oz. cans diced tomatoes, undrained

4-oz. can chopped green chilies

15-oz. can tomato sauce

½ tsp. ground cumin

2 tsp. chili powder

1 Tbsp. unsweetened cocoa powder

1 tsp. ground cinnamon

2 bay leaves

4 hamburger patties, cooked and crumbled into bite-sized pieces

1. Grease interior of slow-cooker crock.

2. Place all ingredients in slow cooker.

3. Cover and cook for 4–5 hours on Low, or until veggies are as soft as you like them and chili is hot in the center.

TIPS

1. Serve with grated cheddar or Mexican-blend cheese on top. We call it Ohio Chili because it's a great mix of Cincinnati chili and the chili you get at Wendy's, the burger chain from Columbus, Ohio.

2. Makes a lot, so the first night we usually just eat it plain in bowls. As a "planned over," the next night we add a little more tomato sauce when reheating it and serve it over spaghetti with cheese and chopped onion, just like the famous 5-way chili in Cincinnati.

Variations:

Add some chopped jalapeños or a few shakes of your favorite hot sauce 30 minutes before end of cooking time.

Corn Chili

Gladys Longacre
Susquehanna, PA

Makes 4-6 servings
Prep. Time: 15 minutes
Cooking Time: 4-5 hours
Ideal slow-cooker size: 4-qt.

1 lb. ground beef

½ cup chopped onions

½ cup chopped green bell peppers

½ tsp. salt

⅛ tsp. pepper

¼ tsp. dried thyme

14½-oz. can diced tomatoes with Italian herbs

6-oz. can tomato paste, diluted with 1 can water

2 cups frozen whole kernel corn

16-oz. can kidney beans

1 Tbsp. chili powder

1. Grease interior of slow-cooker crock.

2. If you have time, sauté ground beef, onions, and green peppers in deep saucepan. Drain and season with salt, pepper, and thyme. Place in crock. If you don't have time, put beef straight into slow cooker. Stir with a wooden spoon to break up clumps. Add onions, green peppers, and seasonings into crock.

3. Stir in tomatoes, tomato paste, corn, kidney beans, and chili powder.

4. Cover. Cook on Low 4–5 hours, or until veggies are as soft as you like them and chili is hot in the center.

TIPS

Top individual servings with dollops of sour cream, or sprinkle with shredded cheese.

Why I like this recipe—
We love corn. And we love the center position corn gets in this chili.

Lotsa-Beans Chili

Jean Weller
State College, PA

Makes 12–15 servings
Prep. Time: 25 minutes
Cooking Time: 4–5 hours
Ideal slow-cooker size: 5- or 6-qt.

1 lb. ground beef

1 lb. uncooked bacon, diced, *or* store-bought and already cooked and crumbled

½ cup chopped onions

½ cup brown sugar

½ cup sugar

½ cup ketchup

2 tsp. dry mustard

1 tsp. salt

½ tsp. pepper

2 15-oz. cans green beans, drained

2 14½-oz. cans baked beans

2 15-oz. cans butter beans, drained

2 16-oz. cans kidney beans, rinsed and drained

1. Grease interior of slow-cooker crock.

2. If you have time, brown ground beef and bacon in skillet. Drain and place in crock. If you don't have time, place beef in crock. Using a wooden spoon break beef into small clumps. Stir in cooked and crumbled bacon.

3. Combine all remaining ingredients in slow cooker.

4. Cover. Cook on Low 4–5 hours, or until chili is hot in the center.

Why I like this recipe—
Boy, does the bacon make this chili sing!

Beef and Sausage Chili

Dorothea K. Ladd
Ballston Lake, NY

Makes 6–8 servings
Prep. Time: 15 minutes
Cooking Time: 4–5 hours
Ideal slow-cooker size: 6- or 7-qt.

1 lb. ground beef
1 lb. bulk pork sausage
1 Tbsp. oil, *optional*
1 large onion, chopped
1 large green pepper, chopped
2–3 ribs celery, chopped
2 15½-oz. cans kidney beans
29-oz. can tomato purée
6-oz. can tomato paste
2 cloves garlic, minced
2 Tbsp. chili powder
2 tsp. salt

1. Grease interior of slow-cooker crock.

2. If you have time, brown ground beef and sausage in skillet. Drain and place meats in crock. If you don't have time, place meats in crock and use a wooden spoon to break them into small clumps.

3. Combine all remaining ingredients in slow cooker.

4. Cover. Cook on Low 4–5 hours.

Serving suggestion:
Top individual servings with shredded sharp cheddar cheese.

TIP

While it takes longer to brown the beef and sausage in a skillet before putting them into the slow cooker, the advantage is that it cooks off a lot of the meats' fat. When you drain off the drippings, you leave the fat behind and put far less into the crock, and therefore into your chili.

Variations:
1. For extra flavor, add 1 tsp. cayenne pepper.
2. For more zest, use mild or hot Italian sausage instead of regular pork sausage.

Pepperoni Pizza Chili

Melissa Cramer
Lancaster, PA

Makes 8 servings
Prep. Time: 15 minutes
Cooking Time: 4 hours
Ideal slow-cooker size: 4- or 5-qt.

1 lb. ground beef

16-oz. can kidney beans, rinsed and drained

15-oz. can pizza sauce

14-oz. can Italian stewed tomatoes, undrained

8-oz. can tomato sauce

1 cup water

3½-oz. pkg. sliced pepperoni

½ cup chopped green bell pepper

½ cup chopped onion

1 tsp. Italian herb seasoning

shredded part-skim mozzarella cheese, for topping

Offer good crusty bread on the side or for dipping.

Why I like this recipe—
Why not bring together two favorites—pizza and chili? This really works!

1. Grease interior of slow-cooker crock.

2. If you have time, brown the beef in a skillet. Drain off drippings. Place browned meat into crock. If you don't have time, place meat in crock and use a wooden spoon to break it into small clumps.

3. Place all other ingredients in slow cooker except cheese and mix together well.

4. Cook on Low 4 hours.

5. Serve in bowls with cheese on top.

Soups, Stews & Chilis

Taco Soup with Corn

Suzanne Slagel
Midway, OH

Makes 6–8 servings
Prep. Time: 15 minutes
Cooking Time: 4 hours
Ideal slow-cooker size: 5- or 6-qt.

1 lb. ground beef

1 large onion, chopped

1 Tbsp. oil

16-oz. can Mexican-style tomatoes, undrained

16-oz. can ranch-style beans, undrained

16-oz. can whole-kernel corn, undrained

16-oz. can kidney beans, undrained

16-oz. can black beans, undrained

16-oz. jar picante sauce

corn *or* tortilla chips

sour cream

shredded cheddar cheese

1. Grease interior of slow-cooker crock.

2. If you have time, brown meat and onions in skillet in oil. Drain off drippings and place meat and onions in crock. If you don't have time, place meat in crock and use a wooden spoon to break it into small clumps.

3. Add other vegetables and picante sauce. Stir well.

4. Cover. Cook on Low 4 hours.

5. Serve with corn or tortilla chips, sour cream, and shredded cheese as toppings.

Why I like this recipe—
We love the variety of color in this very varied veggie soup.

Chicken Barley Chili

Colleen Heatwole
Burton, MI

Makes 6–8 servings
Prep. Time: 20 minutes
Cooking Time: 4 hours
Ideal slow-cooker size: 6-qt.

2 14½-oz. cans tomatoes of your choice

16-oz. jar salsa, your choice of heat

3 cups water

14½-oz. can chicken broth

15½-oz. can black beans, rinsed and drained

15¼-oz. can whole-kernel corn, undrained

1–3 tsp. chili powder, depending on how hot you like your chili

1 tsp. cumin

3 cups cooked chicken *or* turkey, cubed

1 cup quick-cooking barley, uncooked

sour cream

shredded cheese of your choice

1. Grease interior of slow-cooker crock.

2. Combine all ingredients except chicken, barley, sour cream, and shredded cheese in slow cooker.

3. Cover. Cook on Low 4 hours.

4. Thirty minutes before end of cooking time, stir in chicken and barley. Cover. Continue cooking 30 more minutes, or until barley is tender.

5. Serve in individual soup bowls topped with sour cream and shredded cheese.

Why I like this recipe—

I like to roast a good-sized whole chicken now and then, which yields two meals. We love Meal #1, when we eat the meat as is, along with its juice and drippings. This is a perfect recipe for Meal #2, with the "planned-overs."

Soups, Stews & Chilis

Chili, Chicken, Corn Chowder

Jeanne Allen
Rye, CO

Makes 6–8 servings
Prep. Time: 15 minutes
Cooking Time: 3–4 hours
Ideal slow-cooker size: 4-qt.

1 large onion, diced

1 garlic clove, minced

1 rib celery, finely chopped

2 cups frozen *or* canned corn

4-oz. can diced green chilies

½ tsp. black pepper

2 cups chicken broth

salt to taste

2 cups cooked, deboned, diced chicken

1 cup half-and-half

1. Grease interior of slow-cooker crock.

2. Combine all ingredients in slow cooker except cooked chicken and half-and-half.

3. Cover. Heat on Low 3–4 hours, or until onions and celery are cooked as tender as you like them, and the chowder is hot in the middle.

4. Fifteen minutes before end of cooking time, stir in cooked chicken and half-and-half. Do not boil, but be sure chowder is heated through.

Why I like this recipe—
I don't know why chicken and corn are so compatible, but once again, they're a perfect combination here.

Chicken Tortilla Soup

Becky Harder
Monument, CO

Makes 6–8 servings
Prep. Time: 5–10 minutes
Cooking Time: 4–5 hours
Ideal slow-cooker size: 4- or 5-qt.

4 boneless, skinless chicken thighs, about 1½–2 lbs. total

2 15-oz. cans black beans, undrained

2 15-oz. cans Mexican stewed tomatoes *or* tomatoes with green chilies

1 cup salsa, mild, medium, *or* hot, whichever you prefer

4-oz. can chopped green chilies

14½-oz. can tomato sauce

tortilla chips

shredded cheese of your choice

1. Grease interior of slow-cooker crock.

2. Combine all ingredients in large slow cooker.

3. Cover. Cook on Low 4–5 hours, or just until thighs register 160° on instant-read meat thermometer when stuck in center of thigh.

4. Just before serving, remove chicken thighs and slice into bite-sized pieces. Stir back into soup.

5. To serve, put a handful of tortilla chips in each individual soup bowl. Ladle soup over chips. Top with shredded cheese.

TIP

I'm steering you toward chicken thighs because they hold up so well in long, slow cooking.

Soups, Stews & Chilis

Chipotle Chili

Janie Steele
Moore, OK

Makes 6–8 servings
Prep. Time: 30 minutes
Cooking Time: 3–4 hours
Ideal slow-cooker size: 3- or 4-qt.

2 cloves garlic, chopped

1½ lbs. boneless, skinless chicken thighs, cubed

1 lb. butternut squash, peeled and cubed

15-oz. can pinto beans, rinsed and drained

juice and zest of half an orange

2–3 chipotle peppers in adobo sauce, minced

2 Tbsp. tomato paste

2 green onions, sliced

chopped cilantro, *optional*

Why I like this recipe—
Butternut squash really behaves itself in a chili. It doesn't dominate, but it brings a soothing creaminess.

1. Grease interior of slow-cooker crock.

2. Combine garlic, chicken, squash, beans, orange juice, orange zest, peppers, and tomato paste in slow cooker.

3. Cook 3–4 hours on Low, or until chicken is just tender and no longer pink in the center.

4. Mash some of the stew with potato masher to make it thicker.

5. Stir in green onions, and cilantro if you wish, just before serving.

Variations:
Use zest and juice of 1 lime instead of the orange.

Southwest Chicken Soup

Phyllis Good
Lancaster, PA

Makes 6–8 servings
Prep. Time: 15 minutes
Cooking Time: 3–7 hours
Chilling Time: 30 minutes
Ideal slow-cooker size: 6-qt. *oval*

3-lb. whole chicken, *or* 3 large boneless,
    skinless thighs
6 cups water
1 cup onion, chopped
1 cup celery, chopped
1½ Tbsp. olive oil
15½-oz. can black beans, rinsed and drained
10-oz. pkg. frozen corn
15½ -oz. can diced tomatoes, undrained
4-oz. can chopped green chilies, undrained
½ tsp. cumin
½ tsp. black pepper
2 tsp. chili powder
salt to taste
½ cup cilantro, chopped

1. Grease interior of slow-cooker crock.

2. Place whole chicken, or chicken thighs, in slow cooker. Add 6 cups water.

3. Cover cooker. If cooking a whole chicken, cook on Low 4–5 hours, or until instant-read meat thermometer stuck into thickest part of the thigh (without touching the bone) registers 160°. Start checking at 5 hours, and do not overcook. If cooking thighs, cook on Low 2–3 hours, or until instant-read thermometer registers 160° when stuck into center of thighs. Start checking at 1½ hours and do not overcook.

4. Remove whole chicken or thighs from cooker and allow to cool until you can handle the meat without burning yourself. Keep the broth in the cooker for the soup.

5. Chop meat into bite-sized chunks. Set aside.

6. While chicken is cooking, sauté chopped onion and celery in olive oil in a skillet, or cook about 3 minutes on High, covered, in the microwave, just until softened.

7. Add softened vegetables to broth in cooker, along with all remaining ingredients, except the cilantro.

8. Cover. Cook on Low 2 hours, or on High 1 hour, or until everything is heated through.

9. Ten minutes before end of cooking time, stir in cut-up chicken.

10. Top individual servings with chopped fresh cilantro.

Why I like this recipe—
This looks like lots of steps, but it is super easy and takes little prep time. It's probably the soup recipe I make the most because it's the soup that gets the most compliments!

Soups, Stews & Chilis

Sausage and Kale Stew with Mashed Potatoes

Margaret W. High
Lancaster, PA

Makes 6 servings
Prep. Time: 25 minutes
Cooking Time: 5–7 hours
Ideal slow-cooker size: 6-qt.

4 cups canned tomatoes and juice, roughly crushed

1 large onion, chopped

2–3 garlic cloves, roughly chopped

1 lb. sweet *or* hot Italian sausage

freshly ground pepper

2–3 large potatoes, scrubbed

7 cups chopped kale

½ cup olive oil

½ cup milk, room temperature

salt

1. Grease interior of slow-cooker crock.

2. Combine tomatoes, onion, garlic, sausage, and several grinds of pepper in bottom of slow cooker.

3. Nestle the whole, unpeeled potatoes down into the tomato mixture.

4. Put the chopped kale on top of everything—it should come up to the top of the slow cooker.

5. Cover. Cook on Low 5–7 hours, or until potatoes are soft when pricked and kale is cooked down.

TIP

Serve with good bread to mop up the delicious juices.

6. Fish the potatoes out of the stew and place in serving dish. Pour in olive oil and milk, and salt to taste. Mash with potato masher until well combined.

7. Cut sausage in serving pieces. Stir back into stew in cooker.

8. To serve, place dollop of mashed potatoes in soup bowl and add some Potato/Sausage/Kale Stew on top.

Variations:
1. Top with freshly grated Parmesan at the table.
2. Brown sausages before adding to cooker.

Soups, Stews & Chilis

Kielbasa and Veggies Soup

Janie Steele
Moore, OK

Makes 6–8 servings
Prep. Time: 20 minutes
Cooking Time: 4 hours
Ideal slow-cooker size: 4- or 5-qt.

1 lb. kielbasa, sliced thin

8 cups chicken broth

2 14-oz. cans cannellini beans, undrained

1 onion, diced

1 bay leaf

1 tsp. dried thyme

¼ tsp. red pepper flakes

8 oz. rainbow rotini, uncooked

3 cloves garlic, minced

1 lb. chopped fresh spinach

salt and pepper to taste

1. Grease interior of slow-cooker crock.

2. If you have time, brown kielbasa slices in skillet over high heat until some edges are brown. Transfer kielbasa to slow cooker. If you don't have time, place kielbasa slices straight into slow cooker.

3. Add broth, beans, onion, bay leaf, thyme, and red pepper to slow cooker.

4. Cover and cook on Low 3 hours.

5. Add rotini and garlic. Cook 1 more hour on Low, or until pasta is as tender as you like it.

6. Stir in chopped spinach. Add salt and pepper to taste.

7. Remove bay leaf just before serving.

Why I like this recipe—
I'm a grudging pan-washer. Not only is this soup tasty and hearty, I love that you don't need to cook the pasta separately.

Chet's Trucker Stew

Janice Muller
Derwood, MD

Makes 8 servings
Prep. Time: 15 minutes
Cooking Time: 3–4 hours
Ideal slow-cooker size: 4- or 5-qt.

1 lb. bulk pork sausage

1 lb. ground beef

1 Tbsp. oil, *optional*

31-oz. can pork and beans, undrained

16-oz. can light kidney beans, drained

16-oz. can dark kidney beans, drained

14½-oz. can waxed beans, drained

14½-oz. can lima beans, drained

1 cup ketchup

1 cup brown sugar

1 Tbsp. spicy prepared mustard

TIP

While it takes longer to brown the beef and sausage in a skillet before putting them into the slow cooker, the advantage is that it cooks off a lot of the meats' fat. When you drain off the drippings, you leave the fat behind and put far less into the crock, and therefore into your stew.

1. Grease interior of slow-cooker crock.

2. If you have time, brown sausage and ground beef in oil in skillet. Drain and place meats in crock. If you don't have time, place meats in crock and use a wooden spoon to break them into small clumps.

3. Combine all remaining ingredients in slow cooker.

4. Cover. Cook on Low 3–4 hours, or until meats are fully cooked.

Sausage, Tomato, Spinach Soup

Wendy B. Martzall
New Holland, PA

Makes 6–8 servings
Prep. Time: 15–20 minutes
Cooking Time: 3–4 hours
Ideal slow-cooker size: 3- or 4-qt.

½ lb. bulk pork *or* turkey sausage

1 medium onion, chopped

1 small green bell pepper, chopped

1–2 Tbsp. oil, *optional*

28-oz. can diced tomatoes

2 14½-oz. cans beef broth

8-oz. can tomato sauce

½ cup picante sauce

1½ tsp. sugar

1 tsp. dried basil

½ tsp. dried oregano

10-oz. pkg. frozen spinach, thawed and
  squeezed dry

½–¾ cup shredded mozzarella cheese

1. Grease interior of slow-cooker crock.

2. If you have time, brown sausage with onion and pepper in skillet. (If you use turkey sausage, you'll probably need to add 1–2 Tbsp. oil to the pan.) Stir frequently, breaking up clumps of meat. When meat is no longer pink, drain off drippings. (If you don't have time, place sausage into cooker and break up into small clumps with wooden spoon.)

3. Spoon all remaining ingredients into slow cooker except spinach and shredded cheese. Stir until well blended.

4. Cover. Cook on Low 3–4 hours, or until vegetables are as tender as you like them.

5. Fifteen minutes before end of cooking time, stir spinach into soup. Cover and continue cooking on Low.

6. Top each individual serving with a sprinkling of mozzarella cheese.

Why I like this recipe—

There's a versatility opportunity here. Choose sweet or Italian sausage (you can always squeeze it out of its casing if you can't find it loose in the store). Go with Mexican- or Italian-flavored tomatoes if you like, and a hot and spicy picante sauce if you want a punchier flavor yet.

Smoked Sausage Stew

Carol Sherwood
Batavia, NY

Makes 4–5 servings
Prep. Time: 35–40 minutes
Cooking Time: 4–5 hours
Ideal slow-cooker size: 5-qt.

4–5 potatoes, peeled or not, and cubed

2 15-oz. cans green beans, undrained

1 lb. smoked sausage, sliced

1 onion, chopped

2 Tbsp. (¼ stick) butter

1. Grease interior of slow-cooker crock.

2. Layer potatoes, green beans, sausage, and onion in slow cooker in the order they are listed.

3. Dot top with butter.

4. Cook on Low 4–5 hours, or until potatoes are tender but not mushy.

Why I like this recipe—

Smoked sausage gives this mixture a deep-down richness. Making the stew in the slow cooker teases out that flavor and infuses the veggies with it.

Sauerkraut Soup

Norma Grieser
Clarksville, MI

Makes 4 servings
Prep. Time: 10 minutes
Cooking Time: 3–4 hours
Ideal slow-cooker size: 3- or 4-qt.

2 14½-oz. cans stewed tomatoes

2 cups sauerkraut

1 cup diced potatoes

1 lb. fresh *or* smoked sausage, sliced

1 medium-sized onion, chopped, *optional*

⅓ cup brown sugar, *optional*

1. Grease interior of slow-cooker crock.

2. Combine all ingredients in slow cooker.

3. Cover. Cook on Low 3–4 hours, or until potatoes and onions are soft, and the soup is thoroughly heated.

Why I like this recipe—
It's the brown sugar and the way it tames the sauerkraut! The brown sugar is never optional when I'm making this Soup.

Curried Pork and Pea Soup

Kathy Hertzler
Lancaster, PA

Makes 6–8 servings
Prep. Time: 15 minutes
Cooking Time: 4–10 hours
Ideal slow-cooker size: 5-qt.

1½-lb. boneless pork shoulder roast

1 cup yellow *or* green split peas, rinsed and drained

½ cup finely chopped carrots

½ cup finely chopped celery

½ cup finely chopped onions

49½-oz. can (approximately 6 cups) chicken broth

2 tsp. curry powder

½ tsp. paprika

¼ tsp. ground cumin

¼ tsp. pepper

2 cups torn fresh spinach

1. Grease interior of slow-cooker crock.

2. Trim fat from pork and cut pork into 1-inch pieces.

3. Combine split peas, carrots, celery, and onions in slow cooker.

4. Stir in broth, curry powder, paprika, cumin, and pepper. Stir in pork.

5. Cover. Cook on Low 8–10 hours, or on High 4 hours.

6. Stir in spinach. Serve immediately.

Why I like this recipe—

This soup always subtly reminds me that I'm part of a bigger world, thanks to some curry and a dash of cumin.

Soups, Stews & Chilis

Split Pea Soup

Phyllis Good
Lancaster, PA

Makes 8–10 servings
Prep. Time: 20 minutes
Cooking Time: 4¼–8¼ hours
Ideal slow-cooker size: 6-qt.

3 cups dried split peas (a little over 1 pound)
3 quarts water
½ tsp. garlic powder
½ tsp. dried oregano
1 cup diced, or thinly sliced, carrots
½ cup diced onions
1 tsp. salt
¼–½ tsp. pepper (coarsely ground is great)
1 ham shank *or* hock

1. Grease interior of slow-cooker crock.

2. Put all ingredients into slow cooker, except the ham. Stir well.

3. Settle ham into mixture.

4. Cover. Cook on Low 4–8 hours, or until ham is tender and falling off the bone, and the peas are very soft.

5. Use a slotted spoon to lift the ham bone out of the soup. Allow it to cool until you can handle it without burning yourself.

6. Cut the ham into bite-sized pieces. Stir it back into the soup.

7. Heat the soup for 10 minutes, and then serve.

Why I like this recipe—

I grew up eating this soup but always from a big soup pot. No more regularly stirring to make sure nothing's sticking to the bottom of the kettle when you make it in your slow cooker. Go with a big or small ham piece, depending on how much meat you want. You'll get the rich flavor either way.

Minestrone

Bernita Boyts
Shawnee Mission, KS

Makes 8-10 servings
Prep. Time: 15 minutes
Cooking Time: 3-6 hours
Ideal slow-cooker size: 4- or 5-qt.

1 large onion, chopped

4 carrots, sliced

3 ribs celery, sliced

2 garlic cloves, minced

6-oz. can tomato paste

14½-oz. can chicken, beef, *or* vegetable broth

24-oz. can pinto beans, undrained

10-oz. pkg. frozen green beans

2-3 cups chopped cabbage

1 medium zucchini, sliced

8 cups water

2 Tbsp. parsley

2 Tbsp. Italian spice

1 tsp. salt, *or* more if you prefer

½ tsp. pepper

¾ cup dry acini di pepe (small round pasta)

grated Parmesan *or* Asiago cheese

Why I like this recipe—

This is not a fussy, touchy recipe. If I don't have pinto beans, I sub in another kind. If I prefer broccoli to green beans, I make the switch. The acini di pepe takes second place to the veggies, but it's a sturdy presence even so.

1. Grease interior of slow-cooker crock.

2. Combine all ingredients, except pasta and cheese, in slow cooker.

3. Cover. Cook 3–4 hours on High or 5–6 hours on Low, or until veggies are as tender as you like them.

4. Add pasta 1 hour before cooking is complete.

5. Top individual servings with cheese.

Blessing Soup

Alix Nancy Botsford
Seminole, OK

Makes 8–10 servings
Prep. Time: 20 minutes
Soaking Time: 8 hours, or overnight
Cooking Time: 4–8 hours
Ideal slow-cooker size: 4- or 5-qt.

2 cups mixed dried beans (10–18 different kinds, if you can find them!)

2–2½ qts. water

1 cup diced ham

1 large onion, chopped

1 garlic clove, minced

juice of 1 lemon

14½-oz. can Italian tomatoes, chopped

½ cup chopped sweet red bell peppers

½ cup chopped celery

2 carrots, thinly sliced

1 tsp. salt

1 tsp. pepper

1. Grease interior of slow-cooker crock.

2. Wash beans. Discard any stones. Place beans in slow cooker. Cover with water and soak 8 hours or overnight.

3. Drain water off beans.

4. Add 2–2½ qts. water to drained beans. Cook on High 2 hours.

5. Combine all remaining ingredients with beans in slow cooker.

6. Add more water if necessary so that everything is just covered with water.

7. Cover. Cook on High 2–3 hours or on Low 4–6 hours, or until beans and other vegetables are tender but not mushy.

Why I like this recipe—

During one January that was especially dismal, I invited many friends, most of whom didn't know each other, to my home. I put on a video about rose gardens around the world. Then I made this soup and a fresh bread crouton that could be eaten on top of the soup and tossed a large salad.

Garbanzo Souper

Willard E. Roth
Elkhart, IN

Makes 6 servings
Prep. Time: 20 minutes
Soaking Time: 8 hours, or overnight
Cooking Time: 6 hours
Ideal slow-cooker size: 4-qt.

1 lb. dry garbanzo beans
4 oz. raw baby carrots, cut in half
1 large onion, diced
3 ribs celery, cut in 1-inch pieces
1 large green bell pepper, diced
½ tsp. dried basil
½ tsp. dried oregano
½ tsp. dried rosemary
½ tsp. dried thyme
2 28-oz. cans vegetable broth
1 broth can of water
8-oz. can tomato sauce
8 oz. prepared hummus
½ tsp. sea salt

1. Grease interior of slow-cooker crock.

2. Place beans in slow cooker. Cover with water. Soak 8 hours, or overnight.

3. Drain off water. Return soaked beans to slow cooker.

4. Add carrots, onion, celery, and green pepper.

5. Sprinkle with basil, oregano, rosemary, and thyme.

6. Add broth and water.

TIP

Serve with Irish soda bread and lemon curd.

7. Cover. Cook on Low 6 hours, or until beans and vegetables are tender but not overcooked.

8. Half an hour before serving, stir in tomato sauce, hummus, and salt. Continue cooking until hot.

Why I like this recipe—
A fine meal for vegetarians on St. Patrick's Day!

Russian Red Lentil Soup

Naomi E. Fast
Hesston, KS

Makes 8 servings
Prep. Time: 15 minutes
Cooking Time: 3¾–4¾ hours
Ideal slow-cooker size: 4-qt.

1 Tbsp. oil

1 large onion, chopped

3 cloves garlic, minced

½ cup diced, dried apricots

1½ cups dried red lentils

½ tsp. cumin

½ tsp. dried thyme

3 cups water

2 14½-oz. cans chicken *or* vegetable broth

14½-oz. can diced tomatoes

1 Tbsp. honey

¾ tsp. salt

½ tsp. coarsely ground
black pepper

2 Tbsp. chopped fresh mint

1½ cups plain yogurt

1. Grease interior of slow-cooker crock.

2. Combine all ingredients except mint and yogurt in slow cooker.

3. Cover. Heat on High until soup starts to simmer.

4. Turn to Low and cook 3–4 hours, or until lentils and vegetables are tender.

5. When serving, add mint and dollop of yogurt to each individual bowl of soup.

Why I like this recipe—
I just love what some dried apricots and honey do to brighten bashful lentils. And if you don't have fresh mint, use dried. Whichever version, the mint, along with the yogurt, waken up this hearty soup.

Chicken Rice Soup

Karen Ceneviva
Seymour, CT

Makes 8 servings
Prep. Time: 15 minutes
Cooking Time: 2¼–6¼ hours
Ideal slow-cooker size: 4-qt.

½ cup wild rice, uncooked

½ cup long grain rice, uncooked

1 tsp. vegetable oil

1 lb. boneless, skinless chicken thighs, cut into ¾-inch cubes

5¼ cups chicken broth

1 cup celery (about 2 ribs), chopped in ½-inch thick pieces

1 medium onion, chopped

2 tsp. dried thyme leaves

¼ tsp. red pepper flakes

1 cup sour cream

½–¾ cup chopped scallions

1. Grease interior of slow-cooker crock.

2. Mix wild and white rice with oil in slow cooker.

3. Cover. Cook on High 15 minutes.

4. Add chicken, broth, vegetables, and seasonings.

5. Cover. Cook 2–3 hours on High or 4–6 hours on Low, or until rice and chicken are tender but not dry.

6. When serving, add a dollop of sour cream sprinkled with finely chopped scallions on top of each individual serving bowl.

Why I like this recipe—
It's the mix of wild and long grain rices for me!

Chicken Corn Soup

Eleanor Larson
Glen Lyon, PA

Makes 4–6 servings
Prep. Time: 15 minutes
Cooking Time: 3–4 hours
Ideal slow-cooker size: 4- or 5-qt.

2 good-sized whole boneless, skinless chicken thighs, cubed

1 onion, chopped

1 garlic clove, minced

2 carrots, sliced

2 ribs celery, chopped

2 medium potatoes, peeled or not, cubed

1 tsp. mixed dried herbs

⅓ cup tomato sauce

12-oz. can cream-style corn

14-oz. can whole kernel corn

3 cups chicken stock

¼ cup chopped Italian parsley

1 tsp. salt

¼ tsp. pepper

Why I like this recipe—
Another strong partnership between chicken and corn, this time with a tomatoey, pink broth.

1. Grease interior of slow-cooker crock.

2. Combine all ingredients except parsley, salt, and pepper in slow cooker.

3. Cover. Cook on Low 3–4 hours, or until chicken and onions are tender.

4. Add parsley and seasonings 30 minutes before serving.

Soups, Stews & Chilis

Chicken Corn Chowder

Janie Steele
Moore, OK

Makes 6–8 servings
Prep. Time: 10–15 minutes
(with precooked chicken)
Cooking Time: 3–4 hours
Ideal slow-cooker size: 3- or 4-qt.

2 8-oz. pkgs. cream cheese, room-temperature and cubed

2 cups evaporated milk

14½-oz. can tomatoes with green chilies

1 lb. frozen corn

4 good-sized boneless, skinless chicken thighs, cubed

12 oz. cheddar cheese, shredded, *divided*

salt to taste

pepper to taste

hot sauce to taste, *optional*

1. Grease interior of slow-cooker crock.

2. Combine cream cheese, milk, tomatoes with chilies, corn, and cubed chicken in slow cooker.

3. Cover. Cook on Low 3–4 hours, or until chicken is just cooked.

4. Ten minutes before end of cooking time, stir in ⅔ of shredded cheese. Cover. Continue cooking until cheese is melted.

5. Add salt and pepper to taste and hot sauce to taste if you wish.

6. Garnish individual serving bowls with remaining shredded cheddar cheese.

Why I like this recipe—
Here we go again with chicken and corn, but set in a creamy, cheesy broth that really works.

Soups, Stews & Chilis

Smoked Salmon Corn Chowder

**Sandra Haverstraw
Hummelstown, PA**

Makes 8-10 servings
Prep. Time: 30 minutes
Cooking Time: 3-4 hours
Ideal slow-cooker size: 5- or 6-qt.

1 large onion, chopped

½ cup chopped celery

⅓ cup chopped red bell pepper

3 cups cubed potatoes, peeled or not

2 cups chicken broth

15-oz. can creamed corn

16-oz. bag frozen corn

½ tsp. salt, *optional*

½ tsp. ground black pepper

2 Tbsp. (¼ stick) butter

2 tsp. dried dill weed

2 oz. smoked salmon, chopped

1 cup whole milk

1 cup shredded cheddar cheese

½ tsp. hot pepper sauce, *optional*

1 cup sour cream, *optional*

1. Grease interior of slow-cooker crock.

2. Place onion, celery, bell pepper, potatoes, chicken broth, creamed and frozen corn, salt if you wish, pepper, and butter in slow cooker.

3. Cover. Cook on Low 3–4 hours, or until vegetables are as soft as you like them.

4. One-half hour before serving, add dill, smoked salmon, milk, cheese, and hot pepper sauce and sour cream if you wish, to chowder in slow cooker.

5. Cover. Continue cooking 25–30 minutes, or until cheese has melted and chowder is fully heated.

Why I like this recipe—

Our family always goes to Christmas Eve Services, and we enjoy corn chowder on our return home. During a trip to Alaska, I was served a delicious corn chowder with smoked salmon. Now I've added that to our favorite recipe. The rest of the menu for our Christmas Eve Buffet: cold steamed shrimp with cocktail sauce, cocktail meatballs in a small slow cooker, fresh vegetables with ranch dip, assorted cheeses and crackers. Plus hot mulled cider or wine in a large slow cooker. And, of course, coconut cake, fruit, and cookies.

Sweet Potato Chowder

Carol Eberly
Harrisonburg, VA

Makes 12 servings
Prep. Time: 20–25 minutes
Cooking Time: 3–4 hours
Ideal slow-cooker size: 4- or 5-qt.

1 celery rib, chopped

2 Tbsp. (¼ stick) butter, melted

2 14½-oz. cans chicken broth

2 cups water

2 tsp. chicken bouillon granules

4 medium red potatoes, peeled, if you wish, and cubed

1 large sweet potato, peeled, if you wish, and cubed

2 cups ham, fully cooked and cubed

¼ cup chopped onion

½ tsp. garlic powder, *or* 1 clove garlic, minced

½ tsp. seasoning salt

½ tsp. dried oregano

½ tsp. parsley flakes

¼ tsp. pepper

¼ tsp. crushed red pepper flakes

¼ cup flour

2 cups milk

1. Grease interior of slow-cooker crock.

2. Mix all ingredients except flour and milk in slow cooker.

3. Cover. Cook 3–4 hours on Low.

4. One hour before end of cooking time, combine milk and flour in a small bowl, or place in covered jar and shake, until smooth. Stir into hot soup until smooth and thickened.

Why I like this recipe—

Don't mess with the sweet potato! Sure, you could go with all little red guys, but you'd miss that extra touch of sweet creaminess that the sweet potato brings. I'm a no-peeler, by the way. Saves time and nutrients not to do it.

Good Old Potato Soup

Jeanne Hertzog
Bethlehem, PA

Rhonda Lee Schmidt
Scranton, PA

Vera Schmucker
Goshen, IN

Elizabeth Yoder
Millersburg, OH

Marcia S. Myer
Manheim, PA

Mitzi McGlynchey
Downingtown, PA

Kaye Schnell
Falmouth, MA

Makes 8–10 servings
Prep. Time: 15 minutes
Cooking Time: 3–6 hours
Ideal slow-cooker size: 6-qt.

6 potatoes, peeled or not, and cubed
2 leeks, chopped
2 onions, chopped
1 rib celery, sliced
4 chicken bouillon cubes
1 Tbsp. dried parsley flakes
5 cups water
1 Tbsp. salt
pepper to taste
5 ⅔ Tbsp. (⅓ cup) butter
13-oz. can evaporated milk

TIP

Garnish with chopped chives.

Variations:
1. Add one carrot, sliced, to vegetables in Step 2.
2. Instead of water and bouillon cubes, use 4–5 cups chicken stock.

1. Grease interior of slow-cooker crock.

2. Combine all ingredients except milk in slow cooker.

3. Cover. Cook on Low 4–6 hours, or on High 3–4 hours.

4. Stir in milk during last hour.

5. If you wish, mash potatoes with a handheld masher to the degree you want, before serving.

Creamy Potato Soup

Janeen Troyer
Fairview, MI

Makes 6–8 servings
Prep. Time: 30 minutes
Cooking Time: 2¼–3½ hours
Ideal slow-cooker size: 4-qt.

3 cups chopped potatoes, peeled or unpeeled

1 cup water

½ cup chopped celery

½ cup chopped carrots

¼ cup chopped onions

2 cubes chicken, or vegetable, bouillon

1 tsp. parsley

½ tsp. salt

¼ tsp. pepper

1½ cups milk

2 Tbsp. flour

½ lb. cheese, your choice, shredded

1. Grease interior of slow-cooker crock.

2. Combine potatoes, water, celery, carrots, onions, bouillon, parsley, salt, and pepper in slow cooker.

3. Cover. Cook on High 2–3 hours, or until vegetables are tender.

4. In a jar with a tight-fitting lid, add milk to flour. Cover tightly and shake until flour dissolves in milk. When smooth, add mixture to vegetables in cooker. Stir until blended in.

5. Cover. Cook on High another 15–30 minutes, or until soup is thickened and smooth. Stir occasionally to prevent lumps from forming.

6. Add cheese. Stir until melted.

Why I like this recipe—
For the Christmas holidays, I garnish individual soup bowls with fresh parsley and chopped red bell peppers to add a festive touch.

Creamy Tomato Soup

Susie Shenk Wenger
Lancaster, PA

Makes 4 servings
Prep. Time: 10–15 minutes
Cooking Time: 3–4 hours
Ideal slow-cooker size: 3-qt.

28-oz. can tomato sauce, *or* crushed tomatoes,
   or 1 qt. home-canned tomatoes, chopped

1 small onion, chopped

1–2 carrots, sliced thin

2 tsp. brown sugar

1 tsp. Italian seasoning

¼ tsp. salt

¼ tsp. pepper

½ tsp. Worcestershire sauce

1 tsp. freshly chopped parsley

1 cup heavy whipping cream

croutons, preferably homemade

freshly grated Parmesan cheese

TIP

This recipe can easily be doubled.

Why I like this recipe—
Yes, that's heavy whipping cream—and you'll think that what it does to the soup is ethereal. If you prefer a lower-cal version, you can use whole milk, even 2%, but the soup will be less velvety.

1. Grease interior of slow-cooker crock.

2. Combine tomatoes, onion, carrots, brown sugar, Italian seasoning, salt, pepper, and Worcestershire sauce in slow cooker.

3. Cover. Cook on Low 3–4 hours, or until vegetables are soft.

4. Allow soup to cool a bit. Purée with immersion blender.

5. Add parsley and cream and blend lightly again.

6. Serve hot with croutons and Parmesan as garnish.

Tomato Basil Soup

Janet Melvin
Cincinnati, OH

Makes 8–9 servings
Prep. Time: 15 minutes
Cooking Time: 2½–3½ hours
Ideal slow-cooker size: 4-qt.

½ cup very finely diced onion

2 garlic cloves, minced

2 cups vegetable stock

2 28-oz. cans crushed tomatoes

¼ cup chopped fresh basil, plus more for garnish

1 Tbsp. salt

½ tsp. pepper

1 cup heavy cream, room temperature

TIP

Top with croutons or serve with bread.

1. Grease interior of slow-cooker crock.

2. Combine onion, garlic, stock, tomatoes, basil, salt, and pepper in slow cooker.

3. Cover and cook on High 2 or 3 hours. Purée soup at this point if you want a totally smooth soup. Otherwise, leave it chunky as is.

4. Stir in heavy cream and cook an additional 30 minutes on Low. You want to heat the soup through, but not have it boil.

5. Garnish each serving with a few ribbons of fresh basil.

Vegetable Soup

Jean Harris Robinson
Pemberton, NJ

Makes 8–10 servings
Prep. Time: 25 minutes
Cooking Time: 4–6 hours
Ideal slow-cooker size: 4- or 5-qt.

2 Tbsp. olive oil

1 large white onion, Vidalia preferred, diced

2 medium carrots, diced

2 cloves garlic, minced

20-oz. pkg. frozen cubed butternut squash
   or 4 cups chopped fresh

2 cups finely chopped cabbage

1 packed cup chopped kale

½ tsp. ground allspice

1 tsp. salt *or* to taste

14-oz. can diced tomatoes with juice

1 qt. no-salt vegetable broth

¼ tsp. ground ginger *or* 1 Tbsp. finely grated
   fresh ginger

4 sprigs fresh thyme *or* 1 tsp. dried thyme

1. Grease interior of slow-cooker crock.

2. Combine all ingredients in cooker except
ginger and thyme.

3. Cook on Low 4–6 hours or until veggies
are as soft as you like them.

4. Ten minutes before end of cooking time,
stir in ginger and thyme.

Good go-alongs with this recipe:
Add a dollop of Greek yogurt to the top of
each bowl. Place some hot cooked grains,

TIPS

1. Refrigerate for several days or freeze for
later. It is a family pleaser.
2. I like to prep the vegetables the night
before cooking the soup. I often use frozen
vegetables and sometimes add leftover
green beans or broccoli at the last minute
before serving.

such as brown rice or quinoa, in soup bowls
before ladling in soup.

Norma's Vegetarian Chili

Kathy Hertzler
Lancaster, PA

Makes 8–10 servings
Prep. Time: 20 minutes
Cooking Time: 4½ hours
Ideal slow-cooker size: 5-qt.

2 Tbsp. oil

2 cups minced celery

1½ cups chopped green bell pepper

1 cup minced onions

4 garlic cloves, minced

5½ cups stewed tomatoes

2 1-lb. cans kidney beans, undrained

1½–2 cups raisins

¼ cup wine vinegar

1 Tbsp. chopped dried parsley

2 tsp. salt

1½ tsp. dried oregano

1½ tsp. cumin

¼ tsp. pepper

¼ tsp. Tabasco sauce

1 bay leaf

¾ cup broken cashews

1 cup grated cheese, *optional*

Why I like this recipe—

After this chili has cooked for 4 hours, the plumped raisins add a subtle sweetness that sets this soup apart. And as a nut freak, I think the cashews put this chili into a superior place.

1. Grease interior of slow-cooker crock.

2. Combine all ingredients except cashews and cheese in slow cooker.

3. Cover. Simmer on Low 4 hours, or until veggies are as tender as you like them. Add cashews and simmer 30 minutes more.

4. Garnish individual servings with grated cheese.

Black Bean and Butternut Chili

Colleen Heatwole
Burton, MI

Makes 10 servings
Prep. Time: 20 minutes
Cooking Time: 4–5 hours
Ideal slow-cooker size: 5-qt.

1 medium onion, chopped

1 medium red bell pepper, chopped

3 cloves garlic, minced

3 cups vegetable broth

2 15-oz. can black beans, rinsed and drained

5 cups butternut squash, peeled and cubed

14½-oz. can crushed tomatoes

2 tsp. dried parsley flakes

1½ tsp. dried oregano

1½ tsp. cumin

1 tsp. chili powder

½ tsp. salt

1. Grease interior of slow-cooker crock.

2. Combine all ingredients in slow cooker.

3. Cover. Cook on Low 4–5 hours, or until vegetables are done to your liking.

Why I like this recipe—
I'm always struck by how smooth a player butternut squash is in this spicy, beany chili.

Broccoli Cauliflower Soup

Wafi Brandt
Manheim, PA

Makes 4–6 servings
Prep. Time: 15 minutes
Cooking Time: 3¼–4¼ hours
Ideal slow-cooker size: 3- or 4-qt.

16-oz. bag frozen broccoli and cauliflower

2 Tbsp. (¼ stick) butter

½ Tbsp. dried onion

2 cups water

2 chicken bouillon cubes

4 Tbsp. flour

2 cups milk, *divided*

½ tsp. Worcestershire sauce

½ tsp. salt

1 cup grated cheddar cheese

chopped chives

parsley

1. Grease interior of slow-cooker crock.

2. Put broccoli and cauliflower, butter, onion, water, and bouillon cubes in slow cooker.

3. Cover. Cook on Low 3–4 hours.

4. When broccoli and cauliflower are as soft as you want, mix flour and 1 cup milk together in a jar with a tight-fitting lid. Cover jar and shake vigorously until flour dissolves and mixture is smooth.

5. Pour milk mixture into vegetables and stir well. The soup will soon thicken.

6. Then stir in Worcestershire sauce, salt, and cheese.

7. When cheese is melted, stir in last cup of milk. Allow to heat through before serving.

8. Sprinkle chives and parsley over top of each individual serving bowl.

Why I like this recipe—
Creamy, cheesy, comforting. Don't skip the Worcestershire sauce; I usually bump it up to 1 tsp.

Carrot Ginger Soup

Jean Harris Robinson
Pemberton, NJ

Makes 8-10 servings
Prep. Time: 30 minutes
Cooking Time: 3¼–4¼ hours
Ideal slow-cooker size: 5-qt.

2 Tbsp. olive oil

3 lbs. carrots, peeled and thinly sliced (a
   mandoline is great for this)

2 Tbsp. chopped gingerroot

2 Tbsp. minced green onion

3 ribs celery, chopped

49½-oz. can chicken broth

1-3 tsp. kosher salt

1 tsp. ground pepper

2 Tbsp. honey

2 Tbsp. (¼ stick) butter

1 cup heavy cream

1. Grease interior of slow-cooker crock.

2. Pour olive oil into slow cooker. Swirl to cover bottom of cooker.

3. Add carrots, ginger, onion, and celery.

4. Pour in broth. Add salt, pepper, honey, and butter. Stir to mix all ingredients well.

5. Cover. Cook on Low 3–4 hours, or until carrots are soft.

6. Pulse with an immersion blender to purée.

7. Stir in one cup heavy cream. Heat soup 15–20 minutes until heated through, but don't let it boil. Serve immediately.

Why I like this recipe—
I was first introduced to this soup at one of my quilt guild's regular meetings. Even the professed carrot-haters loved it.

Curried Carrot Soup

Ann Bender
Ft. Defiance, VA

Makes 6–8 servings
Prep. Time: 20 minutes
Cooking Time: 3¼–4¼ hours
Ideal slow-cooker size: 4-qt.

2 Tbsp. oil
1 Tbsp. butter
1 garlic clove, minced
1 large onion, chopped
1 tsp. curry powder
1 Tbsp. flour
4 cups chicken *or* vegetable broth
6 large carrots, sliced
¼ tsp. salt
¼ tsp. ground red pepper, *optional*
1½ cups plain yogurt *or* light sour cream

1. Grease interior of slow-cooker crock.

2. Swirl oil and butter into bottom of crock. Turn to High so butter melts.

3. Stir in minced garlic and onion. Allow to cook until vegetables are limp but not brown.

4. Stir in curry powder and flour. Cook 3 minutes, stirring continually.

5. Whisk in chicken broth. When well blended, stir in carrots.

6. Cover. Cook on Low 3–4 hours, or until carrots are soft.

7. Purée mixture with immersion blender.

8. Add seasonings.

9. Add a dollop of yogurt or sour cream to each serving.

Why I like this recipe—

The curry, red pepper, and yogurt (or sour cream) bring out a different character in carrots. The carroty flavor becomes a little subtler than when they're on their own as straight-up vegetables.

Peanut Butter Pumpkin Soup

Carol L. Miller
Lockport, NY

Makes 8–10 servings
Prep. Time: 15 minutes
Cooking Time: 3–4 hours
Ideal slow-cooker size: 4-qt.

2 Tbsp. (¼ stick) butter
4 cups canned pumpkin
2 cups cooked puréed sweet potatoes *or*
   butternut squash
1 cup smooth peanut butter
6 cups chicken broth
1 tsp. black pepper
¼ tsp. salt
croutons for garnish, *optional*
crumbled cooked bacon for garnish, *optional*

1. Grease interior of slow-cooker crock.

2. Place butter, pumpkin, sweet potatoes or squash, peanut butter, broth, pepper, and salt in slow cooker.

3. Cover. Cook on Low 3–4 hours, stirring well after first 2 hours.

4. Serve with croutons or crumbled bacon as garnishes if you wish.

Why I like this recipe—
Pumpkin and butternut squash have pretty quiet flavors. In fact, they can get lost, depending what they're mixed with. Or they can stand up and sing, if they've been blended with peanut butter! The bacon garnish doesn't hurt, either!

TIPS

If you make your own puréed sweet potatoes or squash, add another hour to the Prep Time. Use 2 large sweet potatoes, or a medium-sized butternut squash, in order to get the 2 cups mashed.

Pumpkin Black-Bean Turkey Chili

Rhoda Atzeff
Harrisburg, PA

Makes 8–10 servings
Prep. Time: 20 minutes
Cooking Time: 3–4 hours
Ideal slow-cooker size: 5-qt.

1 cup chopped onions

1 cup chopped yellow bell pepper

3 garlic cloves, minced

2 Tbsp. oil

1½ tsp. dried oregano

1½–2 tsp. ground cumin

2 tsp. chili powder

2 15-oz. cans black beans, rinsed and drained

16-oz. can pumpkin

14½-oz. can diced tomatoes

3 cups chicken broth

2½ cups chopped cooked turkey

1. Grease interior of slow-cooker crock.

2. Place all ingredients, except cooked turkey, into slow cooker. Stir together well.

3. Cover. Cook on Low 3–4 hours, or until veggies are as tender as you like them.

4. Ten minutes before serving, stir in cooked turkey.

Why I like this recipe—

You won't realize you're eating pumpkin. You'll just wonder what makes this more-ish chili so downright creamy.

French Onion Soup

Linda Kosa-Postl
Granite Falls, WA

Makes 6 servings
Prep. Time: 30 minutes
Cooking Time: 6½–6¾ hours
Ideal slow-cooker size: 4-qt.

3 Tbsp. butter
1 Tbsp. olive oil
6 cups thinly sliced onion
6 cups beef stock
1 cup red wine
1 bay leaf
1 tsp. salt
½ tsp. sugar
½ tsp. dried thyme
¼ tsp. fresh ground pepper
3 Tbsp. flour
1 cup water

TIPS

1. Serve with bread and cheese on the side.
2. Or place slices of bread under the broiler. When just turning toasty, place sliced cheese on bread. Broil. When browned and bubbly, cut into cubes and sprinkle on top of French Onion Soup in soup bowls.

1. Grease interior of slow-cooker crock.

2. Place butter, olive oil, and onion in slow cooker. Cover and cook on High 4 hours. Onions should be soft and turning brown at end of cooking time.

3. Add beef stock, wine, bay leaf, salt, sugar, thyme, and pepper.

4. Cover and cook on Low 2 hours.

5. Whisk flour and water together in a small bowl, or place ingredients in a jar with a tight-fitting lid and shake until smooth. Stir mixture into soup. Cook an additional 30–40 minutes on Low until thickened.

Soups, Stews & Chilis

Yummy Spinach

Jeanette Oberholtzer
Manheim, PA

Makes 8 servings
Prep. Time: 10 minutes
Cooking Time: 2½–3 hours
Standing Time: 15 minutes
Ideal slow-cooker size: 4-qt.

10-oz. boxes frozen spinach, thawed and
  squeezed dry

cups cottage cheese

1½ cups grated cheddar cheese

3 eggs

¼ cup flour

1 tsp. salt

¼ cup (½ stick) butter, melted

1. Grease interior of slow-cooker crock.

2. Mix together all ingredients in the slow
cooker.

3. Cover. Cook on Low 2½–3 hours, or
until the dish sets up and is no longer jiggly in
the center.

4. Let stand for 15 minutes so the cheeses
can firm before cutting and serving.

Why I like this recipe—

It's downright tasty, and a perfect dish for
anyone who's cautious about spinach. It's a
finger food. It works for any time of the day.

Barbecued Green Beans

Arlene Wengerd
Millersburg, OH

Makes 4–6 servings
Prep. Time: 20 minutes
Cooking Time: 3–8 hours
Ideal slow-cooker size: 4-qt.

1 lb. bacon

¼ cup chopped onions

¾ cup ketchup

½ cup brown sugar

3 tsp. Worcestershire sauce

¾ tsp. salt

4 cups fresh *or* frozen green beans

1. Grease interior of slow-cooker crock.

2. Brown bacon in skillet until crisp and then break into pieces. Or buy already cooked and crumbled bacon. Set aside.

3. If you've cooked the bacon, reserve 2 Tbsp. bacon drippings. Sauté onions in bacon drippings. Or place raw onions into slow-cooker crock.

4. Combine ketchup, brown sugar, Worcestershire sauce, and salt with onions.

5. Stir green beans into barbecue sauce and mix lightly.

6. Cover. Cook on High 3–4 hours, or on Low 6–8 hours, or until the beans are as tender as you like them.

7. Stir in bacon pieces just before serving.

Why I like this recipe—
Do you see the bacon-green bean ratio here?! How could this not be good? Confession: When we're eating this during ordinary time, I cut back the bacon to a near-garnish amount. But for parties and potlucks, I put in the full amount. Both are yum.

Green Beans Get-Together

Edwina Stoltzfus
Narvon, PA

Makes 4–6 servings
Prep. Time: 20 minutes
Cooking Time: 3–8 hours
Ideal slow-cooker size: 4- or 5-qt.

½ lb. bacon, *or* ham chunks

4 medium onions, sliced

2 quarts fresh, frozen, *or* canned and drained
green beans

4 cups canned stewed tomatoes *or* diced fresh
tomatoes

½–¾ tsp. salt

¼ tsp. pepper

1. Grease interior of slow-cooker crock.

2. Brown bacon until crisp in skillet, or buy already cooked and crumbled bacon. Set bacon or ham chunks aside.

3. If you've cooked the bacon, reserve 2 Tbsp. bacon drippings. Sauté onions in bacon drippings. Or place raw onions into slow-cooker crock.

4. Combine all ingredients except bacon or ham pieces in slow cooker.

5. Cover. If you're using canned green beans, cook on Low 3 hours. If you're using fresh or frozen beans, cook on Low 6–8 hours, or until the beans are as tender as you like them.

6. Stir in bacon or ham pieces just before serving.

Why I like this recipe—
I grew up eating green beans, potatoes, and ham as a seasonal dish from our garden. This recipe introduced me to the addition of tomatoes, and now I often serve the Get-Together on top of steamed or baked potatoes.

Green Beans Caesar

Carol Shirk
Leola, PA

Makes 6–8 servings
Prep. Time: 15 minutes
Cooking Time: 3½– 8½ hours
Ideal slow-cooker size: 4-qt.

1½ lbs. fresh green beans, ends trimmed

2 Tbsp. olive oil

1 Tbsp. red wine vinegar

1 Tbsp. minced garlic

salt and pepper to taste

½ tsp. dried basil

½ tsp. dried oregano

¼ cup plain bread crumbs

¼ cup grated Parmesan cheese

1 Tbsp. butter, melted

Why I like this recipe—
In case you thought green beans were ho-hum, this dressing and topping will change your mind. This is guest-worthy eating.

1. Grease interior of slow-cooker crock.

2. In slow cooker, combine green beans, olive oil, vinegar, garlic, salt and pepper, basil, and oregano.

3. Cover. Cook on High 3–4 hours or on Low 6–8 hours, or until green beans are as soft as you like them. Stir.

4. Combine bread crumbs, Parmesan, and butter in a bowl. Sprinkle over green beans and cook an additional 30 minutes on High with lid off.

Orange-Glazed Carrots

Cyndie Marrara
Port Matilda, PA

Makes 6 servings
Prep. Time: 5–10 minutes
Cooking Time: 3¼–4¼ hours
Ideal slow-cooker size: 3-qt.

32-oz. (2 lbs.) pkg. baby carrots

½ cup packed brown sugar

½ cup orange juice

3 Tbsp. butter, melted

¾ tsp. cinnamon

¼ tsp. nutmeg

2 Tbsp. cornstarch

¼ cup water

1. Grease interior of slow-cooker crock.

2. Combine all ingredients except cornstarch and water in slow cooker.

3. Cover. Cook on Low 3–4 hours, until carrots are tender-crisp.

4. Put carrots in serving dish and keep warm, reserving cooking juices in crock.

5. Turn cooker to High. Cover.

6. Mix cornstarch and water in small bowl until blended. When juices are boiling or nearly so, stir in cornstarch/water mixture. Boil one minute or until thickened, stirring constantly.

7. Pour over carrots and serve.

Why I like this recipe—
If your carrots need a little excitement, this recipe delivers. And you haven't broken a sweat.

Special Times Carrots

Lindsey Spencer
Marrow, OH

Makes 8 servings
Prep. Time: 10–15 minutes
Cooking Time: 3 hours
Ideal slow-cooker size: 3-qt.

2 lbs. carrots
4 Tbsp. (half a stick) butter, melted
½ cup brown sugar
8-oz. can crushed pineapple, undrained
½ cup shredded coconut

1. Grease interior of slow-cooker crock.

2. Peel carrots. Cut into strips ½-inch wide and 2-inch long.

3. For extra flavor, brown carrots in skillet in butter before placing in slow cooker. Or skip doing that and place carrots and butter straight into slow cooker.

4. Add all other ingredients except coconut to slow cooker. Mix together gently but well.

5. Cover. Cook on Low 3 hours, or until carrots are as tender as you like them.

6. Add coconut as garnish to carrots when serving.

Why I like this recipe—

This recipe borders on carrots-as-dessert, but it is irresistible. I've made these without the brown sugar and only half the butter called for, and the natural sugar in the pineapples makes the carrots sing.

Horseradish Carrot Coins

Janet Batdorf
Harrisburg, PA

Makes 4 servings
Prep. Time: 15 minutes
Cooking Time: 3–4 hours
Ideal slow-cooker size: 3- or 4-qt.

12 carrots, cut in coins

¼ cup (½ stick) butter, cubed

⅓ cup honey

2 Tbsp. grated horseradish

1 tsp. vinegar

1 tsp. salt

1. Grease interior of slow-cooker crock.

2. Combine all ingredients in slow cooker. Mix well.

3. Cover and cook on Low 3–4 hours, or until carrots are done to your liking. Stir again before serving.

Why I like this recipe—
I love the balance of flavors here. Horseradish and honey are great partners.

Acorn Squash Straight-Up

Valerie Hertzler
Weyers Cave, VA

Makes 2 servings
Prep. Time: 5 minutes
Cooking Time: 8–10 hours
Ideal slow-cooker size: 4- or 5-qt.

1 acorn squash

salt

cinnamon

butter

Why I like this recipe—
Lots of opportunity for individual seasoning here. It's a great recipe for introducing squash as a vegetable.

1. Grease interior of slow-cooker crock.

2. Place whole, rinsed squash in slow cooker.

3. Cover. Cook on Low 8–10 hours, or until it jags tender when you poke it with a sharp fork.

4. Split and remove seeds. Sprinkle each half with salt and cinnamon, dot with butter, and serve.

Dressed-Up Acorn Squash

Dale Peterson
Rapid City, SD

Makes 4 servings
Prep. Time: 15 minutes
Cooking Time: 6–8 hours
Ideal slow-cooker size: 5- or 6-qt., or 2 4- or
   6-qt., depending on size of squash

2 acorn squash

⅔ cup cracker crumbs

½ cup coarsely chopped pecans

5⅓ Tbsp. (⅓ cup) butter, melted

4 Tbsp. brown sugar

½ tsp. salt

¼ tsp. ground nutmeg

2 Tbsp. orange juice

1. Grease interior of slow-cooker crock.

2. Cut squash in half through the middle. Remove seeds.

3. Combine remaining ingredients in a bowl. Spoon into squash halves.

4. Place squash halves in slow cooker side by side.

5. Cover. Cook on Low 6–8 hours, or until squash is tender.

Why I like this recipe—

Because squash is so mildly flavored, it accepts the citrus/butter/nutty additions well. Again, adapt this recipe to fit the taste preferences of the people around your table. Just follow Steps 1, 2, 4, and 5, and you'll have perfectly cooked squash. Do what you want with Step 3.

Fix-It and Forget-It Slow Cooker Champion Recipes   **351**

Summer Squash Delish

Sharon Anders
Alburtis, PA

Makes 4-6 servings
Prep. Time: 15 minutes
Cooking Time: 3-4 hours
Ideal slow-cooker size: 4-qt.

2 lbs. yellow summer squash *or* zucchini, thinly sliced (about 6 cups)

half a medium onion, chopped

1 cup peeled, shredded carrot

10¾-oz. can condensed cream of chicken soup*

1 cup sour cream

¼ cup flour

8-oz. pkg. seasoned stuffing crumbs, *divided*

½ cup (1 stick) butter, melted

1. Grease interior of slow-cooker crock.

2. Combine squash, onion, carrots, and soup in large bowl.

3. Mix together sour cream and flour. Stir into vegetables.

4. Toss stuffing mix with butter. Spread half in bottom of slow cooker.

5. Top with vegetable mixture.

6. Spread remaining crumbs over top.

7. Cover. Cook on Low 3-4 hours.

*To make your own Cream Soup, see recipes on pages 561–564.

Why I like this recipe—

Zucchini has been the butt of too many jokes. Serve this, and you'll put the scorn to rest, promise!

Zucchini Special

Louise Stackhouse
Benten, PA

Makes 4 servings
Prep. Time: 10 minutes
Cooking Time: 3–4 hours
Ideal slow-cooker size: 4-qt.

1 medium to large zucchini, peeled (or not) and sliced

1 medium onion, sliced

1 quart stewed tomatoes with juice, *or* 2 14½-oz. cans stewed tomatoes with juice

¼ tsp. salt

1 tsp. dried basil

8 oz. mozzarella cheese, shredded

1. Grease interior of slow-cooker crock.

2. Layer zucchini, onion, and tomatoes in slow cooker.

3. Sprinkle with salt, basil, and cheese.

4. Cover. Cook on Low 3–4 hours.

Why I like this recipe—

If you've got more than one zucchini on your hands, put in two or three (sliced, of course) and up the seasoning proportionately—it's that flexible a recipe. I like to serve this over pasta, and pass grated Parm for topping.

Scalloped Cabbage

Edwina Stoltzfus
Lebanon, PA

Makes 6–8 servings
Prep. Time: 25 minutes
Cooking Time: 3–5 hours
Ideal slow-cooker size: 5-qt.

1 Tbsp. butter

12 cups chopped cabbage

¼ cup chopped onion

1 cup grated sharp cheese

¼ cup flour

12-oz. can evaporated milk

¼ cup chopped fresh parsley

½ cup diced, cooked bacon, *optional*

1. Grease interior of slow-cooker crock with 1 Tbsp. butter.

2. Combine cabbage, onion, and cheese in slow cooker.

3. In a mixing bowl, whisk together flour and milk until lump-free.

4. Pour milk mixture over cabbage mixture.

5. Cover and cook on Low 3–5 hours, or until cabbage is soft and sauce is thick.

6. Sprinkle with parsley, and bacon if you wish, before serving.

Why I like this recipe—
If you like a crunchy, even raw, flavor and bite to your cabbage, plan to eat this after three hours of cooking. If you're after a softer, creamier dish, go the whole way to five hours. This sauce brings some well-deserved respect to cabbage.

Sweet and Tangy Cabbage

Irma H. Schoen
Windsor, CT

Makes 6 servings
Prep. Time: 20 minutes
Cooking Time: 3–5 hours
Ideal slow-cooker size: 5- or 6-qt.

1 medium-sized head red *or* green cabbage, shredded

2 onions, chopped

4 tart apples, peeled and quartered

½ cup raisins

¼ cup lemon juice

¼ cup cider *or* apple juice

3 Tbsp. honey

1 Tbsp. caraway seeds

⅛ tsp. allspice

½ tsp. salt

1. Grease interior of slow-cooker crock.

2. Combine all ingredients in slow cooker.

3. Cook on Low 3–5 hours, depending upon how crunchy or soft you want the cabbage and onions.

Why I like this recipe—
This is kind of like cooked coleslaw. I like to pair it with beef or pork roasts or sandwiches.

Sweet and Sour Red Cabbage

Kaye Taylor
Florissant, MO

Makes 6–8 servings
Prep. Time: 30–45 minutes
Cooking Time: 3–5 hours
Ideal slow-cooker size: 5- or 6-qt.

4 slices bacon, diced

¼ cup brown sugar

2 Tbsp. flour

1 tsp. salt

⅛ tsp. pepper

½ cup water

¼ cup vinegar

1 medium head red cabbage, shredded (6–8 cups)

1 small onion, finely chopped

1. Grease interior of slow-cooker crock.

2. Sauté bacon in skillet until crisp. Or buy already cooked and crumbled bacon. Set bacon aside.

3. If you've cooked your own bacon, reserve 1 Tbsp. drippings. Combine 1 Tbsp. bacon drippings in slow cooker with brown sugar, flour, salt, and pepper. Stir in water and vinegar. If you don't have bacon drippings, mix brown sugar, flour, salt, and pepper together in a bowl. Then stir in water and vinegar.

4. Add cabbage and onion to slow cooker and stir.

5. Cover. Cook on Low 3–5 hours, or until cabbage and onion are as tender as you like them.

6. Sprinkle cooked bacon on top just before serving.

Why I like this recipe—
For my taste, this balances sweet and sour perfectly. I often serve it instead of a salad.

Vegetable Party

Janie Steele
Moore, OK

Makes 6–8 servings
Prep. Time: 25–30 minutes
Cooking Time: 1½–2 hours
Ideal slow-cooker size: 5-qt.

arge raw potato, peeled and cut into small cubes

2 onions, chopped

2 carrots, sliced thin

¼ cup uncooked long grain rice

2 Tbsp. lemon juice

⅓ cup, plus 2 Tbsp., olive oil

2 1-lb. cans diced tomatoes, *divided*

1 cup water, *divided*

arge green bell pepper, chopped

2 zucchini squash, chopped

1 Tbsp. salt

half a 1-lb. pkg. frozen green peas

1 cup cheese, grated

2 Tbsp. fresh parsley, chopped

hot sauce, *optional*

1. Grease interior of slow-cooker crock.

2. Combine potato, onions, carrots, rice, lemon juice, olive oil, 1 can of tomatoes, and ½ cup water in slow cooker.

3. Cover. Cook on High 1 hour.

4. Stir in chopped green pepper, chopped zucchini, salt, and remaining tomatoes. Add remaining water if you want a juicy outcome.

5. Cover. Cook on High 30–60 minutes, or until vegetables are somewhat tender but not mushy.

6. Ten minutes before end of cooking time, stir in peas and cheese.

7. Just before serving, stir in fresh parsley.

8. Pass hot sauce so individuals can add it to their servings if they wish.

Why I like this recipe—
You can include more delicate vegetables in your slow-cooking. Just add them later so they keep their character, crunch, and flavor. Like here.

Vegetable Curry

Sheryl Shenk
Harrisonburg, VA

Makes 8–10 servings
Prep. Time: 15 minutes
Cooking Time: 3–10 hours
Ideal slow-cooker size: 6- or 7-qt.

16-oz. pkg. baby carrots

3 medium potatoes, cubed

1 lb. fresh *or* frozen green beans, cut in
   2-inch pieces

1 green bell pepper, chopped

1 onion, chopped

1–2 cloves garlic, minced

15-oz. can garbanzo beans, drained

28-oz. can crushed tomatoes

3 Tbsp. minute tapioca

3 tsp. curry powder

2 tsp. salt

2 tsp. chicken bouillon granules, *or* 2 chicken
   bouillon cubes

1¾ cups boiling water

1. Grease interior of slow-cooker crock.

2. Combine carrots, potatoes, green beans,
chopped pepper, onion, garlic, garbanzo
beans, and crushed tomatoes in slow cooker.

3. Stir in tapioca, curry powder, and salt.

4. Dissolve bouillon in boiling water. Pour
over vegetables. Mix well.

5. Cover. Cook on Low 8–10 hours, or on
High 3–4 hours, or until vegetables are done
to your liking.

Serving suggestion:
Serve with cooked rice.

Variation:
Substitute canned green beans for fresh
beans, but add toward the end of the cooking
time.

Baked Stuffed Tomatoes

Leslie Scott
Troy, NY

Makes 6 servings
Prep. Time: 30 minutes
Cooking Time: 2–3 hours
Ideal slow-cooker size: 5-qt., *oval*

6 medium-sized tomatoes

3 Tbsp. butter, melted

2 tsp. chopped fresh basil

2 tsp. chopped fresh oregano

2 tsp. chopped fresh parsley

2 garlic cloves, minced

1 cup grated Parmesan cheese

¾ cup fine bread crumbs

salt and pepper to taste

1. Grease interior of slow-cooker crock.

2. Remove cores from tomatoes, and cut away an additional inch or so underneath the core to make a cavity in each tomato.

3. Mix together butter, herbs, garlic, Parmesan, bread crumbs, and salt and pepper.

4. Gently stuff each tomato with mixture.

5. Set tomatoes in lightly greased slow cooker.

6. Cover and cook on Low 2–3 hours, until tomatoes are soft and heated through.

Variation:
If you don't have fresh herbs, use ⅔ tsp. each of dried basil, oregano, and parsley instead.

Mushrooms Italian

Connie Johnson
Loudon, NH

Makes 4–5 servings
Prep. Time: 20 minutes
Cooking Time: 4–6 hours
Ideal slow-cooker size: 5-qt.

2 large onions, chopped

3 large red bell peppers, chopped

3 large green bell peppers, chopped

2–3 Tbsp. oil

12-oz. pkg. oyster mushrooms, cleaned and
    chopped

4 garlic cloves, minced

3 fresh bay leaves

10 fresh basil leaves, chopped

1 Tbsp. salt

1½ tsp. pepper

28-oz. can Italian plum tomatoes, crushed, *or*
    chopped

1. Grease interior of slow-cooker crock.

2. Place onions and peppers in cooker.
Cover. Cook on Low 2 hours, or until no
longer crisp.

3. Stir all remaining ingredients into
veggies.

4. Cover. Cook on Low 4–6 more hours, or
until quite soft.

5. Remove bay leaves before serving.

6. Serve as an appetizer with a spoon, or
spread on pita bread. For a main dish, serve
over rice or pasta.

Why I like this recipe—
Mushrooms make a great main dish in this
very vegetable-y combination.

Saucy Mushrooms

Donna Lantgen
Arvada, CO

Makes 4 servings
Prep. Time: 15 minutes
Cooking Time: 3¼–4¼ hours
Ideal slow-cooker size: 3- or 4-qt.

1 lb. small, whole, fresh mushrooms, cleaned

4 cloves garlic, minced

¼ cup chopped onion

1 Tbsp. olive oil

¾ cup red wine

½ tsp. salt

⅛ tsp. pepper

¼ tsp. dried thyme

¼ cup water

2 Tbsp. cornstarch

1. Grease interior of slow-cooker crock.

2. Combine mushrooms, garlic, onion, olive oil, red wine, salt, pepper, and thyme in slow cooker.

3. Cover. Cook on Low 3–4 hours, or until mushrooms are soft but still holding their shape.

4. In a small bowl, whisk together water and cornstarch. Turn cooker to High and stir in cornstarch mixture. Cook, stirring occasionally, until thickened, 10–15 minutes.

5. Serve as a sauce over pasta, or as a side dish with steak and baked potatoes.

Why I like this recipe—
No competition here from other strong flavors. The mushrooms step forward.

Wild Rice

Ruth S. Weaver
Reinholds, PA

Makes 4 servings
Prep. Time: 10 minutes
Cooking Time: 2½–3 hours
Ideal slow-cooker size: 3-qt.

1 cup wild rice *or* wild rice mixture, uncooked

½ cup sliced fresh mushrooms

½ cup diced onions

½ cup diced green *or* red peppers

1 Tbsp. oil

½ tsp. salt

¼ tsp. pepper

2½ cups chicken broth

1. Grease interior of slow-cooker crock.

2. Layer rice and vegetables in slow cooker. Pour oil, salt, and pepper over vegetables. Stir.

3. Heat chicken broth. Pour over ingredients in slow cooker.

4. Cover. Cook on High 2½–3 hours, or until rice is soft and liquid is absorbed.

Why I like this recipe—
The vegetable presence here adds subtle flavor and helps to keep the rice from getting dry.

Wild Rice Bake

Edith Romano
Westminster, MD

Makes 4 servings
Prep. Time: 30 minutes
Cooking Time: 2½–3 hours
Ideal slow-cooker size: 4-qt.

1½ cups uncooked long-grain rice

½ cup uncooked wild rice

1 envelope dry onion soup mix

4 cups water

¼ cup chopped green onions

8 oz. fresh *or* canned sliced mushrooms

¼ cup (½ stick) melted butter

1–3 Tbsp. cut-up fresh parsley

1. Grease interior of slow-cooker crock.

2. Combine all ingredients, except parsley, in crock.

3. Cover. Cook on High 2½-3 hours, or until rice is tender but not dry.

4. Ten minutes before end of cooking time, stir in parsley.

Why I like this recipe—
I've added this recipe to my keeper file. It's much tastier than plain rice but requires very little additional effort.

—Kelly Bailey

TIP

This is a good go-along with chicken.

Party Wild Rice

**Susan Kasting
Jenks, OK**

Makes 4 servings
Prep. Time: 10 minutes
Cooking Time: 2½–3 hours
Ideal slow-cooker size: 4-qt.

1½ cups wild rice, uncooked

3 cups chicken stock

3 Tbsp. orange zest

2 Tbsp. orange juice

½ cup raisins (I like golden raisins)

1½ tsp. curry powder

1 Tbsp. butter, softened

½ cup fresh parsley

½ cup chopped pecans

½ cup chopped green onion

1. Grease interior of slow-cooker crock.

2. Mix rice, chicken stock, orange zest, orange juice, raisins, curry powder, and butter in slow cooker.

3. Cover and cook on High 2½–3 hours, or until rice is tender and has absorbed most of the liquid, but is not dry.

4. Stir in parsley, pecans, and green onion just before serving.

Why I like this recipe—
I love how fruit brightens wild rice!

Fruity Wild Rice with Pecans

Dottie Schmidt
Kansas City, MO

Makes 4 servings
Prep. Time: 15 minutes
Cooking Time: 2–2½ hours
Ideal slow-cooker size: 4-qt.

½ cup chopped onions

2 Tbsp. (¼ stick) butter, cut in chunks

6-oz. pkg. long grain and wild rice, uncooked

seasoning packet from wild rice pkg.

1½ cups hot water

⅔ cup apple juice

1 large tart apple, chopped

¼ cup raisins

¼ cup coarsely chopped pecans

1. Grease interior of slow-cooker crock.

2. Combine all ingredients except pecans in slow cooker.

3. Cover. Cook on High 2–2½ hours, or until rice is fully cooked and tender.

4. Stir in pecans. Serve.

Why I like this recipe—

I make this during the week, all year long; it's so easy in a slow cooker. I used to think that a dish like this was just for special meals.

Risotto in the Crock

Carolyn Spohn
Shawnee, KS

Makes 4 servings
Prep. Time: 20 minutes
Cooking Time: 1½–2½ hours
Ideal slow-cooker size: 3- or 4-qt.

½ medium onion, chopped

1 Tbsp. olive oil

1 cup uncooked Arborio rice

2½ cups chicken *or* vegetable broth, *divided*

⅓ cup grated Parmesan cheese

½ tsp. salt, *optional*

¼ tsp. pepper, *optional*

1. Grease interior of slow-cooker crock.

2. Stir onion, olive oil, rice, and 2 cups broth into slow cooker.

3. Cover. Cook on High 1½–2½ hours, or until rice is just tender. Stir once or twice during cooking time.

TIP

This makes a good side dish to take the place of potatoes or regular rice.

4. When rice is cooked but still a bit firm, stir in grated cheese and enough broth to reach the consistency you want.

5. Taste before serving. Add salt and pepper as needed.

Peas and Rice

Cyndie Marrara
Port Matilda, PA

Makes 6 servings
Prep. Time: 10–15 minutes
Cooking Time: 2¼–3¼ hours
Ideal slow-cooker size: 4-qt.

1½ cups converted long-grain white rice, uncooked

¾ cup chopped onions

2 garlic cloves, minced

2 14½-oz. cans reduced-sodium chicken broth

⅓ cup water

¾ tsp. Italian seasoning

½ tsp. dried basil leaves

½ cup frozen baby peas, thawed

¼ cup grated Parmesan cheese

1. Grease interior of slow-cooker crock.

2. Combine rice, onions, garlic, broth, water, Italian seasoning, and basil in slow cooker.

3. Cover. Cook on Low 2–3 hours, or until rice is tender but not dry and liquid is absorbed.

4. Stir in peas. Cover. Cook 15 minutes.

5. Just before serving, stir in cheese.

Why I like this recipe—
Rice plays nice with so many other ingredients. The peas and Parm add so much flavor and color. Add them just a few minutes before serving.

Butter-Rubbed Baked Potatoes

Lucille Metzler
Wellsboro, PA

Glenda S. Weaver
Manheim, PA

Elizabeth Yutzy
Wauseon, OH

Mary Jane Musser
Manheim, PA

Esther Becker
Gordonville, PA

Makes 6 servings
Prep. Time: 5 minutes
Cooking Time: 3–10 hours
Ideal slow-cooker size: 5-qt.

6 uncooked medium baking potatoes
butter

1. Grease interior of slow-cooker crock.

2. Prick potatoes with fork. Rub each all over with butter. Place in slow cooker.

3. Cover. Cook on High 3–5 hours, or on Low 6–10 hours, or until all potatoes jag tender in the center when poked with a sharp-tined fork.

Why I like this recipe—

Because I can't imagine a simpler way to have cooked potatoes—for making potato salad or a grated potato-cheese bake—or to eat with dinner at the end of a day away.

Foil-Wrapped Baked Potatoes

Valerie Hertzler
Weyers Cave, VA

Carol Peachey
Lancaster, PA

Janet L. Roggie
Lowville, NY

Prep. Time: 5 minutes
Cooking Time: 3–10 hours
Ideal slow-cooker size: depends on how many potatoes you're doing

uncooked potatoes

1. Prick potatoes with fork and wrap in foil.

2. Cover. Do not add water.

3. Cook on High 3–5 hours, or on Low 6–10 hours.

Why I like this recipe—
Super and utterly convenient.

Cottage Potatoes

Margaret W. High
Lancaster, PA

Makes 6–8 servings
Prep. Time: 15 minutes
Cooking Time: 3 hours
Ideal slow-cooker size: 5-qt.

5–6 large cooked* potatoes, peeled or
    unpeeled, and diced

1 onion, diced

½ green bell pepper, diced, *optional*

2 cups diced bread, preferably dry and stale

2 cups diced sharp cheese

¾ tsp. salt

¼ tsp. pepper

1 tsp. dried rosemary

¼ cup (½ stick) butter, melted

1. In lightly greased slow cooker, combine all ingredients except melted butter. Stir gently.

2. Pour melted butter over all.

3. Cover and cook on High 2½ hours. Remove lid and cook uncovered an additional 30 minutes.

*See recipes for cooking potatoes in your slow cooker on pages 369 and 370.

Why I like this recipe—

We eat this as a vegetarian main dish with a green vegetable and cranberry applesauce on the side. It's also wonderful with baked ham.

TIP

I make extra baked potatoes at one meal in order to have enough for this dish later in the week.

Potatoes O'Brien

Rebecca Meyerkorth
Wamego, KS

Makes 6 servings
Prep. Time: 10 minutes
Cooking Time: 3–4 hours
Ideal slow-cooker size: 4-qt.

32-oz. pkg. shredded potatoes*
¼ cup chopped onions
¼ cup chopped green bell peppers
2 Tbsp. chopped pimento, *optional*
1 cup chopped ham, *optional*
¾ tsp. salt
¼ tsp. pepper
3 Tbsp. butter
3 Tbsp. flour
½ cup milk, *divided*
10¾-oz. can cream of mushroom soup**
1 cup shredded cheddar cheese, *divided*

1. Grease interior of slow-cooker crock.

2. Place potatoes, onions, and green peppers—and pimento and ham if you wish—in slow cooker. Sprinkle with salt and pepper.

3. Melt butter in saucepan. Stir in flour; then add half of milk. Stir rapidly to remove all lumps.

4. Stir in remaining milk. Stir in mushroom soup and ½ cup cheese. Pour over potatoes.

*To make your own shredded potatoes, see recipe on page 570.
**To make your own Cream Soup, see recipes on pages 561 and 562.

5. Cover. Cook on Low 3–4 hours, or until potatoes are hot in the center of the crock.

6. Sprinkle remaining cheese on top about ½ hour before serving.

Why I like this recipe—
I've taken this to potlucks and neighborhood gatherings and tailgatings and family holiday meals. And I'm always asked for the recipe, it's so downright good.

Creamy Scalloped Potatoes

Dede Peterson
Rapid City, SD

Makes 8–10 servings
Prep. Time: 15 minutes
Cooking Time: 6–7 hours
Ideal slow-cooker size: 6-qt.

5 lbs. uncooked red potatoes, peeled or unpeeled and sliced, *divided*

2 cups water

1 tsp. cream of tartar

¼ lb. bacon, cut in 1-inch squares, browned until crisp, and drained, *or* store-bought, *divided*

dash of salt

½ pt. whipping cream

1 pt. half-and-half

1. Grease interior of slow-cooker crock.

2. In large bowl, toss sliced potatoes in water and cream of tartar. Drain.

3. Layer half of potatoes and half of bacon in large slow cooker. Sprinkle each layer with salt.

3. Repeat layers using all remaining potatoes and bacon.

4. Mix whipping cream and half-and-half in bowl. Pour over potatoes.

5. Cover. Cook on Low 6–7 hours, or until potatoes jag tender when you poke those in the center of the crock.

Variations:

For added flavor, cut one large onion into thin rings. Sauté in bacon drippings; then layer onion along with potatoes and bacon into slow cooker. Sprinkle each layer of potatoes with salt and pepper. Continue with Step 4.

Mashed Potatoes

Alice Miller
Stuarts Draft, VA

Makes 4–5 servings
Prep. Time: 15 minutes
Cooking Time: 3–5 hours
Ideal slow-cooker size: 3- or 4-qt.

8 large potatoes, uncooked, peeled and cut into 1-inch chunks

water

¼ cup (half a stick) butter, softened

1½ cups milk, heated until skin forms on top, but not boiling

1 tsp. salt

1. Grease interior of slow-cooker crock.

2. Place potatoes in slow cooker; add water to cover.

3. Cover. Cook on High 3–5 hours, or until potatoes are very tender.

4. Lift potatoes out with a slotted spoon into a bowl. Beat with electric mixer on high speed, scraping down sides.

5. Cut butter in chunks. Add to potatoes.

6. Slowly add milk, being careful not to splash yourself with the hot milk. Add salt. Beat until creamy.

TIP

Put the potatoes in the slow cooker, and forget about them while you're occupied otherwise. Come back to the kitchen 3–5 hours later, and you've got soft potatoes, ready to mash!

Garlic Mashed Potatoes

Katrine Rose
Woodbridge, VA

Makes 6 servings
Prep. Time: 10 minutes
Cooking Time: 4–7 hours
Ideal slow-cooker size: 4-qt.

2 lbs. uncooked baking potatoes, unpeeled
   and cut into ½-inch cubes

¼ cup water

3 Tbsp. butter, sliced

1 tsp. salt

¼ tsp. garlic powder

¼ tsp. black pepper

1 cup milk

1. Grease interior of slow-cooker crock.

2. Combine all ingredients, except milk, in slow cooker. Toss to combine.

TIP

For added garlic flavor, mince 2 cloves garlic. Stir in with milk in Step 4.

3. Cover. Cook on Low 7 hours, or on High 4 hours.

4. Add milk to potatoes during last 30 minutes of cooking time.

5. Mash potatoes with potato masher or electric mixer until fairly smooth.

Make-Ahead Mixed Potatoes Florentine

Becky Frey
Lebanon, PA

Makes 8–10 servings
Prep. Time: 45–60 minutes
Cooking Time: 8–10 hours
Ideal slow-cooker size: 5- or 6-qt.

medium-sized white potatoes, uncooked
medium-sized sweet potatoes, uncooked
large onion, chopped
–2 cloves garlic, pressed
Tbsp. (¼ stick) butter
Tbsp. olive oil
oz. low-fat or nonfat cream cheese, at room temperature
½ cup nonfat sour cream
½ cup nonfat plain yogurt
tsp. salt or to taste
–1½ tsp. dill weed
¼ tsp. black pepper
0-oz. pkg. frozen, chopped spinach, thawed and squeezed dry

1. Grease interior of slow-cooker crock.

2. Peel and quarter both white and sweet potatoes. Place in slow cooker. Barely cover with water.

3. Cover. Cook on Low 6–8 hours, or until potatoes are falling-apart-tender.

4. Meanwhile, in a saucepan, sauté onion and garlic in butter and olive oil on low heat, until soft and golden. Or place in a microwave-safe bowl and cook for 2 minutes on High, or until tender.

5. In an electric mixer bowl, combine sautéed onion and garlic with cream cheese,

TIP

You can use 1 cup plain yogurt and omit the sour cream, or vice versa. The more yogurt, the greater the savory tang.

sour cream, yogurt, salt, dill weed, and pepper. Whip until well blended. Set aside.

6. Drain off some of the potato cooking water in the slow cooker. Reserve.

7. Mash potatoes in some of their cooking water until soft and creamy. Add more cooking water if you'd like them to be more creamy.

8. Stir onion-cheese mixture into mashed potatoes.

9. Fold spinach into potato mixture.

10. Turn into greased slow cooker. Cover. Cook 2 hours on Low, or until heated through. Serve!

11. Or, if you've made the recipe a day or so in advance of serving it, refrigerate it until the day you need it. Then heat potatoes in slow cooker, covered, for 3–4 hours on Low, or until hot in the middle.

Garlicky Potatoes

Donna Lantgen
Chadron, NE

Makes 4–5 servings
Prep. Time: 30 minutes
Cooking Time: 4½–6 hours
Ideal slow-cooker size: 3- or 4-qt.

6 uncooked potatoes, peeled and cubed

6 garlic cloves, minced

¼ cup diced onion, *or* one medium-sized onion, chopped

2 Tbsp. olive oil

1. Spray interior of slow cooker with nonstick cooking spray.

2. Combine all ingredients in slow cooker.

3. Cover and cook on Low 4½–6 hours, or until potatoes are tender but not mushy or dry.

Why I like this recipe—

Funny what some cloves of garlic can do to keep people coming back for more of this dish. We like to eat it with a touch of ketchup on top.

Creamy Red Potatoes

Kayla Snyder
North East, PA

Makes 8 servings
Prep. Time: 20–30 minutes
Cooking Time: 3½–5 hours
Ideal slow-cooker size: 4- or 5-qt.

3 Tbsp. butter

3 Tbsp. flour

1 cup milk

½ tsp. garlic powder

¾ tsp. salt

1 Tbsp. dried onion flakes

1 tsp. parsley flakes

2 3-oz. pkgs. cream cheese, at room temperature

2 lbs. uncooked red potatoes

TIPS

Mix up the sauce ahead of time and refrigerate it. Then when you're ready, cut up the potatoes, and put them and the sauce in your slow cooker.

1. Grease interior of slow-cooker crock.

2. Make a white sauce in a saucepan by melting butter, stirring in flour, and adding milk. Whisk to get rid of lumps, and stir until smooth and thickened.

3. Add seasonings. Beat in cream cheese until smooth.

4. Cut up unpeeled potatoes into 1–2-inch cubes.

5. Layer potatoes and sauce in slow cooker.

6. Cover. Cook on High 3½ hours, on Low 4–5 hours, or until potatoes are as soft as you like them.

Lemon Red Potatoes

Carol Leaman
Lancaster, PA

Makes 6 servings
Prep. Time: 15–20 minutes
Cooking Time: 2½–3½ hours
Ideal slow-cooker size: 3- or 4-qt.

10-12 small to medium-sized, uncooked red potatoes

¼ cup water

¼ cup (half a stick) butter, melted

1 Tbsp. lemon juice

3 Tbsp. fresh *or* dried parsley

salt and pepper to taste

1. Grease interior of slow-cooker crock.

2. Cut a strip of peel from around the middle of each potato, using a potato peeler.

3. Place potatoes and water in slow cooker.

4. Cover and cook on High 2½–3½ hours, or until tender. Do not overcook.

5. Drain off water.

6. Combine butter, lemon juice, and parsley in a small bowl. Mix well. Pour over potatoes and toss to coat.

7. Season with salt and pepper.

Why I like this recipe—
We love the zip of lemon juice on these potatoes. I make them often to go with Sunday dinner.

QUICK
and
EASY

Rosemary New Potatoes

Carol Shirk
Leola, PA

Makes 4–5 servings
Prep. Time: 15 minutes
Cooking Time: 2–5 hours
Ideal slow-cooker size: 3- or 4-qt.

1½ lbs. new red potatoes, uncooked and
  unpeeled

1 Tbsp. olive oil

1 Tbsp. fresh chopped rosemary *or* 1 tsp. dried
  rosemary

1 tsp. garlic and pepper seasoning, *or* 1 large
  clove garlic, minced, plus ½ tsp. salt and
  ¼ tsp. pepper

1. Grease interior of slow-cooker crock.

2. If potatoes are larger than golf balls, cut
them in half or in quarters.

3. Toss potatoes with olive oil in slow
cooker, coating well.

4. Add rosemary and garlic and pepper
seasoning (or the minced garlic, salt, and
pepper). Toss again until the potatoes are well
coated.

5. Cover. Cook on High 2–3 hours, or on
Low 4–5 hours, or until potatoes are tender
but not mushy or dry.

Why I like this recipe—
We always grow potatoes in our garden, and
this is the first recipe we use to make them
when they're ready.

Parmesan Potato Wedges

Carol and John Ambrose
McMinnville, OR

Makes 6 servings
Prep. Time: 15 minutes
Cooking Time: 3½–4 hours
Ideal slow-cooker size: 4-qt.

2 lbs. uncooked red potatoes, cut into ½-inch wedges *or* strips

¼ cup chopped onion

2 Tbsp. (¼ stick) butter, cut into pieces

1½ tsp. dried oregano

¼ cup grated Parmesan cheese

1. Grease interior of slow-cooker crock.

2. Layer potatoes, onion, butter, and oregano in slow cooker.

3. Cover and cook on High 3½–4 hours, or until potatoes are tender but not dry or mushy.

4. Spoon into serving dish and sprinkle with cheese.

Why I like this recipe—

It was my daughter's idea to add oregano to this recipe, and I love it. I have also used Italian herb seasoning, which is good, too.

Potatoes Perfect

Naomi Ressler
Harrisonburg, VA

Makes 4-6 servings
Prep. Time: 15 minutes
Cooking Time: 3-8 hours
Ideal slow-cooker size: 4- or 5-qt.

¼ lb. bacon, diced and browned in a skillet until crisp, or store-bought, *divided*

2 medium-sized onions, thinly sliced, *divided*

6-8 medium-sized uncooked potatoes, thinly sliced, *divided*

½ lb. cheddar cheese, thinly sliced, *divided*

salt to taste

pepper to taste

2-4 Tbsp. (¼-½ stick) butter

1. Grease interior of slow-cooker crock.

2. Layer half of bacon, onions, potatoes, and cheese in greased slow cooker. Season to taste.

3. Dot with butter. Repeat layers.

4. Cover. Cook on Low 6–8 hours or on High 3–4 hours, or until potatoes are soft.

Why I like this recipe—
Making these potatoes in the slow cooker blends the flavors so perfectly. I make most of my potato dishes in the slow cooker now.

Colcannon

Margaret W. High
Lancaster, PA

Makes 6–8 servings
Prep. Time: 20 minutes
Cooking Time: 4–6 hours
Ideal slow-cooker size: 6-qt.

6 cups chopped kale, ribs removed

6 cups chopped uncooked potatoes, peeled or not

2 leeks, chopped

1½ tsp. salt

¼ tsp. black pepper

1 cup chicken stock

3 Tbsp. butter

3 Tbsp. olive oil

TIP

Colcannon is an Irish version of mashed potatoes. It's often served on St. Patrick's Day, and some people use cabbage instead of kale and serve it with additional butter melted on top.

1. Grease interior of slow-cooker crock.

2. Combine kale, potatoes, leeks, salt, pepper, and chicken stock in slow cooker.

3. Cover. Cook on Low 4–6 hours, or until potatoes are tender.

4. Add butter and olive oil.

5. Mash well with potato masher.

Simply Sweet Potatoes

Leona Yoder
Hartville, OH

Makes 4 servings
Prep. Time: 5 minutes
Cooking Time: 2–4 hours
Ideal slow-cooker size: 3-qt.

3 large uncooked sweet potatoes

¼ cup water

1. Grease interior of slow-cooker crock.

2. Place unpeeled sweet potatoes into slow cooker.

3. Add ¼ cup water.

4. Cover. Cook on High 2 hours or on Low 3–4 hours, or until potatoes are tender in their centers.

Why I like this recipe—
I will never bake sweet potatoes in my oven again! This is such an easy method, and the sweet potatoes get perfectly moist and fudgy in texture. Perfect.

Fruity Sweet Potatoes

Jean Butzer
Batavia, NY

Evelyn Page
Lance Creek, WY

Makes 6 servings
Prep. Time: 15 minutes
Cooking Time: 4–6 hours
Ideal slow-cooker size: 4-qt.

2 lbs. (about 6 medium-sized) uncooked sweet potatoes *or* yams

1¼ cups applesauce

⅔ cup brown sugar

3 Tbsp. butter, melted

1 tsp. cinnamon

chopped nuts, *optional*

1. Grease interior of slow-cooker crock.

2. Peel sweet potatoes if you wish. Cut into cubes or slices. Place in slow cooker.

3. In a bowl, mix together applesauce, brown sugar, butter, and cinnamon. Spoon over potatoes.

4. Cover. Cook on Low 4–6 hours, or until potatoes are tender.

5. Mash potatoes and sauce together if you wish with a large spoon, or spoon cooked potatoes into serving dish and top with the sauce.

6. Sprinkle with nuts, if you want.

Variation:
Instead of raw sweet potatoes, substitute a 40-oz. can of cut-up sweet potatoes, drained. Then cook on Low for only 2–3 hours.
—Shelia Heil, Lancaster, PA

Autumn Sweet Potatoes

Melinda Wenger
Middleburg, PA

Makes 4 servings
Prep. Time: 20 minutes
Cooking Time: 2–3½ hours
Ideal slow-cooker size: 4-qt.

uncooked medium sweet potatoes, peeled and sliced thin

large Granny Smith apple, peeled and diced

½ cup raisins

est and juice of half an orange

Tbsp. maple syrup

oasted, chopped walnuts, for serving, *optional*

1. Grease interior of slow-cooker crock.

2. Place sweet potatoes in cooker.

3. Top with apple, raisins, and orange zest. Drizzle with maple syrup and orange juice.

4. Cover and cook on High 2–3 hours, on Low 3–3½ hours, or until sweet potatoes are tender.

5. Serve sprinkled with walnuts if you wish.

Why I like this recipe—
We really like the flavor of this dish. I love that it uses fresh ingredients that are easy to come by in autumn and winter.

Mom's New England Baked Beans

Debbie Zeida
Mashpee, MA

Makes 6–8 servings
Prep. Time: 20 minutes
Cooking Time for dried beans: 3–6 hours
Cooking Time for baked beans: 2–8 hours
Ideal slow-cooker size: 6-qt.

3 cups dried navy beans

9 cups water

1 medium onion, chopped

1 cup ketchup

1 cup brown sugar

1 cup water

2 tsp. dry mustard

2 Tbsp. dark molasses

1 Tbsp. salt

¼ lb. bacon, diced

1. Grease interior of slow-cooker crock.

2. Cover. Cook beans in water in slow cooker on Low for 3–6 hours, or until beans are as tender as you want.

3. Drain. Return cooked beans to slow cooker.

4. Stir in remaining ingredients. Mix well.

5. Cover. Cook on Low 4–8 hours, or on High 2–3 hours, stirring occasionally.

Variation:
Use 1 lb. dried great northern beans instead of 3 cups dried navy beans.
—Dorothy Miller, Gulfport, M

Barbecued Lima Beans

Hazel L. Propst
Oxford, PA

Makes 10 servings
Prep. Time: 1 hour
Soaking Time: 8 hours, or overnight
Cooking Time: 11–13 hours
Ideal slow-cooker size: 5-qt.

1½ lbs. dried lima beans
3½ cups water
2¼ cups chopped onions
1¼ cups brown sugar
1½ cups ketchup
13 drops Tabasco sauce
1 cup dark corn syrup
1 Tbsp. salt
½ lb. uncooked bacon, diced, *or* already
  cooked and crumbled bacon

1. Grease interior of slow-cooker crock.

2. Pour dried beans into slow cooker. Cover them with water that comes at least 2 inches above the beans. Cover cooker and soak beans for 8 hours, or overnight.

3. Pour off soaking water. Add 3½ cups fresh water.

4. Stir in all ingredients except bacon.

5. Cover. Cook on Low 11–13 hours, or until beans are tender. Stir occasionally.

6. If you have time, fry the bacon until crisp. Remove from drippings and place on a paper-towel-covered plate to drain. Break bacon into pieces.

7. Fifteen minutes before end of beans' cooking time, stir in either the bacon you fried, or the bacon you bought cooked and crumbled.

Why I like this recipe—
This is a favorite dish to take to potlucks year-round because people enjoy it a lot, and I always have the ingredients on hand.

Red Beans and Rice

Margaret A. Moffitt
Bartlett, TN

Makes 8–10 servings
Prep. Time: 5 minutes
Soaking Time: 8 hours
Cooking Time: 9–11 hours
Ideal slow-cooker size: 4- or 5-qt.

1-lb. pkg. dried red beans
2½ cups water
salt pork, *or* ham hocks, *or* sausage, cut into
    small chunks
2 tsp. salt
1 tsp. pepper
3–4 cups water
6-oz. can tomato paste
8-oz. can tomato sauce
4 garlic cloves, minced

TIPS

1. Serve over rice.
2. These beans freeze well.

1. Grease interior of slow-cooker crock.

2. Pour dried beans into slow cooker. Cover them with water that comes at least 2 inches above the beans. Cover cooker and soak beans for 8 hours, or overnight.

3. Pour off soaking water. Add 2½ cups fresh water.

4. Mix all remaining ingredients with beans and water in slow cooker.

5. Cover. Cook on Low 9–11 hours, or until beans are soft.

Variation:
Use canned red kidney beans instead of dried red beans. Cook 3 hours on Low, or until meat is fully cooked.

Homemade Refried Beans

Emily Fox
Bethel, PA

Makes 15 servings
Prep. Time: 15 minutes
Cooking Time: 4–8 hours
Ideal slow-cooker size: 6-qt.

1 onion, peeled and halved

3 cups dry pinto *or* black beans, rinsed

½ fresh *or* frozen jalepeño, chopped

2 cloves garlic

3–4 tsp. salt

1¾ tsp. black pepper

⅛ tsp. ground cumin

9 cups water

1. Grease interior of slow-cooker crock.

2. Place all ingredients in slow cooker and stir to combine.

3. Cook on Low 4–8 hours.

4. Drain off liquid, reserving it. Mash beans with potato masher, adding liquid as needed to reach the consistency you want.

Why I like this recipe—
These are much better than canned refried beans! Eat alone or with rice and tortillas, or use in other recipes.

Meatless Baked Beans

Jeannine Janzen
Elbing, KS

Makes 8–10 servings
Prep. Time: 10 minutes
Cooking Time: 3–4 hours
Ideal slow-cooker size: 3- or 4-qt.

16-oz. can kidney beans, drained

15-oz. can lima beans, drained

¼ cup vinegar

2 Tbsp. molasses

2 heaping Tbsp. brown sugar

2 Tbsp. minced onion

mustard to taste

Tabasco sauce to taste

1. Grease interior of slow-cooker crock.

2. Place beans in slow cooker.

3. Add remaining ingredients to slow cooker and combine well.

4. Cover. Cook on Low 3–4 hours.

Variation:
Add 1 lb. browned ground beef in Step 3 to make this a meaty main dish.

Barbecued Beans

Jane Steiner
Orrville, OH

Makes 12–15 servings
Prep. Time: 5–10 minutes
Cooking Time: 4 hours
Ideal slow-cooker size: 5-qt.

4 11-oz. cans pork and beans, undrained
/4 cup brown sugar
1 tsp. dry mustard
6 slices bacon, diced
1/2 cup ketchup

1. Grease interior of slow-cooker crock.

2. Pour 2 cans pork and beans into slow cooker.

3. In a small bowl, combine brown sugar and mustard. Sprinkle half of mixture over beans.

4. Cover with remaining cans of pork and beans. Sprinkle with rest of brown sugar and mustard.

5. Layer bacon over top. Spread ketchup over all.

6. Cut through bean mixture a bit before heating to lightly blend ingredients.

7. Cover. Cook on Low 4 hours.

Why I like this recipe—
This is deep rich flavor. And you don't have to pre-cook the bacon!

Beans with Turkey Bacon

Frances B. Musser
Newmanstown, PA

Makes 6–8 servings
Prep. Time: 15 minutes
Cooking Time: 2–3 hours
Ideal slow-cooker size: 4-qt.

½ cup ketchup

1 Tbsp. prepared mustard

½ cup brown sugar

1 small onion, chopped

1 tsp. salt

¼ tsp. ground ginger

½ cup molasses

1 lb. turkey bacon, chopped

40-oz. can great northern beans, drained

1. Grease interior of slow-cooker crock.

2. Combine all ingredients in slow cooker.

3. Cover. Cook on Low 2–3 hours.

Why I like this recipe—

My sister cooks for a threshing crew every
summer, and this is one of the recipes she
makes for them. She gets compliments from
the crew every time.

Maple Baked Beans

Dot Hess
Willow Street, PA

Makes 20 servings
Prep. Time: 15–20 minutes
Cooking Time: 2–4 hours
Ideal slow-cooker size: 6-qt.

10 strips bacon, cooked and crumbled

½ cup onion, chopped

½ cup maple syrup

4 tsp. dry mustard

8 15-oz. cans pork and beans, undrained

1. Grease interior of slow-cooker crock.

2. Cook bacon in skillet until crisp and crumbly. Or use already cooked and crumbled bacon. Scatter into slow cooker.

3. Stir in onion, maple syrup, mustard, and beans.

4. Cover and cook on Low for 3–4 hours or 2 hours on High.

Why I like this recipe—
My friend lives in upstate New York and brings us maple syrup every spring when she comes to visit. I've enjoyed using it for foods other than pancakes and waffles.

Four Beans and Sausage

Mary Seielstad
Sparks, NV

Makes 8 servings
Prep. Time: 10 minutes
Cooking Time: 2–4 hours
Ideal slow-cooker size: 5-qt.

1-lb. can great northern beans, drained

1-lb. can black beans, rinsed and drained

1-lb. can red kidney beans, drained

1-lb. can butter beans, drained

1½ cups ketchup

½ cup chopped onions

1 green bell pepper, chopped

1 lb. smoked sausage, cut into ½-inch-thick slices

¼ cup brown sugar

2 garlic cloves, minced

1 tsp. Worcestershire sauce

½ tsp. dry mustard

½ tsp. Tabasco sauce

1. Grease interior of slow-cooker crock.

2. Combine all ingredients in slow cooker.

3. Cover. Cook on Low 4 hours, or on High 2 hours.

Why I like this recipe—

I first tasted these beans at a carry-in supper at my knitting club. They looked so nice because of the different kinds of beans, and the flavor of the sausage is a nice change from bacon. Now I make this recipe when I need to take a dish somewhere!

Cajun Sausage and Beans

Melanie Thrower
McPherson, KS

Makes 4–6 servings
Prep. Time: 10 minutes
Cooking Time: 4–5 hours
Ideal slow-cooker size: 4-qt.

1 lb. smoked sausage, sliced into ¼-inch-thick pieces

16-oz. can red beans, rinsed and drained

16-oz. can crushed tomatoes with green chilies, undrained

1 cup chopped celery

half an onion, chopped

2 Tbsp. Italian seasoning

Tabasco sauce to taste

1. Grease interior of slow-cooker crock.

2. Combine all ingredients in slow cooker.

3. Cover. Cook on Low 4–5 hours.

TIPS

Serve over rice or as a thick, zesty soup.

Six-Bean Barbecue

Gladys Longacre
Susquehanna, PA

Makes 15–18 servings
Prep. Time: 10–15 minutes
Cooking Time: 4–6 hours
Ideal slow-cooker size: 6-qt.

1-lb. can kidney beans, drained

1-lb. can pinto beans, drained

1-lb. can great northern beans, drained

1-lb. can butter beans, drained

1-lb. can navy beans, drained

1-lb. can pork and beans, undrained

¼ cup barbecue sauce

¼ cup prepared mustard

⅓ cup ketchup

1 small onion, chopped

1 small bell pepper, chopped

¼ cup molasses, *or* sorghum molasses

1 cup brown sugar

1. Grease interior of slow-cooker crock.

2. Mix together all ingredients in slow cooker.

3. Cover. Cook on Low 4–6 hours.

Why I like this recipe—

We have a number of family picnics in the summer, and I often make these beans as my contribution. I sometimes double this recipe and borrow a second slow cooker.

Calico Beans with Corn

Carol Sommers
Millersburg, OH

Makes 10–12 servings
Prep. Time: 20 minutes
Cooking Time: 4–6 hours
Ideal slow-cooker size: 5-qt.

½ lb. bacon *or* ground beef

32-oz. can pork and beans, undrained

1-lb. can green lima beans, drained

16-oz. can kidney beans, drained

1-lb. can whole kernel corn, drained

1 tsp. prepared mustard

2 medium onions, chopped

¾ cup brown sugar

1 cup ketchup

1. Grease interior of slow-cooker crock.

2. If you have time, brown bacon or ground beef in skillet. Drain and crumble. Or cut bacon into chunks and scatter it, or crumble ground beef into slow cooker.

3. Stir beans and corn into slow cooker with meat.

4. In a bowl, combine mustard, onions, brown sugar, and ketchup. Pour over beans. Mix well.

5. Cover. Cook on Low 4–6 hours.

Why I like this recipe—
We love to have a slow cooker full of these beans when we do a cookout at the cabin in the fall. The adults and teenagers get the wood chopped for the winter, while the rest of us get the food ready. It's easy to have these beans waiting in the slow cooker to carry outside to the bonfire.

Apple Bean Bake

Barbara A. Yoder
Goshen, IN

Makes 10 servings
Prep. Time: 20 minutes
Cooking Time: 2–4 hours
Ideal slow-cooker size: 4- or 5-qt.

4 Tbsp. (½ stick) butter, melted
2 large Granny Smith *or* other tart and crisp
 apples, cubed
½ cup brown sugar
¼ cup sugar
½ cup ketchup
1 tsp. cinnamon
1 Tbsp. molasses
1 tsp. salt
24-oz. can great northern beans, undrained
24-oz. can pinto beans, undrained
ham chunks, *optional*

1. Grease interior of slow-cooker crock.

2. Pour melted butter and apple cubes into cooker. Stir in brown sugar, sugar, ketchup, cinnamon, molasses, and salt.

3. Add beans and ham chunks. Mix well.

4. Cover. Cook on High 2–4 hours, or until apples are as tender as you like them, and bake is hot in the center.

Why I like this recipe—

I love the subtle apple cinnamon flavor in these beans. My husband often grills sausages to go with them.

Super Creamed Corn

Ruth Ann Penner
Hillsboro, KS

Alix Nancy Botsford
Seminole, OK

Makes 8–12 servings
Prep. Time: 5–10 minutes
Cooking Time: 4 hours
Ideal slow-cooker size: 3- or 4-qt.

2–3 lbs. frozen corn

8-oz. pkg. cream cheese, cubed

4 Tbsp. (½ stick) butter, melted

2–3 Tbsp. sugar *or* honey

2–3 Tbsp. water, *optional*

TIP

Serve with meat loaf, turkey, or hamburgers.

1. Grease interior of slow-cooker crock.

2. Combine all ingredients in slow cooker.

3. Cover. Cook on Low 4 hours.

Variation:
Add ¼ lb. mild cheese, shredded, to Step 2.
—Marlene Weaver, Lititz, PA

Why I like this recipe—
A great addition to a holiday meal that is easy and requires no last-minute preparation. It also frees the stove and oven for other food preparation.

Baked Corn

Velma Stauffer
Akron, PA

Makes 8 servings
Prep. Time: 5–10 minutes
Cooking Time: 3 hours
Ideal slow-cooker size: 3- or 4-qt.

1 qt. fresh, *or* 2 1-lb. bags frozen, corn

2 eggs, beaten

1 tsp. salt

1 cup milk

1/8 tsp. pepper

2 tsp. oil

3 Tbsp. sugar

3 Tbsp. flour

1. Grease interior of slow-cooker crock.

2. Combine all ingredients well in greased slow cooker.

3. Cover. Cook on Low 3 hours.

If you use homegrown sweet corn, you can reduce the amount of sugar to 1 Tbsp.

Mexican Corn

Betty K. Drescher
Quakertown, PA

Makes 4–5 servings
Prep. Time: 10 minutes
Cooking Time: 2 hours
Ideal slow-cooker size: 3-qt.

2 10-oz. pkgs. frozen corn, partially thawed
4-oz. jar chopped pimentos, drained
⅓ cup chopped green bell peppers
⅓ cup water
1 tsp. salt
¼ tsp. pepper
½ tsp. paprika
½ tsp. chili powder

1. Grease interior of slow-cooker crock.

2. Combine all ingredients in slow cooker.

3. Cover. Cook on Low 2 hours. Stir occasionally if you're home and able to do so.

Variations:
1. For more fire, add ⅓ cup salsa to ingredients.
2. Increase amounts of pepper, paprika, and chili powder to match your taste.

Succotash

Andy Wagner
Quarryville, PA

Makes 5–6 servings
Prep. Time: 15 minutes
Cooking Time: 2½–3¾ hours
Ideal slow-cooker size: 4-qt.

16-oz. pkg. frozen corn
16-oz. pkg. frozen lima beans
14¾-oz. can cream-style corn
¼ cup minced red bell pepper
¼ cup minced sweet onion
½ tsp. salt
pinch black pepper
½ cup whole milk, room temperature
2 Tbsp. flour

1. Grease interior of slow-cooker crock.

2. Combine corn, lima beans, cream-style corn, bell pepper, onion, salt, and pepper in slow cooker.

3. Cover and cook on Low for 2–3 hours, or until corn is tender and dish is hot in the center.

4. Separately, whisk together milk and flour. Stir into corn mixture.

5. Cover and cook on Low for an additional 30–40 minutes, stirring occasionally, until thickened.

Variations:
Add ½ cup grated smoked cheddar cheese in Step 4.

Broccoli Corn Mix

Gerry Bauman
Grimes, IA

Makes 4 servings
Prep. Time: 25 minutes
Cooking Time: 3½–3¾ hours
Ideal slow-cooker size: 4-qt.

0-oz. pkg. frozen chopped broccoli

cups cream-style corn

cup cracker crumbs, *divided*

egg, beaten

½ tsp. salt

½ tsp. dried rosemary

½ tsp. dried thyme

green onions, diced

Tbsp. grated Parmesan cheese

Tbsp. butter, melted

1. Grease interior of slow-cooker crock.

2. Break broccoli apart if it has clumped, but keep it frozen.

3. In slow cooker, combine corn, ½ cup cracker crumbs, egg, salt, rosemary, and thyme. Stir well.

4. Add broccoli and stir gently.

5. Cover. Cook on Low 3 hours, or until set.

6. Combine remaining ½ cup cracker crumbs, green onions, Parmesan, and melted butter. Sprinkle on top of mix.

7. Remove lid, turn cooker to High, and cook an additional 30–40 minutes, or until topping is set.

Why I like this recipe—
This reminds me of a casserole my grandmother used to make. I like to serve it with meat loaf and pickles.

Quick Broccoli Fix

Willard E. Roth
Elkhart, IN

Makes 6 servings
Prep. Time: 15 minutes
Cooking Time: 3–4 hours
Ideal slow-cooker size: 4-qt.

1 lb. fresh *or* frozen broccoli florets

10¾-oz. can cream of mushroom soup*

½ cup mayonnaise

½ cup plain yogurt

½ lb. sliced fresh mushrooms

1 cup shredded cheddar cheese, *divided*

1 cup crushed saltine crackers

sliced almonds, *optional*

1. Grease interior of slow-cooker crock.

2. Place broccoli in greased slow cooker.

3. In a bowl, combine soup, mayonnaise, yogurt, mushrooms, and ½ cup cheese in mixing bowl.

4. Pour over broccoli. Stir together gently but well.

5. Cover. Cook on Low 3–4 hours, or until broccoli is tender and mixture is hot in the center.

6. Top with remaining cheese and crackers for last half hour of cooking time. Cook uncovered during these 30 minutes.

7. If you wish, top with sliced almonds, just before serving.

Why I like this recipe—

This is a favorite winter lunch for us when we are a little tired of soup.

*To make your own Cream Soup, see recipes on pages 561 and 562.

Cauliflower Cassoulet

Susie Shenk Wenger
Lancaster, PA

Makes 6 servings
Prep. Time: 30 minutes
Cooking Time: 3–4 hours
Ideal slow-cooker size: 6-qt.

1 cup uncooked brown rice
½ tsp. salt
2 cups water
1 cup sliced fresh mushrooms
1 large sweet onion, chopped
½ cup chopped red bell pepper
3 cloves garlic, chopped
salt and pepper to taste
1 Tbsp. butter
1 Tbsp. olive oil
1 large head cauliflower, chopped
½ cup diced Parmesan cheese
1 tsp. dried basil
½ tsp. dried oregano
juice and zest of 1 lemon

1. Grease interior of slow-cooker crock.

2. Put rice and ½ tsp. salt into cooker. Pour water over rice.

3. Scatter in mushrooms, onion, bell pepper, and garlic. Sprinkle lightly with salt and pepper. Dot with butter and drizzle with olive oil.

4. Scatter in cauliflower and diced Parmesan. Sprinkle with basil and oregano, adding more salt and pepper to taste.

5. Cover and cook on Low 3–4 hours, until rice is cooked and cauliflower is tender.

6. Drizzle with lemon juice and zest before serving.

Why I like this recipe—
I can get yellow cauliflower at the roadside farm stand nearby, which makes this dish look even more interesting.

Beets with Capers

Mary Clair Wenger
Kimmswick, MO

Makes 6 servings
Prep. Time: 20 minutes
Cooking Time: 3 –4 hours
Ideal slow-cooker size: 3-qt.

8 cups diced fresh, uncooked beets,
   peeled or not
3 Tbsp. olive oil
4 garlic cloves, chopped
¼ tsp. fresh ground pepper
½ tsp. salt
1 tsp. dried rosemary
1–2 Tbsp. capers with brine

1. Grease interior of slow-cooker crock.

2. In slow cooker, mix together beets, olive oil, garlic, pepper, salt, and rosemary.

3. Cover and cook on High until beets are tender, 3–4 hours.

4. Stir in capers and brine. Taste for salt. Add more if needed.

5. Serve beets hot or at room temperature.

Why I like this recipe—
My neighbor made these beets for me one time. I tweaked the recipe to make it in my slow cooker because it's so easy.

Mediterranean Onions

Barbara Warren
Folsom, PA

Makes 4–6 servings
Prep. Time: 25 minutes
Cooking Time: 4–8 hours
Ideal slow-cooker size: 3-qt.

large yellow onions, sliced in thin rings

½ tsp. freshly ground pepper

tsp. salt

¼ tsp. turmeric

tsp. dried thyme

½ tsp. dried basil

Tbsp. butter

Tbsp. olive oil

Tbsp. fresh lemon juice

⅓ cup chopped fresh parsley

⅓ cup crumbled feta cheese

oil-cured black olives, pitted, chopped, *optional*

TIPS

We serve the onions hot on pasta or couscous the first night. We serve any leftovers at room temperature with crusty bread, or tucked into a pita pocket with hummus and lettuce.

Variations:
Add more lemon juice or even some lemon zest if the onions need some brightening up.

1. Grease interior of slow-cooker crock.

2. Combine onions, pepper, salt, turmeric, thyme, basil, butter, and olive oil in slow cooker.

3. Cover and cook on Low for 4–8 hours, stirring once or twice, until onions are soft and browning.

4. Remove onions to serving dish. Gently stir in lemon juice and parsley. Sprinkle with feta, and black olives if you wish.

5. Serve hot or at room temperature.

Armenian Eggplant

Donna Treloar
Muncie, IN

Makes 6 servings
Prep. Time: 30 minutes
Cooking Time: 3–4 hours
Ideal slow-cooker size: 4- or 5-qt.

1 large sweet onion, diced

4 garlic cloves, chopped

4 ribs celery, diced

2 cups fresh green beans in 2-inch pieces

3 Tbsp. olive oil

2 tsp. dried basil

¼ tsp. black pepper

1 tsp. salt

1 medium eggplant, cubed

28-oz. can tomatoes with juice

2 Tbsp. lemon juice

2 Tbsp. capers

3 Tbsp. chopped fresh parsley

1. Grease interior of slow-cooker crock.

2. In slow cooker, combine onion, garlic, celery, green beans, olive oil, basil, black pepper, and salt.

3. Layer in eggplant. Pour tomatoes and juice over all.

4. Cover and cook on Low 3–4 hours, until vegetables are tender.

5. Add lemon juice and capers. Stir gently. Sprinkle with parsley just before serving.

6. Serve hot or at room temperature with good bread and olive oil for dipping.

Why I like this recipe—
This makes two meals for my husband and me, and the leftovers only improve with age. This has become our favorite way of fixing and eating eggplant.

Hot Fruit

Michele Ruvola
Vestal, NY

Makes 10 servings
Prep. Time: 5 minutes
Cooking Time: 2–3 hours
Ideal slow-cooker size: 5- or 6-qt.

2 24-oz. jars unsweetened, chunky applesauce

2 15-oz. cans pears, cut into bite-sized pieces, drained

2 15-oz. cans peaches, cut into bite-sized pieces, drained

14-oz. can tart pitted cherries, drained

1 Tbsp. ground cinnamon

¼ cup (½ stick) butter, sliced into 6–8 pieces

1. Grease interior of slow-cooker crock.

2. Combine applesauce and fruits in slow cooker. Stir in cinnamon.

This is great with a holiday ham dinner.

3. Space pats of butter over top.

4. Cook on High 2–3 hours, or until hot in the center and butter is melted. Stir once more before serving.

Pumpkin Chutney

Ginny Birky
Cortez, CO

Makes 12–16 servings
Prep. Time: 25 minutes
Cooking Time: 4–6 hours
Ideal slow-cooker size: 3-qt.

4 cups diced, peeled raw pumpkin *or* winter squash
2 cups diced, peeled apples
1 cup raisins
1 cup chopped dried apricots, dates, prunes, and/*or* pineapple (a mixture is fine)
1 small onion, diced finely
1-inch piece fresh ginger, diced finely
⅓ cup dark brown sugar
2 Tbsp. apple cider vinegar
1 tsp. curry powder
½ tsp. salt

1. Grease interior of slow-cooker crock.

2. Combine all ingredients in slow cooker.

3. Cover. Cook on Low 4–6 hours, or until pumpkin and apple are soft. Stir occasionally.

TIPS

1. Serve hot or cold as a side dish with roast pork or turkey.
2. This is also good as an appetizer with crackers and cream cheese.

Cranberry Applesauce

Margaret W. High
Lancaster, PA

Makes 6–8 servings
Prep. Time: 20 minutes
Cooking Time: 3–4 hours
Ideal slow-cooker size: 4-qt.

12-oz. bag fresh *or* frozen cranberries
4–6 apples, mixed varieties
⅓–½ cup sugar, depending how sweet your
   apples are and how tart you like your sauce

1. Grease interior of slow-cooker crock.

2. Cut apples into eighths; no need to core or peel.

3. Combine apple slices and cranberries in slow cooker.

4. Cover. Cook on Low 3–4 hours, or until apples are totally soft.

5. Put hot apples and cranberries through a food mill or applesauce sieve.

6. Add sugar to taste to the hot/warm sauce, depending how tart or sweet you like things.

7. Serve at room temperature or chilled.

Why I like this recipe—
This is our favorite way to have cranberry sauce at Thanksgiving!

Variations:
1. Use only 4 apples for a really deep red sauce with strong cranberry flavor, or use 6 (or more) apples to get more applesauce flavor and a lighter red finish.
2. If you don't have a food mill or strainer, simply peel and core the apples before cooking.

TIP

This is a great side for creamed chicken over cornbread, split pea soup and biscuits, or Swedish meatballs and egg noodles.

3. When the cranberries and apples are soft, mash them with a potato masher for a chunky texture or purée them with an immersion blender for a silky texture.

Healthy Whole Wheat Bread

Esther Becker
Gordonville, PA

Makes 8 servings
Prep. Time: 20 minutes
Cooking Time: 2½–3 hours
Ideal slow-cooker size: 6-qt. oval

2 cups warm reconstituted powdered milk

2 Tbsp. vegetable oil

¼ cup honey *or* brown sugar

¼ tsp. salt

1 pkg. yeast

2½ cups whole wheat flour, *divided*

1¼ cups white flour, *divided*

1. Mix together milk, oil, honey or brown sugar, salt, yeast, and half the flour in electric mixer bowl. Beat with mixer for 2 minutes. Add remaining flour. Mix well.

2. Place dough in well-greased bread or cake pan that will fit into your slow cooker. Cover with greased tinfoil. Let stand for 5 minutes. Place in slow cooker crock.

3. Cover cooker. Bake on High 2½–3 hours. You'll know the loaf is finished when it springs back when touched and the whole loaf has pulled away from the sides of the pan.

4. Remove pan and uncover. Let stand for 15 or more minutes. Slice and serve warm.

Why I like this recipe—
This is a versatile bread, great for sandwiches or breakfast toast. I always keep a loaf on hand in the freezer.

Cornbread from Scratch

Dorothy M. Van Deest
Memphis, TN

Makes 6 servings
Prep. Time: 15 minutes
Cooking Time: 2–3 hours
Ideal slow-cooker size: 5- or 6-qt.

1¼ cups flour

¾ cup yellow cornmeal

¼ cup sugar

4½ tsp. baking powder

1 tsp. salt

1 egg, slightly beaten

1 cup milk

⅓ cup melted butter *or* oil

1. In mixing bowl sift together flour, cornmeal, sugar, baking powder, and salt. Make a well in the center.

2. Pour egg, milk, and butter into well. Mix into the dry mixture until just moistened.

3. Pour mixture into a greased 2-quart mold that fits into your slow-cooker crock. Cover with a plate. Place on a trivet or rack in the bottom of slow cooker.

4. Cover. Cook on High 2–3 hours, or until tester inserted into center of bread comes out clean.

Why I like this recipe—
I can get stone-ground cornmeal from a local mill. That adds to the flavor and makes this bread more special for us.

Broccoli Cornbread

Winifred Ewy
Newton, KS

Makes 8 servings
Prep. Time: 15 minutes
Cooking Time: 6 hours
Ideal slow-cooker size: 3- or 4-qt.

½ cup (1 stick butter), melted

10-oz. pkg. chopped broccoli, cooked and drained

1 onion, chopped

1 box cornbread mix

4 eggs, well beaten

8 oz. cottage cheese

1¼ tsp. salt

1. Combine all ingredients. Mix well.

2. Pour into greased slow cooker crock.

3. Cover. Cook on Low 6 hours, or until toothpick inserted in center comes out clean.

TIPS

Serve like spoon bread, or invert the pot, remove bread, and cut into wedges.

Dilly Cornbread

Paula Winchester
Kansas City, MO

Makes 10 servings
Prep. Time: 30 minutes
Cooking Time: 3–4 hours
Standing Time: 20 minutes
Ideal slow-cooker size: 6-qt., *oval*

1 cup flour
1 cup stone-ground cornmeal
3 tsp. baking powder
3 Tbsp. sugar
1 tsp. salt
2 Tbsp. dried dill weed
1 cup corn kernels, thawed if frozen, drained
2 eggs
²/₃ cup milk
¹/₃ cup oil

1. In a mixing bowl, stir together flour, cornmeal, baking powder, sugar, salt, dill, and corn.

2. Separately, whisk together eggs, milk, and oil.

3. Make a well in dry ingredients and pour egg mixture into well. Mix just until combined; streaks of flour are fine.

4. Make sure your loaf pan fits into your oval 6-quart slow cooker, or will hang on the upper edge. Grease and flour loaf pan.

5. Pour batter into prepared loaf pan.

6. Put lid on cooker, propping it open at one end with a chopstick or wooden spoon handle.

7. Cook on High 3–4 hours, or until tester inserted in middle comes out clean.

8. Wearing oven mitts (to protect your knuckles!), remove hot pan from hot cooker and allow to cool for 10 minutes. Run a knife around the edge and turn loaf out on cooling rack to cool for an additional 10 minutes before slicing.

Good go-alongs with this recipe:
Whipped butter, cream of tomato soup, and a green salad.

Pineapple Cheddar Cornbread

Moreen and Christina Weaver
Bath, NY

Makes 10–12 servings
Prep. Time: 25 minutes
Cooking Time: 3–4 hours
Ideal slow-cooker size: 6-qt., *oval*

cup whole wheat flour

cup yellow cornmeal

Tbsp. sugar

tsp. baking powder

tsp. salt

½ cup (1 stick) butter, softened to room temperature

eggs, beaten

4-oz. can cream-style corn

-oz. can crushed pineapple, drained

cup shredded cheddar cheese

1. In mixing bowl, combine flour, cornmeal, sugar, baking powder, and salt.

2. Separately, beat butter well in a large bowl. Add eggs and beat again.

3. Stir corn, pineapple, and cheese into butter mixture.

4. Add flour mixture, stirring gently until just combined.

5. Prepare a loaf pan that fits in your slow cooker by greasing it and flouring it.

TIP

Leftover bread is great the next day toasted with butter for breakfast.

6. Pour batter into prepared pan.

7. Cover. Raise lid at one end with a wooden chopstick or wooden spoon handle so lid is vented.

8. Cook on High 3–4 hours, or until tester inserted in middle of loaf comes out clean.

9. Wearing oven gloves to protect your knuckles, remove hot pan from cooker and allow to cool 10 minutes. Run a knife around the edge and turn loaf out onto cooling rack. Serve warm.

Good go-alongs with this recipe:
Spicy chili.

Greek Bread

Nancy Raleigh
Belcamp, MD

Makes 10 servings
Prep. Time: 30 minutes
Cooking Time: 3–4 hours
Standing Time: 40 minutes
Ideal slow-cooker size: 6-qt., *oval*

2 cups whole wheat flour

1 cup flour

2 Tbsp. sugar

3 tsp. baking powder

1 tsp. salt

⅛ tsp. pepper

2 tsp. dried thyme

1 Tbsp. dried oregano

1 Tbsp. dried parsley

12-oz. beer, any kind, room temperature

2 Tbsp. olive oil

1. In a mixing bowl, combine flours, sugar, baking powder, salt, pepper, thyme, oregano, and parsley.

2. Add beer and mix.

3. Grease and flour a loaf pan that fits in your oval 6-quart cooker, either on the bottom of the crock or hanging on the top edge.

4. Pour batter into prepared pan. Smooth top. Drizzle with olive oil.

5. Place pan of batter in crock. Cover. Place wooden chopstick or spoon handle under lid to vent at one end.

6. Cook on High 3–4 hours, or until tester inserted in middle of loaf comes out clean.

7. Wearing oven mitts to protect your knuckles, remove hot pan from cooker. Allow to cool 10 minutes. Run a knife around the edge, and turn loaf out onto cooling rack for 30 more minutes before slicing. Serve warm.

Variations:
1. Add ½ cup chopped black olives in Step 2.
2. Substitute Italian herb seasoning for thyme and oregano.
3. Add ½ cup chopped sun-dried tomatoes in Step 2, and sprinkle some grated cheese on top of the olive oil in Step 4. Call it pizza bread!

Hearty Irish Soda Bread

Margaret W. High
Lancaster, PA

Makes 8–10 servings
Prep. Time: 20 minutes
Cooking Time: 2–3 hours
Ideal slow-cooker size: 4-qt.

cups whole wheat flour

Tbsp. brown sugar

½ tsp. salt

tsp. baking soda

egg

½ cup plain yogurt

Variations:
Add ½ tsp. ground cardamom, *or* ½ tsp. caraway seeds, in Step 1.

Good go-alongs with this recipe:
Lemon curd, jam, butter. This is a wonderful accompaniment to corned beef and cabbage.

1. In mixing bowl, mix together flour, sugar, salt, and baking soda.

2. Separately, mix egg and yogurt together.

3. Stir together wet and dry mixtures until soft dough forms.

4. Cut a large square of parchment paper and grease the middle. Tuck it inside the slow cooker, greased side up, to line it.

5. Nudge the dough out of the mixing bowl into the center of the greased parchment in the cooker. Shape and smooth it as needed so it makes a low loaf.

6. Cover the cooker and tuck a chopstick or wooden spoon under one end of the lid to vent it.

7. Cook on High 2–3 hours, until bread is firm on top and lightly browned.

8. Carefully lift parchment and bread out of the cooker. Allow to rest for 10 minutes, then slice and serve warm.

Boston Brown Bread

Jean Butzer
Batavia, NY

Makes 3 loaves
Prep. Time: 15–20 minutes
Cooking Time: 4 hours
Ideal slow-cooker size: large enough to hol
3 cans upright, with the cooker lid on

3 15½-oz., or 16-oz., vegetable cans, cleaned
and emptied

½ cup rye flour

½ cup yellow cornmeal

½ cup whole wheat flour

3 Tbsp. sugar

1 tsp. baking soda

¾ tsp. salt

½ cup chopped walnuts

½ cup raisins

1 cup buttermilk*

⅓ cup molasses

1. Spray insides of vegetable cans, and one side of three 6-inch-square pieces of foil, with nonstick cooking spray. Set aside.

2. Combine rye flour, cornmeal, whole wheat flour, sugar, baking soda, and salt in a large bowl.

3. Stir in walnuts and raisins.

* To substitute for buttermilk, pour 1 Tbsp. lemon juice into a 1-cup measure. Add enough milk to fill the cup. Let stand 5 minutes before mixing with molasses.

4. Whisk together buttermilk and molasses in a separate bowl. Add to dry ingredients. Stir until well mixed. Spoon into prepared cans.

5. Place one piece of foil, greased side down, on top of each can. Secure foil with rubber bands or cotton string. Place upright in slow cooker.

6. Pour boiling water into slow cooker to come halfway up sides of cans. (Make sure foil tops do not touch boiling water.)

7. Cover cooker. Cook on Low 4 hours, or until skewer inserted in center of bread come out clean.

8. To remove bread, lay cans on their sides. Roll and tap gently on all sides until bread releases. Cool completely on wire racks.

9. Serve with butter or cream cheese.

Why I like this recipe—
Traditionally, this bread is part of a New England baked bean supper. We prefer to eat it for breakfast or tea with butter or cream cheese.

Old-Fashioned Gingerbread

Mary Ann Westerberg
Rosamond, CA

Makes 6–8 servings
Prep. Time: 15 minutes
Cooking Time: 2½–3 hours
Ideal slow-cooker size: 4-qt.

½ cup (1 stick) butter, softened
½ cup sugar
1 egg
1 cup light molasses
2½ cups flour
1½ tsp. baking soda
1 tsp. ground cinnamon
2 tsp. ground ginger
½ tsp. ground cloves
½ tsp. salt
1 cup hot water

1. Cream together butter and sugar. Add egg and molasses. Mix well.

2. Stir in flour, baking soda, cinnamon, ginger, cloves, and salt. Mix well.

3. Add hot water. Beat well.

4. Pour batter into greased and floured 2-pound coffee can.

5. Stand can upright in cooker. Cover top of can with 8 paper towels. Cover cooker. Cook on High 2½–3 hours, or until tester inserted into center of gingerbread comes out clean.

Serve with applesauce. Top slices of gingerbread with whipped cream and sprinkle with nutmeg.

Date and Nut Bread

Jean Butzer
Batavia, NY

Makes 16 servings
Prep. Time: 20 minutes
Cooking Time: 3½–4 hours
Ideal slow-cooker size: large enough to hold
  2 coffee cans, or your baking insert

½ cups boiling water
½ cups chopped dates
¼ cups sugar
 egg
 tsp. baking soda
½ tsp. salt
 tsp. vanilla
 Tbsp. melted butter
½ cups flour
 cup walnuts, chopped
 cups hot water

1. In a large mixing bowl, pour 1½ cups boiling water over dates. Let stand 5–10 minutes.

2. Stir in sugar, egg, baking soda, salt, vanilla, and butter.

3. In a separate bowl, combine flour and nuts. Stir into date mixture and combine well.

4. Pour into 2 greased 11½-oz. coffee cans, or one 8-cup baking insert.

5. If using coffee cans, cover with foil and tie securely with kitchen twine. If using baking insert, cover with its lid.

6. Stand cans upright in cooker, or place insert in cooker.

7. Pour 2 cups hot water around cans or insert, up to half their/its height.

8. Cover slow cooker tightly. Cook on High 3½–4 hours, or until tester inserted into loaves of bread comes out clean. If it does, the bread is finished. If it doesn't, allow to cook 30 more minutes. Check again to see if bread is done. If not, continue cooking in 30-minute intervals.

9. When bread is finished, remove cans or insert from cooker. Let bread stand in coffee cans or baking insert for 10 minutes. Turn out onto cooling rack.

10. When warm, or thoroughly cooled, slice. Spread with butter, cream cheese, or peanut butter.

Why I like this recipe—

There's something magical about dates in baked goods. They don't taste like dates, really, but just sweet and buttery and delicious.

Zucchini Bread

Esther J. Yoder
Hartville, OH

Makes 10 servings
Prep. Time: 25 minutes
Cooking Time: 3–4 hours
Cooling Time: 40 minutes
Ideal slow-cooker size: 6-qt., *oval*

2 eggs

2 cups shredded zucchini (no need to peel zucchini)

1 cup brown sugar

⅓ cup oil

1 tsp. vanilla extract

1 cup chopped walnuts, *optional*

8-oz. pkg. cream cheese, at room temperature

1½ cups whole wheat flour

½ cup rolled oats

1 tsp. baking powder

1 tsp. baking soda

1½ tsp. ground cinnamon

½ tsp. nutmeg

1 tsp. salt

1. Mix eggs, zucchini, sugar, oil, vanilla, and nuts (if using) in a big bowl.

2. Cut cream cheese into cubes. Using an electric mixer or food processor, beat in until smooth.

3. Separately, mix flour, oats, baking powder, baking soda, cinnamon, nutmeg, and salt.

4. Combine wet and dry ingredients, mixing gently until just combined.

TIP

When the garden is really churning out zucchini, I make sure I shred some and put it in the freezer in 2-cup amounts. Then, in the winter, we enjoy the scent of this zucchini bread baking.

5. Make sure you have a loaf pan that fits in your oval 6-quart cooker. Grease and flour loaf pan.

6. Pour batter into prepared pan and place in cooker, either on the bottom or hanging from the top edge.

7. Prop lid open at one end with a chopstick or wooden spoon handle.

8. Cook on High 3–4 hours, or until tester inserted in middle comes out clean.

9. Wearing oven mitts to protect your knuckles, remove hot pan and allow to sit for 10 minutes.

10. Run knife around edges and turn loaf out to cool for 30 more minutes before slicing.

Special Banana Bread

Phyllis Good
Lancaster, PA

Makes: 1 loaf
Prep. Time: 20 minutes
Cooking Time: 3½–4½ hours
Ideal slow-cooker size: 6-qt., *oval*

1⅓ cups flour

⅓ cup whole wheat flour

¾ tsp. baking soda

½ tsp. salt

1 cup mashed, very ripe banana (2-3 medium)

½ cup creamy peanut butter

½ cup sugar

⅓ cup buttermilk

⅓ cup vegetable oil

2 eggs

1 tsp. vanilla extract

1 cup semisweet chocolate chips

1. In a mixing bowl, combine flours, baking soda, and salt.

2. In another mixing bowl, stir together banana, peanut butter, sugar, buttermilk, oil, eggs, and vanilla. When well-mixed, stir in chocolate chips.

3. Add wet ingredients to dry (or the other way around) and be very careful to stir briefly, just until mixed. A few streaks of flour may remain.

4. Pour batter into greased loaf pan, 9x5-inch or 8x4-inch, whatever size fits in your cooker. Or use small, individual bakers.

5. Place loaf pan or bakers in cooker. Prop slow cooker lid open at one end with a wooden spoon handle or chopstick.

6. Cook on High 3½–4½ hours, or until tester inserted in middle comes out clean.

7. Carefully, wearing oven gloves, remove the hot loaf pan or bakers from the hot cooker. Let stand 10 minutes. Run a knife around the edge of the bread and turn the loaf out onto a wire rack to finish cooling. Slices best when cool, if you can wait that long!

8. Spread cream cheese on slices if you wish.

Why I like this recipe—

What's better than banana, peanut butter, and chocolate? I love these three together. This is a wonderfully flavored bread that you don't have to feel guilty eating—serve it for breakfast or an after-school snack. I usually eat it straight up, but you could spread cream cheese on it, too.

Lemon Bread

Ruth Ann Gingrich
New Holland, PA

Makes 6 servings
Prep. Time: 15 minutes
Cooking Time: 2–2¼ hours
Ideal slow-cooker size: 4-qt.

½ cup shortening

¾ cup sugar

2 eggs, beaten

1⅔ cups flour

1⅔ tsp. baking powder

½ tsp. salt

½ cup milk

½ cup chopped nuts

grated peel from 1 lemon

Glaze:
¼ cup powdered sugar

juice of 1 lemon

1. Cream together shortening and sugar. Add eggs. Mix well.

2. Sift together flour, baking powder, and salt. Add flour mixture and milk alternately to shortening mixture.

3. Stir in nuts and lemon peel.

4. Spoon batter into well-greased 2-pound coffee can and cover with well-greased tin foil.

Serve plain or with cream cheese.

5. Stand upright in cooker. Cover cooker with its lid. Cook on High 2–2¼ hours, or until tester inserted in center of bread comes out clean.

6. Remove can from cooker. Let stand 10 minutes. Run knife around edge of bread. Turn bread out onto a wire rack to finish cooling.

7. When bread reaches room temperature, mix together powdered sugar and lemon juice. Drizzle over loaf.

Poppy Seed Tea Bread

Julie Hurst
Leola, PA

Makes 10 servings
Prep. Time: 30 minutes
Cooking Time: 3–4 hours
Cooling Time: 30 minutes
Ideal slow-cooker size: 6-qt., *oval*

½ cup whole wheat flour

1½ cups flour

¾ cup sugar

2 tsp. baking powder

¼ tsp. salt

¼ cup poppy seeds

2 eggs at room temperature

½ cup (1 stick) salted butter, melted

¾ cup whole milk at room temperature

½ tsp. almond extract

½ tsp. vanilla extract

1. In a mixing bowl, combine flours, sugar, baking powder, salt, and poppy seeds.

2. Separately, whisk together eggs, butter, milk, and extracts.

3. Pour wet ingredients into flour mixture, stirring until just combined.

4. Make sure your loaf pan fits in your oval 6-quart slow cooker, or can be hung from its top edge. Grease and flour loaf pan.

5. Pour batter into prepared loaf pan.

6. Put lid on cooker, propping it open at one end with a chopstick or wooden spoon handle.

TIP

Serve with pineapple whipped cream cheese and tea.

7. Cook on High 3–4 hours, or until tester inserted in middle comes out clean.

8. Wearing oven mitts (to protect your knuckles!), remove hot pan from hot cooker and allow it to cool for 10 minutes. Run a knife around the edge and turn loaf out on cooling rack to cool for an additional 20 minutes before slicing.

Dutch Apple Batter Bread

Margaret W. High
Lancaster, PA

Makes 10 servings
Prep. Time: 25 minutes
Cooking Time: 3–4 hours
Cooling Time: 40 minutes
Ideal slow-cooker size: 6-qt., *oval*

½ cup (1 stick) butter
1 cup sugar
2 eggs
1 cup whole wheat flour
1 cup flour
1 tsp. baking soda
½ tsp. salt
½ tsp. ground cinnamon
¼ tsp. ground nutmeg
1 cup chopped apples, peeled or not
½ cup chopped walnuts
⅓ cup buttermilk

1. Cream together butter, sugar, and eggs.

2. Separately, combine flours, baking soda, salt, cinnamon, nutmeg, apples, and walnuts.

3. Add flour mixture to creamed mixture alternately with buttermilk.

4. Make sure you have a loaf pan that fits in your 6-quart cooker, either sitting on the bottom or hanging from its top edge.

5. Grease and flour loaf pan.

6. Pour batter into pan and place pan in cooker. Prop lid open at one end with a wooden chopstick or spoon handle.

7. Cook on High 3–4 hours, or until tester inserted in middle comes out clean.

TIP

Great with butter or cream cheese, or toasted for breakfast.

8. Wearing oven mitts to protect your knuckles, remove hot pan and set aside to cool for 10 minutes. Run knife around the edge and turn bread out of pan to cool an additional 30 minutes on rack before slicing.

Variations:
Add ⅓ cup chopped raw cranberries or raisins in Step 2.

Breads

Raspberry Chocolate Chip Bread

Rosanna Martin
Morgantown, WV

Makes 10 servings
Prep. Time: 25 minutes
Cooking Time: 3–4 hours
Cooling Time: 40 minutes
Ideal slow-cooker size: 6-qt., *oval*

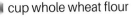 cup whole wheat flour

⅓ cup flour

¼ cup rolled oats

⅓ cup sugar

2 tsp. baking powder

1 tsp. baking soda

½ tsp. salt

½ tsp. ground cinnamon

¾ cup fresh *or* unsweetened frozen raspberries
    (do not thaw)

⅔ cup chocolate chips

1 egg, lightly beaten

¾ cup buttermilk

⅓ cup canola oil

1 tsp. vanilla extract

1. In large bowl, mix flours, oats, sugar, baking powder, baking soda, salt, and cinnamon. Gently stir in raspberries and chocolate chips.

2. Separately, mix egg, buttermilk, oil, and vanilla together.

3. Gently stir wet ingredients into dry just until barely mixed—streaks of flour are fine.

TIPS

Serve with butter or cream cheese, if you wish, but I love it by itself with a glass of milk.

4. Make sure your loaf pan fits into the bottom of your oval 6-quart slow cooker, or hangs on its to edge.

5. Grease and flour loaf pan. Pour batter into prepared loaf pan.

6. Put lid on cooker, propping it open at one end with a chopstick or wooden spoon handle.

7. Cook on High 3–4 hours, or until tester inserted in middle comes out clean.

8. Wearing oven mitts to protect your knuckles, remove hot pan from hot cooker and allow it to cool for 10 minutes. Run a knife around the edge and turn loaf out on cooling rack to cool for an additional 30 minutes before slicing.

Slow-Cooker Cinnamon Rolls

Margaret High
Lancaster, PA

Makes 6–8 servings
Prep. Time: 30 minutes
Cooking Time: 1½–2½ hours
Rising Time: 30 minutes
Ideal slow-cooker size: 6-qt.

½ cup warm milk

½ cup warm water

4 Tbsp. (½ stick) melted butter, *divided*

1 egg

1 Tbsp. instant yeast

1 tsp. salt

2 Tbsp. sugar

3½ cups unbleached all-purpose flour, *divided*

⅓ cup brown sugar

1 Tbsp. ground cinnamon

Frosting:

1 Tbsp. butter, softened

¼ cup cream cheese, softened

½ tsp. vanilla

2 cups powdered sugar

1-2 Tbsp. milk, *divided*

1. In a mixing bowl, combine milk, water, 2 Tbsp. butter, egg, yeast, salt, sugar, and 1 cup flour.

2. Beat well for 1 minute.

3. Gradually stir in remaining flour, stopping when batter comes together in a soft dough.

4. Knead dough 3–5 minutes.

5. Set dough aside in covered bowl to rise for 30 minutes.

6. Turn slow cooker on High to preheat while you roll out dough.

7. Turn dough out onto floured counter. Roll gently into a 10x8-inch rectangle.

8. Spread dough with remaining 2 Tbsp. melted butter. Separately, combine brown sugar and cinnamon. Sprinkle evenly over buttered dough.

9. Starting with long side, roll dough up into log. Slice into 1½-inch-thick pieces.

10. Grease a large square of parchment paper. Tuck it into the slow cooker, greased side up.

11. Nestle the cinnamon roll pieces, lying on their cut sides, on the parchment.

12. Lay a paper towel or two over the top of the slow cooker before putting on lid (to catch condensation).

13. Cover. Cook on High 1½–2½ hours, checking rolls at 1½ hours by gently prying apart two rolls in the middle to be sure they're not still doughy. If they are, continue cooking in 30-minute intervals until they're firm in their centers, but not dry.

14. Wearing oven gloves to protect your knuckles, lift parchment and rolls from cooker and set on wire rack.

15. Mix frosting ingredients in a small bowl, using milk as needed to reach spreading consistency.

16. Spread frosting over warm rolls and serve.

Why I like this recipe—

These rolls are one of our favorite summer breakfasts because the slow cooker doesn't heat up the house the way the oven would. We eat them with fresh fruit on the side – lots to choose from in the summer!

Breads

Caramel Rolls

Jessalyn Wantland
Paris, TX

Makes 6–8 servings
Prep. Time: 20 minutes
Cooking Time: 2–3 hours
Ideal slow-cooker size: 5-qt.

½ cup brown sugar

½ tsp. ground cinnamon

4 Tbsp. (½ stick) butter

2 8-oz. pkgs. refrigerator biscuits

1. Mix sugar and cinnamon together in small bowl.

2. Melt butter in another small bowl.

3. Dip individual biscuits into melted butter and then into cinnamon and sugar mixture.

4. Place each covered biscuit in greased slow cooker.

5. Cover. Cook on High 2–3 hours, or until rolls are done. Check rolls in center after 2 hours to see if they are still doughy in the center. If they are, continue cooking in 30-minute intervals until they're firm in the center, but not dry.

Why I like this recipe—

I love to make these rolls on vacation because they're so easy, yet smell and taste so special. My daughter is 8 and she can make these by herself because they're so easy and she's watched me do it before.

Welsh Rarebit

Sharon Timpe
Mequon, WI

Makes 6-8 servings
Prep. Time: 5 minutes
Cooking Time: 1⅓–2½ hours
Ideal slow-cooker size: 4-qt.

2-oz. can beer

Tbsp. dry mustard

tsp. Worcestershire sauce

½ tsp. salt

⅛ tsp. black *or* white pepper

lb. American cheese, cubed

lb. sharp cheddar cheese, cubed

1. Grease interior of slow cooker crock. Combine beer, mustard, Worcestershire sauce, salt, and pepper in crock.

2. Cover and cook on High 1–2 hours, or until mixture boils.

3. Add cheese, a little at a time, stirring constantly until all the cheese melts.

TIPS

Serve hot over toasted English muffins or over toasted bread cut into triangles. Garnish with strips of crisp bacon and tomato slices.

4. Heat on High 20–30 minutes with cover off, stirring frequently.

Why I like this recipe—

This is a good dish for brunch with fresh fruit, juice, and coffee. Also makes a great lunch or late-night light supper. Serve with a tossed green salad, especially fresh spinach and orange slices with a vinaigrette dressing.

Breakfast Skillet

Sue Hamilton
Minooka, IL

Makes 4 servings
Prep. Time: 15 minutes
Cooking Time: 2½–6 hours
Ideal slow-cooker size: 3½-qt.

3 cups milk

5½-oz. box au gratin potatoes

1 tsp. hot sauce

5 eggs, lightly beaten

1 Tbsp. prepared mustard

4-oz. can sliced mushrooms, drained

8 slices bacon, fried and crumbled, DIY, *or* buy it crumbled

1 cup cheddar cheese, shredded

1. Grease interior of slow cooker crock. Combine milk, au gratin sauce packet, hot sauce, eggs, and mustard in slow cooker until well blended.

2. Stir in dried potatoes, drained mushrooms, and bacon.

3. Cover. Cook on High 2½–3 hours, or on Low 5–6 hours.

4. Sprinkle cheese over top. Cover and let stand a few minutes until cheese melts.

Why I like this recipe—
I get up first in our household, and I'm not usually hungry for the first 2 hours or so. I like to mix this recipe up the night before; then take the crock out of the fridge, place it into the slow cooker, and flip the switch to High before I hop in the shower. As the house comes alive, this sturdy dish is making the place smell sooo good.

Egg and Cheese Bake

Iva Schmidt
Fergus Falls, MN

Makes 6 servings
Prep. Time: 15 minutes
Cooking Time: 3–4 hours
Ideal slow-cooker size: 3- or 4-qt.

slices bread (crusts removed), cubed, *or* torn
 into squares

cups (8 oz.) grated cheddar, Swiss, *or*
 American cheese

cup cooked, chopped ham

eggs

cup light cream *or* milk

cup evaporated milk

¼ tsp. salt

Tbsp. parsley

aprika

1. Lightly grease slow cooker. Alternate
layers of bread and cheese and ham in the
cooker.

2. Beat together eggs, milk, salt, and
parsley. Pour over bread in slow cooker.

3. Sprinkle with paprika.

4. Cover and cook on Low 3–4 hours. (The
longer cooking time yields a firmer, dryer
dish.)

Why I like this recipe—
This is such a flexible dish. I like it best when
I use a sturdy, whole-grain bread, very sharp
cheese, and either browned sausage or ham.
I've used browned ground beef, sometimes,
too. (Ever wonder why we eat pork, but
seldom beef, for breakfast?)

Western Omelet

Mary Louise Martin
Boyd, WI

Jan Mast
Lancaster, PA

Makes 10 servings
Prep. Time: 15 minutes
Cooking Time: 4–6 hours
Ideal slow-cooker size: 5-qt.

32-oz. bag frozen hash brown potatoes, *divided**

1 lb. cooked ham, cubed, *divided*

1 medium onion, diced, *divided*

1½ cups shredded cheddar cheese, *divided*

18 eggs

1½ cups milk

1 tsp. salt

1 tsp. pepper

1. Grease interior of slow-cooker crock. Layer ⅓ each of frozen potatoes, ham, onion, and cheese in bottom of slow cooker.

2. Repeat 2 times.

3. Beat together eggs, milk, salt, and pepper in a large mixing bowl. Pour over mixture in slow cooker.

4. Cover. Cook on Low 4–6 hours, or until potatoes are fully cooked and omelet is firm but not dry or overcooked.

*See recipe for making your own hash browns on page 570.

Why I like this recipe—
This is a great breakfast, served along with orange juice and fresh fruit.

Egg and Broccoli

Joette Droz
Kalona, IA

Makes 6 servings
Prep. Time: 15 minutes
Cooking Time: 3½–4 hours
Ideal slow-cooker size: 4-qt.

24-oz. carton small-curd cottage cheese

10-oz. pkg. frozen chopped broccoli, thawed and drained

2 cups (8 oz.) shredded cheddar cheese

6 eggs, beaten

⅓ cup flour

¼ cup (4 Tbsp.) melted butter

3 Tbsp. finely chopped onion

½ tsp. salt

1. Grease interior of slow-cooker crock. Combine all ingredients in cooker.

2. Cover and cook on High 1 hour.

3. Stir. Reduce heat to Low. Cover and cook 2½–3 hours, or until temperature reaches 160° in the center and the eggs are set.

Why I like this recipe—

I think that eggs, broccoli, and cheese are just a fantastic combination. So savory; so satisfying.

TIP

Sprinkle with shredded cheese, if you like, and serve.

Spinach Frittata

Shirley Unternahrer
Wayland, IA

Makes 4-6 servings
Prep. Time: 15 minutes
Cooking Time: 1½–2 hours
Ideal slow-cooker size: 5-qt.

Breakfasts & Brunches

4 eggs

½ tsp. salt

½ tsp. dried basil

freshly ground pepper to taste

3 cups chopped fresh spinach, stems removed

½ cup chopped tomato, liquid drained off

⅓ cup freshly grated Parmesan cheese

1. Whisk eggs well in mixing bowl. Whisk in salt, basil, and pepper.

2. Gently stir in spinach, tomato, and Parmesan.

3. Grease interior of slow-cooker crock. Pour mixture into cooker.

4. Cover and cook on High 1½–2 hours, or until middle is set. Serve hot.

Variations:
1. Add 1 cup browned, crumbled sausage to Step 2.
2. Add ½ tsp. minced garlic to Sep 2.

Good go-alongs with this recipe:
Biscuits or hash brown potatoes.

Huevos Rancheros in the Crock

Pat Bishop
Bedminster, PA

Makes 6 servings
Prep. Time: 25 minutes
Cooking Time: 2 hours
Ideal slow-cooker size: 4-qt.

cups salsa, room temperature
cups cooked beans, drained, room
   temperature
eggs, room temperature
alt and pepper to taste
 cup grated Mexican-blend cheese, *optional*
  tortillas, for serving

1. Grease interior of slow cooker crock. Mix salsa and beans in slow cooker.

2. Cook on High 1 hour, or until steaming.

3. With a spoon, make 6 evenly spaced dents in the salsa mixture; try not to expose the bottom of the crock. Break an egg into each dent.

4. Salt and pepper eggs. Sprinkle with cheese if you wish.

5. Cover and continue to cook on High until egg whites are set and yolks are as firm as you like them, approximately 20–40 minutes.

6. To serve, scoop out an egg with some beans and salsa. Serve with warm tortillas.

Variation:
Serve with hot cooked rice instead of tortillas.

TIP

If you want, sprinkle with chopped cilantro or chopped spring onions after cooking.

Overnight Veggie Omelet

Doug Garrett
Palmyra, PA

Makes 6 servings
Prep. Time: 30 minutes
Chilling Time: 4–8 hours, or overnight
Cooking Time: 3–4 hours
Ideal slow-cooker size: 4- or 5-qt.

6 slices whole-grain bread, torn into pieces

½ cup diced onion

1 medium carrot, pared and sliced thinly

¼ stick (2 Tbsp). butter

2 cups fresh broccoli florets, cut small

¾ cup grape tomatoes, sliced lengthwise

4 oz. cream cheese

1 cup grated Colby cheese

6 eggs

1½ cups milk

½ tsp. dry mustard

½ tsp. salt

dash cayenne pepper

1. Grease interior of slow-cooker crock.

2. Distribute torn bread in bottom of greased crock.

3. If you have time, sauté diced onion and carrots in butter in skillet, until onion is light brown and softened. If you don't have time, spread diced veggies over bread pieces in cooker.

4. Drop broccoli and grape tomatoes evenly over top of other vegetables.

5. Cut cream cheese into small pieces. Sprinkle it and grated cheese evenly over broccoli and tomatoes.

6. In a bowl, mix eggs, milk, mustard, salt, and cayenne together. Pour over all other ingredients in crock.

7. Cover. Refrigerate 4–8 hours, or overnight.

8. Cook on Low 3–4 hours, or until eggs are set in center.

9. Twenty minutes before end of cooking time, remove lid so that top of omelet can dry

Good go-alongs with this recipe:
Breakfast pastries, such as sticky buns or muffins.

French Toast with Apples and Nuts

Michele Ruvola
Vestal, NY

Makes 9 servings
Prep. Time: 30 minutes
Cooking Time: 2–4 hours
Ideal slow-cooker size: 5– 6½-qt.

eggs
egg whites
½ cups milk, preferably 2%
Tbsp. honey, *divided*
tsp. vanilla extract
tsp. ground cinnamon, *divided*
slices bread of your choice
cups finely diced apple
tsp. lemon juice
⅓ cup chopped, toasted pecans

1. In a mixing bowl, whisk together eggs, egg whites, milk, 2 Tbsp. honey, vanilla, and ½ tsp. cinnamon.

2. Separately, combine apple, lemon juice, pecans, remaining 3 Tbsp. honey, and remaining ½ tsp. cinnamon. Set aside.

3. Grease interior of slow-cooker crock. Place one layer of bread into crock, cutting to fit (triangles are good).

4. Layer in ¼ of the apple filling. Repeat layers, making 3 layers of bread and 4 of filling, ending with filling on top.

5. Pour egg mixture gently over all.

6. Cover and cook on High 2–2½ hours, or on Low 4 hours, or until bread has soaked up the liquid and apples are soft.

TIP

Serve with maple syrup.

Variations:
1. Use 3 diced bananas instead of apples.
2. Use soy milk or almond milk instead of cow's milk.

Cubed French Toast

Donna Suter
Pandora, OH

Makes 6 servings
Prep. Time: 20 minutes
Cooking Time: 3¼–5¼ hours
Ideal slow-cooker size: 6-qt.

1 loaf white bread, cut into 1-inch cubes
8 eggs
1½ cups milk
½ cup heavy cream
¼ cup maple syrup
zest of 1 orange
½ cup chopped, toasted pecans
3 Tbsp. butter, cut into cubes
maple syrup, for serving
whipped cream, for serving
sliced bananas, for serving

1. Place bread cubes on a baking sheet and toast in 400° oven for 8–10 minutes, or until golden brown. Remove from oven and cool.

2. In large bowl, whisk together eggs, milk, cream, maple syrup, and orange zest.

3. Add in the toasted bread cubes and toss to coat with the egg mixture.

4. Stir in pecans.

5. Grease slow cooker well. Pour bread and egg mixture into cooker. Dot top with cubed butter.

6. Cook on High 3 hours, or on Low 5 hours, or until set.

7. Serve hot, topped with maple syrup, whipped cream, and bananas.

Why I like this recipe—
Toasting the bread cubes before putting them into the slow cooker adds some of the browned flavor of traditional French toast when it's made in a skillet or on a griddle.

Oatmeal Morning

Barbara Forrester Landis
Lititz, PA

Makes 4–5 servings
Prep. Time: 5 minutes
Cooking Time: 2½–6 hours
Ideal slow-cooker size: 3-qt.

1 cup uncooked steel cut oats

1 cup dried cranberries

1 cup broken walnuts

½ tsp. salt

1 Tbsp. cinnamon

4 cups liquid—milk, water, or combination of the two

1. Grease interior of slow cooker crock. Combine all dry ingredients in slow cooker. Stir well.

2. Pour in liquid ingredient(s). Mix together well.

3. Cover. Cook on High 2½ hours, or on Low 5–6 hours, or until oats are as tender as you like them.

Variation:
If you wish, substitute fresh or dried blueberries or raisins, for the dried cranberries.

Why I like this recipe—
Steel-cut oats have such great body and texture. If you haven't tried them, use this sturdy, flavorful recipe to get acquainted.

Apple Oatmeal

Sheila Plock
Boalsburg, PA

Makes 6–8 servings
Prep. Time: 15 minutes
Cooking Time: 6 hours
Ideal slow-cooker size: 5-qt.

3-4 apples, peeled and sliced

½ cup brown sugar

1 tsp. nutmeg

1 tsp. cinnamon

¼ stick (2 Tbsp.) butter

½ cup walnuts

3 cups uncooked rolled oats

6 cups milk

1. Grease interior of slow-cooker crock. Layer apples in bottom of slow cooker.

2. Sprinkle with brown sugar, nutmeg, and cinnamon.

3. Dot with butter.

4. Scatter walnuts evenly over top.

5. Layer dry oatmeal over fruit and nuts.

6. Pour milk over oatmeal. Stir together until well blended.

7. Cover. Cook on Low 6 hours.

Why I like this recipe—
Wake up to what smells like freshly baked apple pie!

Apple Cider Cinnamon Steel-Cut Oatmeal

Jenny Unternahrer
Wayland, IA

Makes 4-6 servings
Prep. Time: 15 minutes
Cooking Time: 6 hours
Ideal slow-cooker size: 5- or 6-qt.

medium Granny Smith apples, peeled and chopped

cups apple cider

½ cups water

cup steel-cut oats

¼ tsp. ground cinnamon

⅛ tsp. salt

Tbsp. sugar

maple syrup, *optional*

hopped pecans *or* walnuts, *optional*

1. Pour a little water in slow cooker crock. Grease a heat-safe baking dish that will fit into your crock.

2. Combine apples, cider, water, oats, cinnamon, salt, and sugar in baking dish.

3. Cover baking dish, either with its lid or aluminum foil, and the slow-cooker lid. Cook on Low 6 hours, or until oats are tender. Stir gently before serving.

4. Serve with a drizzle of maple syrup and a sprinkle of nuts over each individual dish, if you wish.

TIP

You can put all of the ingredients into the slow cooker before bed, or program your slow cooker. The oatmeal cooks without effort while you sleep, and in the morning, you will have an aroma that smells like baked apple pie filling your kitchen.

Variation:
Use 3½ cups apple cider and omit water.

Steel-Cut Oats with Bananas

April Green
Aurora, CO

Makes 4 servings
Prep. Time: 5 minutes
Cooking Time: 2½–6 hours
Ideal slow-cooker size: 4-qt.

2 cups water

2 cups vanilla soy milk

1 cup uncooked steel-cut oats

¼ tsp. salt

2 bananas, mashed

2 Tbsp. ground flaxseed

2 tsp. cinnamon

2 Tbsp. pure maple syrup

1½ tsp. vanilla extract

1. Grease interior of slow-cooker crock.

2. Combine water, soy milk, oats, salt, bananas, and flaxseed in slow cooker.

3. Cover. Cook on High 2½ hours, or on Low 5–6 hours, or until oats are as tender as you like them.

4. Remove from heat. Stir in cinnamon, syrup, and vanilla before serving.

Good go-alongs with this recipe:
Serve with your favorite hot-cereal toppings such as raisins, walnuts, granola, or brown sugar.

Granola in the Slow Cooker

Earnie Zimmerman
Mechanicsburg, PA

Makes 10–12 servings
Prep. Time: 10 minutes
Cooking Time: 3–8 hours
Ideal slow-cooker size: 6-qt.

5 cups uncooked rolled oats

1 Tbsp. flaxseeds

/4 cup slivered almonds

/4 cup chopped pecans *or* walnuts

/4 cup unsweetened shredded coconut

/4 cup maple syrup *or* honey

4 Tbsp. (½ stick) melted butter *or* oil of your choice

½ cup dried fruit

1. Grease interior of slow cooker crock. Mix together oats, flaxseeds, almonds, pecans, and coconut in slow cooker.

2. Separately, combine maple syrup and butter. Pour over dry ingredients in cooker and toss well.

3. Place lid on slow cooker with a wooden spoon handle or chopstick venting one end of the lid.

4. Cook on High 3–4 hours, stirring every 30 minutes, or on Low 8 hours, stirring every hour. You may need to stir more often or cook for less time, depending on how hot your cooker cooks.

5. When granola smells good and toasty, pour it out onto a baking sheet to cool.

6. Add dried fruit to cooled granola and store in airtight container.

TIP

Tired of burning granola in the oven? Give your slow cooker a try!

Variations:
Add whatever fruit or nuts you like. I've used dried cranberries, apples, and apricots. Pecans, walnuts, almonds, and sunflower seeds all taste delicious. This is wonderful with milk or yogurt for breakfast.

Soy-Flax Granola

Doug Garrett
Palmyra, PA

Makes 10 cups
Prep. Time: 20 minutes
Cooking Time: 2–7 hours
Standing Time: 2 hours
Ideal slow-cooker size: 4-qt.

12 oz. soybeans, roasted without salt

4 cups uncooked rolled oats

¾ cup soy flour

¾ cup ground flaxseed

1¼ cups brown sugar

1 tsp. salt

2 tsp. cinnamon

⅔ cup walnuts, coarsely chopped

⅔ cup whole pecans

½ cup canola oil

¾ cup applesauce

2 tsp. vanilla extract

dried cranberries, dried cherries, chopped
   dried apricots, chopped dried figs, or raisins,
   optional

1. Put roasted soybeans in a blender and blend briefly until coarsely chopped. Place in large mixing bowl.

2. Add oats, flour, flaxseed, brown sugar, salt, cinnamon, walnuts, and pecans. Mix thoroughly with spoon, breaking up any brown sugar lumps.

3. In a 2-cup measuring cup, combine oil, applesauce, and vanilla extract.

TIP

You can be very flexible with this granola's dry ingredients. Just keep the dry/wet proportions similar.

4. Thoroughly mix dry and wet ingredients together until mixture is uniformly moist.

5. Grease interior of slow-cooker crock. Turn granola mixture into the crock.

6. Cover. Cook on Low 7 hours, or on High 2–3 hours. Stir every hour. Granola is done when it smells toasty.

7. Pour cooked granola onto a baking sheet to cool for at least 2 hours. Then add dried fruit if you wish.

8. Store in airtight containers.

Good go-alongs with this recipe:
Top granola with some yogurt and fresh fruit—it's like dessert for breakfast!

Grain and Fruit Cereal

Cynthia Haller
New Holland, PA

Makes 4–5 servings
Prep. Time: 5 minutes
Cooking Time: 3½ hours
Ideal slow-cooker size: 4-qt.

⅓ cup uncooked quinoa
⅓ cup uncooked millet
⅓ cup uncooked brown rice
cups water
¼ tsp. salt
½ cup raisins *or* dried cranberries
¼ cup chopped nuts, *optional*
 tsp. vanilla extract, *optional*
½ tsp. ground cinnamon, *optional*
 Tbsp. maple syrup, *optional*
½ cup milk

Why I like this recipe—
My dad grew up on a farm and did several hours of work before eating breakfast. So he was super-hungry when he came to the table. Grandma often made hot cereal that stuck to the ribs. Dad thought we kids should eat hot cereal, too, before we went to school. I was not a big fan. But now I've grown up to love these grains and the way they satisfy me until the next meal.

1. Rinse the quinoa, millet, and brown rice well.

2. Grease interior of slow-cooker crock. Place the grains, water, and salt into the crock.

3. Cook on Low about 3 hours, or until most of the water has been absorbed.

4. Add dried fruit, any optional ingredients, and milk.

5. Cover. Cook for 30 minutes more. If the mixture is too thick, add a little more water or milk.

6. Serve hot or cold.

Breakfast Polenta with Bacon

Margaret W. High
Lancaster, PA

Makes 8–10 servings
Prep. Time: 20 minutes
Cooking Time: 2½ hours
Ideal slow-cooker size: 5- or 6-qt.

eggs, room temperature

cups whole milk, room temperature

cups stone-ground (coarse) cornmeal

⅓ cup shredded Parmesan cheese, *divided*

cups boiling water

½ cup cooked, diced bacon

Tbsp. finely diced onion

cups chopped fresh spinach

tsp. salt

epper to taste

1. In a large mixing bowl, beat eggs. Whisk
milk, cornmeal, and ⅓ cup Parmesan.

2. Whisk in boiling water.

3. Gently stir in bacon, onion, spinach, salt,
nd pepper.

4. Grease interior of slow cooker. Pour
nixture into cooker.

5. Cover. Cook on High 2 hours, stirring
nce to be sure cornmeal is evenly distributed
s it cooks.

6. When polenta is thick, sprinkle with
remaining ⅓ cup Parmesan.

7. Remove lid and allow to cook on High
an additional 30 minutes as cheese melts and
any extra liquid evaporates.

8. Polenta will be softer when hot, but
will firm up as it cools. Serve hot, warm, or
chilled.

Why I like this recipe—
In case you thought polenta was for lunch
or dinner, you'll discover what a delectable
and filling meal it makes for breakfast when
blended with bacon and spinach.

Cheese Grits

Janie Steele
Moore, OK

Makes 6 servings
Prep. Time: 20 minutes
Cooking Time: 2–3 hours
Ideal slow-cooker size: 3- or 4-qt.

4 cups water

1 tsp. salt

1 cup regular (not instant) grits, uncooked

3 eggs

¼ cup (½ stick) butter, cut in chunks

1¾ cups grated sharp cheese

¼ tsp. pepper, *optional*

1. In saucepan, bring water and salt to boil. Slowly add grits, stirring.

2. Cook until grits are thick and creamy, 5–10 minutes.

3. Beat eggs in small bowl. Add spoonful of hot grits to eggs, stirring. This tempers the eggs.

4. Slowly stir egg mixture into rest of hot grits, stirring.

5. Add butter, cheese, and optional pepper. Stir.

6. Grease interior of slow-cooker crock. Pour grits mixture into slow cooker.

7. Cover. Cook on High 2–3 hours, or until grits are set in middle and lightly browned around edges.

Variation:
Use pepper-jack cheese for a kick.

Mexican-Style Grits

Mary Sommerfeld
Lancaster, PA

Makes 10–12 servings
Prep. Time: 10 minutes
Cooking Time: 2–6 hours
Ideal slow-cooker size: 3-qt.

½ cups instant grits

lb. Velveeta cheese, cubed

½ tsp. garlic powder

4-oz. cans diced chilies, drained

stick (8 Tbsp.) butter, cut in chunks

1. Prepare grits according to package directions.

2. Stir in cheese, garlic powder, and chilies, until cheese is melted.

3. Stir in butter.

4. Grease interior of slow-cooker crock. Pour mixture into cooker.

5. Cover. Cook on High 2–3 hours, or on Low 4–6 hours, or until grits are firm but not dry.

Why I like this recipe—
Grits are kind of tame on their own. But add some bold seasonings and chilies and you've got a good dish on its own, or as a partner to eggs any style.

Breakfast Apple Cobbler

Anona M. Teel
Bangor, PA

Makes 6–8 servings
Prep. Time: 15 minutes
Cooking Time: 2–9 hours
Ideal slow-cooker size: 3½- or 4-qt.

8 medium apples, cored, peeled, and sliced

¼ cup sugar

dash of cinnamon

juice of 1 lemon

½ stick (4 Tbsp.) butter, melted

2 cups of your favorite granola

1. Grease interior of slow-cooker crock.
Combine all ingredients in slow cooker.

2. Cover. Cook on Low 7–9 hours (while
you sleep), or on High 2–3 hours (after you're
up in the morning), or until mixture smells
toasty.

Why I like this recipe—
The apples turn to applesauce here, replacing
the need for milk. But sometimes I add milk
anyway, especially if I can't wait to eat the
cobbler until it's had time to cool off.

Breakfasts & Brunches

462   **Breakfasts and Brunches**

Plums for Breakfast

Jo Haberkamp
Fairbank, IA

Makes 6 servings
Prep. Time: 10 minutes
Cooking Time: 8–10 hours
Ideal slow-cooker size: 2-qt.

2 cups orange juice
¼ cup orange marmalade
1 tsp. ground cinnamon
¼ tsp. ground cloves
¼ tsp. ground nutmeg
1 cup water
12-oz. pkg. pitted dried plums (1¾ cups)
2 thin lemon slices

1. Combine orange juice, marmalade, cinnamon, cloves, nutmeg, and water in slow cooker.

2. Stir in dried plums and lemon slices.

3. Cover. Cook on Low 8–10 hours, or overnight, until the dried plums are as tender as you like them.

4. Serve warm as a breakfast food, or warm or chilled as a side dish with a meal later in the day.

Variation:

If you prefer more citrus flavor, eliminate the ground cloves and reduce the cinnamon to ½ tsp. and the nutmeg to ⅛ tsp.

Pumpkin Breakfast Custard

Audrey Hess
Gettysburg, PA

Makes 4-6 servings
Prep. Time: 20 minutes
Cooking Time: 1½-2 hours
Ideal slow-cooker size: 2½- or 3-qt.

2½ cups cooked pumpkin *or* winter squash

2 Tbsp. blackstrap molasses

3 Tbsp. sugar

¼ cup half-and-half

3 eggs

1 tsp. cinnamon

½ tsp. ground ginger

½ tsp. ground nutmeg

¼ tsp. ground cloves

¼ tsp. salt

1. Purée ingredients in blender until smooth.

2. Grease interior of slow-cooker crock. Pour mixture into cooker.

3. Cook on High 1½–2 hours, or until set in the middle and just browning at edges.

4. Serve warm in scoops over hot cereal, baked oatmeal, or as a breakfast side dish with toast or muffins.

TIPS

1. Toasted walnuts are a nice topping if you're serving this as a side dish.
2. Leftover custard will weep a little in the fridge, but it's still fine to use.
3. This is also good served chilled.

Apple Cobbler

Kendra Dreps
Liberty, PA

Makes 8 servings
Prep. Time: 25 minutes
Cooking Time: 2–4 hours
Ideal slow-cooker size: 4- or 5-qt.

7–8 apples, peeled and sliced

1¼ cups sugar, *divided*

¾ tsp. cinnamon, *divided*

2 cups flour

2 tsp. baking powder

¾ tsp. salt

2 eggs

⅔ cup butter, melted

TIPS

Serve like spoon bread, or invert the pot, remove bread, and cut into wedges.

1. Grease interior of slow-cooker crock.

2. Combine apples, ½ cup sugar, and ½ tsp. cinnamon in crock.

3. Combine ¾ cup sugar, ¼ tsp. cinnamon, flour, baking powder, salt, and eggs in a bowl. Pour evenly over top of apples.

4. Pour melted butter over all.

5. Cover. Cook on Low 2–4 hours, or until apples are tender and tester comes out clean when stuck into the center of the topping.

Why I like this recipe—
I like to use a mix of apples—some sweet and some tart—and then I usually don't need a full half cup of sugar in Step 2. I put in ¼ cup sugar, then taste the mixture to see if I need to add more.

Black and Blue Cobbler

Renee Shirk
Mount Joy, PA

Makes 6 servings
Prep. Time: 20 minutes
Cooking Time: 2–2½ hours
Ideal slow-cooker size: 5-qt.

1 cup flour

1½ cups sugar, *divided*

1 tsp. baking powder

¼ tsp. salt

¼ tsp. ground cinnamon

¼ tsp. ground nutmeg

2 eggs, beaten

2 Tbsp. milk

2 Tbsp. vegetable oil

2 cups fresh *or* frozen blueberries

2 cups fresh *or* frozen blackberries

¾ cup water

1 tsp. grated orange peel

1. Grease interior of slow-cooker crock.

2. Combine flour, ¾ cup sugar, baking powder, salt, cinnamon, and nutmeg in a good-sized bowl.

3. Combine eggs, milk, and oil in another bowl. Stir into dry ingredients just until moistened.

4. Spread the batter evenly over bottom of greased slow cooker.

5. In saucepan, combine berries, water, orange peel, and ¾ cup sugar. Bring to boil. Remove from heat and pour over batter. Cover.

6. Cook on High 2–2½ hours, or until toothpick inserted into batter comes out clean. Turn off cooker.

7. Uncover and let stand 30 minutes before serving.

TIP

Spoon from cooker and serve with whipped topping or ice cream.

Why I like this recipe—
Sometimes I use 1 cup strawberries and use only 1½ cups of both the blueberries and the blackberries. It adds color and flavor.

Quick Yummy Peaches

Willard E. Roth
Elkhart, IN

Makes 6 servings
Prep. Time: 10 minutes
Cooking Time: 5 hours
Ideal slow-cooker size: 3½-qt.

⅓ cup buttermilk baking mix

⅔ cup dry quick oats

½ cup brown sugar

1 tsp. cinnamon

4 cups sliced peaches, canned *or* fresh

½ cup peach juice, *or* water

1. Grease interior of slow-cooker crock.

2. Mix together baking mix, oats, brown sugar, and cinnamon in greased slow cooker.

3. Stir in peaches and peach juice.

4. Cook on Low for up to 5 hours. (If you like a drier cobbler, remove lid for last 15–30 minutes of cooking.)

TIP

Serve with frozen yogurt or ice cream.

Why I like this recipe—
I like this for breakfast with milk—or as an after-school snack.

Extra-Crispy Apple Crisp

Christina Gerber
Apple Creek, OH

Makes 4 servings
Prep. Time: 15 minutes
Cooking Time: 3–6 hours
Ideal slow-cooker size: 5-qt.

5–6 cups tart apple slices

¾ cup (1½ sticks) butter

1 cup rolled *or* quick oats

1½ cups flour

1 cup brown sugar, packed

3 tsp. ground cinnamon

1. Grease interior of slow-cooker crock.

2. Place apples in lightly greased slow cooker.

3. Melt butter in microwave or on stove-top. Add rest of ingredients and mix well.

4. Crumble topping over apples.

5. Cover and cook on High for 3 hours or Low for 4–6 hours. If you like a drier topping, remove lid for last hour of cooking.

6. Let crisp stand uncovered for about 30 minutes before serving, so it's not hot, but still warm.

Why I like this recipe—
This is the recipe for people who can never get enough crisp topping on their apple crisp!

TIP

Serve with ice cream or whipped cream.

Variations:
Add 1 tsp. salt to topping in Step 3.

Cherry Delight

Anna Musser
Manheim, PA

Marianne J. Troyer
Millersburg, OH

Makes 10–12 servings
Prep. Time: 5 minutes
Cooking Time: 2–4 hours
Ideal slow-cooker size: 4-qt.

21-oz. can cherry pie filling

1 pkg. yellow cake mix

½ cup (1 stick) butter, melted

⅓ cup walnuts, *optional*

1. Grease interior of slow-cooker crock.

2. Place pie filling in greased slow cooker.

3. Combine dry cake mix and butter (mixture will be crumbly) in a bowl. Sprinkle over filling. If you wish, scatter walnuts over top.

4. Cover. Cook on Low 4 hours, or on High 2 hours.

TIPS

1. For a less rich, less sweet dessert, use only half the cake mix and only ¼ cup (half a stick) melted butter.
2. Allow to cool, then serve in bowls with scoops of ice cream.

Sweets & Desserts

Sour Cherry Cobbler

**Margaret W. High
Lancaster, PA**

Makes 6–8 servings
Prep. Time: 20 minutes
Cooking Time: 2 hours
Ideal slow-cooker size: 5-qt.

½ cup whole wheat flour

¼ cup all-purpose flour, *divided*

 Tbsp. sugar, plus ⅔ cup sugar, *divided*

 tsp. baking powder

¼ tsp. salt

¼ tsp. ground cinnamon

¼ tsp. almond extract

 egg

¼ cup milk

 Tbsp. (¼ stick) melted butter

 cups pitted sour cherries, thawed and
  drained if frozen

1. Grease interior of slow-cooker crock.

2. In mixing bowl, combine whole wheat
flour and ½ cup all-purpose flour. Mix in
 Tbsp. sugar, baking powder, salt, and
cinnamon.

3. Separately, combine almond extract, egg,
milk, and butter. Stir into dry ingredients just
until moistened.

4. Spread batter in bottom of greased slow
cooker.

5. Separately, mix remaining ¼ cup all-
purpose flour with ⅔ cup sugar. Add cherries.
Spoon cherry mixture evenly over batter in
slow cooker.

6. Cover. Cook on High 2 hours, or until
edges are lightly browned and juice is
bubbling from cherries.

Why I like this recipe—
Cobblers are wonderful served warm with
vanilla ice cream, whipped cream, or custard
sauce.

Variations:
Use blueberries instead of sour cherries.
Reduce sugar to ½ cup and use vanilla extract
instead of almond.

Sweets & Desserts

Apple Cake

Esther Becker
Gordonville, PA

Wanda S. Curtin
Bradenton, FL

Makes 8–10 servings
Prep. Time: 15 minutes
Cooking Time: 3½–4 hours
Ideal slow-cooker size: 4- or 5-qt.

2 cups sugar

1 cup oil

2 eggs

1 tsp. vanilla

2 cups chopped apples

2 cups flour

1 tsp. salt

1 tsp. baking soda

1 tsp. nutmeg

1 cup chopped walnuts, *or* pecans

1. Beat together sugar, oil, and eggs in a large bowl. Add vanilla.

2. Add apples. Mix well.

3. In a separate bowl, sift together flour, salt, baking soda, and nutmeg. Add dry ingredients and nuts to apple mixture. Stir well.

4. Pour batter into greased and floured bread or cake pan that fits into your slow cooker. Cover with pan's lid, or greased tinfoil. Place pan in slow cooker. Cover cooker.

5. Bake on High 3½–4 hours, or until tester inserted into center of cake comes out clean. (Remove cooker cover with a strong swoop to keep condensation on inside of lid from dripping onto the cake.)

6. Let cake stand in pan for 5 minutes after removing from slow cooker before removing from pan or slicing.

Why I like this recipe—
I almost have apples on hand—and I often put a batch of this in the slow cooker when we go out to an evening event—so we can invite friends home for dessert after the play or concert.

Easy Autumn Cake

Janice Muller
Derwood, MD

Makes 8 servings
Prep. Time: 15 minutes
Cooking Time: 3–5 hours
Ideal slow-cooker size: 4-qt.

16-oz. cans sliced apples, undrained (not pie filling)
18¼-oz. pkg. spice cake mix
½ cup (1 stick) butter, melted
½ cup chopped pecans

1. Spray interior of slow cooker with nonstick cooking spray.

2. Spoon apples and their juice into slow cooker, spreading evenly over the bottom.

3. Sprinkle with dry spice cake mix.

4. Pour melted butter over dry mix. Top with chopped pecans.

5. Cover. Cook on Low 3–5 hours, or until toothpick inserted into topping comes out dry.

6. Serve warm from cooker.

Why I like this recipe—
No icing needed! And no one will miss it because of the saucy bottom layer and the crunch of the top layer.

Hot Fudge Cake

Maricarol Magill
Freehold, NJ

Makes 6–8 servings
Prep. Time: 10 minutes
Cooking Time: 2–3 hours
Ideal slow-cooker size: 4-qt.

¾ cups packed brown sugar, *divided*

cup flour

Tbsp. plus ¼ cup cocoa powder, *divided*

tsp. baking powder

½ tsp. salt

½ cup milk

Tbsp. (¼ quarter stick) melted butter

½ tsp. vanilla

¾ cups boiling water

TIP

Serve warm with vanilla ice cream.

Why I like this recipe—
This never gets old. Watch the faces around
the table beam when you spoon out the cake
and its oozy, gooey, chocolate sauce.

1. Grease interior of slow-cooker crock.

2. In a good-sized bowl, mix together 1 cup brown sugar, flour, 3 Tbsp. cocoa, baking powder, and salt.

3. Stir in milk, butter, and vanilla. Spread over bottom of slow cooker.

4. In a clean bowl, mix together remaining ¼ cup brown sugar and ¼ cup cocoa powder. Sprinkle over mixture in slow cooker.

5. Slowly pour in boiling water. Do *not* stir.

6. Cover. Cook on High 2–3 hours, or until a toothpick inserted in center of cake comes out clean.

Sweets & Desserts

Fudgy Peanut Butter Cake

Betty Moore
Plano, IL

Makes 4 servings
Prep. Time: 15 minutes
Cooking Time: 1½ hours
Ideal slow-cooker size: 3-qt.

¼ cup sugar, *divided*
½ cup flour
¼ tsp. baking powder
⅓ cup milk
¼ cup peanut butter
1 Tbsp. oil
½ tsp. vanilla
2 Tbsp. dry cocoa powder
1 cup boiling water

1. Butter or spray interior of slow-cooker crock.

2. Mix ¼ cup sugar, flour, and baking powder together in a small bowl.

3. In another larger bowl, mix milk, peanut butter, oil, and vanilla together. Beat well.

4. Stir dry ingredients into milk-peanut butter mixture just until combined. Spread in buttered slow cooker.

5. In bowl, combine cocoa powder and remaining ½ cup sugar. Add boiling water, stirring until well mixed. Pour slowly into slow cooker. Do *not* stir.

6. Cover. Cook on High 1½ hours, or until toothpick inserted in center of cake comes out clean.

TIP

Serve warm with vanilla ice cream.

Why I like this recipe—

1. I take this to potlucks, and it is always a hit.

2. I was pretty sure my kids would love this, so I doubled the recipe. I cooked that larger recipe for 2 hours. The kids came back for second and third helpings!

3. This is a pretty sturdy cake. I kept one of my test cakes for over an hour before serving it, and it was just as good, if not better, than the one we ate right away.

Sweets & Desserts

Self-Frosting Fudge Cake

Mary Puterbaugh
Elwood, IN

Makes 8–10 servings
Prep. Time: 10 minutes
Cooking Time: 2–3 hours
Ideal slow-cooker size: 5- or 6-qt.

2½ cups of 18½-oz. pkg. chocolate fudge pudding cake mix

2 eggs

¾ cup water

3 Tbsp. oil

⅓ cup pecan halves

¼ cup chocolate syrup

¼ cup warm water

3 Tbsp. sugar

1. Combine cake mix, eggs, ¾ cup water, and oil in electric mixer bowl. Beat 2 minutes.

2. Pour into greased and floured bread or cake pan that will fit into your slow cooker.

3. Sprinkle nuts over mixture.

4. Blend together chocolate syrup, ¼ cup water, and sugar. Spoon over batter. Do *not* stir.

5. Cover. Bake on High 2–3 hours, or until tester inserted into center of cake comes out clean.

TIP

Serve warm from slow cooker.

Why I like this recipe—
This is the first cake I made in a slow cooker. I took the filled cooker to the office that day so I could keep an eye on it while it cooked, because I wasn't convinced that this recipe would produce an edible cake. Not only did the recipe work, but the baking smell drew a hungry crowd. And we ate it all on the spot, with no crumbs or sauce left!

QUICK and EASY

Black Forest Cake

Marla Folkerts
Holland, OH

Makes 8–10 servings
Prep. Time: 10 minutes
Cooking Time: 2¼ hours
Ideal slow-cooker size: 4- or 5-qt.

20-oz. can cherry pie filling (lite *or* regular)

18¼-oz. box chocolate cake mix, butter-style

1. Spray interior of baking insert that fits into your slow cooker with nonstick cooking spray.

2. In a bowl, stir together pie filling and cake mix until mix is thoroughly moistened. Spoon into insert.

3. Place insert into cooker. Cover insert with 8 paper towels. Cover slow cooker.

4. Cook on High for 1¾ hours. Remove paper towels and cooker lid. Continue cooking for another 30 minutes, or until a toothpick inserted in the center of the cake comes out clean.

5. Remove baking insert from cooker.

6. Let cake cool for 20–30 minutes. Serve warm directly from the insert.

Why I like this recipe—

You cannot beat this for simplicity. Keep a box of the cake mix and a can of pie filling in your pantry, and you'll always feel prepared for guests.

Carrot Cake

Colleen Heatwole
Burton, MI

Makes 6–8 servings
Prep. Time: 20 minutes
Cooking Time: 3–4 hours
Ideal slow-cooker size: large enough to hold your baking insert or a bread pan

½ cup vegetable oil

2 eggs

1 Tbsp. hot water

½ cup grated raw carrots

¾ cup flour plus 2 Tbsp. flour, *divided*

¾ cup sugar

½ tsp. baking powder

⅛ tsp. salt

¼ tsp. ground allspice

½ tsp. ground cinnamon

⅛ tsp. ground cloves

½ cup chopped nuts

½ cup raisins *or* chopped dates

2 Tbsp. flour

1. In large bowl, beat oil, eggs, and hot water for 1 minute.

2. Add carrots. Mix well.

3. In a separate bowl, stir together flour, sugar, baking powder, salt, allspice, cinnamon, and cloves. Add to creamed mixture.

4. Toss nuts and raisins in bowl with 2 Tbsp. flour. Add to creamed mixture. Mix well.

TIPS

1. If your bread pan doesn't fit down into your oval slow cooker, you might be able to hang it onto the upper edge of the crock. If you can, proceed with Step 6 above.
2. Use your favorite cream cheese frosting on top of the cooled cake.

5. Pour into greased and floured baking dish or bread pan that fits into your slow cooker. Place baking dish or bread pan in slow cooker.

6. Cover insert with its lid, or cover with 8 paper towels, folded down over edge of slow cooker to absorb moisture. Cover paper towels with cooker lid.

7. Cook on High 3–4 hours, or until toothpick inserted in center of cake comes out clean.

8. Remove can or insert from cooker and allow to cool on rack for 10 minutes. Run knife around edge of cake. Invert onto serving plate.

Creamy Orange Cheesecake

Jeanette Oberholtzer
Manheim, PA

Makes 10 servings
Prep. Time: 15 minutes
Cooking Time: 2½–3 hours
Standing Time: 1–2 hours
Chilling Time: 2–4 hours
Ideal slow-cooker size: large enough to hold your springform pan

Crust:

¼ cup graham cracker crumbs

2 Tbsp. sugar

3 Tbsp. melted butter

Filling:

2 8-oz. pkgs. cream cheese, at room temperature

⅓ cup sugar

2 eggs

1 egg yolk

¼ cup frozen orange juice concentrate

1 tsp. orange zest

1 Tbsp. flour

½ tsp. vanilla

1. Combine crust ingredients in a small bowl.

2. Grease a 7- or 9-inch springform pan, whichever size fits into your slow cooker, and then pat the crust into the bottom of the pan and up the sides an inch or so if you can.

3. In a large mixing bowl, cream together cream cheese and sugar. Add eggs and yolk. Beat 3 minutes.

TIP

Serve with thawed frozen whipped topping and fresh or mandarin orange slices.

4. Add juice concentrate, zest, flour, and vanilla. Beat 2 more minutes.

5. Pour batter into crust. Place on rack (or jar rings) in slow cooker.

6. Cover. Cook on High 2½–3 hours, or until cake is firm in center and sides are beginning to pull away from sides of pan.

7. Turn off cooker. Let stand 1–2 hours, or until cool enough to remove pan from cooker.

8. Cool cake completely before removing sides of pan.

9. Chill before serving.

Orange Slice Cake

Steven Lantz
Denver, CO

Makes 10–12 servings
Prep. Time: 20 minutes
Cooking Time: 2–3 hours
Cooling Time: 3–4 hours
Ideal slow-cooker size: 4-qt.

1 cup chopped dates

½ lb. candied orange slices, cut into thirds

½ cup chopped walnuts

1 cup flaked, unsweetened coconut

1 Tbsp. grated orange rind, *optional*

1¾ cups flour, *divided*

8 Tbsp. (1 stick) butter, at room temperature

1 cup sugar

2 eggs

½ tsp. baking soda

¼ cup buttermilk

1. In a good-sized mixing bowl, combine dates, orange slices, nuts, coconut, and orange rind if you wish.

2. Pour ¼ cup flour over mixture and stir together.

3. In a separate big bowl, cream butter and sugar together. Add eggs and beat well.

4. In a small bowl, dissolve baking soda in buttermilk.

5. Add remaining 1½ cups flour and buttermilk in which soda has been dissolved to creamed mixture.

TIPS

Chop the dates and nuts in a food processor, then spoon them into a mixing bowl and combine them with the other ingredients in Steps 1 and 2. Continue using food processor for Steps 3 and 5. No need to wash it in between! I believe in saving time whenever I can.

6. Stir in fruit and nut mixture.

7. Pour into greased slow cooker.

8. Cover. Cook on High 2–3 hours, or until toothpick inserted in center comes out clean.

9. Allow cake to cool completely before removing from slow cooker.

Why I like this recipe—
This cake is perfect with coffee in the morning or later in the day as dessert.

Sweets & Desserts

Lemon Pudding Cake

Jean Butzer
Batavia, NY

Makes 5–6 servings
Prep. Time: 15 minutes
Cooking Time: 2–3 hours
Ideal slow-cooker size: 3- or 4-qt.

eggs, separated
tsp. grated lemon peel
¼ cup lemon juice
Tbsp. melted butter
½ cups milk
¼ cup sugar
¼ cup flour
⅛ tsp. salt

TIP

Serve with a spoon straight from the cooker.

Why I like this recipe—
Lemony, light, and airy! (Don't skimp on the grated lemon peel.)

1. Grease interior of slow-cooker crock.

2. Beat egg whites until stiff peaks form. Set aside.

3. Beat egg yolks in a good-sized bowl. Blend in lemon peel, lemon juice, butter, and milk.

4. In separate bowl, combine sugar, flour, and salt. Add to egg-lemon mixture, beating until smooth.

5. Fold into beaten egg whites.

6. Spoon into slow cooker.

7. Cover and cook on High 2–3 hours, or until tester inserted in center of cake comes out clean.

Gingerbread Pudding Cake

Katrina Eberly
Wernersville, PA

Makes 6–8 servings
Prep. Time: 20 minutes
Cooking Time: 2–2½ hours
Standing Time: 15 minutes
Ideal slow-cooker size: 4-qt.

Tbsp. (½ stick) butter, softened

¼ cup sugar

egg white

tsp. vanilla extract

½ cup molasses

cup water

¼ cups flour

¼ tsp. baking soda

½ tsp. ground cinnamon

½ tsp. ground ginger

¼ tsp. salt

¼ tsp. ground allspice

⅛ tsp. ground nutmeg

½ cup chopped pecans

Tbsp. brown sugar

Topping:

¼ cup hot water

⅔ Tbsp. (⅓ cup) butter, melted

1. Spray interior of slow cooker with cooking spray.

2. In a large mixing bowl, cream butter and sugar together until light and fluffy. Beat in egg white and vanilla.

TIP

I use blackstrap molasses, and the flavor doesn't overpower the cake.

3. In a separate bowl, combine molasses and water until blended.

4. In another bowl, combine flour, baking soda, and spices. Add to creamed mixture alternately with molasses mixture, beating well after each addition.

5. Fold in pecans. Spoon into slow cooker. Sprinkle with brown sugar.

6. In a small bowl, combine hot water and 5⅔ Tbsp. butter. Pour over batter. Do *not* stir.

7. Cover. Cook on High 2–2½ hours, or until toothpick inserted in center of cake comes out clean.

8. Turn off cooker. Let stand 15 minutes. Serve cake warm.

Sweets & Desserts

Seven-Layer Bars

Mary W. Stauffer
Ephrata, PA

Makes 6–8 servings
Prep. Time: 5–10 minutes
Cooking Time: 2–3 hours
Ideal slow-cooker size: large enough to
   hold your baking insert or bread pan

¼ cup (½ stick) butter, melted

½ cup graham cracker crumbs

½ cup chocolate chips

½ cup butterscotch chips

½ cup flaked coconut

½ cup chopped nuts

½ cup sweetened condensed milk

Why I like this recipe—

You can customize this—according to your
taste preferences, or according to what
you've got in your pantry. If you have only
butterscotch chips—or chocolate chips—use
them! Choose the nuts you like most. Either
sweetened or unsweetened flaked coconut
will work.

1. Grease interior of baking insert or bread
pan.

2. Layer ingredients into a baking insert or
bread pan that fits in your slow cooker, in the
order listed. Do not stir.

3. Cover and bake on High 2–3 hours, or
until firm. Remove pan and uncover. Let
stand 5 minutes.

4. Run knife around all sides of bars to
loosen from pan. Unmold carefully on plate
and cool.

Banana Chocolate Chip Bars

Carol Huber
Austin, TX

Makes 12–15 servings
Prep. Time: 20 minutes
Cooking Time: 2–3 hours
Ideal slow-cooker size: 6- or 7-qt., *oval*

¾ cup (1½ sticks) butter, softened
⅓ cup granulated sugar
⅓ cup brown sugar
 eggs
 tsp. vanilla
 ripe bananas, mashed
 cups flour
 tsp. baking powder
½ tsp. salt
2-oz. pkg. semisweet chocolate chips

1. Grease a loaf pan that will either hang on the edges of your oval slow-cooker crock, or will sit down in the slow-cooker crock on metal jar rings or small trivet.

2. In a good-sized mixing bowl, cream together butter and sugars.

3. Add eggs and vanilla. Mix well.

4. Stir in mashed bananas and stir well.

5. In a medium bowl, sift together flour, baking powder, and salt.

6. Stir dry ingredients into creamed mixture.

7. Stir in chocolate chips.

8. Pour into greased loaf pan.

9. Suspend pan on edges of slow-cooker crock, or place on trivet or jar rings on bottom of crock.

10. Vent slow-cooker lid at one end by propping it open with a wooden spoon handle or chopstick.

11. Cook on High 2–3 hours, or until toothpick inserted in center comes out clean.

12. Uncover pan and remove from cooker. Let cool before slicing into bars.

Why I like this recipe—

Whenever I have a really ripe banana, I mash it and put it in a labeled box in the freezer. I add to it when another too-ripe banana turns up on the counter. When I've got three, I make this recipe, knowing that these bars provide some nutrition along with their matchless flavor!

Sweets & Desserts

Gooey Cookie Dessert

Sue Hamilton
Benson, AZ

Makes 8 servings
Prep. Time: 10 minutes
Cooking Time: 2 hours
Ideal slow-cooker size: 5-qt.

3½ cups full-fat vanilla ice cream (half of 1¾ -quart container)

16½-oz. roll of refrigerated ready-to-bake chocolate chip cookie dough

1. Grease interior of slow-cooker crock.

2. Turn empty slow cooker to High to preheat.

3. Place ice cream in warmed crock, spreading and pushing it to make it a layer. Lumps are fine—they will melt.

4. Slice cookie dough into 12 slices.

5. Press the slices into the ice cream.

6. Cover and cook on High for 2 hours, until edges are browning and the center is cooked.

TIPS

1. Great served warm with whipped cream. It might be good cold but there is never any left.
2. Instead of measuring the ice cream, I cut the container in half. It saves the mess of measuring.

Variations:
Use different ice creams and different cookies—there are many flavor options!

Sweets & Desserts

Bread Pudding

Winifred Ewy
Newton, KS

Helen King
Fairbank, IA

Elaine Patton
West Middletown, PA

Makes 6 servings
Prep. Time: 20 minutes
Cooking Time: 3–4 hours
Ideal slow-cooker size: 4-qt.

3 slices bread (raisin bread is especially good), cubed

4 eggs

2 cups milk

¼ cup sugar

4 Tbsp. (½ stick) butter, softened

½ cup raisins (use only ¼ cup if using raisin bread)

½ tsp. cinnamon

Sauce:
2 Tbsp. (¼ stick) butter

2 Tbsp. flour

1 cup water

¾ cup sugar

1 tsp. vanilla

1. Grease interior of slow-cooker crock.

2. Place bread cubes into slow cooker.

3. Beat together eggs and milk. Stir in sugar, butter, raisins, and cinnamon. Pour over bread and stir.

4. Cover and cook on High 1 hour. Reduce heat to Low and cook 2–3 hours, or until instant-read thermometer reaches 160° when stuck into center of bread pudding.

5. Make sauce just before pudding is done baking. Melt butter in saucepan. Stir in flour until smooth. Gradually add water, sugar, and vanilla, stirring continually. Bring to boil. Cook, stirring constantly for 2 minutes, or until thickened.

6. Serve sauce over individual dishes of warm bread pudding.

Variations:
1. Use dried cherries instead of raisins. Use cherry flavoring in sauce instead of vanilla.
—Char Hagnes, Montague, MI

2. Use ¼ tsp. ground cinnamon and ¼ tsp. ground nutmeg instead of ½ tsp. ground cinnamon in pudding.

3. Use 8 cups day-old unfrosted cinnamon rolls instead of bread.
—Beatrice Orgist, Richardson, TX

Sweets & Desserts

White Chocolate Bread Pudding

Linda E. Wilcox
Blythewood, SC

Makes 5–6 servings
Prep. Time: 30 minutes
Cooking Time: 2–3 hours
Cooling Time: 30 minutes, and then 1–2 hours
Ideal slow-cooker size: 3- or 4-qt.

½ cup dried cranberries, *or* dried cherries
3 Tbsp. apple cider *or* brandy
8-oz. white chocolate bar
2 Tbsp. (¼ stick) butter
4 cups stale French bread, cubed, *divided*
4 eggs
½ cup sugar
1 cup half-and-half
1 tsp. vanilla

1. Combine dried fruit with cider or brandy in a microwave-safe bowl.

2. Microwave on High for 30 seconds. Set aside to cool (about 30 minutes).

3. Coarsely chop the chocolate. Set aside.

4. Drain the dried fruit. Set aside.

5. Spray interior of slow cooker with cooking spray.

6. Cover bottom of slow cooker with half the bread cubes.

7. Sprinkle half the chocolate and half the fruit over bread cubes.

8. Layer in remaining bread cubes. Top with all remaining fruit and then all remaining chocolate.

TIP

If you don't have stale French bread, cut a fresh loaf into slices. Then tear up the slices, leaving some crust on each piece if you can. Spread them on a towel on your counter, or on a baking sheet for a day—and you'll have stale pieces that are ready to go.

9. In a bowl beat eggs with whisk. Add sugar, half-and-half, and vanilla to eggs. Mix together thoroughly.

10. Pour over bread mixture and press down to make sure egg mixture covers all bread.

11. Cover and cook on High 2–3 hours.

12. Cool until warm or at room temperature.

Why I love this recipe—
My grandchildren love this dessert.

Apple-Nut Bread Pudding

Ruth Ann Hoover
New Holland, PA

Makes 6–8 servings
Prep. Time: 15 minutes
Cooking Time: 3–4 hours
Cooling Time: 1–2 hours
Ideal slow-cooker size: 4-qt.

8 slices raisin bread, cubed

2–3 medium-sized tart apples, peeled or unpeeled, and sliced

1 cup chopped pecans, toasted

1 cup sugar

1 tsp. ground cinnamon

½ tsp. ground nutmeg

3 eggs, lightly beaten

2 cups half-and-half

¼ cup apple juice

4 Tbsp. (½ stick) butter, melted

TIP

Ice cream is a great accompaniment.

1. Place bread cubes, apples, and pecans in greased slow cooker and mix together gently.

2. Combine sugar, cinnamon, and nutmeg in a good-sized mixing bowl.

3. Combine remaining ingredients in a bowl, mixing well.

4. Pour over bread mixture. Stir gently to mix thoroughly.

5. Cover. Cook on Low 3–4 hours, or until knife inserted in center comes out clean.

6. Serve warm (but not hot) or at room temperature.

QUICK
and
EASY

Easy Rice Pudding

Michele Ruvola
Vestal, NY

Makes 6 servings
Prep. Time: 5 minutes
Cooking Time: 4 hours
Ideal slow-cooker size: 5-qt.

2 quarts whole milk

1 cup uncooked Arborio rice

1 cup sugar

3 Tbsp. butter

1 tsp. vanilla

½ tsp. ground cinnamon

dash salt

1. Grease interior of slow-cooker crock.

2. Combine all ingredients in slow cooker. Stir to mix well.

3. Cover. Cook on Low 4 hours, or until creamy and thickened. Serve warm or chilled.

Variations:

1. Add raisins, nuts, or cranberries in Step 2 for different variations of rice pudding.
2. Add ½ tsp. ground cardamom for another variation.
3. For an adult version, add rum-soaked raisins to pudding and cook for 15 minutes more to heat through.
4. Use vanilla soy milk in place of cow's milk, although the pudding will be less creamy.

Chocolate Rice Pudding

Michele Ruvola
Selden, NY

Makes 4 servings
Prep. Time: 10 minutes
Cooking Time: 2½–3½ hours
Chilling Time: 2–5 hours
Ideal slow-cooker size: 3-qt.

4 cups cooked white rice

¾ cup sugar

¼ cup baking cocoa powder

3 Tbsp. butter, melted

1 tsp. vanilla

2 12-oz. cans evaporated milk

1. Combine all ingredients in greased slow cooker.

2. Cover. Cook on Low 2½–3½ hours, or until liquid is absorbed.

TIP

Serve warm or chilled. Top individual servings with a dollop of whipped cream, sliced toasted almonds, and/or a maraschino cherry if you wish.

Sweets & Desserts

Deluxe Tapioca Pudding

Michelle Showalter
Bridgewater, VA

Makes 16 servings
Prep. Time: 10 minutes
Cooking Time: 3½ hours
Chilling Time: 4–5 hours, or longer
Ideal slow-cooker size: 4-qt.

qts. milk
¼ cup dry small pearl tapioca
½ cups sugar
eggs, beaten
tsp. vanilla
3–4 cups whipped cream, *or* frozen whipped topping, thawed
chocolate candy bar

1. Grease interior of slow-cooker crock.

2. Combine milk, tapioca, and sugar in low cooker.

3. Cook on High 3 hours.

4. In a medium-sized mixing bowl, add a little hot milk mixture to beaten eggs. Stir.

5. Whisk eggs into milk mixture in slow cooker. Stir in vanilla.

6. Cover. Cook on High 20–30 minutes.

7. Cool to room temperature. Chill in refrigerator.

8. When fully chilled, beat with hand mixer to fluff pudding.

9. Fold in whipped cream or whipped topping. Garnish with chopped candy bar.

Why I like this recipe—
We have a family tradition that the kids pick out some of their Halloween candy bars and hand them over to me for this pudding. We do make this pudding at other times of the year, too, because it's so yummy.

Blushing Apple Tapioca

Julie Weaver
Reinholds, PA

Makes 8–10 servings
Prep. Time: 15–20 minutes
Cooking Time: 3–4 hours
Ideal slow-cooker size: 4- or 5-qt.

8–10 tart apples

½ cup sugar

4 Tbsp. quick-cooking raw tapioca

4 Tbsp. red cinnamon candy

½ cup water

1. Grease interior of slow-cooker crock.

2. Pare and core apples. Cut into eighths lengthwise and place in slow cooker.

3. Mix together sugar, tapioca, candy, and water. Pour over apples.

4. Cook on High 3–4 hours.

TIPS

Serve warm or cold. Top with whipped cream, if you wish.

QUICK and EASY

Marshmallow Applesauce Dessert

Marla Folkerts
Holland, OH

Makes 6-8 servings
Prep. Time: 5 minutes
Cooking Time: 1½-4 hours
Ideal slow-cooker size: 4-qt.

4 cups applesauce

¼ tsp. allspice

½ tsp. cinnamon

2 cups mini-marshmallows

1. Spray slow cooker with nonfat cooking spray.

2. In the cooker, mix applesauce, allspice, and cinnamon together.

3. Sprinkle marshmallows on top.

4. Cook on Low 3-4 hours, or on High 1½-2 hours.

TIP

Serve warm from slow cooker.

Why I like this recipe—
This is delicious over ice cream and cake.
We've even used it as a fondue for fruit.

Zesty Pears

Barbara Walker
Sturgis, SD

Makes 6 servings
Prep. Time: 15 minutes
Cooking Time: 4–6 hours
Ideal slow-cooker size: 2- or 3-qt.

6 fresh pears

½ cup raisins

¼ cup brown sugar

1 tsp. grated lemon peel

¼ cup brandy

½ cup sauterne wine

½ cup macaroon crumbs

sour cream, *optional*

1. Grease interior of slow-cooker crock.

2. Peel and core pears. Cut into thin slices and place in bowl.

3. In a separate small bowl, combine raisins, sugar, and lemon peel. Layer alternately with pear slices in slow cooker.

4. Pour brandy and wine over top.

5. Cover. Cook on Low 4–6 hours.

6. Spoon into serving dishes. Cool. Sprinkle with macaroons. Serve plain or topped with sour cream.

Why I like this recipe—
I love to make this dessert when company's coming. It's handy to have the slow cooker off to the side taking care of dessert while I use the stove for the rest of the meal. Plus, the pears look beautiful in their glass dessert dishes.

Sweets & Desserts

Raisin Nut-Stuffed Apples

Margaret Rich
North Newton, KS

Makes 6 servings
Prep. Time: 15 minutes
Cooking Time: 6–8 hours
Ideal slow-cooker size: 5-qt.

 baking apples, cored
 Tbsp. (¼ stick) butter, melted
¼ cup packed brown sugar
¼ cup raisins
 Tbsp. chopped walnuts
½ cup water

1. Grease interior of slow-cooker crock.

2. Peel a strip around each apple about one-third of the way below the stem end to prevent splitting.

3. Mix together butter and brown sugar. Stir in raisins and walnuts. Stuff into apple cavities.

4. Stand apples in slow cooker. Add water.

5. Cover and cook on Low 6–8 hours, or until apples are tender but still holding their shape.

Why I like this recipe—
This is a lovely fall and winter dessert. My friend Barbara makes this whole recipe for herself and her husband, and then they eat the apples with oatmeal for breakfast throughout the week.

Rhubarb Sauce

Esther Porter
Minneapolis, MN

Makes 4–6 servings
Prep. Time: 10 minutes
Cooking Time: 4–5 hours
Ideal slow-cooker size: 3-qt.

1½ lbs. rhubarb

⅛ tsp. salt

½ cup water

½–⅔ cup sugar

1. Grease interior of slow-cooker crock.

2. Cut rhubarb into ½-inch-thick slices.

3. Combine all ingredients in slow cooker. Cook on Low 4–5 hours, or until rhubarb is soft but not mushy.

4. Serve chilled.

Variation:
Add 1 pint sliced strawberries about 30 minutes before removing from heat.

Sweets & Desserts

Strawberry Rhubarb Sauce

Tina Snyder
Manheim, PA

Makes 6–8 servings
Prep. Time: 10 minutes
Cooking Time: 4–5 hours
Ideal slow-cooker size: 3-qt.

cups rhubarb, cut into ½-inch-thick slices

cup sugar

cinnamon stick

½ cup white grape juice

cups sliced strawberries

1. Grease interior of slow-cooker crock.

2. Place rhubarb in slow cooker. Pour sugar ver rhubarb. Add cinnamon stick and grape uice. Stir well.

3. Cover and cook on Low 3–4 hours, or ntil rhubarb is almost tender.

4. Stir in strawberries. Cook 1 hour longer.

5. Remove cinnamon stick. Chill.

6. Serve as is, or over cake or ice cream.

Why I like this recipe—
My neighbor has a prolific rhubarb plant, and every spring, she gives me a bag. This is our favorite way to eat it.

Sweets & Desserts

Fresh Fruit Compote

**Beatrice Orgish
Richardson, TX**

Makes 8 servings
Prep. Time: 15 minutes
Cooking Time: 3–4 hours
Ideal slow-cooker size: 3- or 4-qt.

2 medium tart apples, peeled

2 medium fresh peaches, peeled and cubed

2 cups unsweetened pineapple chunks

1¼ cups unsweetened pineapple juice

¼ cup honey

2 ¼-inch-thick lemon slices.

3½-inch-long cinnamon stick

1 medium firm banana, thinly sliced

1. Grease interior of slow-cooker crock.

2. Cut apples into ¼-inch slices and then in half horizontally. Place in slow cooker.

3. Add peaches, pineapple chunks, pineapple juice, honey, lemon slices, and cinnamon. Cover and cook on Low 3–4 hours.

4. Stir in banana slices just before serving.

Garnish with whipped cream, sliced almonds, and maraschino cherries, if you wish.

Sweets & Desserts

Fruit Medley

Angeline Lang
Greeley, CO

Makes 6–8 servings
Prep. Time: 10 minutes
Cooking Time: 2¼–3¼ hours
Ideal slow-cooker size: 3-qt.

½ lbs. mixed dried fruit

½ cups water

cup sugar

Tbsp. honey

eel of half a lemon, cut into thin strips

⅛ tsp. nutmeg

cinnamon stick

Tbsp. cornstarch

¼ cup cold water

¼ cup Cointreau

TIPS

Serve warm or chilled. Serve as a side dish with the main course, as a dessert on its own, or as a topping for ice cream.

1. Grease interior of slow-cooker crock.

2. Place dried fruit in slow cooker. Pour in water.

3. Stir in sugar, honey, lemon peel, nutmeg, and cinnamon.

4. Cover and cook on Low 2–3 hours. Turn cooker to High.

5. In a small bowl, mix cornstarch into water until smooth. Stir into fruit mixture. Cook on High 10 minutes, or until thickened.

6. Stir in Cointreau.

Scandinavian Fruit Soup

Willard E. Roth
Elkhart, IN

Makes 12 servings
Prep. Time: 5 minutes
Cooking Time: 8 hours
Ideal slow-cooker size: 4-qt.

1 cup dried apricots

1 cup dried sliced apples

1 cup dried pitted dried plums

1 cup canned pitted red cherries

½ cup quick-cooking tapioca

1 cup grape juice *or* red wine

3 cups water *or* more

½ cup orange juice

¼ cup lemon juice

1 Tbsp. grated orange peel

½ cup brown sugar

1. Grease interior of slow-cooker crock.

2. Combine apricots, apples, dried plums, cherries, tapioca, and grape juice in slow cooker.

TIPS

Serve warm or cold, as a soup or dessert. Delicious served chilled over vanilla ice cream or frozen yogurt.

3. Cover with water.

4. Cook on Low for at least 8 hours.

5. Before serving, stir in remaining ingredients.

Sweets & Desserts

Festive Applesauce

Dawn Day
Westminster, CA

Makes 12 servings
Prep. Time: 25 minutes
Cooking Time: 6 hours
Ideal slow-cooker size: 5-qt.

medium apples, mixed varieties, peeled and
  cubed

pears, peeled and cubed

cup fresh *or* frozen cranberries

-inch piece fresh ginger root, minced

Tbsp. dark brown sugar

/2 cup apple cider

tsp. ground cinnamon

/4 tsp. ground nutmeg

/4 tsp. ground cloves

pinch salt

juice and zest of 1 lemon

1. Grease interior of slow-cooker crock.

2. Combine all ingredients in slow cooker
except lemon zest and juice.

3. Cover and cook on Low 6 hours, or until
apples and pears are soft and falling apart.

4. Stir in lemon zest and juice. Serve hot,
warm, or chilled.

Why I like this recipe—
This is a good side dish with pork or chicken
for a holiday—or, really, any time.

Chunky Cranberry Applesauce

Christie Anne Detamore-Hunsberger
Harrisonburg, VA

Makes 6 servings
Prep. Time: 15 minutes
Cooking Time: 3–4 hours
Ideal slow-cooker size: 4-qt.

6 McIntosh, *or* Winesap, *or* your favorite baking apple, peeled *or* unpeeled, cut into 1-inch cubes

½ cup apple juice

½ cup fresh *or* frozen cranberries

¼ cup sugar

¼ tsp. ground cinnamon, *optional*

1. Grease interior of slow-cooker crock.

2. Combine all ingredients in slow cooker.

3. Cover and cook on Low 3–4 hours, or until apples are as soft as you like them.

4. Serve warm, or refrigerate and serve chilled. Serve the sauce as a side dish during the main course. Or have it for dessert, topping pound cake or ice cream.

Why I like this recipe—
My aunt requested this recipe from me, and she always makes it for her Thanksgiving dinner. It's delicious and so easy.

Sweets & Desserts

Whole Cranberry Sauce

Sherril Bieberly
Salina, KS

Makes 5–6 servings
Prep. Time: 5 minutes
Cooking Time: 5–6 hours
Chilling Time: 6–8 hours, or overnight
Ideal slow-cooker size: 2-qt.

2-oz pkg. cranberries

 cups sugar

½ cup brandy, *or* white grape juice, *or* apple
 juice

½–¼ cup walnuts, *optional*

1. Grease interior of slow-cooker crock.

2. Place first 3 ingredients in slow cooker.
Cook on Low 5–6 hours, stirring occasionally
if you're home and able to do so.

3. Spoon cooked cranberries into dish and
refrigerate overnight. Serve cold.

4. If you wish, chop the nuts. Spread out
in a single layer in a dry nonstick skillet over
medium heat. Stir occasionally, heating nuts
until toasted.

5. Allow to cool, and then stir into
cranberry sauce before serving.

TIPS

You can prepare this several days
ahead of serving it, and then refrigerate
it until you're ready for it. But wait to stir
in the nuts until just before serving so
they don't get soft.

Cranberry Sauce with Red Wine and Oranges

Donna Treloar
Muncie, IN

Makes 3-4 servings
Prep. Time: 5-10 minutes
Cooking Time: 2-2½ hours
Ideal slow-cooker size: 2-qt.

12-oz. bag fresh cranberries, rinsed
1½ cups sugar
1 cup dry red wine
1 cinnamon stick
grated zest of one orange, then cut orange in
   half
4 whole cloves

1. Grease interior of slow-cooker crock.

2. Combine cranberries, sugar, wine,
cinnamon stick, and zest in slow cooker.

3. Place 2 cloves in each orange half. Push
orange pieces down into cranberry mixture.

4. Cover. Cook on High 2–2½ hours, or
until cranberries have popped. Turn off
cooker.

5. Discard cinnamon stick and orange
halves with cloves.

6. Remove lid and let sauce cool to room
temperature.

7. Serve chilled or at room temperature
over ice cream or pound cake.

Why I like this recipe—
We love the flavor of this sauce, a bit different
from the typical dessert sauces.

Southwest Cranberries

Bernita Boyts
Shawnee Mission, KS

Makes 8 servings
Prep. Time: 5 minutes
Cooking Time: 2–3 hours
Ideal slow-cooker size: 2-qt.

16-oz. can whole berry cranberry sauce

10½-oz. jar jalapeño jelly

2 Tbsp. chopped fresh cilantro

1. Grease interior of slow-cooker crock.

2. Combine ingredients in slow cooker.

3. Cover. Cook on Low 2–3 hours.

4. Cool. Serve at room temperature.

TIP

Serve these spicy cranberries as a side dish or as a marinade for poultry or pork.

Sweets & Desserts

Dates in Cardamom Coffee Syrup

Margaret W. High
Lancaster, PA

Makes 12 servings
Prep. Time: 15 minutes
Cooking Time: 7–8 hours
Ideal slow-cooker size: 3-qt.

2 cups pitted, whole dried dates

2½ cups very strong, hot coffee

2 Tbsp. sugar

15 whole green cardamom pods

4-inch cinnamon stick

plain Greek yogurt, for serving

1. Combine dates, coffee, sugar, cardamom, and cinnamon in slow cooker.

2. Cover and cook on High for 1 hour. Remove lid and continue to cook on High for 5–7 hours until sauce has reduced.

3. Pour dates and sauce into container and chill in fridge.

4. To serve, put a scoop of Greek yogurt in a small dish and add a few dates on top. Drizzle with a little sauce.

TIPS

1. I make decaf coffee for this recipe, using a few extra scoops of ground coffee when I make it.
2. The dates get tastier the longer they sit in the sauce, up to 2 weeks in the fridge.

Chocolate Nut Clusters from the Crock

A. Catherine Boshart
Lebanon, PA

Makes 24 servings
Prep. Time: 15 minutes
Cooking Time: 2 hours
Chilling Time: 45 minutes
Ideal slow-cooker size: 4-qt.

1½-lb. pkg. almond bark
4-oz. pkg. sweet German chocolate bar
8 oz. dark chocolate chips
8 oz. peanut butter chips
1 lb. salted peanuts
1 lb. unsalted peanuts

1. Layer ingredients into slow cooker in order as listed.

2. Cover. Cook on Low for 2 hours. Do not stir or lift lid during cooking time.

3. At end of 2 hours, stir and mix well.

4. Drop by teaspoonsful or tablespoonsful on wax paper or parchment paper.

5. Refrigerate for 45 minutes until hard.

6. Store in tight container in cool place.

Why I like this recipe—
We mix up a batch of these clusters on our cookie-baking day in December. They work so well because they don't require the oven and they look beautiful with the assortment of cookies.

Easy Chocolate Clusters

Marcella Stalter
Flanagan, IL

Makes 3½ dozen clusters
Prep. Time: 5 minutes
Cooking Time: 2 hours
Standing Time: 2 hours
Ideal slow-cooker size: 4-qt.

2 lbs. white coating chocolate, broken into small pieces

2 cups (12 oz.) semisweet chocolate chips

4-oz. pkg. sweet German chocolate bar, broken

24-oz. jar roasted peanuts

1. Combine coating chocolate, chocolate chips, and German chocolate bar in slow cooker.

2. Cover and cook on High 1 hour.

3. Reduce heat to Low and cook 1 hour longer, or until chocolate is melted, stirring every 15 minutes. Make sure chocolate doesn't begin to scorch or burn.

4. Stir in peanuts. Mix well.

5. Drop by teaspoonsful onto wax paper. Let stand until set. Store at room temperature.

Why I like this recipe—
The flavors of chocolate are wonderful together here, and the coating chocolate makes it easy to work with. We make these every Christmas.

Chocolate Covered Pretzels

Beth Maurer
Harrisonburg, VA

Makes 10–12 servings
Prep. Time: 10 minutes
Cooking Time: 30+ minutes
Ideal slow-cooker size: 2-qt.

1 lb. white chocolate bark coating

2 blocks chocolate bark coating

1 bag pretzel rods

1. Chop white chocolate into small chunks. Place in slow cooker.

2. Cover. Heat on Low setting, stirring occasionally until melted, about 30 minutes. Turn off cooker.

3. Using a spoon, coat ¾ of each pretzel rod with chocolate. Place on wax paper to cool.

4. Chop chocolate bark into small chunks. Microwave on High in a microwave-safe bowl for 1½ minutes. Stir. Microwave on High 1 more minute. Stir.

5. Microwave on High in 30-second intervals until chocolate is smooth when stirred. (Do not allow chocolate to get too hot or it will scorch.)

6. Put melted chocolate in small bag. Snip off corner of bag. Drizzle chocolate over white chocolate covered pretzels.

TIP

These are easy to make. They also taste wonderful and are good holiday gifts when thoroughly cooled and placed in small gift bags!

Maple Apple Topping

Donna Lantgen
Arvada, CO

Makes 6 servings
Prep. Time: 10–12 minutes
Cooking Time: 6 hours
Ideal slow-cooker size: 4-qt.

6–8 cups apples, cored, peeled, and chopped

¾ cup brown sugar

1 cup apple cider

½ cup maple syrup

1. Put apples in slow cooker.

2. Mix brown sugar, apple cider, and maple syrup in a bowl.

3. Drizzle cider mixture over apples.

4. Cook 6 hours on Low.

TIP

This is great on top of vanilla ice cream or on waffles.

Sweets & Desserts

Apple Caramel Peanut Topping

Jeanette Oberholtzer
Manheim, PA

Makes 7 servings
Prep. Time: 15 minutes
Cooking Time: 6 hours
Ideal slow-cooker size: 2-qt.

½ cup apple juice

7 ozs. caramels, unwrapped

1 tsp. vanilla

⅛ tsp. ground cardamom

½ tsp. ground cinnamon

⅓ cup creamy peanut butter

2 medium apples, peeled, cored, and cut in wedges

Serve about ⅓ cup warm mixture over individual slices of angel food cake, and then top each with ice cream.

1. Combine apple juice, caramel candies, vanilla, and spices in slow cooker.

2. Drop peanut butter, 1 Tbsp. at a time, into slow cooker. Stir well after each addition.

3. Gently stir in apple wedges.

4. Cover. Cook on Low 5 hours.

5. Stir well.

6. Cover. Then cook 1 more hour on Low.

Bold Butterscotch Sauce

Margaret W. High
Lancaster, PA

Makes 16 servings
Prep. Time: 10 minutes
Cooking Time: 2–3 hours
Ideal slow-cooker size: 3-qt.

/₂ cup (1 stick) salted butter
1 cup dark brown sugar, packed
1 cup heavy cream
/₂ tsp. salt, *or* more to taste
2 tsp. vanilla extract, *or* more to taste

1. Cut butter in slices. Add to heatproof bowl that will fit in your slow cooker.

2. Add sugar, cream, and salt.

3. Place bowl with butter mixture in crock. Add water so that it comes halfway up the sides of the bowl.

4. Cover and cook on High 2–3 hours, until sauce is steaming hot.

5. Wearing oven mitts to protect your knuckles, remove hot bowl from cooker.

6. Add vanilla. Stir. Taste. Add more vanilla and/or salt to achieve a bold butterscotch flavor.

TIP

Store butterscotch sauce in lidded jar in fridge for several weeks. Warm and stir before serving.

Why I like this recipe—
This sauce is fabulous poured over chocolate cake, gingerbread, angel food cake with berries, vanilla ice cream, sliced pears, and graham cracker pudding (and also eaten straight from the fridge, cold!).

Chocolate Fondue with Kirsch

Eleanor J. Ferreira
North Chelmsford, MA

Makes 6 servings
Prep. Time: 5 minutes
Cooking Time: 1–1½ hours
Ideal slow-cooker size: 2-qt.

1 pkg. (8 squares) semisweet chocolate

4-oz. pkg. sweet cooking chocolate

¾ cup sweetened condensed milk

¼ cup sugar

2 Tbsp. kirsch

1. Break both chocolates into pieces and place in cooker. Set cooker to High and stir chocolate constantly until it melts.

2. Turn cooker to Low and stir in milk and sugar. Stir until thoroughly blended.

3. Stir in kirsch. Cover and cook on Low 1–1½ hours or until fondue comes to a very gentle simmer.

TIP

Bring fondue to table, along with fresh cherries with stems and sponge cake squares to dip into it.

Chocolate Fondue with Almonds and Marshmallows

Vera Schmucker
Goshen, IN

Vicki Dinkel
Sharon Springs, KS

Makes 8–10 servings
Prep. Time: 10 minutes
Cooking Time: 3–7 hours
Ideal slow-cooker size: 3½-qt.

Tbsp. butter

6 1-oz. chocolate candy bars with almonds, unwrapped and broken

0 large marshmallows

⅓ cups milk, *divided*

ngel food cake cubes; strawberries; chunks of pineapple, bananas, apples, oranges; pretzel pieces

1. Grease slow cooker with butter. Turn to High for 10 minutes.

2. Add chocolate, marshmallows, and ⅓ up milk.

3. Cover. Turn cooker to Low. Stir after 30 minutes.

4. Continue cooking for another 30 minutes, or until mixture is melted and smooth.

5. Gradually add remaining milk.

6. Cover. Cook on Low 2–6 hours.

7. Bring cooker to table, along with angel food cake, fruit chunks, and pretzels for dipping.

Why I like this recipe—

My son requested this fondue for his ninth birthday party. All the boys enjoyed this so much, although I kept wipes on the table because their hands got messy quickly.

Sweets & Desserts

Hot Fudge Sauce

Beth Nafziger
Lowville, NY

Makes 1½ cups
Prep. Time: 15 minutes
Ideal slow-cooker size: 1-qt.

¾ cup semisweet chocolate chips

4 Tbsp. (½ stick) butter

⅔ cup sugar

5-oz. can (⅔ cup) evaporated milk

1. In a small heavy saucepan melt chocolate and butter together.

2. Add sugar. Gradually stir in evaporated milk.

3. Bring mixture to a boil, and then reduce heat. Boil gently over low heat for 8 minutes, stirring frequently.

4. Remove pan from heat. Pour sauce into slow cooker.

5. Set cooker control to Warm—the ideal temperature for serving.

TIP

Use as a dipping sauce for angel food cake cubes, banana chunks, pineapple chunks, and mini-pretzels.

Why I like this recipe—
I have served this for many years as part of our family Christmas Eve celebration.

Sweets & Desserts

Texas Queso Dip

Donna Treloar
Muncie, IN

Janie Steele
Moore, OK

Makes 2 quarts dip
Prep. Time: 10 minutes
Cooking Time: 2 hours
Ideal slow-cooker size: 4-qt.

1 lb. loose spicy ground pork sausage (squeeze it out of its casings if that's the only way you can find it.)

2-lb. block Mexican-style Velveeta cheese, cubed

10-oz. can diced tomatoes with chilies

½ cup milk

1. Grease interior of slow-cooker crock.

2. Brown sausage in skillet, breaking it into small chunks as it browns.

3. Drain off drippings.

4. Combine cheese, tomatoes, and milk in slow cooker.

5. Stir in browned sausage.

6. Cover and cook 2 hours on Low.

Hot Cheese and Bacon Dip

Lee Ann Hazlett
Freeport, IL

Makes 6–8 servings
Prep. Time: 15 minutes
Cooking Time: 1 hour
Ideal slow-cooker size: 2- or 3-qt.

16 slices bacon, diced, either store-bought or done yourself

2 8-oz. pkgs. cream cheese, cubed and softened

4 cups shredded mild cheddar cheese

1 cup half-and-half

2 tsp. Worcestershire sauce

1 tsp. dried minced onion

½ tsp. dry mustard

½ tsp. salt

2–3 drops Tabasco

Serve with fruit slices or French bread slices. (Dip fruit in lemon juice to prevent browning.)

1. Grease interior of slow-cooker crock.

2. Brown and drain bacon if you've decided to DIY. Set aside.

3. Mix remaining ingredients in slow cooker.

4. Cover. Cook on Low 1 hour, stirring occasionally until cheese melts.

5. Stir in bacon.

Appetizers, Snacks,
Spreads & Beverages

QUICK
and
EASY

Championship Bean Dip

**Renee Shirk
Mt. Joy, PA**

**Ada Miller
Sugarcreek, OH**

Makes 4½ cups dip
Prep. Time: 10 minutes
Cooking Time: 2 hours
Ideal slow-cooker size: 3-qt.

15-oz. can refried beans

1 cup picante sauce

1 cup (4 oz.) shredded Monterey Jack cheese

1 cup (4 oz.) shredded cheddar cheese

¾ cup sour cream

3-oz. pkg. cream cheese, softened

1 Tbsp. chili powder

¼ tsp. ground cumin

1. Grease interior of slow-cooker crock.

2. Combine all ingredients in a bowl. Transfer to slow cooker.

3. Cover. Cook on Low 2 hours, or until heated through, stirring once or twice.

TIP

Serve with tortilla chips and salsa.

Creamy Taco Dip

**Elaine Rineer
Lancaster, PA**

Makes 10–12 servings
Prep. Time: 15 minutes
Cooking Time: 2–3 hours
Ideal slow-cooker size: 2-or 3-qt.

1½ lbs. ground beef

1 envelope dry taco seasoning mix

16-oz. jar of salsa

2 cups sour cream

1 cup cheddar cheese, grated

1. Grease interior of slow-cooker crock.

2. Brown ground beef in nonstick skillet. Drain.

3. Place beef in cooker. Stir in taco seasoning and salsa.

4. Stir in sour cream and cheese.

5. Cover and cook on Low 2–3 hours, or until hot in the center.

6. Serve with tortilla chips.

Why I like this recipe—
This is just a traditional crowd-pleaser. It's straightforward, delicious, and versatile. Serve it with veggies or crackers, too, or on top of salad as a taco salad.

Hot Chili Dip

Lavina Hochstedler
Grand Blanc, MI

Anna Stoltzfus
Honey Brook, PA

Kathi Rogge
Alexandria, IN

Makes 5–6 cups
Prep. Time: 5–10 minutes
Cooking Time: 1–2 hours
Ideal slow-cooker size: 3-qt.

24-oz. jar hot salsa
15-oz. can chili with beans
2 2-oz. cans sliced ripe olives, drained
12 ozs. mild cheese, cubed
tortilla chips

1. Grease interior of slow-cooker crock.

2. Combine all ingredients except tortilla chips in slow cooker.

3. Cover. Cook on Low 1–2 hours, or until cheese is melted, stirring halfway through.

4. Serve with tortilla chips.

Why I like this recipe—
The addition of black olives kicks this dip up a notch. For extra pizzazz, sprinkle with chopped cilantro as a garnish.

Cheese and Crab Dip

Donna Lantgen
Rapid City, SD

Makes 5 cups
Prep. Time: 10 minutes
Cooking Time: 2 hours
Ideal slow-cooker size: 3-qt.

3 8-oz. pkgs. cream cheese, softened

2 6-oz. cans crabmeat, drained

1 can broken shrimp, drained

6 Tbsp. finely chopped onions

1 tsp. horseradish

½ cup toasted almonds

broken assorted crackers and/or bread cubes

1. Grease interior of slow-cooker crock.

2. Combine all ingredients, except crackers and/or bread cubes, in slow cooker.

3. Cover. Cook on Low 2 hours.

4. Serve with crackers or bread cubes.

Variation:
Add 2 tsp. Worcestershire sauce to Step 2 for added zest.

    —Dorothy VanDeest, Memphis, TN

Creamy Artichoke Dip

Jessica Stoner
West Liberty, OH

Makes 7–8 cups
Prep. Time: 15–20 minutes
Cooking Time: 1–1½ hours
Ideal slow-cooker size: 3-qt.

2 14-oz. cans water-packed artichoke hearts, coarsely chopped (drain one can; stir juice from other can into dip)

2 cups (8 oz.) shredded, part-skim mozzarella cheese

8-oz. pkg. cream cheese, softened and cubed

1 cup grated Parmesan cheese

½ cup shredded Swiss cheese

½ cup mayonnaise

2 Tbsp. lemon juice

2 Tbsp. plain yogurt

1 Tbsp. seasoned salt

1 Tbsp. chopped, seeded jalapeño pepper

1 tsp. garlic powder

tortilla chips

Variation:
Add 2 10-oz. pkgs. frozen chopped spinach, thawed and squeezed dry, to Step 2.
—Steven Lantz, Denver, CO

1. Grease interior of slow-cooker crock.

2. In slow cooker, combine artichoke hearts and reserved juice, cheeses, mayonnaise, lemon juice, yogurt, salt, jalapeño pepper, and garlic powder.

3. Cover. Cook on Low 1 hour, or until cheeses are melted and dip is hot in the center.

4. Serve with tortilla chips.

Fix-It and Forget-It Slow Cooker Champion Recipes 537

Italiano Spread

Nanci Keatley
Salem, OR

Makes 8 servings
Prep. Time: 15 minutes
Cooking Time: 2–3 hours
Ideal slow-cooker size: 2- or 3-qt.

2 8-oz. pkgs. cream cheese, softened and cubed

1 cup prepared pesto

3 medium tomatoes, chopped

1 cup mozzarella cheese, shredded

½ cup Parmesan cheese, shredded

2 Tbsp. olive oil

Spread on crackers or slices of Italian bread.

1. Grease interior of slow-cooker crock.

2. Spread cream cheese cubes over bottom of slow cooker.

3. Drop spoonfuls of pesto over cream cheese.

4. Add a layer of chopped tomatoes over cream cheese and pesto.

5. Sprinkle shredded cheeses on top of tomatoes.

6. Drizzle olive oil over top.

7. Cook on Low 2–3 hours or until cheeses are melted.

Roasted Pepper and Artichoke Spread

Sherril Bieberly
Sauna, KS

Makes 3 cups, or about 12 servings
Prep. Time: 10 minutes
Cooking Time: 1 hour
Ideal slow-cooker size: 2- or 3-qt.

1 cup grated Parmesan cheese

1/2 cup mayonnaise

8-oz. pkg. cream cheese, softened and cubed

1 garlic clove, minced

14-oz. can artichoke hearts, drained and chopped finely

1/3 cup finely chopped roasted red bell peppers (from 7¼-oz. jar)

TIP

Use as spread for crackers, cut-up fresh vegetables, or snack bread slices.

1. Grease interior of slow-cooker crock.

2. Combine Parmesan cheese, mayonnaise, cream cheese, and garlic in food processor. Process until smooth. Place mixture in slow cooker.

3. Add artichoke hearts and red bell pepper. Stir well.

4. Cover. Cook on Low 1 hour or until hot in center. Stir again just before serving.

Hot Cheddar Mushroom Spread

Amber Swarey
Honea Path, SC

Makes 3¼–3½ cups
Prep. Time: 10 minutes
Cooking Time: 1–1½ hours
Ideal slow-cooker size: 2-qt.

1 cup mayonnaise

1 cup (4 oz.) shredded cheddar cheese

⅓ cup grated Parmesan cheese

2 4-oz. cans sliced mushrooms, drained

half an envelope ranch salad dressing mix

minced fresh parsley

assorted crackers

1. Grease interior of slow-cooker crock.

2. Combine mayonnaise, cheeses, mushrooms, and dressing mix in slow cooker.

3. Cover. Cook on Low 1 hour, or until cheeses are melted and dip is heated through.

4. Sprinkle with parsley and serve with crackers.

Why I like this recipe—
My husband has been known to make grilled cheese sandwiches with this spread in the place of cheese. Decadent and delicious!

Crab Spread

Jeanette Oberholtzer
Manheim, PA

Makes 8 servings
Prep. Time: 20 minutes
Cooking Time: 1 hour
Ideal slow-cooker size: 2- or 3-qt.

½ cup mayonnaise

-oz. pkg. cream cheese, softened

Tbsp. apple juice

onion, minced

lb. lump crabmeat, picked over to remove
cartilage and shell bits

nack crackers, snack bread, and/or crudités

1. Grease interior of slow-cooker crock.

2. Mix mayonnaise, cheese, and juice in
nedium-sized bowl until blended.

3. Stir in onions, mixing well. Gently stir
n crabmeat.

4. Place in slow cooker. Cover and cook on
Low for 1 hour, or until hot in the center.

5. Serve with snack crackers, snack bread,
and/or crudités.

Why I like this recipe—
We were first introduced to this crab spread
at the beach, when our friends had gotten
fresh crabmeat and wanted to keep its flavor
front and center in the recipe. It's a family
favorite of ours now!

Appetizers, Snacks,
Spreads & Beverages

Sausages in Wine

Mary E. Wheatley
Mashpee, MA

Makes 6 servings or 24 appetizers
Prep. Time: 15 minutes
Cooking Time: 45 minutes–1 hour
Ideal slow-cooker size: 3-qt.

1 cup dry red wine

2 Tbsp. currant jelly

6-8 mild Italian sausages, *or* Polish sausages

1. Grease interior of slow cooker crock.

2. Place wine and jelly in slow cooker. Heat until jelly is dissolved and sauce begins to simmer. Add sausages.

3. Cover. Cook on High 45 minutes to 1 hour, or until sausages are cooked through and lightly glazed.

4. Transfer sausages to a cutting board and slice. Serve with juices spooned over.

Why I like this recipe—
I love the simplicity of this recipe—the flavor it yields is definitely more than the sum of its parts! You can vary the flavors according to what sausage you choose, of course. One of my friends uses turkey sausages with sage.

Curried Almonds

Barbara Aston
Ashdown, AR

Makes 4 cups nuts
Prep. Time: 5 minutes
Cooking Time: 3 hours
Ideal slow-cooker size: 3-qt.

2 Tbsp. (¼ stick) melted butter

1 Tbsp. curry powder

½ tsp. seasoned salt

1 lb. blanched almonds

1. Grease interior of slow-cooker crock.

2. In a small bowl, combine butter with curry powder and seasoned salt.

3. Pour over almonds in slow cooker. Mix to coat well.

4. Cover. Cook on Low 2 hours.

5. Turn to High. Uncover cooker and cook 1 hour.

TIP

Serve hot or cold.

Spicy Nut and Pretzel Mix

Sharon Miller
Holmesville, OH

Makes 13 cups
Prep. Time: 15 minutes
Cooking Time: 3–4 hours
Ideal slow-cooker size: 4- or 5-qt.

6 Tbsp. (¾ stick) butter, melted

1-oz. packet taco seasoning mix

¾ tsp. ground cinnamon

⅛-¼ tsp. cayenne, depending on your taste preferences

2 cups pecan halves

2 cups roasted cashews, unsalted

2 cups walnut halves

2 cups whole almonds, unblanched

3 cups Goldfish, *or* bite-sized cheese, crackers

2 cups pretzel nuggets *or* sticks

1. Grease interior of slow-cooker crock.

2. Mix butter and seasonings in slow cooker.

TIP

You can make this a day before your party. Just be sure to store it in an airtight container.

3. Add all remaining ingredients and toss together gently.

4. Cook uncovered on Low 3–4 hours, stirring every 30 minutes until nuts are toasted. Turn off heat.

5. Serve from slow cooker with large spoon, or pour into big serving bowl.

Pumpkin Butter

Emily Fox
Bethel, PA

Makes approximately 6½ cups
Prep. Time: 5–10 minutes
Cooking Time: 11–12 hours
Ideal slow-cooker size: 3-qt.

3 cups pumpkin purée

2¾ cups light brown sugar

2½ tsp. pumpkin pie spice

1. Grease interior of slow-cooker crock.

2. Mix pumpkin purée, brown sugar, and pumpkin pie spice together in slow cooker.

3. Cook *uncovered* on Low for 11–12 hours, depending on how thick you'd like the butter to be. Cool.

4. Serve on bread or rolls for seasonal eating.

TIPS

1. Refrigerate or freeze until ready to use.
2. You could replace 3 cups pumpkin purée with 3 cups applesauce for a different twist on pumpkin butter.

Apricot Butter

Janet L. Roggie
Lowville, NY

Makes 15 cups
Prep. Time: 10 minutes
Cooking Time: 8 hours
Ideal slow-cooker size: 5-qt.

4 28-oz. cans apricots, drained

3 cups sugar

2 tsp. cinnamon

½ tsp. ground cloves

2 Tbsp. lemon juice

1. Grease interior of slow-cooker crock.

2. Purée fruit in food processor. Pour into slow cooker.

3. Stir in remaining ingredients.

4. Cover and cook on Low 8 hours.

5. Pour into hot, sterilized 1-cup or 1-pt. jars. Process according to standard canning methods.

6. Serve as a spread with bread, or as a sauce with pork or chicken dishes.

Why I like this recipe—
Apricot Butter has such a decadent texture and flavor and it's so easy to make! I make it any time of year.

Hot Caramel Dip

**Marilyn Yoder
Archbold, OH**

Makes about 3 cups dip
Prep. Time: 5 minutes
Cooking Time: none
Ideal slow-cooker size: 2½-qt.

½ cup (1 stick) butter
½ cup light corn syrup
 cup brown sugar
 can sweetened condensed milk
apple slices

1. Grease interior of slow-cooker crock.

2. Mix together all ingredients except apples in saucepan. Bring to boil over medium to low heat. I recommend creating the caramel dip on the stovetop so you can adjust the heat to prevent sticking and burning, and so you can stir frequently. Things happen fast, so stay nearby.

3. When the dip comes to a boil, pour it into your slow cooker.

4. Set on Low and serve.

TIP

Dip fresh apple slices into hot caramel.

Variation:
Add ½ cup peanut butter in Step 2.

Slow-Cooker Chai

Kathy Hertzler
Lancaster, PA

Makes 18 servings
Prep. Time: 10 minutes
Cooking Time: 1–1½ hours
Ideal slow-cooker size: 5-qt.

1 gallon water
16 regular black tea bags
8 opened cardamom pods
9 whole cloves
3 Tbsp. gingerroot, freshly grated *or* chopped
   fine
3 cinnamon sticks
8-oz. can sweetened condensed milk
12-oz. can evaporated milk (regular *or* fat-free
   are equally good)

1. Pour one gallon water into slow cooker. Turn cooker to High and bring water to a boil.

2. Tie tea bag strings together. Remove paper tags. Place in slow cooker, submerging in boiling water.

3. Place cardamom seeds and pods, cloves, and ginger in a tea ball.

4. Place tea ball and cinnamon sticks in boiling water in slow cooker. Reduce heat to Low and steep, along with tea bags, for 10 minutes.

5. After 10 minutes, remove tea bags. Allow spices to remain in cooker. Increase heat to High.

6. Add condensed milk and evaporated milk. Bring mixture just to the boiling point.

7. Immediately turn back to Low. Remove spices 30 minutes later.

8. Serve tea from the slow cooker, but do not allow it to boil.

Why I like this recipe—
We love this after leaf-raking or for a fall party, especially when we serve it with muffins and fruit.

Hot Spicy Lemonade Punch

Mary E. Herr
The Hermitage
Three Rivers, MI

Makes 9–10 1-cup servings
Prep. Time: 5–10 minutes
Cooking Time: 3–4 hours
Ideal slow-cooker size: 4-qt.

4 cups cranberry juice

/₃–²/₃ cup sugar

12-oz. can lemonade concentrate, thawed

4 cups water

1–2 Tbsp. honey

6 whole cloves

2 cinnamon sticks, broken

1 lemon, sliced

1. Combine juice, sugar, lemonade concentrate, water, and honey in slow cooker.

2. Place cloves and cinnamon sticks in small cheesecloth square and tie shut.

3. Add spice bag and lemon slices to slow cooker.

4. Cover and cook on Low 3–4 hours. Remove spice bag before serving.

TIP

Keep hot in slow cooker until ready to serve.

Spicy Citrus Warmer

Jean Butzer
Batavia, NY

Barbara Walker
Sturgis, SD

Makes 12 servings
Prep. Time: 5–10 minutes
Cooking Time: 2–3 hours
Ideal slow-cooker size: 5-qt.

2½ qts. water

1½ cups sugar

1½ cups orange juice (with pulp is great!)

⅔ cup freshly squeezed lemon juice

⅓ cup pineapple juice

6-inch-long cinnamon stick, *or* two 3-inch sticks

1 tsp. whole cloves

1. Combine water, sugar, and juices in slow cooker. Stir until sugar is dissolved.

2. Add cinnamon stick to cooker. Place cloves in a tea ball. Close tightly and place in slow cooker.

3. Cover. Cook on Low 2–3 hours, or until heated through.

TIP

Add a half slice of orange or lime on the edge of each individual cup before serving.

Ginger Tea

**Evelyn Page
Gillette, WY**

Makes 8 cups
Prep. Time: 5–15 minutes
Cooking Time: 2 hours
Ideal slow-cooker size: 3-qt.

4 cups boiling water

15 single green tea bags

4 cups white grape juice

1-2 Tbsp. honey, according to your taste
    preference

1 Tbsp. minced fresh gingerroot

candied ginger pieces, *optional*

1. Place boiling water and tea bags in slow cooker. Cover and let stand 10 minutes. Discard tea bags.

2. Stir in juice, honey, and gingerroot.

3. Cover. Cook on Low 2 hours, or until heated through.

4. Strain if you wish before pouring into individual cups.

5. Garnish each cup with candied ginger, if you wish.

Why I like this recipe—
The women's group at church has a spring tea, and I am always asked to bring this Ginger Tea. It's a beautiful pale gold color, perfect for our clear glass mugs.

Pomegranate Punch

Lindsey Spencer
Marrow, OH

Makes 8 servings
Prep. Time: 5–7 minutes
Cooking Time: 1–2 hours
Ideal slow-cooker size: 3-qt.

3 cups pomegranate juice

1–1½ cups cranberry juice cocktail, according to your taste preference

½ cup orange juice

3-inch-long cinnamon stick

1 tsp. grated ginger

1. Put all ingredients in slow cooker.

2. Cover. Cook on Low 1–2 hours, or until heated through.

Why I like this recipe—
I like to make this punch for my cousins and their spouses when we get together for popcorn on Sunday evenings. It tastes special, but it's so easy to throw together!

Hot Cranberry Cider

Kristi See
Weskan, KS

Makes 10–12 servings
Prep. Time: 10 minutes
Cooking Time: 5 hours
Ideal slow-cooker size: 4-qt.

½ gallon apple cider, *or* apple juice

2 cups cranberry juice

½–¾ cup sugar, according to your taste
   preference

2 cinnamon sticks

1 tsp. whole allspice

whole orange studded with cloves

1. Put all ingredients except orange studded with cloves in slow cooker.

2. Cover. Cook on High 1 hour, and then on Low 4 hours, or until thoroughly hot.

3. Float clove-studded orange (instructions in Tip) in cooker. Serve hot.

TIP

To garnish cider with an orange, insert ten to twelve ½-inch-long whole cloves halfway into orange. Place studded orange in flat baking pan with sides. Pour in ¼ cup water. Bake at 325° for 30 minutes. Just before serving, float orange on top of hot Cider.

Why I like this recipe—

I come from a family of eight children, and every Christmas we all get together. We eat dinner, and then play games while drinking hot cranberry cider.

Appetizers, Snacks,
Spreads & Beverages

Matthew's Hot Mulled Cider

Shirley Unternahrer
Wayland, IA

Makes 12 servings
Prep. Time: 5 minutes
Cooking Time: 5 hours
Ideal slow-cooker size: 3½-qt.

2 qts. apple cider

¼ cup brown sugar

½ tsp. vanilla

1 cinnamon stick

4 cloves

1. Combine all ingredients in slow cooker.

2. Cover. Cook on Low 5 hours. Stir.

Why I like this recipe—

Our kids just tried hot mulled cider for the first time this past Christmas, thanks to our friend Matthew. They loved it. It's fun to try new old things.

Triple Delicious Hot Chocolate

Jennifer Freed
Harrisonburg, VA

Makes 6 servings
Prep. Time: 15 minutes
Cooking Time: 2¼ hours
Ideal slow-cooker size: 2- or 3-qt.

⅓ cup sugar

¼ cup unsweetened cocoa powder

¼ tsp. salt

3 cups milk, *divided*

¼ tsp. vanilla

1 cup heavy cream

1 square (1 oz.) bittersweet chocolate

1 square (1 oz.) white chocolate

¼ cup whipped topping

6 tsp. mini-chocolate chips, *or* shaved
    bittersweet chocolate

1. Combine sugar, cocoa powder, salt, and ½ cup milk in medium-sized bowl. Stir until smooth. Pour into slow cooker.

2. Add remaining 2½ cups milk and vanilla to slow cooker. Cover. Cook on Low 2 hours.

3. Stir in cream. Cover. Cook on Low 10 minutes.

4. Stir in bittersweet and white chocolates until melted.

5. Pour hot chocolate into 6 mugs. Top each with 2 Tbsp. whipped topping and 1 tsp. mini-chocolate chips or shavings.

Why I like this recipe—
I make this hot chocolate when I am longing for snowy mountains. It's cozy and delicious to have a mug of this in my hands.

Vanilla Steamer

Anita Troyer
Fairview, MI

Makes 8 servings
Prep. Time: 5–10 minutes
Cooking Time: 2–3 hours
Ideal slow-cooker size: 3-qt.

cups milk

⅛ tsp. cinnamon, *or* 2 3-inch-long cinnamon
sticks

Tbsp. sugar

Tbsp. vanilla

inch of salt

inch of nutmeg

whipped topping, *optional*

sprinkling of ground cinnamon, *optional*

1. Put all ingredients except whipped
topping and sprinkling of ground cinnamon
in slow cooker.

2. Cover. Cook on Low 2–3 hours, watching
near end of cooking time to make sure it
doesn't boil.

3. Garnish individual servings with
whipped topping and a sprinkling of
cinnamon if you wish.

Why I like this recipe—
I found this recipe when my children wanted
hot chocolate in the evening, but I didn't want
them to get hyper from the chocolate. It's a
total hit with them and the adults! Vanilla
Steamers are soothing and relaxing and
totally delicious.

TIP

I usually make a larger recipe than I will need,
and then refrigerate the leftovers. We like it
either reheated, or as creamer in our coffee.

Appetizers, Snacks,
Spreads & Beverages

Viennese Coffee

Evelyn Page
Gillette, WY

Makes 4 servings
Prep. Time: 15 minutes
Cooking Time: 3 hours
Ideal slow-cooker size: 1½- or 2-qt.

3 cups strong brewed coffee

3 Tbsp. chocolate syrup

1 tsp. sugar

⅓ cup heavy whipping cream

¼ cup crème de cacao, *or* Irish cream liqueur

whipped cream, *optional*

chocolate curls, *optional*

1. In a slow cooker, combine coffee, chocolate syrup, and sugar.

2. Cover. Cook on Low 2½ hours.

3. Stir in heavy cream and crème de cacao.

4. Cover. Cook 30 minutes more on Low, or until heated through.

5. Ladle into mugs. Garnish if you wish with whipped cream and chocolate curls.

Why I like this recipe—
This coffee is a special treat that I make as dessert for adult dinner parties in the winter. It's so easy, smells delicious, and usually leads to people reminiscing about the coffee they've had and loved.

Homemade Cream
of Mushroom Soup
on the stove

Makes about 1¼ cups (10 oz.)
Cooking Time: 20–30 minutes

3 Tbsp. butter

¼ cup fresh mushrooms, chopped

1 Tbsp. onion, chopped

3 Tbsp. flour

1 cup milk (skim, 1%, 2%, *or* whole)

1. In a small saucepan, melt butter.

2. Sauté mushrooms and onion in butter until tender. Stir frequently.

3. Add flour and stir until smooth. Cook over low heat for a minute or so to cook off the raw flour taste.

4. Continuing over low heat, gradually add milk, stirring the whole time.

5. Stir frequently to keep soup from sticking. When soup begins to bubble, stir continuously until it thickens to a creamy consistency.

Homemade Cream of Mushroom Soup
in the microwave

Makes about 1¼ cups (10 oz.)
Cooking Time: 10 minutes

3 Tbsp. butter

¼ cup fresh mushrooms, chopped

1 Tbsp. onion, chopped

3 Tbsp. flour

1 cup milk (skim, 1%, 2%, *or* whole)

1. In a 1- or 2-qt. microwave-safe container, melt 3 Tbsp. butter on High for 30 seconds.

2. Stir chopped mushrooms and onions into melted butter.

3. Microwave on High for 1 minute, or just enough to make the vegetables tender.

4. Stir in flour until well blended.

5. Microwave on High for 1 minute, just enough to overcome the raw flour taste.

6. Gradually stir in milk until as well blended as possible.

7. Microwave on 50% for 45 seconds.

8. Stir until well blended.

TIP

If your microwave is fairly new and powerful, you will probably have a creamy soup by the end of Step 8 or 10 below. If you're working with an older, less powerful, microwave, you will likely need to go through Step 12, and maybe Step 13.

9. Microwave on 50% for another 45 seconds. The mixture should be starting to bubble and thicken.

10. Stir again until well blended.

11. If the mixture isn't fully bubbling and thickened, microwave on High for 20 seconds

12. Stir. If the mixture still isn't fully bubbling and thickened, microwave on High for 20 more seconds.

13. Repeat Step 12 if needed.

Homemade Cream
of Celery Soup
on the stove

Makes about 1¼ cups (10 oz.)
Cooking Time: 20–30 minutes

3 Tbsp. butter

¼ cup fresh celery, finely chopped

1 Tbsp. onion, chopped

3 Tbsp. flour

1 cup milk (skim, 1%, 2%, *or* whole)

1. In a small saucepan, melt butter.

2. Sauté celery and onion in butter until tender. Stir frequently.

3. Add flour and stir until smooth. Cook over low heat for a minute or so to cook off the raw flour taste.

4. Continuing over low heat, gradually add milk, stirring the whole time.

5. Stir frequently to keep soup from sticking. When soup begins to bubble, stir continuously until it thickens to a creamy consistency.

Homemade Cream of Celery Soup
in the microwave

Makes about 1¼ cups (10 oz.)
Cooking Time: 10 minutes

3 Tbsp. butter

¼ cup fresh celery, finely chopped

1 Tbsp. onion, chopped

3 Tbsp. flour

1 cup milk (skim, 1%, 2%, *or* whole)

1. In a 1- or 2-qt. microwave-safe container, melt 3 Tbsp. butter on High for 30 seconds.

2. Stir chopped celery and onions into melted butter.

3. Microwave on High for 1 minute, or just enough to make the vegetables tender.

4. Stir in flour until well blended.

5. Microwave on High for 1 minute, just enough to overcome the raw flour taste.

6. Gradually stir in milk until as well blended as possible.

7. Microwave on 50% for 45 seconds.

8. Stir until well blended.

TIP

If your microwave is fairly new and powerful, you will probably have a creamy soup by the end of Step 8 or 10 below. If you're working with an older, less powerful, microwave, you will likely need to go through Step 12, and maybe Step 13.

9. Microwave on 50% for another 45 seconds. The mixture should be starting to bubble and thicken.

10. Stir again until well blended.

11. If the mixture isn't fully bubbling and thickened, microwave on High for 20 seconds.

12. Stir. If the mixture still isn't fully bubbling and thickened, microwave on High for 20 more seconds.

13. Repeat Step 12 if needed.

Chicken or Beef Stock

Makes 20 cups
Prep. Time: 10 minutes
Cooking Time: 12–36 hours
Chilling Time: 1–2 hours
Ideal slow-cooker size: 6-qt.

lbs. chicken parts, such as backs, necks, and wings, *or* meaty beef bones

-2 onions, unpeeled, cut in chunks

garlic cloves, unpeeled

tsp. salt

peppercorns

bay leaf

Tbsp. vinegar

/ater

1. Place all ingredients in slow cooker, dding water to come up to 1-inch from top of rock.

2. Cover and cook on Low for at least 12 ours and up to 36, adding more water as eeded. Especially large beef bones will need he full 36 hours to fully extract the good tuff.

3. Allow stock to cool for an hour or two efore straining. The bones will be so tender hat they will break as you press on the solids o extract the stock. This is good! Be sure to nclude any marrow if you are using large eef bones.

4. To de-fat the stock, either use a fat separator to strain off fat, or else refrigerate the stock. When it has chilled, the fat will be in a solid layer on top. Lift off the fat with a shallow spoon and discard it.

5. Store stock in fridge for up to a week, or portion it out and freeze it for several months.

Cook's notes—
- If you roast a chicken or turkey, save the carcass and make stock from that. The roasting makes for extra flavorful stock.
- Don't skip the vinegar: its presence is not detected in the flavor, but rather in its ability to help extract the minerals and good stuff from the bones.

TIP

Some people do not care for the smell of stock cooking. You can set your slow cooker in your garage, basement, or other space removed from the kitchen. Just be sure to write yourself a note to check on it at regular intervals!

Vegetable Broth

Makes 10 cups
Prep. Time: 15 minutes
Cooking Time: 8½–10½ hours
Ideal slow-cooker size: 6-qt.

1 yellow onion, unpeeled, cut in chunks

1 large potato, unpeeled, cut in chunks

2 carrots, unpeeled, cut in chunks

1 Tbsp. oil

3 dried mushrooms, such as shiitake

2 ribs celery, diced

2 bay leaves

8 peppercorns

2 Tbsp. soy sauce

9 cups water

1 cup white wine

1. Mix onion, potato, and carrots together with oil and spread on baking sheet. Roast at 400° for 20–30 minutes, stirring twice, until softened and browned in spots.

2. Scrape vegetables into slow cooker, being sure to get all the browned bits.

3. Add rest of ingredients.

4. Cover and cook on Low 8–10 hours. Remove crock from electrical unit and remove lid. Allow to sit for up to an hour to cool.

5. Strain the broth through a mesh strainer, pressing on the solids in the strainer to get all the good liquid out. Discard solids.

6. Store in refrigerator for up to 1 week, or portion out and freeze for several months.

TIPS

1. If you prefer, you can skip the wine and use another cup of water instead.
2. You can skip the roasting step if you wish, but the broth will not be as deeply flavored or colored.

Why I like this recipe—

I understand the process for making meat stocks, but I was curious about how vegetables gave up their juices for broth. Turns out, the process is not that hard, and the results are delicious.

Slow-Cooked Dried Beans

Makes 6 cups
Prep. Time: 5 minutes
Cooking Time: 3–6 hours
Standing Time: 1 hour or so
Ideal slow-cooker size: 5-qt.

2 cups dried beans such as navy, black, kidney, *or* pinto

7 cups water

1. Rinse the dried beans and pick out any stones or debris.

2. Place beans in slow cooker. Add water.

3. Cover and cook on Low 3–6 hours. The amount of time and water depends on the age of the bean (older will take longer and more water), how hot your cooker cooks, and how soft you like your beans. Fortunately, you have a long grace period with a slow cooker!

4. Start checking the beans at 3 hours. You might need to add more water to keep it just level with the beans.

5. When beans are cooked to the tenderness you want, remove hot crock from electrical base, remove lid, and allow beans to cool if you have time. They're easier to handle when they've cooled off.

6. Portion beans and their cooking liquid in containers. Keep in the refrigerator for up to a week, or freeze for several months.

TIP

If you like your beans soft, do not add salt or anything acidic to them until they are finished cooking as soft as you like them. The salt and acid keep the beans firm.

Cook's notes—

- Sometimes I add a bay leaf or a chopped onion, depending on what I have in mind for the finished beans. But often, I am simply cooking beans to store them in the freezer for future recipes instead of buying canned beans, which are more expensive and high in sodium.
- Another way to freeze the beans is to strain off the liquid entirely and spread them in a single layer on a baking sheet. Freeze. When the beans are frozen, scrape them into a freezer bag and return to the freezer. Then you can scoop out the amount you need.

Millet in the Slow Cooker

Makes 4 cups
Prep. Time: 5 minutes
Cooking Time: 6–9 hours
Ideal slow-cooker size: 2- or 3-qt.

1 cup millet

4 cups water

½ tsp. salt, *optional*

1. Place millet, water, and optional salt in slow cooker.

2. Cover and cook on Low 6–9 hours, or until millet is fluffy and water is mostly absorbed.

3. Drain off and discard any water remaining. Cooked millet will keep up to two weeks in the fridge, or it can be frozen.

TIP

Use cooked millet in recipes that call for cooked rice, or serve hot with a pat of butter as a side dish.

Cook's note—

What can you do with cooked millet? Serve hot with milk, honey, and fruit for breakfast. Add to soups instead of rice or barley. Chill and add veggies and dressing to make a sturdy salad.

Wheat Berries (or Farro or Spelt or Rye or Barley) in the Slow Cooker

Makes 4 cups
Prep. Time: 5 minutes
Cooking Time: 4–12 hours
Ideal slow-cooker size: 3- or 4-qt.

1 cup wheat berries, farro, spelt, rye, *or* hulled/
   pearl barley

3 cups water

¼ tsp. salt, *optional*

1. Place wheat berries or other grain, water, and optional salt in slow cooker.

2. Cover and cook on Low 8–12 hours or High 4–5 hours. The wheat berries are done when they are soft and chewy. There may be water left that can just be drained off and discarded.

Cook's note—
Cooked wheat berries will keep in the fridge for up to 2 weeks, or they can be frozen. Make a sturdy salad with wheat berries. They are also nice reheated for breakfast with milk and honey, served instead of rice at dinner, and used as a ground-meat extender in recipes like meat loaf or chili.

Homemade Frozen Hash Browns

Makes 8 servings
Prep. Time: 30 minutes
Cooking Time: 3–6 hours
Standing Time: 2 hours
Chilling Time: 2–3 hours
Ideal slow-cooker size: 3-qt.

2 lbs. potatoes, scrubbed well

1. Prick each potato with fork.

2. Place in lightly greased slow cooker.

3. Cover and cook on Low for 3–6 hours, or until potatoes are tender but firm. Start checking at 3 hours. The time really varies with the size and variety of the potatoes you are using.

4. When potatoes are cooked but firm, remove them from cooker and allow to cool to room temperature, about 2 hours. Refrigerate for 2–3 hours, or until potatoes are thoroughly chilled. Cold potatoes are much easier to grate than warm or room-temperature ones.

5. Grate potatoes. Portion into containers, label, and freeze.

TIP

Use these Hash Browns in any recipe calling for frozen hash browns. Follow recipe directions for whether or not to thaw. To serve hash browns by themselves, heat some oil in a skillet. Place frozen hash browns directly in hot skillet and fry over high heat, breaking them up as the potatoes thaw and brown. Fry until hot and browned. Serve with eggs and toast for breakfast.

Homemade Cornbread Mix

Makes the equivalent of an 8½-oz.
box of Jiffy cornbread mix
Prep. Time: 5 minutes
Cooking Time: 20 minutes

⅓ cup flour

½ cup cornmeal

3 Tbsp. sugar

 Tbsp. baking powder

¼ tsp. salt

2 Tbsp. oil

To make muffins from this mix, add:

1 egg

⅓ cup milk

1. Combine ingredients, and stir just until mixed.

2. Fill muffin cups half-full.

3. Bake at 400° for 15–20 minutes, or until toothpick inserted in center of muffins comes out clean.

Why I like this recipe—
Super-easy. Super-economical.

Easy Ketchup

Makes 3 cups
Prep. Time: 25 minutes
Cooking Time: 7–10 hours
Ideal slow-cooker size: 5-qt.

2 lbs. very ripe red tomatoes

1 large onion, coarsely chopped

2 celery ribs, coarsely chopped

1 red bell pepper, coarsely chopped

¼ cup apple cider vinegar

¼ cup red wine vinegar

1 garlic clove, crushed

1 Tbsp. honey

1 Tbsp. brown sugar

1 tsp. Dijon mustard

⅛ tsp. ground cloves

⅛ tsp. celery seed

⅛ tsp. ground allspice

⅛ tsp. ground cinnamon

½ teaspoon salt

pinch red pepper flakes

1. Combine all ingredients in blender or food processor and process until entirely smooth.

2. Pour into slow cooker.

3. Cover and cook on High for 1 hour to get it hot.

4. Turn cooker to Low and prop lid open at one end with a wooden spoon handle or chopstick.

5. Stir occasionally, being sure that the condensation on the lid does not drip into the ketchup when you move the lid. You are thickening the ketchup by evaporating the water out of it. Cook on Low for 6–9 hours, or until it has thickened and gotten darker.

6. Taste the ketchup and add more spices, sugar, or salt if you wish.

7. Store ketchup in fridge for several months. Ketchup can be canned by following guidelines from the USDA or other reputable source.

Why I like this recipe—

I'm recalling my childhood when my mother boiled down vats of ketchup to can. However, that was a big kitchen commitment with lots of splatters and stirring. Making ketchup in the slow cooker is so much easier! I don't need to pay much attention to it, and I can make a small batch and it will keep fine in the fridge.

Slow-Cooked Apple Butter

Makes 6–8 cups
Prep. Time: 20–30 minutes
Cooking Time: 8–8½ hours
Ideal slow-cooker size: 4-qt.

12 apples
¼–⅓ cup water
½ cup sugar
2 tsp. cinnamon
½ cup brown sugar

1. Wash, core, and peel apples. Cut into quarters. Place in slow cooker.

2. Mix all other ingredients together well in a bowl, using the lesser amount of water. Pour over the apples and stir together. You may need to add more water during the cooking process, depending on how juicy your apples are.

3. Cook on Low 8 hours, or until the mixture smells deep and darkly sweet. Check to see if the apple butter is thick enough for you. If you want it to be thicker, cook it with the lid off for 30 minutes or so to evaporate more moisture.

4. Store in fridge for up to 2 weeks, or otherwise freeze it or can it according to your canner's instructions.

Why I like this recipe—

We eat this spread on toast and over cottage cheese. I also love it in toasted cheese sandwiches. Spread it on the inside of the bottom bread slices before topping them with cheese.

Cheese Sauce

**Carol Eveleth
Hillsdale, WY**

Makes 6 servings
Prep. Time: 10 minutes
Cooking Time: 2–3 hours
Ideal slow-cooker size: 3-qt.

3 Tbsp. flour

1½ cups milk

3 Tbsp. butter, diced

1½ cups grated sharp cheddar cheese

1 tsp. salt

¼ tsp. paprika

1 tsp. ketchup

pepper to taste, *optional*

1. In slow cooker, mix flour and milk together until smooth.

2. Add butter, cheese, salt, paprika, and ketchup.

3. Cook in slow cooker for 2–3 hours on Low, stirring occasionally, until thickened.

TIPS

Put on Warm setting to serve this cheese sauce. Serve with baked potatoes, taco salad, haystacks, or soft pretzels— anywhere you want some warm, gooey cheese!

DIY Velveeta Cheese

Makes 14 ounces
Prep. Time: 25 minutes
Cooking Time: 3–5 minutes

¼ cup whole milk

1 tsp. unflavored gelatin

12 oz. shredded cheddar *or* Colby cheese

¼ tsp. salt

1. Prepare a 9x4-inch loaf pan by lining it with plastic wrap *or* use a glass loaf pan.

2. Pour milk in small saucepan and sprinkle gelatin on milk. Set aside for 5 minutes to soften.

3. Combine cheese and salt in food processor and pulse several times to combine.

4. Over low heat, warm milk and gelatin until just steaming, stirring several times. Do not boil.

5. With the food processor on, slowly pour the hot milk/gelatin into the cheese and process until cheese is completely melted and smooth.

6. Immediately scrape mixture into prepared pan and cover. Refrigerate for at least 3 hours to set completely before using. Store in the fridge for up to 2 weeks.

Why I like this recipe—
As we all get more nervous about eating processed foods—but miss some of the old-timey things we used to eat innocently—it's kinda fun and reassuring to find ways to bring back the cherished food, but with less guilt.

Homemade Applesauce

Makes 12–15 servings
Prep. Time: 30 minutes
Cooking Time: 5–9 hours
Ideal slow-cooker size: 6-qt.

cooking spray

10–14 large apples, of mixed varieties

¼ cup water

sugar, *optional*

1. Lightly spray the inside of the slow-cooker crock.

2. Peel, core, and chop the apples.

3. Place the apples and water in the slow cooker. The apples should come to the top of the crock.

4. Cover and cook on Low 5–9 hours, stirring once or twice. The time depends on the ripeness and varieties of the apples. When the apples can easily be smashed against the side of the inner crock with the cooking spoon, turn off the heat.

5. Use an immersion blender or a handheld masher to mash or blend the apples until you make an applesauce as smooth or as chunky as you like.

6. Taste the applesauce to see if you want to add any sugar. This also depends on the varieties of apples you used and on personal taste. Add the sugar while the applesauce is hot so it dissolves easily.

7. Pour applesauce into a bowl to cool. Serve warm, at room temperature, or chilled. Applesauce may be frozen for several months It will keep in the fridge for up to a week.

Why I like this recipe—

My friend goes to her local orchard and buys a mixture of seconds, aiming for a balance of natural flavors, as apple season progresses. She cuts out any bruises or bad spots and makes a pot of applesauce every two weeks or so. She always makes one batch especially for the Community Meal we serve at our church every Monday night. Delish!

Homemade Yogurt

Makes 8½ cups
Prep. Time: 15 minutes
Cooking Time: 2½ hours
Standing Time: 3 hours, and then 8–12 hours
Ideal slow-cooker size: 3- or 4-qt.

½ gallon (8 cups) 2% *or* whole milk

½ cup plain yogurt with live cultures, *or* freeze-dried yogurt starter

1. Place milk in slow cooker. Cover and cook on Low 2½ hours.

2. Turn the cooker off and unplug it, but keep the lid on. Allow to sit in this manner for 3 hours.

3. The milk should be in the lukewarm range (105°–115°) before you introduce the yogurt cultures. If you're unsure, check it with a kitchen candy thermometer.

4. Scoop a cup of the lukewarm milk into a small mixing bowl. Add the yogurt or yogurt starter. Whisk well.

5. Return the milk/yogurt mixture to the low cooker. Whisk again to distribute the starter through all of the milk.

6. Put the lid on. Swaddle the entire, unplugged slow cooker in a beach towel or two. Allow to sit for 8–12 hours undisturbed.

7. The yogurt is done when it's thick and gelatinous. It will thicken more with chilling or a longer incubation (but it will get more tart the longer it is incubated!).

8. Gently scoop the yogurt into containers, but try to avoid stirring it, as that breaks down its natural gel and it will get runnier.

9. Refrigerate. Keeps in the fridge for 2–3 weeks, but it gets more tart as it ages.

Cook's notes—
• You can use ½ cup homemade yogurt as the starter for your next batch, although some people think it's helpful to renew the starter with a commercial yogurt every few batches or so.
• Make Greek yogurt with your homemade yogurt: line a mesh strainer with cheesecloth and set it over a bowl. Pour yogurt into the lined strainer. Allow the whey to strain into the bowl. Allow to strain for 1 hour, or up to 12 hours for really thick yogurt (yogurt cheese, some people call it, and use it like cream cheese). The whey is quite nutritious and can be used instead of buttermilk for some baked goods.
• Another thickening option is to add a packet of unflavored, powdered gelatin at the end of the yogurt incubation. Whisk it gently through the yogurt, and after it's been refrigerated for a few hours, the yogurt will set up more firmly.

Home-Style Tomato Juice

Wilma Haberkamp
Fairbank, IA

Makes: 4 cups
Prep. Time: 20 minutes
Cooking Time: 4–6 hours
Ideal slow-cooker size: 3-qt.

10–12 large ripe tomatoes

1 tsp. salt

1 tsp. seasoned salt

¼ tsp. pepper

1 Tbsp. sugar

1. Wash and drain tomatoes. Remove cores and blossom ends.

2. Place the whole tomatoes in your slow cooker. (Do not add water.)

3. Cover and cook on Low 4–6 hours, or until tomatoes are very soft.

4. Press them through a sieve or food mill.

5. Add seasonings. Chill.

TIP

If you have more than 10–12 tomatoes, you can use a larger slow cooker and increase the amounts of the other ingredients proportionately. The cooking time will probably be somewhat longer.

Slow-Cooked Salsa

Andy Wagner
Quarryville, PA

Makes 2 cups
Prep. Time: 15 minutes
Cooking Time: 2½–3 hours
Standing Time: 2 hours
Ideal slow-cooker size: 3-qt.

0 plum tomatoes

garlic cloves

small onion, cut into wedges

–2 jalapeño peppers

¼ cup chopped fresh cilantro

½ tsp. salt, *optional*

TIP

Wear disposable gloves when cutting hot peppers; the oils can burn your skin. Avoid touching your face when you've been working with hot peppers.

1. Core tomatoes. Cut a small slit in two omatoes. Insert a garlic clove into each slit.

2. Place all tomatoes and onions in a 3-qt. low cooker.

3. Cut stems off jalapeños. (Remove seeds f you want a milder salsa.) Place jalapeños in he slow cooker.

4. Cover and cook on High 2½ to 3 hours, r until vegetables are softened. Some may rown slightly. Cool at least 2 hours with the id off.

5. In a blender, combine the tomato mixture, cilantro, and salt if you wish. Cover nd process until blended.

5. Refrigerate leftovers.

Pico de Gallo

MaryAnn Beachy
Dover, OH

Makes 4 cups
Prep. Time: 15 minutes

1 large onion, chopped

1½ cups tomatoes, chopped

1-1½ cups chopped fresh cilantro

½ tsp. salt

juice of one lime

1-2 jalapeños, minced, *optional,* if you like the
heat

Why I like this recipe—
I can't go to our farmers market during the
summer without coming home with tomatoes.
I try to always make at least one batch
of homemade pico de gallo to serve with
whatever we're grilling.

1. Combine onions, tomatoes, cilantro,
salt, lime juice, and optional jalapeños. Stir
together.

2. Taste and add salt as needed.

3. Serve with tortilla chips.

Garlic Hummus

Donna Suter
Pandora, OH

Samantha Seifried
Lancaster, PA

Lindsay Spencer
Morrow, OH

Makes 2 cups
Prep. Time: 10 minutes

15-oz. can garbanzo beans

¼ cup tahini (nut butter made from sesame seeds)

1-4 garlic cloves, depending on your taste preference

½ cup olive oil

3 Tbsp. lemon juice

½ tsp. salt

dash pepper, *optional*

½ tsp. roasted garlic powder, *optional*

1 tsp. ground cumin, *optional*

1. Drain the garbanzos, but reserve ½ cup liquid.

2. Combine beans, tahini, garlic, oil, lemon juice, salt, optional pepper, optional garlic powder, and optional cumin in a food processor or blender.

3. Blend until smooth. Add a little bean liquid if needed to reach desired spreading or dipping consistency.

4. Store in the refrigerator. Serve with pita bread or homemade pita chips.

TIPS

1. To make homemade pita chips, cut pita bread into 8 triangles. Drizzle with olive oil, sprinkle with Mrs. Dash seasoning or seasoned salt, and bake in a 350° oven for 20 minutes.
—Donna Suter

2. Add 1 cup chopped red bell peppers to hummus. Omit olive. Purée as directed.
—Lindsay Spencer

3. To make Tex-Mex Hummus, replace garbanzos with black beans. Add 6 oz. plain Greek yogurt and ½ packet taco seasoning. Reduce tahini to 1 Tbsp. Omit cumin, salt, pepper, and olive oil.
—Samantha Seifried

Hot Bacon Salad Dressing

Makes 3-4 cups
Prep. Time: 15 minutes
Cooking Time: 2½-3½ hours
Ideal slow-cooker size: 2-qt.

½ lb. bacon, chopped

2 cups water

¾ cup apple cider vinegar

1 cup sugar

1 Tbsp. prepared mustard

2 eggs

4 Tbsp. flour

1. Fry bacon in a skillet until crisp. Scrape it and the drippings into the slow cooker.

2. Whisk together remaining ingredients until smooth.

3. Cover and cook on High for 2–3 hours, or until thickened and bubbly, stirring twice.

4. Serve warm over lettuce, spinach, or early spring dandelion greens.

Why I like this recipe—

My grandma used to entice me to eat lettuce by putting a good-sized spoonful of this dressing over top! My dad liked to eat dandelion greens in the spring, but my mom didn't. She'd get herself and us kids through the dish with generous toppings of this dressing. Now that I'm a convinced greens-eater, I like just a small dollop to brighten my salad—and to relive those moments around our table as a kid.

202
Chicken Azteca, 37
Chicken Barley Chili, 305
Chicken Tortilla Soup, 307
Chipotle Chili, 308
Crock-o-Beans, 253
Easy Black Bean Lasagna, 231
Enchilada Stack-Up, 151
Filled Acorn Squash, 273
Four Beans and Sausage, 396
Homemade Refried Beans, 391
Mexican Chicken Bake, 65
Mexican Rice and Beans, 251
Pumpkin Black-Bean Turkey Chili, 339
Quinoa, and Black Beans, 268
Slow-Cooked Dried Beans, 568
Taco Soup with Corn, 304
black-eyed peas
Creamy Black-Eyed Peas, 259
butter, 398
Lotsa-Beans Chili, 301
cannellini
Kielbasa and Veggies Soup, 311
Pasta Bean Pot, 242
garbanzo
Crock-o-Beans, 253
Curried Lentils, 266
Garbanzo Souper, 320
Garlic Hummus, 581
Lotsa Veggies Spaghetti, 224
Minestra Di Ceci, 243
Moroccan Sweet Potato Medley, 271
Thai Veggie Curry, 261
Vegetable Curry, 359
great northern
Apple Bean Bake, 400
Six-Bean Barbecue, 398
green
Armenian Eggplant, 411
Barbecued Green Beans, 344
Beefy Vegetable Soup, 281
Easy Veggie-Beef Soup, 291
Green Beans Caesar, 346
Green Beans Get-Together, 345
Lotsa-Beans Chili, 301
Minestrone, 318
Pork Loin with Savory

Fruit Sauce, 176
Potatoes and Green Beans with Ham, 203
Santa Fe Stew, 117
Smoked Sausage Stew, 314
Vegetable Beef Borscht, 282
Green Beans and Sausage, 214
Huevos Rancheros, 447
kidney
Beef and Sausage Chili, 302
Calico Beans with Corn, 399
Chet's Trucker Stew, 312
Corn Chili, 300
Cornbread-Topped Frijoles, 250
Crock-o-Beans, 253
Enchilada Stack-Up, 151
Four Beans and Sausage, 396
Lotsa-Beans Chili, 301
Meatless Baked Beans, 392
Norma's Vegetarian Chili, 333
Pasta Bean Pot, 242
Pepperoni Pizza Chili, 303
Six-Bean Barbecue, 398
Slow-Cooked Dried Beans, 568
Taco Soup with Corn, 304
Trail Chili, 295
lima
Barbecued Lima Beans, 388
Calico Beans with Corn, 399
Chet's Trucker Stew, 312
Meatless Baked Beans, 392
Succotash, 404
Mexican-style
Arroz con Queso, 246
mixed, 319
navy
Mom's New England Baked Beans, 388
Six-Bean Barbecue, 398
Slow-Cooked Dried Beans, 568
northern
Beans with Turkey Bacon, 394
Four Beans and Sausage, 396
pinto
Apple Bean Bake, 400
Best Bean Chili, 297
Chipotle Chili, 308

Cornbread-Topped Frijoles, 250
Homemade Refried Beans, 391
Minestrone, 318
Ohio Chili, 299
Six-Bean Barbecue, 398
Slow-Cooked Dried Beans, 568
pork and beans
Barbecued Beans, 393
Calico Beans with Corn, 399
Chet's Trucker Stew, 312
Maple Baked Beans, 395
Six-Bean Barbecue, 398
ranch
Ohio Chili, 299
Taco Soup with Corn, 304
red
Cajun Sausage and Beans, 397
Red Beans and Pasta, 241
Red Beans and Rice, 390
red kidney
Best Bean Chili, 297
Creamy Ham and Red Beans Over Rice, 205
Jamaican Rice and Beans, 252
Ohio Chili, 299
refried
Championship Bean Dip, 533
Homemade Refried Beans, 391
Lasagna Mexicana, 149
waxed
Chet's Trucker Stew, 312
white kidney
Tuscan Beef Stew, 114
Beans with Turkey Bacon, 394
Beef, ground
Beef and Sausage Chili, 302
Best Bean Chili, 297
Calico Beans with Corn, 399
Cheesy Meat Loaf, 147
Chet's Trucker Stew, 312
Corn Chili, 300
Creamy Taco Dip, 534
Easy Veggie-Beef Soup, 291
Enchilada Stack-Up, 151
Festive Meatballs, 148
Flavorful Meat Loaf, 146
Lasagna Mexicana, 149
Lotsa-Beans Chili, 301
Pepperoni Pizza Chili, 303
Spaghetti Sauce with a Kick, 152
Taco Soup with Corn, 304
Tasty Meatball Stew, 293
Trail Chili, 295

Beef, stewing
Barbecued Pork and Beef Sandwiches, 184
Beef and Sausage Chili, 302
Beef Barley Soup, 289
Beef brisket
Apple Corned Beef and Cabbage, 109
Autumn Brisket, 103
Corned Beef and Cabbage, 108
Cranberry Brisket, 104
Good-Time Beef Brisket, 105
Spicy Beef Roast, 94
Beef Burgundy, 121
Beef chuck roast
Barbecued Roast Beef, 142
Bavarian Beef, 67
Beef Barley Soup, 289
Beef Burgundy, 121
Beef Roast with Mushroom Barley, 89
Beefy Vegetable Soup, 281
Can't Beet Beef Stew, 285
Classic Beef Stew, 113
Easy Creamy Beef, 118
Fruity Beef Tagine, 120
Hearty New England Dinner, 90
Italian Beef Stew, 123
Layered Herby Stew, 111
Machaca Beef, 96
Melt-in-Your-Mouth Mexican Meat Dish, 101
Mexican Pot Roast, 93
Middle East Sandwiches, 145
Moroccan Beef Stew, 286
New Mexico Beef & Pork Stew, 123
Peppery Roast, 91
Piquant Chuck Roast, 92
Plum Roast, 97
Pot-Roast Complete, 102
Powerhouse Beef Roast with Tomatoes, Onions, and Peppers, 87
Ranch Hand Beef, 143
Ready-When-You-Get-Home Dinner, 115
Santa Fe Stew, 117
Spanish Round Steak, 127
Tuscan Beef Stew, 114
Vegetable Beef Borscht, 282
Wine Tender Roast, 95
Winter's Night Beef Stew, 283
Beef flank steak
Fruity Flank Steak, 135
Slow-Cooker Beef with Mushrooms, 137
Stuffed Flank Steak, 134
Three-Pepper Steak, 139
Beef Ribs with Sauerkraut, 133
Beef Roast with Mushroom

Fix-It and Forget-It Slow Cooker Champion Recipes

Barley, 89
Beef round steak
  Fajita Steak, 141
  Hungarian Goulash, 119
  Round Steak Roll-Ups, 138
  Slow-Cooker Beef with
    Mushrooms, 137
Beef round tip roast
  Spicy Beef Roast, 94
Beef short ribs
  Beef Ribs with Sauerkraut,
    133
  Old-Fashioned Vegetable
    Beef Soup, 287
  Slow-Cooked Short Ribs,
    131
  Zingy Short Ribs, 129
Beef stock, 565
  French Onion Soup, 340
  Italian Beef Stew, 123
Beefy Vegetable Soup, 281
Beer
  Good-Time Beef Brisket,
    105
  Greek Bread, 422
  Ranch Hand Beef, 143
Beets
  Can't Beet Beef Stew, 285
  Vegetables with Red
    Quinoa, 269
Beets with Capers, 408
Best Bean Chili, 297
Biscuit baking mix
  Zucchini Torte, 275
Biscuits, refrigerator
  Caramel Rolls, 438
Black and Blue Cobbler, 469
Black Bean and Butternut Chili,
    334
Black Bean Burritos, 248
Black Beans with Ham, 202
Black Forest Cake, 481
Blackberries
  Black and Blue Cobbler, 469
Black-eyed peas
  Creamy Black-Eyed Peas,
    259
Blessing Soup, 319
Blueberries
  Black and Blue Cobbler, 469
Blushing Apple Tapioca, 504
Bold Butterscotch Sauce, 525
Boston Brown Bread, 424
Bread
  Apple-Nut Bread Pudding,
    500
  Cubed French Toast, 450
  Egg and Cheese Bake, 443
  French Toast with Apples
    and Nuts, 449
  White Chocolate Bread
    Pudding, 499
Bread crumbs
  Amish Wedding Chicken, 48
  Baked Stuffed Tomatoes,
    360

Baked Tomato Rarebit, 277
Cheese and Crab Dip, 536
Cottage Potatoes, 371
Festive Meatballs, 148
Green Beans Caesar, 346
Summer Squash Delish, 352
Tasty Meatball Stew, 293
Bread Pudding, 497
Breakfast Apple Cobbler, 462
Breakfast Polenta with Bacon,
    459
Breakfast Skillet, 442
Brisket. See Beef brisket
Broccoli
  Brown Rice Vegetable
    Dinner, 255
  Egg and Broccoli, 445
  Overnight Veggie Omelet,
    448
  Pork Chops with a Hint of
    Asia, 175
  Quick Broccoli Fix, 406
  Tortellini with Broccoli, 244
  Veggie Mac and Cheese,
    238
Broccoli Cauliflower Soup, 335
Broccoli Corn Mix, 405
Broccoli Cornbread, 419
Brown Bread, 424
Brown Rice Vegetable Dinner,
    255
Buffalo wing sauce
  Cheesy Buffalo Chicken
    Pasta, 57
Bulgur
  Moroccan Sweet Potato
    Medley, 271
Burritos
  Black Bean Burritos, 248
  Sweet Pepper Burritos, 249
Butter Chicken, 41
Butternut squash
  Autumn Harvest Pork
    Loin, 177
  Black Bean and Butternut
    Chili, 334
  Chipotle Chili, 308
  Golden Autumn Stew, 215
  Peanut Butter Pumpkin
    Soup, 338
  Vegetable Soup, 332
  Vegetables with Red
    Quinoa, 269
Butter-Rubbed Baked Potatoes,
    369
Butterscotch chips
  Seven-Layer Bars, 491

C
Cabbage
  Apple Corned Beef and
    Cabbage, 109
  Autumn Brisket, 103
  Corned Beef and Cabbage,
    108
  Hearty New England

Dinner, 90
  Scalloped Cabbage, 354
  Sweet and Sour Red
    Cabbage, 356
  Sweet and Tangy Cabbage,
    355
  Vegetable Beef Borscht, 282
  Vegetable Soup, 332
Cajun Sausage and Beans, 397
Cake mix
  Black Forest Cake, 481
  Easy Autumn Cake, 475
  Self-Frosting Fudge Cake,
    480
Calico Beans with Corn, 399
Can't Beet Beef Stew, 285
Capers
  Armenian Eggplant, 411
  Beets with Capers, 408
  Tomato-Glazed Pork with
    Grilled Corn Salsa,
    180–181
Caramel Rolls, 438
Caramels
  Apple Caramel Peanut
    Topping, 524
Carrot Cake, 483
Carrot Ginger Soup, 336
Carrots
  Apple Corned Beef and
    Cabbage, 109
  Basil Chicken, 24
  Can't Beet Beef Stew, 285
  Carrot Ginger Soup, 336
  Chicken Corn Soup, 323
  Classic Beef Stew, 113
  Corned Beef and Cabbage,
    108
  Curried Carrot Ginger
    Soup, 337
  Easy Veggie-Beef Soup, 291
  Garbanzo Souper, 320
  Horseradish Carrot Coins,
    349
  Lentils Swiss Style, 265
  New Mexico Beef & Pork
    Stew, 123
  Orange-Glazed Carrots,
    347
  Overnight Veggie Omelet,
    448
  Special Times Carrots, 348
  Summer Squash Delish, 352
  Sunday Chicken Stew with
    Dumplings, 50–51
  Sunshine Dish, 257
  Tasty Meatball Stew, 293
  Thai Veggie Curry, 261
  Tuscan Beef Stew, 114
  Vegetable Beef Borscht, 282
  Vegetable Curry, 359
  Zucchini Torte, 275
Cashew butter
  Butter Chicken, 41
Cashews
  Brown Rice Vegetable

Dinner, 255
  Norma's Vegetarian Chili,
    333
  Spicy Nut and Pretzel Mix,
    544
  Vegetables with Red
    Quinoa, 269
Cauliflower
  Broccoli Cauliflower Soup,
    335
  Brown Rice Vegetable
    Dinner, 255
  Cauliflower Cassoulet, 407
  Veggie Mac and Cheese,
    238
Cauliflower Cassoulet, 407
Championship Bean Dip, 533
Cheese
  American
    Cheesy Meat Loaf, 147
    Egg and Cheese Bake,
      443
    Potatoes and Green
      Beans with Ham,
      203
    Welsh Rarebit, 441
  Asiago
    Minestrone, 318
  Black Bean Burritos, 248
  cheddar
    Baked Lentils with
      Cheese, 267
    Baked Tomato Rarebit,
      277
    Barley with Mushrooms,
      270
    Breakfast Skillet, 442
    Broccoli Cauliflower
      Soup, 335
    Brown Rice Vegetable
      Dinner, 255
    Championship Bean
      Dip, 533
    Cheese Sauce, 574
    Cheesy Buffalo Chicken
      Pasta, 57
    Cheesy Meat Loaf, 147
    Chicken Corn Chowder,
      325
    Creamy Mac and
      Cheese, 240
    Creamy Taco Dip, 534
    DIY Velveeta Cheese,
      575
    Easy Black Bean Lasagna,
      231
    Egg and Broccoli, 445
    Egg and Cheese Bake,
      443
    Enchilada Stack-Up, 151
    Herbal Apple Cheese
      Dish, 278
    Herbed Rice and Lentil
      Bake, 260
    Horseradish Mac and
      Cheese, 239

Hot Cheddar Mushroom Spread, 540
Hot Cheese and Bacon Dip, 532
Lentils Swiss Style, 265
Mexican Chicken Bake, 65
Mexican Rice and Beans, 251
Pineapple Cheddar Cornbread, 421
Potatoes O'Brien, 372
Potatoes Perfect, 383
Sausage Town, 217
Scalloped Potatoes and Ham, 204
Smoked Salmon Corn Chowder, 326
Summer Veggie Bake, 276
Sweet Pepper Burritos, 249
Taco Soup with Corn, 304
Tastes-Like-Chili-Rellenos, 245
Turkey Fajitas, 84
Veggie Mac and Cheese, 238
Welsh Rarebit, 441
Western Omelet, 444
Yummy Spinach, 343
Chicken Barley Chili, 305
Chicken Tortilla Soup, 307
Colby
    DIY Velveeta Cheese, 575
    Overnight Veggie Omelet, 448
    Summer Squash Lasagna, 233
cottage
    Broccoli Cornbread, 419
    Crustless Spinach Quiche, 274
    Egg and Broccoli, 445
    Summer Squash Lasagna, 233
    Summer Veggie Bake, 276
    Yummy Spinach, 343
Cottage Potatoes, 371
cream
    Championship Bean Dip, 533
    Cheese and Crab Dip, 536
    Chicken Azteca, 37
    Chicken Corn Chowder, 325
    Chicken Tacos, 64
    Crab Spread, 541
    Creamy Artichoke Dip, 537
    Creamy Orange

Cheesecake, 485
Creamy Red Potatoes, 379
Creamy Sausage and Potatoes, 212
Creamy Ziti in the Crock, 237
Hot Cheese and Bacon Dip, 532
Italiano Spread, 538
Make-Ahead Mixed Potatoes Florentine, 377
Overnight Veggie Omelet, 448
Roasted Pepper and Artichoke Spread, 539
Slow-Cooker Cinnamon Rolls, 436–437
Summer Squash Lasagna, 233
Super Creamed Corn, 401
Sweet Pepper Burritos, 249
Zucchini Bread, 429
Creamy Potato Soup, 329
Crustless Spinach Quiche, 274
feta
    Chicken with Feta, 39
    Mediterranean Onions, 409
Gouda
    Creamy Mac and Cheese, 240
Havarti
    Pasta with Tomatoes, Olives, and Two Cheeses, 223
horseradish
    Horseradish Mac and Cheese, 239
Hot Chili Dip, 535
Italian blend
    Herbed Rice and Lentil Bake, 260
    Summer Squash Lasagna, 233
Mexican blend
    Huevos Rancheros, 447
    Lasagna Mexicana, 149
Monterey Jack
    Arroz con Queso, 246
    Championship Bean Dip, 533
    Double Corn Tortilla Bake, 247
    Filled Acorn Squash, 273
    Mexican Stuffed Chicken, 42
    Tastes-Like-Chili-Rellenos, 245
mozzarella
    Barbecued Chicken

Pizza, 71
Classic Spinach Lasagna, 229
Creamy Artichoke Dip, 537
Creamy Ziti in the Crock, 237
Easy Black Bean Lasagna, 231
Italiano Spread, 538
Pepperoni Pizza Chili, 303
Sausage, Tomato, Spinach Soup, 313
Zucchini Special, 353
Norma's Vegetarian Chili, 333
Parmesan
    Baked Stuffed Tomatoes, 360
    Broccoli Corn Mix, 405
    Cauliflower Cassoulet, 407
    Creamy Artichoke Dip, 537
    Creamy Tomato Soup, 330
    Creamy Ziti in the Crock, 237
    Green Beans Caesar, 346
    Hot Cheddar Mushroom Spread, 540
    Italiano Spread, 538
    Lotsa Veggies Spaghetti, 224
    Melt-in-Your-Mouth Sausages, 207
    Mexican Stuffed Chicken, 42
    Minestrone, 318
    Mushroom Spaghetti Sauce, 225
    Parmesan Potato Wedges, 382
    Pasta with Tomatoes, Olives, and Two Cheeses, 223
    Peas and Rice, 368
    Risotto in the Crock, 367
    Roasted Pepper and Artichoke Spread, 539
    Southern Italy Sauce, 228
    Spinach Frittata, 446
    Zucchini Torte, 275
ricotta
    Summer Squash Lasagna, 233
Salsa Lentils, 263
Scalloped Cabbage, 354
So-Simple Salsa Chicken, 61
Spinach Rice Bake, 262

Sunshine Dish, 257
Swiss
    Creamy Artichoke Dip, 537
    Egg and Cheese Bake, 443
    Horseradish Mac and Cheese, 239
    Lentils Swiss Style, 265
Vegetable Party, 357
Velveeta
    DIY Velveeta Cheese, 575
    Mexican-Style Grits, 461
    Texas Queso Dip, 531
Cheese and Crab Dip, 536
Cheese Grits, 460
Cheese Sauce, 574
Cheesy Buffalo Chicken Pasta, 57
Cheesy Meat Loaf, 147
Cherries
    Hot Fruit, 412
    Scandinavian Fruit Soup, 512
    Sour Cherry Cobbler, 473
    Soy-Flax Granola, 456
    White Chocolate Bread Pudding, 499
Cherry Delight, 472
Cherry jam
    Barbecued Ribs, 194
Cherry pie filling
    Black Forest Cake, 481
Cherry Tomato Spaghetti Sauce, 227
Chet's Trucker Stew, 312
Chicken
    Amish Wedding Chicken, 48
    Barbecued Chicken Pizza, 71
    Chicken Barley Chili, 305
    Chili, Chicken, Corn Chowder, 306
    Curried Chicken with Fruit, 27
    Dad's Spicy Chicken Curry, 29
    Herby Barbecued Chicken, 67
    Old-Fashioned Stewed Chicken, 47
    Sunday Chicken Stew with Dumplings, 50–51
    Sunday Roast Chicken, 11
Chicken, Sweet Chicken, 59
Chicken Azteca, 37
Chicken Barley Chili, 305
Chicken breast
    So-Simple Salsa Chicken, 61
Chicken Cacciatore with Mushrooms, 55
Chicken Corn Chowder, 325
Chicken Corn Soup, 323
Chicken Curry with Rice, 31
Chicken Dijon Dinner, 16
Chicken Marengo, 22

Fix-It and Forget-It Slow Cooker Champion Recipes   587

Chicken Rice Soup, 322
Chicken stock, 565
   Chicken Corn Soup, 323
   Colcannon, 384
   Good Old Potato Soup, 328
   Party Wild Rice, 365
   Sunday Roast Chicken, 11
Chicken Tacos, 64
Chicken thighs
   African Chicken Treat, 66
   Bacon Ranch Slow-Cooked
     Chicken, 43
   Barbecued Chicken
     Sandwiches, 69
   Chicken, Sweet Chicken, 59
   Chicken Azteca, 37
   Chicken Cacciatore with
     Mushrooms, 55
   Chicken Corn Chowder,
     325
   Chicken Corn Soup, 323
   Chicken Curry with Rice,
     31
   Chicken Dijon Dinner, 16
   Chicken Marengo, 22
   Chicken Rice Soup, 322
   Chicken Tacos, 64
   Chicken Tikka Masala, 35
   Chicken Tortilla Soup, 307
   Chicken with Feta, 39
   Chicken with Fresh Fruit,
     26
   Chicken with Raspberry
     Jam, 25
   Chipotle Chili, 308
   Cornbread Chicken, 45
   Creamy Herbed Chicken,
     52
   Flaming Chicken Bombay,
     33
   Garlic Lime Chicken, 13
   Garlic Mushroom Chicken
     Thighs, 15
   Herby Barbecued Chicken,
     67
   Honey Garlic Chicken, 19
   Honey-Mustard Chicken,
     17, 18
   Lemon Greek Chicken, 20
   Maui Chicken, 23
   Mexican Chicken Bake, 65
   Mexican Stuffed Chicken, 42
   Our Favorite Chicken and
     Stuffing, 49
   Salsa Chicken Curry, 30
   Szechwan Chicken and
     Broccoli, 53
   Tangy Chicken, 21
   Teriyaki Chicken, 61
   Tex-Mex Chicken and
     Rice, 63
   Thai Chicken, 60
Chicken Tikka Masala, 35
Chicken Tortilla Soup, 307
Chicken wings
   Barbecued Chicken Wings,

73
Chicken with Feta, 39
Chicken with Fresh Fruit, 26
Chicken with Raspberry Jam,
   25
Chicken with Red Onions,
   Potatoes, and
   Rosemary, 38
Chili
   Beef and Sausage Chili, 302
   Best Bean Chili, 297
   Black Bean and Butternut
     Chili, 334
   Chicken Barley Chili, 305
   Chipotle Chili, 308
   Corn Chili, 300
   Lotsa-Beans Chili, 301
   Norma's Vegetarian Chili,
     333
   Ohio Chili, 299
   Pepperoni Pizza Chili, 303
   Trail Chili, 295
Chili, Chicken, Corn Chowder,
   306
Chili paste
   Pork Chops with a Hint of
     Asia, 175
Chili-Taco Soup, 294
Chipotle Chili, 308
Chipotle peppers
   Chipotle Chili, 308
Chocolate
   Triple Delicious Hot
     Chocolate, 555
Chocolate bar
   Chocolate Nut Clusters
     from the Crock, 520
   Easy Chocolate Clusters,
     521
Chocolate cake mix
   Black Forest Cake, 481
Chocolate chips
   Banana Chocolate Chip
     Bars, 493
   Chocolate Nut Clusters
     from the Crock, 520
   Easy Chocolate Clusters,
     521
   Hot Fudge Sauce, 528
   Raspberry Chocolate Chip
     Bread, 435
   Special Banana Bread, 431
   Triple Delicious Hot
     Chocolate, 555
Chocolate Covered Pretzels,
   522
Chocolate Fondue with
   Almonds and
   Marshmallows, 527
Chocolate Fondue with Kirsch,
   526
Chocolate Nut Clusters from
   the Crock, 520
Chocolate Rice Pudding, 502
Chocolate syrup
   Self-Frosting Fudge Cake,

480
   Vietnamese Coffee, 558
Chuck roast. See Beef chuck
   roast
Chunky Cranberry Applesauce,
   514
Classic Beef Stew, 113
Classic Spinach Lasagna, 229
Cobbler
   Apple Cobbler, 467
   Black and Blue Cobbler, 469
   Sour Cherry Cobbler, 473
Cocoa powder
   Chocolate Rice Pudding,
     502
   Fudgy Peanut Butter Cake,
     479
   Hot Fudge Cake, 477
   Ohio Chili, 299
   Triple Delicious Hot
     Chocolate, 555
Coconut
   Granola in the Slow
     Cooker, 455
   Special Times Carrots, 348
Coconut milk
   Jamaican Rice and Beans,
     252
   Thai Veggie Curry, 261
Coffee
   Dates in Cardamom Coffee
     Syrup, 519
   Vietnamese Coffee, 558
Cointreau
   Fruit Medley, 511
Cola
   Plum Roast, 97
Colcannon, 384
Cookie dough
   Gooey Cookie Dessert,
     495
Corn
   Baked corn, 402
   Beefy Vegetable Soup, 281
   Broccoli Corn Mix, 405
   Calico Beans with Corn,
     399
   Chicken Azteca, 37
   Chicken Barley Chili, 305
   Chicken Corn Soup, 323
   Corn Chili, 300
   Crock-o-Beans, 253
   Dilly Cornbread, 420
   Double Corn Tortilla Bake,
     247
   Mexican Chicken Bake, 65
   Mexican Corn, 403
   Mexican Rice and Beans,
     251
   Old-Fashioned Vegetable
     Beef Soup, 287
   Pineapple Cheddar
     Cornbread, 421
   Quinoa, and Black Beans,
     268
   Smoked Salmon Corn

     Chowder, 326
   Stuffed Pork Chops and
     Corn, 158
   Succotash, 404
   Summer Veggie Bake, 276
   Sunshine Dish, 257
   Super Creamed Corn, 401
   Taco Soup with Corn, 304
Corn Chili, 300
Corn chips
   Salsa Lentils, 263
   Taco Soup with Corn, 304
Cornbread
   Broccoli Cornbread, 419
   Creamy Black-Eyed Peas,
     259
   Dilly Cornbread, 420
Cornbread Chicken, 45
Cornbread from Scratch, 418
Cornbread Mix, Homemade,
   571
Cornbread stuffing
   Stuffed Flank Steak, 134
Cornbread-Topped Frijoles,
   250
Corned Beef and Cabbage, 108
Cornflakes
   Cheesy Meat Loaf, 147
Cottage Potatoes, 371
Couscous
   Winter's Night Beef Stew,
     283
Crab
   Cheese and Crab Dip, 536
Crab Spread, 541
Cranberries
   Chunky Cranberry
     Applesauce, 514
   Festive Applesauce, 513
   Grain and Fruit Cereal, 457
   Southwest Cranberries, 518
   Soy-Flax Granola, 456
   White Chocolate Bread
     Pudding, 499
   Whole Cranberry Sauce,
     515
Cranberry Applesauce, 414
Cranberry Brisket, 104
Cranberry juice
   Hot Spicy Lemonade Punch,
     549
   Pomegranate Punch, 552
Cranberry Orange Pork Roast,
   190
Cranberry Sauce with Red
     Wine and Oranges, 517
Cream
   Bold Butterscotch Sauce,
     525
   Carrot Ginger Soup, 336
   Chicken Tikka Masala, 35
   Creamy Scalloped Potatoes,
     373
   Tomato Basil Soup, 331
   Vietnamese Coffee, 558
Cream cheese

Championship Bean Dip, 533
Cheese and Crab Dip, 536
Chicken Azteca, 37
Chicken Corn Chowder, 325
Chicken Tacos, 64
Crab Spread, 541
Creamy Artichoke Dip, 537
Creamy Orange Cheesecake, 485
Creamy Red Potatoes, 379
Creamy Sausage and Potatoes, 212
Creamy Ziti in the Crock, 237
Hot Cheese and Bacon Dip, 532
Italiano Spread, 538
Make-Ahead Mixed Potatoes Florentine, 377
Overnight Veggie Omelet, 448
Roasted Pepper and Artichoke Spread, 539
Slow-Cooker Cinnamon Rolls, 436–437
Summer Squash Lasagna, 233
Super Creamed Corn, 401
Sweet Pepper Burritos, 249
Zucchini Bread, 429
Cream of celery soup, 563, 564
Autumn Brisket, 103
Easy Veggie-Beef Soup, 291
homemade
  in microwave, 565
  on stove, 564
Ranch Hand Beef, 143
Scalloped Potatoes and Ham, 204
Cream of chicken soup
Bacon Ranch Slow-Cooked Chicken, 43
Chicken Tacos, 64
Creamy Herbed Chicken, 52
Our Favorite Chicken and Stuffing, 49
Summer Squash Delish, 352
Cream of mushroom soup, 561, 562
Creamy Herbed Chicken, 52
Easy Creamy Beef, 118
homemade
  in microwave, 563
  on stove, 562
Our Favorite Chicken and Stuffing, 49
Pork Chops with Mushroom Sauce, 171
Potatoes O'Brien, 372
Quick Broccoli Fix, 406
Scalloped Potatoes and Ham, 204

Slow-Cooked Turkey Dinner, 83
Stuffed Pork Chops and Corn, 158
Creamy Artichoke Dip, 537
Creamy Black-Eyed Peas, 259
Creamy Ham and Red Beans Over Rice, 205
Creamy Herbed Chicken, 52
Creamy Mac and Cheese, 240
Creamy Orange Cheesecake, 485
Creamy Potato Soup, 329
Creamy Red Potatoes, 379
Creamy Sausage and Potatoes, 212
Creamy Scalloped Potatoes, 373
Creamy Taco Dip, 534
Creamy Tomato Soup, 330
Creamy Ziti in the Crock, 237
Crock-o-Beans, 253
Crustless Spinach Quiche, 274
Cubed French Toast, 450
Cucumber
  Middle East Sandwiches, 145
Currant jelly
  Sausages in Wine, 542
Curried Almonds, 543
Curried Carrot Ginger Soup, 337
Curried Chicken with Fruit, 27
Curried Lentils, 266
Curried Pork and Pea Soup, 316

D
Dad's Spicy Chicken Curry, 29
Date and Nut Bread, 427
Dates
  Carrot Cake, 483
  Date and Nut Bread, 427
  Orange Slice Cake, 486
  Pumpkin Chutney, 413
Dates in Cardamom Coffee Syrup, 519
Deluxe Tapioca Pudding, 503
Dilly Cornbread, 420
DIY Velveeta Cheese, 575
Double Corn Tortilla Bake, 247
Dr. Pepper
  Pulled Pork with Dr. Pepper, 187
Dressed-Up Acorn Squash, 351
Dried fruit
  Turkey with Sweet Potatoes and Dried Fruit, 82
Dumplings
  Sunday Chicken Stew with Dumplings, 50–51
Dutch Apple Batter Bread, 434

E
Easy Autumn Cake, 475
Easy Black Bean Lasagna, 231

Easy Chocolate Clusters, 521
Easy Creamy Beef, 118
Easy Ketchup, 572
Easy Rice Pudding, 501
Easy Veggie-Beef Soup, 291
Egg and Broccoli, 445
Egg and Cheese Bake, 443
Eggplant
  Armenian Eggplant, 411
Eggs
  Breakfast Skillet, 442
  Cheese Grits, 460
  Huevos Rancheros, 447
  Overnight Veggie Omelet, 448
  Spinach Frittata, 446
  Western Omelet, 444
Enchilada Stack-Up, 151
Extra-Crispy Apple Crisp, 471

F
Fajita Steak, 141
Farro, 570
Festive Applesauce, 513
Festive Meatballs, 148
Figs
  Soy-Flax Granola, 456
Filled Acorn Squash, 273
Flaming Chicken Bombay, 33
Flank steak. See Beef flank steak
Flavorful Meat Loaf, 146
Foil-Wrapped Baked Potatoes, 370
Four Beans and Sausage, 396
French Onion Soup, 340
French Toast, Cubed, 450
French Toast with Apples and Nuts, 449
Fresh Fruit Compote, 510
Fresh Vegetables Pasta Sauce, 221
Frosting, 436–437
Fruit, dried
  Fruit Medley, 511
  Granola in the Slow Cooker, 455
  Soy-Flax Granola, 456
  Turkey with Sweet Potatoes and Dried Fruit, 82
Fruit, mixed
  Fruity Flank Steak, 135
  Pork Loin with Savory Fruit Sauce, 176
Fruit Medley, 511
Fruity Beef Tagine, 120
Fruity Flank Steak, 135
Fruity Sweet Potatoes, 386
Fruity Wild Rice with Pecans, 366
Fudgy Peanut Butter Cake, 479

G
Garbanzo Souper, 320
Garlic Hummus, 581
Garlic Lime Chicken, 13

Garlic Mashed Potatoes, 375
Garlic Mushroom Chicken Thighs, 15
Garlicky Potatoes, 378
Ginger, fresh
  Carrot Ginger Soup, 336
  Festive Applesauce, 513
  Ginger Tea, 551
  Pomegranate Punch, 552
  Pork Loin with Savory Fruit Sauce, 176
  Pumpkin Chutney, 413
  Slow-Cooker Chai, 548
  Thai Chicken, 60
Ginger ale
  Barbecued Ham Steaks, 200
Ginger Tea, 551
Gingerbread, 425
Gingerbread Pudding Cake, 489
Gingersnaps
  Sauerbraten, 110
Golden Autumn Stew, 215
Golden raisins
  Apple Raisin Ham, 197
Good Old Potato Soup, 328
Good-Time Beef Brisket, 105
Gooey Cookie Dessert, 495
Graham cracker
  Creamy Orange Cheesecake, 485
  Seven-Layer Bars, 491
Grain and Fruit Cereal, 457
Granola
  Breakfast Apple Cobbler, 462
  Soy-Flax Granola, 456
Granola in the Slow Cooker, 455
Grape juice
  Scandinavian Fruit Soup, 512
  Strawberry Rhubarb Sauce, 509
Greek Bread, 422
Green beans
  Armenian Eggplant, 411
  Barbecued Green Beans, 344
  Beefy Vegetable Soup, 281
  Easy Veggie-Beef Soup, 291
  Green Beans Caesar, 346
  Green Beans Get-Together, 345
  Lotsa-Beans Chili, 301
  Minestrone, 318
  Pork Loin with Savory Fruit Sauce, 176
  Potatoes and Green Beans with Ham, 203
  Santa Fe Stew, 117
  Smoked Sausage Stew, 314
  Vegetable Beef Borscht, 282
Green Beans and Sausage, 214
Green Beans Caesar, 346
Green Beans Get-Together, 345

Green chilies
  Arroz con Queso, 246
  Chicken Corn Chowder, 325
  Chicken Tortilla Soup, 307
  Chicken with Fresh Fruit, 26
  Chili, Chicken, Corn Chowder, 306
  Chipotle Chili, 308
  Double Corn Tortilla Bake, 247
  Enchilada Stack-Up, 151
  Fajita Steak, 141
  Machaca Beef, 96
  Melt-in-Your-Mouth Mexican Meat Dish, 101
  Mexican Stuffed Chicken, 42
  New Mexico Beef & Pork Stew, 123
  Ohio Chili, 299
  Santa Fe Stew, 117
  Tastes-Like-Chili-Rellenos, 245
  Tex-Mex Chicken and Rice, 63
  Trail Chili, 295
  Turkey Fajitas, 84
Grits
  Cheese Grits, 460
  Mexican-Style Grits, 461
Ground beef
  Beef and Sausage Chili, 302
  Best Bean Chili, 297
  Calico Beans with Corn, 399
  Cheesy Meat Loaf, 147
  Chet's Trucker Stew, 312
  Corn Chili, 300
  Creamy Taco Dip, 534
  Easy Veggie-Beef Soup, 291
  Enchilada Stack-Up, 151
  Festive Meatballs, 148
  Flavorful Meat Loaf, 146
  Lasagna Mexicana, 149
  Lotsa-Beans Chili, 301
  Pepperoni Pizza Chili, 303
  Spaghetti Sauce with a Kick, 152
  Taco Soup with Corn, 304
  Tasty Meatball Stew, 293
  Trail Chili, 295
Ground chuck
  Cheesy Meat Loaf, 147

H
Ham
  Apple Raisin Ham, 197
  Black Beans with Ham, 202
  Blessing Soup, 319
  Creamy Ham and Red Beans Over Rice, 205
  deviled
    Festive Meatballs, 148
  Green Beans Get-Together, 345

Honey-Dijon Holiday Ham, 198
Potatoes and Green Beans with Ham, 203
Red Beans and Rice, 390
Scalloped Potatoes and Ham, 204
Split Pea Soup, 317
Sweet Potato Chowder, 327
Western Omelet, 444
Ham in Cider, 201
Ham with Sweet Potatoes and Oranges, 199
Hamburger
  Ohio Chili, 299
Healthy Whole Wheat Bread, 417
Hearty Irish Soda Bread, 423
Hearty New England Dinner, 90
Herbal Apple Cheese Dish, 278
Herbed Rice and Lentil Bake, 260
Herb-Roasted Turkey Breast, 75
Herby Barbecued Chicken, 67
Homemade Applesauce, 576
Homemade Cornbread Mix, 571
Homemade Frozen Hashbrowns, 571
Homemade Refried Beans, 391
Homemade Yogurt, 577
Home-Style Tomato Juice, 578
Honey Barbecue Pork Chops, 155
Honey Garlic Chicken, 19
Honey-Dijon Holiday Ham, 198
Honey-Mustard Chicken (Deluxe Version), 17
Honey-Mustard Chicken (Quick and Easy Version), 18
Horseradish Carrot Coins, 349
Horseradish jam
  Zingy Short Ribs, 129
Horseradish Mac and Cheese, 239
Hot Bacon Salad Dressing, 582
Hot Caramel Dip, 547
Hot Cheddar Mushroom Spread, 540
Hot Cheese and Bacon Dip, 532
Hot Chili Dip, 535
Hot Cranberry Cider, 553
Hot Fruit, 412
Hot Fudge Cake, 477
Hot Fudge Sauce, 528
Hot Spicy Lemonade Punch, 549
Huevos Rancheros, 447
Hummus
  Garbanzo Souper, 320
  Garlic Hummus, 581

Hungarian Goulash, 119

I
Ice cream
  Gooey Cookie Dessert, 495
Indonesian Turkey, 79
Irish Soda Bread, 423
Italian Beef Stew, 123
Italian Sausage Spaghetti, 209
Italiano Spread, 538

J
Jamaican Rice and Beans, 252
Just Peachy Ribs, 193

K
Kale
  Colcannon, 384
  Sausage and Kale Stew with Mashed Potatoes, 310
  Vegetable Soup, 332
Ketchup, 572
  Apple Bean Bake, 400
  Baked beans and Chops, 163
  Barbecued Beans, 393
  Barbecued Chicken Sandwiches, 69
  Barbecued Green Beans, 344
  Barbecued Roast Beef, 142
  Barbecued Turkey Cutlets, 80
  Beef Burgundy, 121
  Calico Beans with Corn, 399
  Chet's Trucker Stew, 312
  Flavorful Meat Loaf, 146
  Four Beans and Sausage, 396
  Lemon Sweet Pork Chops, 173
  Pork Chops in Orange Sauce, 165
  Pulled Pork BBQ, 185
  Round Steak Roll-Ups, 138
  Six-Bean Barbecue, 398
  Smoked Beef Brisket, 107
Kielbasa
  Pork and Apricots with Mashed Sweet Potatoes, 188–189
  Kielbasa and Veggies Soup, 311
Kiwi
  Chicken with Fresh Fruit, 26

L
Lasagna
  Classic Spinach Lasagna, 229
  Easy Black Bean Lasagna, 231
  Summer Squash Lasagna, 233
  Vegetarian Lasagna, 235

Lasagna Mexicana, 149
Layered Herby Stew, 111
Leeks
  Colcannon, 384
  Good Old Potato Soup, 32
Lemon Bread, 432
Lemon Greek Chicken, 20
Lemon Pudding Cake, 487
Lemon Red Potatoes, 380
Lemon Sweet Pork Chops, 17.
Lemonade
  Hot Spicy Lemonade Punch, 549
Lentils
  Baked Lentils with Cheese, 267
  Curried Lentils, 266
  Herbed Rice and Lentil Bake, 260
  Russian Red Lentil Soup, 321
  Salsa Lentils, 263
  Sausage Town, 217
Lentils Swiss Style, 265
Lettuce
  Middle East Sandwiches, 145
Lotsa Veggies Spaghetti, 224
Lotsa-Beans Chili, 301

M
Mac and Cheese
  Creamy Mac and Cheese, 240
  Horseradish Mac and Cheese, 239
Machaca Beef, 96
Make-Ahead Mixed Potatoes Florentine, 377
Maple Apple Topping, 523
Maple Baked Beans, 395
Maple syrup
  Autumn Sweet Potatoes, 387
  Cubed French Toast, 450
  Grain and Fruit Cereal, 457
  Maple Apple Topping, 523
  Maple Baked Beans, 395
  Maple-Glazed Turkey Breast with Rice, 78
  Steel-Cut Oats with Bananas, 454
Maple-Glazed Turkey Breast with Rice, 78
Marmalade
  Plums for Breakfast, 463
  Pork Chops in Orange Sauce, 165
  Pork Chops with a Hint of Asia, 175
Marshmallow Applesauce Dessert, 505
Marshmallows
  Chocolate Fondue with Almonds and Marshmallows, 527

Indexes

ashed Potatoes, 374
Matthew's Hot Mulled Cider, 554
Maui Chicken, 23
Mayonnaise
  Crab Spread, 541
  Creamy Artichoke Dip, 537
  Hot Cheddar Mushroom Spread, 540
  Quick Broccoli Fix, 406
  Tomato-Glazed Pork with Grilled Corn Salsa, 180–181
Meat loaf
  Cheesy Meat Loaf, 147
  Flavorful Meat Loaf, 146
Meatless Baked Beans, 392
Mediterranean Onions, 409
Melt-in-Your-Mouth Mexican Meat Dish, 101
Melt-in-Your-Mouth Sausages, 207
Mexican Chicken Bake, 65
Mexican Corn, 403
Mexican Pot Roast, 93
Mexican Rice and Beans, 251
Mexican Stuffed Chicken, 42
Mexican-Style Grits, 461
Middle East Sandwiches, 145
Milk, condensed
  Chocolate Fondue with Kirsch, 526
  Hot Caramel Dip, 547
  Seven-Layer Bars, 491
  Slow-Cooker Chai, 548
Milk, evaporated
  Chicken Corn Chowder, 325
  Chocolate Rice Pudding, 502
  Creamy Mac and Cheese, 240
  Festive Meatballs, 148
  Good Old Potato Soup, 328
  Horseradish Mac and Cheese, 239
  Hot Fudge Sauce, 528
  Scalloped Cabbage, 354
  Slow-Cooker Chai, 548
  Tastes-Like-Chili-Rellenos, 245
Millet
  Grain and Fruit Cereal, 457
  Millet in the Slow Cooker, 568
Minestra Di Ceci, 243
Minestrone, 318
Molasses
  Apple Bean Bake, 400
  Beans with Turkey Bacon, 394
  Meatless Baked Beans, 392
  Mom's New England Baked Beans, 388
  Old-Fashioned Ginger Bread, 425
  Pumpkin Breakfast Custard,

464
Six-Bean Barbecue, 398
Mom's New England Baked Beans, 388
Moroccan Beef Stew, 286
Moroccan Sweet Potato Medley, 271
Mushroom Spaghetti Sauce, 225
Mushrooms
  Barley with Mushrooms, 270
  Beef Burgundy, 121
  Beef Roast with Mushroom Barley, 89
  Breakfast Skillet, 442
  Cauliflower Cassoulet, 407
  Chicken Cacciatore with Mushrooms, 55
  Chicken Dijon Dinner, 16
  Easy Creamy Beef, 118
  Garlic Mushroom Chicken Thighs, 15
  Hot Cheddar Mushroom Spread, 540
  Mushrooms Italian, 361
  Oxford Canal Chops Deluxe, 167
  Pork Chops with Mushroom Sauce, 171
  Pot-Roast Complete, 102
  Quick Broccoli Fix, 406
  Ranch Hand Beef, 143
  Ready-When-You-Get-Home Dinner, 115
  Slow-Cooker Beef with Mushrooms, 137
  Summer Squash Lasagna, 233
  Wild Rice, 363
  Wild Rice Bake, 364
Mushrooms Italian, 361
Mustard
  Baked beans and Chops, 163
  Barbecued Ribs, 194
  Bavarian Beef, 67
  BBQ Pork Ribs, 196
  Beans with Turkey Bacon, 394
  Breakfast Skillet, 442
  Calico Beans with Corn, 399
  Chet's Trucker Stew, 312
  Chicken Dijon Dinner, 16
  Cranberry Brisket, 104
  Honey-Dijon Holiday Ham, 198
  Honey-Mustard Chicken, 17, 18
  Horseradish Mac and Cheese, 239
  Hot Bacon Salad Dressing, 582
  Meatless Baked Beans, 392
  North Carolina Barbecue,

183
Six-Bean Barbecue, 398
Smoked Beef Brisket, 107
Spicy Pork Chops, 157
Tasty Meatball Stew, 293
Tomato-Glazed Pork with Grilled Corn Salsa, 180–181
Veggie Mac and Cheese, 238

N
New Mexico Beef & Pork Stew, 123
Noodles. See also Pasta
  Bacon Ranch Slow-Cooked Chicken, 43
  Cheesy Buffalo Chicken Pasta, 57
  Classic Spinach Lasagna, 229
  Lasagna Mexicana, 149
  Pork Chops with a Hint of Asia, 175
  Sausage Tortellini, 218
Norma's Vegetarian Chili, 333
North Carolina Barbecue, 183

O
Oatmeal Morning, 451
Oats
  Apple Cider Cinnamon Steel-Cut Oatmeal, 453
  Apple Oatmeal, 452
  Extra-Crispy Apple Crisp, 471
  Granola in the Slow Cooker, 455
  Quick and Yummy Peaches, 470
  Raspberry Chocolate Chip Bread, 435
  Soy-Flax Granola, 456
Ohio Chili, 299
Old World Sauerkraut Supper, 211
Old-Fashioned Ginger Bread, 425
Old-Fashioned Stewed Chicken, 47
Old-Fashioned Vegetable Beef Soup, 287
Olives
  Fresh Vegetables Pasta Sauce, 221
  Hot Chili Dip, 535
  Lasagna Mexicana, 149
  Mediterranean Onions, 409
  Pasta with Tomatoes, Olives, and Two Cheeses, 223
  Southern Italy Sauce, 228
Onion soup, French, 340
Onion soup mix
  Easy Creamy Beef, 118
  Hearty New England Dinner, 90
  Pork Roast with Sauerkraut,

191
Savory Slow Cooker Pork Tenderloin, 179
Wild Rice Bake, 364
Onions
  Chicken with Red Onions, Potatoes, and Rosemary, 38
  French Onion Soup, 340
  Mediterranean, 409
Orange juice
  Chicken with Fresh Fruit, 26
  Creamy Orange Cheesecake, 485
  Dressed-Up Acorn Squash, 351
  Ham with Sweet Potatoes and Oranges, 199
  Orange-Glazed Carrots, 347
  Piquant Chuck Roast, 92
  Plums for Breakfast, 463
  Pomegranate Punch, 552
  Pork Chops in Orange Sauce, 165
  Pork Chops with a Hint of Asia, 175
  Spicy Citrus Warmer, 550
  Turkey Breast with Orange Sauce, 76
  Turkey with Sweet Potatoes and Dried Fruit, 82
Orange Slice Cake, 486
Orange-Glazed Carrots, 347
Oranges
  Chocolate Fondue with Almonds and Marshmallows, 527
  Ham with Sweet Potatoes and Oranges, 199
Our Favorite Chicken and Stuffing, 49
Overnight Veggie Omelet, 448
Oxford Canal Chops Deluxe, 167

P
Parmesan Potato Wedges, 382
Parsley, Sage, and Ginger Turkey, 81
Parsnips
  Can't Beet Beef Stew, 285
Party Wild Rice, 365
Pasta
  Bacon Ranch Slow-Cooked Chicken, 43
  Cheesy Buffalo Chicken Pasta, 57
  Cherry Tomato Spaghetti Sauce, 227
  Classic Spinach Lasagna, 229
  Creamy Mac and Cheese, 240
  Creamy Ziti in the Crock, 237

Fix-It and Forget-It Slow Cooker Champion Recipes   591

Easy Black Bean Lasagna, 231
Fresh Vegetables Pasta Sauce, 221
Horseradish Mac and Cheese, 239
Kielbasa and Veggies Soup, 311
Lasagna Mexicana, 149
Lotsa Veggies Spaghetti, 224
Minestrone, 318
Mushroom Spaghetti Sauce, 225
Pork Chops with a Hint of Asia, 175
Red Beans and Pasta, 241
Sausage Tortellini, 218
Southern Italy Sauce, 228
Summer Squash Lasagna, 233
Tortellini with Broccoli, 244
Vegetarian Lasagna, 235
Veggie Mac and Cheese, 238
Pasta Bean Pot, 242
Pasta with Tomatoes, Olives, and Two Cheeses, 223
Peach jam
Spicy Pork Olé, 182
Peaches
Curried Chicken with Fruit, 27
Fresh Fruit Compote, 510
Hot Fruit, 412
Just Peachy Ribs, 193
Quick and Yummy Peaches, 470
Peanut butter
African Chicken Treat, 66
Apple Caramel Peanut Topping, 524
Butter Chicken, 41
Fudgy Peanut Butter Cake, 479
Indonesian Turkey, 79
Thai Chicken, 60
Peanut butter chips
Chocolate Nut Clusters from the Crock, 520
Peanut Butter Pumpkin Soup, 338
Peanuts
Chocolate Nut Clusters from the Crock, 520
Easy Chocolate Clusters, 521
Thai Chicken, 60
Pearl barley, 570
Barley with Mushrooms, 270
Beef Roast with Mushroom Barley, 89
Pears
Festive Applesauce, 513
Hot Fruit, 412
Zesty Pears, 506

Peas
Beefy Vegetable Soup, 281
Chicken Curry with Rice, 31
Italian Beef Stew, 123
split
Curried Pork and Pea Soup, 316
Sunday Chicken Stew with Dumplings, 50–51
Thai Veggie Curry, 261
Vegetable Party, 357
Peas and Rice, 368
Pecans
Apple Cake, 474
Apple Cider Cinnamon Steel-Cut Oatmeal, 453
Apple-Nut Bread Pudding, 500
Cubed French Toast, 450
Dressed-Up Acorn Squash, 351
Easy Autumn Cake, 475
French Toast with Apples and Nuts, 449
Fruity Wild Rice with Pecans, 366
Gingerbread Pudding Cake, 489
Granola in the Slow Cooker, 455
Party Wild Rice, 365
Soy-Flax Granola, 456
Pepper jam
Southwest Cranberries, 518
Zingy Short Ribs, 129
Pepperoni Pizza Chili, 303
Peppers
Black Bean Burritos, 248
Chipotle Chili, 308
Creamy Artichoke Dip, 537
Homemade Refried Beans, 391
Pico de Gallo, 580
Powerhouse Beef Roast with Tomatoes, Onions, and Peppers, 87
Salsa Lentils, 263
Slow-Cooked Salsa, 579
Three-Pepper Steak, 139
Peppery Roast, 91
Pesto
Italiano Spread, 538
Picante sauce
Championship Bean Dip, 533
Sausage, Tomato, Spinach Soup, 313
Szechwan Chicken and Broccoli, 53
Taco Soup with Corn, 304
Pico de Gallo, 580
Pie filling
Apple Raisin Ham, 197
Black Forest Cake, 481
Cherry Delight, 472

Pimento
Mexican Corn, 403
Potatoes O'Brien, 372
Pine nuts
Filled Acorn Squash, 273
Pineapple
Chicken with Fresh Fruit, 26
Chocolate Fondue with Almonds and Marshmallows, 527
Fresh Fruit Compote, 510
Maui Chicken, 23
Pumpkin Chutney, 413
Special Times Carrots, 348
Pineapple Cheddar Cornbread, 421
Pineapple juice
Spicy Citrus Warmer, 550
Piquant Chuck Roast, 92
Pizza
Barbecued Chicken Pizza, 71
Plum Roast, 97
Plums
Curried Chicken with Fruit, 27
Fruity Beef Tagine, 120
Pork Loin with Savory Fruit Sauce, 176
Scandinavian Fruit Soup, 512
Plums for Breakfast, 463
Polenta
Breakfast Polenta with Bacon, 459
Pomegranate Punch, 552
Poppy Seed Tea Bread, 433
Pork and Apricots with Mashed Sweet Potatoes, 188–189
Pork and beans
Barbecued Beans, 393
Calico Beans with Corn, 399
Chet's Trucker Stew, 312
Maple Baked Beans, 395
Six-Bean Barbecue, 398
Pork and Sweet Potatoes, 159
Pork butt roast
Cranberry Orange Pork Roast, 190
North Carolina Barbecue, 183
Pulled Pork BBQ, 185
Pulled Pork with Dr. Pepper, 187
Pork chops
Apples, Sauerkraut, and Chops, 169
Honey Barbecue Pork Chops, 155
Lemon Sweet Pork Chops, 173
Oxford Canal Chops Deluxe, 167
Pork and Sweet Potatoes,

159
Spicy Pork Chops, 157
Stuffed Pork Chops and Corn, 158
Pork Chops in Orange Sauce, 165
Pork Chops Pierre, 161
Pork Chops with a Hint of Asia, 175
Pork Chops with Mushroom Sauce, 171
Pork cubes
Barbecued Pork and Beef Sandwiches, 184
Pork loin
Autumn Harvest Pork Loin, 177
Savory Slow Cooker Pork Tenderloin, 179
Spicy Pork Olé, 182
Tomato-Glazed Pork with Grilled Corn Salsa, 180–181
Pork Loin with Savory Fruit Sauce, 176
Pork ribs, country-style
BBQ Pork Ribs, 196
Sesame Pork Ribs, 195
Pork Roast with Sauerkraut, 191
Pork sausage
Beef and Sausage Chili, 302
Chet's Trucker Stew, 312
Flavorful Meat Loaf, 146
New Mexico Beef & Pork Stew, 123
Red Beans and Rice, 390
Texas Queso Dip, 531
Pork shoulder roast
Curried Pork and Pea Soup, 316
Pork and Apricots with Mashed Sweet Potatoes, 188–189
Pork Roast with Sauerkraut, 191
Pork spareribs
Barbecued Ribs, 194
Just Peachy Ribs, 193
Saucy Spareribs, 192
Portobello mushrooms
Summer Squash Lasagna, 233
Potatoes. See also Sweet potatoes
Apple Corned Beef and Cabbage, 109
Breakfast Skillet, 442
Butter-Rubbed Baked Potatoes, 369
Chicken Corn Soup, 323
Chicken with Red Onions, Potatoes, and Rosemary 38
Classic Beef Stew, 113
Colcannon, 384

Indexes

Cottage Potatoes, 371
Creamy Potato Soup, 329
Creamy Red Potatoes, 379
Creamy Sausage and
    Potatoes, 212
Creamy Scalloped Potatoes,
    373
Dad's Spicy Chicken Curry,
    29
Flavorful Meat Loaf, 146
Foil-Wrapped Baked
    Potatoes, 370
Garlic Mashed Potatoes,
    375
Garlicky Potatoes, 378
Golden Autumn Stew, 215
Good Old Potato Soup, 328
Homemade Frozen
    Hashbrowns, 571
Layered Herby Stew, 111
Lemon Red Potatoes, 380
Make-Ahead Mixed
    Potatoes Florentine, 377
Mashed Potatoes, 374
New Mexico Beef & Pork
    Stew, 123
Parmesan Potato Wedges,
    382
Rosemary New Potatoes,
    381
Sauerkraut Soup, 315
Sausage and Kale Stew with
    Mashed Potatoes, 310
Scalloped Potatoes and
    Ham, 204
Slow-Cooked Turkey
    Dinner, 83
Smoked Salmon Corn
    Chowder, 326
Smoked Sausage Stew, 314
Sweet Potato Chowder,
    327
Tasty Meatball Stew, 293
Thai Veggie Curry, 261
Vegetable Curry, 359
Vegetable Party, 357
otatoes and Green Beans
    with Ham, 203
otatoes O'Brien, 372
otatoes Perfect, 383
ot-Roast Complete, 102
owerhouse Beef Roast with
    Tomatoes, Onions, and
    Peppers, 87
reserves
    Barbecued Ribs, 194
    Tangy Chicken, 21
retzels
    Chocolate Covered
    Pretzels, 522
    Chocolate Fondue
    with Almonds and
    Marshmallows, 527
    Spicy Nut and Pretzel Mix,
    544
runes

Curried Chicken with
    Fruit, 27
Moroccan Beef Stew, 286
Pumpkin Chutney, 413
Pulled Pork BBQ, 185
Pulled Pork with Dr. Pepper,
    187
Pumpkin
    Peanut Butter Pumpkin
    Soup, 338
Pumpkin Black-Bean Turkey
    Chili, 339
Pumpkin Breakfast Custard,
    464
Pumpkin Butter, 545
Pumpkin Chutney, 413

Q
Quick and Yummy Peaches, 470
Quick Broccoli Fix, 406
Quinoa
    Grain and Fruit Cereal, 457
    Vegetables with Red
    Quinoa, 269
Quinoa, and Black Beans, 268

R
Raisin bread
    Apple-Nut Bread Pudding,
    500
Raisin Nut-Stuffed Apples, 507
Raisins
    Apple Raisin Ham, 197
    Boston Brown Bread, 424
    Bread Pudding, 497
    Carrot Cake, 483
    Fruity Wild Rice with
    Pecans, 366
    Ham in Cider, 201
    Moroccan Sweet Potato
    Medley, 271
    Party Wild Rice, 365
    Pumpkin Chutney, 413
    Soy-Flax Granola, 456
    Sweet and Tangy Cabbage,
    355
    Zesty Pears, 506
Ranch dressing mix
    Bacon Ranch Slow-Cooked
    Chicken, 43
    Creamy Sausage and
    Potatoes, 212
    Hot Cheddar Mushroom
    Spread, 540
Ranch Hand Beef, 143
Rarebit
    Baked Tomato Rarebit, 277
    Welsh Rarebit, 441
Raspberry Chocolate Chip
    Bread, 435
Raspberry jam
    Chicken with Raspberry
    Jam, 25
Ready-When-You-Get-Home
    Dinner, 115
Red Beans and Pasta, 241

Red Beans and Rice, 390
Red onions
    Chicken with Red Onions,
    Potatoes, and Rosemary,
    38
Refrigerator biscuits
    Caramel Rolls, 438
Rhubarb
    Strawberry Rhubarb Sauce,
    509
Rhubarb Sauce, 508
Ribs. See Beef short ribs; Pork
    spareribs
Rice
    Arborio
        Easy Rice Pudding, 501
        Risotto in the Crock,
        367
    Arroz con Queso, 246
    brown
        Brown Rice Vegetable
        Dinner, 255
        Cauliflower Cassoulet,
        407
        Grain and Fruit Cereal,
        457
        Herbed Rice and Lentil
        Bake, 260
        Mexican Chicken Bake,
        65
        Mexican Rice and Beans,
        251
    Chicken Curry with Rice,
        31
    Chicken Rice Soup, 322
    Chocolate Rice Pudding,
        502
    Creamy Ham and Red
        Beans Over Rice, 205
    Crock-o-Beans, 253
    Flaming Chicken Bombay,
        33
    Jamaican Rice and Beans,
        252
    Maple-Glazed Turkey Breast
        with Rice, 78
    Peas and Rice, 368
    Red Beans and Rice, 390
    Sausage Town, 217
    Spinach Rice Bake, 262
    Sunshine Dish, 257
    Sweet Pepper Burritos, 249
    Tex-Mex Chicken and
        Rice, 63
    Thai Veggie Curry, 261
    Vegetable Party, 357
    wild
        Chicken Rice Soup, 322
        Fruity Wild Rice with
        Pecans, 366
        Maple-Glazed Turkey
        Breast with Rice, 78
        Party Wild Rice, 365
        Ready-When-You-Get-
        Home Dinner, 115
        Wild Rice, 363

Wild Rice Bake, 363
Rice Pudding, 502
Risotto in the Crock, 367
Roasted Pepper and Artichoke
    Spread, 539
Rosemary
    Chicken with Red Onions,
    Potatoes, and Rosemary,
    38
Rosemary New Potatoes, 381
Round steak. See Beef round
    steak
Round Steak Roll-Ups, 138
Round tip roast. See Beef
    round tip roast
Russian Red Lentil Soup, 321
Rutabaga
    Golden Autumn Stew, 215
Rye, 570

S
Salmon, smoked
    Smoked Salmon Corn
    Chowder, 326
Salsa
    Chicken Azteca, 37
    Chicken Barley Chili, 305
    Chicken Tacos, 64
    Creamy Taco Dip, 534
    Fajita Steak, 141
    Hot Chili Dip, 535
    Huevos Rancheros, 447
    Lasagna Mexicana, 149
    Machaca Beef, 96
    Mexican Pot Roast, 93
    Mexican Rice and Beans,
    251
    Powerhouse Beef Roast
    with Tomatoes, Onions,
    and Peppers, 87
    Slow-Cooked Salsa, 579
    So-Simple Salsa Chicken, 61
    Spicy Pork Olé, 182
    Sweet Pepper Burritos, 249
    Tangy Chicken, 21
    Thai Chicken, 60
    Tomato-Glazed Pork with
    Grilled Corn Salsa,
    180–181
Salsa Chicken Curry, 30
Salsa Lentils, 263
Saltines
    Quick Broccoli Fix, 406
Sandwich
    Barbecued Chicken
    Sandwiches, 69
    Barbecued Pork and Beef
    Sandwiches, 184
    Middle East Sandwiches,
    145
Santa Fe Stew, 117
Saucy Mushrooms, 362
Saucy Spareribs, 192
Sauerbraten, 110
Sauerkraut
    Apples, Sauerkraut, and

Chops, 169
Beef Ribs with Sauerkraut, 133
Old World Sauerkraut Supper, 211
Pork Roast with Sauerkraut, 191
Sauerkraut Soup, 315
Sausage
Beef and Sausage Chili, 302
Cajun Sausage and Beans, 397
Chet's Trucker Stew, 312
Creamy Sausage and Potatoes, 212
Flavorful Meat Loaf, 146
Four Beans and Sausage, 396
Golden Autumn Stew, 215
Green Beans and Sausage, 214
Italian
Italian Sausage Spaghetti, 209
Melt-in-Your-Mouth Sausages, 207
Sausage and Kale Stew with Mashed Potatoes, 310
Sausages in Wine, 542
Spaghetti Sauce with a Kick, 152
kielbasa
Kielbasa and Veggies Soup, 311
Pork and Apricots with Mashed Sweet Potatoes, 188–189
New Mexico Beef & Pork Stew, 123
Polish
Old World Sauerkraut Supper, 211
Sausages in Wine, 542
Red Beans and Rice, 390
Sauerkraut Soup, 315
Sausage, Tomato, Spinach Soup, 313
Smoked Sausage Stew, 314
Texas Queso Dip, 531
turkey
Sausage, Tomato, Spinach Soup, 313
Sausage, Tomato, Spinach Soup, 313
Sausage and Kale Stew with Mashed Potatoes, 310
Sausage and Sweet Potatoes, 213
Sausage Tortellini, 218
Sausage Town, 217
Sausages in Wine, 542
Savory Slow Cooker Pork Tenderloin, 179
Scalloped Cabbage, 354
Scalloped Potatoes and Ham, 204

Scandinavian Fruit Soup, 512
Self-Frosting Fudge Cake, 480
Sesame Pork Ribs, 195
Seven-Layer Bars, 491
7-Up
Barbecued Ham Steaks, 200
Short ribs. See Beef short ribs
Shrimp
Cheese and Crab Dip, 536
Simply Sweet Potatoes, 385
Six-Bean Barbecue, 398
Slow-Cooked Apple Butter, 573
Slow-Cooked Dried Beans, 567
Slow-Cooked Salsa, 579
Slow-Cooked Short Ribs, 131
Slow-Cooked Turkey Dinner, 83
Slow-Cooker Beef with Mushrooms, 137
Slow-Cooker Chai, 548
Slow-Cooker Cinnamon Rolls, 436–437
Smoked Beef Brisket, 107
Smoked Salmon Corn Chowder, 326
Smoked Sausage Stew, 314
Snow peas
Pork Chops with a Hint of Asia, 175
Teriyaki Chicken, 61
Soda
7-Up
Barbecued Ham Steaks, 200
cola
Plum Roast, 97
Dr. Pepper, 187
ginger ale
Barbecued Ham Steaks, 200
Sprite
Barbecued Ham Steaks, 200
Soda Bread, 423
So-Simple Salsa Chicken, 61
Sour Cherry Cobbler, 473
Sour cream
Butter Chicken, 41
Championship Bean Dip, 533
Chicken Barley Chili, 305
Curried Carrot Ginger Soup, 337
Festive Meatballs, 148
Hungarian Goulash, 119
Lasagna Mexicana, 149
Make-Ahead Mixed Potatoes Florentine, 377
Salsa Chicken Curry, 30
Salsa Lentils, 263
Smoked Salmon Corn Chowder, 326
Vegetable Beef Borscht, 282
Zesty Pears, 506
Southern Italy Sauce, 228
Southwest Cranberries, 518
Soy-Flax Granola, 456

Spaghetti Sauce with a Kick, 152
Spanish Round Steak, 127
Special Banana Bread, 431
Special Times Carrots, 348
Spelt, 570
Spice cake mix
Easy Autumn Cake, 475
Spicy Beef Roast, 94
Spicy Citrus Warmer, 550
Spicy Nut and Pretzel Mix, 544
Spicy Pork Chops, 157
Spicy Pork Olé, 182
Spinach
Breakfast Polenta with Bacon, 459
Classic Spinach Lasagna, 229
Crustless Spinach Quiche, 274
Curried Lentils, 266
Curried Pork and Pea Soup, 316
Dad's Spicy Chicken Curry, 29
Kielbasa and Veggies Soup, 311
Make-Ahead Mixed Potatoes Florentine, 377
Pot-Roast Complete, 102
Sausage, Tomato, Spinach Soup, 313
Yummy Spinach, 343
Spinach Frittata, 446
Spinach Rice Bake, 262
Split Pea Soup, 317
Split peas
Curried Pork and Pea Soup, 316
Sprite
Barbecued Ham Steaks, 200
Sriracha sauce
Saucy Spareribs, 192
Steak. See Beef flank steak; Beef round steak
Steel-Cut Oats with Bananas, 454
Stew
Can't Beet Beef Stew, 285
Chet's Trucker Stew, 312
Classic Beef Stew, 113
Golden Autumn Stew, 215
Italian Beef Stew, 123
Layered Herby Stew, 111
Moroccan Beef Stew, 286
New Mexico Beef & Pork Stew, 123
Santa Fe Stew, 117
Sausage and Kale Stew with Mashed Potatoes, 310
Smoked Sausage Stew, 314
Sunday Chicken Stew with Dumplings, 50–51
Tasty Meatball Stew, 293
Tuscan Beef Stew, 114
Winter's Night Beef Stew, 283
Strawberry Rhubarb Sauce, 509

Stuffed Flank Steak, 134
Stuffed Pork Chops and Corn, 158
Stuffed Turkey Breast, 77
Stuffing, cornbread
Stuffed Flank Steak, 134
Stuffing mix
Our Favorite Chicken and Stuffing, 49
Stuffed Pork Chops and Corn, 158
Succotash, 404
Summer squash
Fresh Vegetables Pasta Sauce, 221
Summer Squash Delish, 352
Summer Squash Lasagna, 233
Summer Veggie Bake, 276
Sunday Chicken Stew with Dumplings, 50–51
Sunday Roast Chicken, 11
Sunshine Dish, 257
Super Creamed Corn, 401
Sweet and Sour Red Cabbage, 356
Sweet and Tangy Cabbage, 355
Sweet Pepper Burritos, 249
Sweet Potato Chowder, 327
Sweet potatoes
Autumn Brisket, 103
Autumn Sweet Potatoes, 387
Chicken, Sweet Chicken, 5
Fruity Sweet Potatoes, 386
Golden Autumn Stew, 215
Ham with Sweet Potatoes and Oranges, 199
Make-Ahead Mixed Potatoes Florentine, 377
Moroccan Sweet Potato Medley, 271
Peanut Butter Pumpkin Soup, 338
Pork and Apricots with Mashed Sweet Potatoes, 188–189
Pork and Sweet Potatoes, 159
Sausage and Sweet Potatoes, 213
Simply Sweet Potatoes, 385
Sweet Potato Chowder, 327
Turkey with Sweet Potatoes and Dried Fruit, 82
Szechwan Chicken and Broccoli, 53

T
Taco seasoning
Chicken Tacos, 64
Mexican Pot Roast, 93
Salsa Lentils, 263
Spicy Nut and Pretzel Mix, 544
Spicy Pork Olé, 182
Tangy Chicken, 21

Indexes

Tex-Mex Chicken and
Rice, 63
Turkey Fajitas, 84
ıco Soup with Corn, 304
ıngy Chicken, 21
ıpioca
Blushing Apple Tapioca, 504
Classic Beef Stew, 113
Deluxe Tapioca Pudding,
503
Layered Herby Stew, 111
Pork Chops with
Mushroom Sauce, 171
Scandinavian Fruit Soup, 512
Szechwan Chicken and
Broccoli, 53
Vegetable Curry, 359
astes-Like-Chili-Rellenos, 245
asty Meatball Stew, 293
ea
Ginger Tea, 551
Slow-Cooker Chai, 548
ea Bread, 433
eriyaki Chicken, 61
exas Queso Dip, 531
ex-Mex Chicken and Rice, 63
hai Chicken, 60
hai Veggie Curry, 261
hree-Pepper Steak, 139
omato Basil Soup, 331
omato juice, 581. See also
Vegetable juice
Beef Barley Soup, 289
Mexican Rice and Beans,
251
Vegetable Beef Borscht, 282
omato sauce
Cranberry Brisket, 104
Creamy Tomato Soup, 330
Garbanzo Souper, 320
Good-Time Beef Brisket,
105
Italian Beef Stew, 123
Italian Sausage Spaghetti,
209
Melt-in-Your-Mouth
Sausages, 207
Ohio Chili, 299
Pepperoni Pizza Chili, 303
Red Beans and Rice, 390
Sausage, Tomato, Spinach
Soup, 313
Sausage Tortellini, 218
Spaghetti Sauce with a
Kick, 152
Tortellini with Broccoli, 244
Tomato soup
Creamy Tomato Soup, 330
Tomato Basil Soup, 331
Tuscan Beef Stew, 114
Tomatoes
Armenian Eggplant, 411
Arroz con Queso, 246
Baked Lentils with Cheese,
267
Baked Stuffed Tomatoes,
360

Baked Tomato Rarebit, 277
Black Bean and Butternut
Chili, 334
Black Bean Burritos, 248
Black Beans with Ham, 202
Blessing Soup, 319
Butter Chicken, 41
Cajun Sausage and Beans,
397
Can't Beet Beef Stew, 285
Cherry Tomato Spaghetti
Sauce, 227
Chicken Barley Chili, 305
Chicken Cacciatore with
Mushrooms, 55
Chicken Corn Chowder,
325
Chicken Marengo, 22
Chicken Tikka Masala, 35
Chicken Tortilla Soup, 307
Chipotle Chili, 308
Classic Beef Stew, 113
Classic Spinach Lasagna, 229
Corn Chili, 300
Cornbread-Topped Frijoles,
250
Creamy Ziti in the Crock,
237
Easy Black Bean Lasagna,
231
Enchilada Stack-Up, 151
Filled Acorn Squash, 273
Flaming Chicken Bombay,
33
Fresh Vegetables Pasta
Sauce, 221
Green Beans Get-Together,
345
Home-Style Tomato Juice,
578
Hungarian Goulash, 119
Italian Sausage Spaghetti,
209
Italiano Spread, 538
Layered Herby Stew, 111
Lentils Swiss Style, 265
Lotsa Veggies Spaghetti, 224
Mexican Chicken Bake, 65
Moroccan Beef Stew, 286
Moroccan Sweet Potato
Medley, 271
Mushroom Spaghetti Sauce,
225
Mushrooms Italian, 361
Norma's Vegetarian Chili,
333
Ohio Chili, 299
Old-Fashioned Vegetable
Beef Soup, 287
Overnight Veggie Omelet,
448
Pasta Bean Pot, 242
Pasta with Tomatoes, Olives,
and Two Cheeses, 223
Pepperoni Pizza Chili, 303
Pico de Gallo, 580
Pork Chops Pierre, 161

Powerhouse Beef Roast
with Tomatoes, Onions,
and Peppers, 87
Pumpkin Black-Bean Turkey
Chili, 339
Russian Red Lentil Soup,
321
Santa Fe Stew, 117
Sauerkraut Soup, 315
Sausage, Tomato, Spinach
Soup, 313
Sausage and Kale Stew with
Mashed Potatoes, 310
Sausage Tortellini, 218
Slow-Cooked Salsa, 579
Southern Italy Sauce, 228
Spaghetti Sauce with a
Kick, 152
Spanish Round Steak, 127
Spinach Frittata, 446
Summer Squash Lasagna,
233
Summer Veggie Bake, 276
Taco Soup with Corn, 304
Tastes-Like-Chili-Rellenos,
245
Texas Queso Dip, 531
Tex-Mex Chicken and
Rice, 63
Thai Veggie Curry, 261
Three-Pepper Steak, 139
Tomato Basil Soup, 331
Trail Chili, 295
Turkey Fajitas, 84
Tuscan Beef Stew, 114
Vegetable Beef Borscht, 282
Vegetable Curry, 359
Vegetable Party, 357
Vegetable Soup, 332
Winter's Night Beef Stew,
283
Zingy Short Ribs, 129
Zucchini Special, 353
Tomato-Glazed Pork with
Grilled Corn Salsa,
180–181
Top round roast
Sauerbraten, 110
Tortellini
Sausage Tortellini, 218
Tortellini with Broccoli, 244
Tortillas
Black Bean Burritos, 248
Double Corn Tortilla Bake,
247
Sweet Pepper Burritos, 249
Turkey Fajitas, 84
Trail Chili, 295
Triple Delicious Hot
Chocolate, 555
Turkey
Chicken Barley Chili, 305
Turkey bacon
Beans with Turkey Bacon,
394
Turkey breast
Herb-Roasted Turkey

Breast, 75
Indonesian Turkey, 79
Maple-Glazed Turkey Breast
with Rice, 78
Stuffed Turkey Breast, 77
Turkey Breast with Orange
Sauce, 76
Turkey cutlets
Barbecued Turkey Cutlets,
80
Turkey Fajitas, 84
Turkey sausage
Sausage, Tomato, Spinach
Soup, 313
Turkey tenderloin
Turkey Fajitas, 84
Turkey thighs
Parsley, Sage, and Ginger
Turkey, 81
Slow-Cooked Turkey
Dinner, 83
Turkey with Sweet Potatoes
and Dried Fruit, 82
Turkey with Sweet Potatoes
and Dried Fruit, 82
Tuscan Beef Stew, 114

V
Vanilla Steamer, 557
Vegetable Beef Borscht, 282
Vegetable broth, 566
Vegetable Curry, 359
Vegetable juice
Beef Barley Soup, 289
Mexican Rice and Beans,
251
Tasty Meatball Stew, 293
Vegetable Party, 357
Vegetable Soup, 332
Vegetable stock
Thai Veggie Curry, 261
Tomato Basil Soup, 331
Vegetables with Red Quinoa,
269
Vegetarian Lasagna, 235
Veggie Mac and Cheese, 238
Venison roast
Middle East Sandwiches,
145
Peppery Roast, 91
Vietnamese Coffee, 558

W
Walnuts
Apple Cake, 474
Apple Cider Cinnamon
Steel-Cut Oatmeal, 453
Apple Oatmeal, 452
Autumn Sweet Potatoes,
387
Boston Brown Bread, 424
Cherry Delight, 472
Date and Nut Bread, 427
Granola in the Slow
Cooker, 455
Herbal Apple Cheese Dish,
278

Oatmeal Morning, 451
Orange Slice Cake, 486
Raisin Nut-Stuffed Apples,
507
Spicy Nut and Pretzel Mix,
544
Whole Cranberry Sauce,
515
Zucchini Bread, 429
Water chestnuts
Teriyaki Chicken, 61
Welsh Rarebit, 441
Western Omelet, 444
Wheat Berries in the Slow
Cooker, 569
White chocolate
Chocolate Covered
Pretzels, 522
Easy Chocolate Clusters,
521
Triple Delicious Hot
Chocolate, 555
White Chocolate Bread
Pudding, 499
White raisins
Ham in Cider, 201
Whole Cranberry Sauce, 515
Wild rice
Chicken Rice Soup, 322
Fruity Wild Rice with
Pecans, 366
Party Wild Rice, 365
Ready-When-You-Get-
Home Dinner, 115
Wild Rice, 363
Wild Rice Bake, 363

Wild rice mix
Maple-Glazed Turkey Breast
with Rice, 78
Wine
burgundy
Beef Burgundy, 121
Oxford Canal Chops
Deluxe, 167
red
Bavarian Beef, 99
Classic Spinach Lasagna,
229
Cranberry Sauce with
Red Wine and
Oranges, 517
Easy Creamy Beef, 118
French Onion Soup, 340
Italian Beef Stew, 123
Layered Herby Stew, 111
Middle East Sandwiches,
145
Saucy Mushrooms, 362
Sausage Tortellini, 218
Sausages in Wine, 542
Savory Slow Cooker
Pork Tenderloin, 179
Scandinavian Fruit Soup,
512
Winter's Night Beef
Stew, 283
Zingy Short Ribs, 129
sauterne
Zesty Pears, 506
Slow-Cooked Short Ribs,
131
white

Basil Chicken, 24
Chicken Cacciatore with
Mushrooms, 55
Chicken Marengo, 22
Herbed Rice and Lentil
Bake, 260
Herb-Roasted Turkey
Breast, 75
Parsley, Sage, and Ginger
Turkey, 81
Pork Chops with
Mushroom Sauce,
171
Stuffed Turkey Breast, 77
Wine Tender Roast, 95
Wing sauce
Cheesy Buffalo Chicken
Pasta, 57
Winter's Night Beef Stew, 283

Y
Yams. See also Sweet potatoes
Fruity Sweet Potatoes, 386
Turkey with Sweet Potatoes
and Dried Fruit, 82
Yellow squash
Brown Rice Vegetable
Dinner, 255
Fresh Vegetables Pasta
Sauce, 221
Summer Squash Delish, 352
Yogurt, 577
Chicken Tikka Masala, 35
Creamy Artichoke Dip, 537
Curried Carrot Ginger
Soup, 337

Curried Lentils, 266
Dad's Spicy Chicken Curry,
29
Dates in Cardamom Coffee
Syrup, 519
Hearty Irish Soda Bread,
423
Make-Ahead Mixed
Potatoes Florentine, 377
Middle East Sandwiches,
145
Quick Broccoli Fix, 406
Russian Red Lentil Soup,
321
Vegetables with Red
Quinoa, 269
Yummy Spinach, 343

Z
Zesty Pears, 506
Zingy Short Ribs, 129
Zucchini
Brown Rice Vegetable
Dinner, 255
Minestrone, 318
Santa Fe Stew, 117
Sausage Tortellini, 218
Summer Squash Delish, 35
Summer Squash Lasagna,
233
Summer Veggie Bake, 276
Vegetable Party, 357
Zucchini Bread, 429
Zucchini Special, 353
Zucchini Torte, 275

Quick & Easy Recipe Index

A
Apple Raisin Ham, 197

B
Bacon Ranch Slow-Cooked
Chicken, 43
Basil Chicken, 24
BBQ Pork Ribs, 196
Beef Ribs with Sauerkraut,
133
Black Forest Cake, 481

C
Caramel Rolls, 438
Championship Bean Dip, 533
Cherry Delight, 472
Chicken, Sweet Chicken, 59
Chicken Dijon Dinner, 16
Chili-Taco Soup, 294
Chocolate Rice Pudding, 502
Cranberry Brisket, 104

Cranberry Orange Pork
Roast, 190
Curried Almonds, 543

E
Easy Autumn Cake, 475
Easy Creamy Beef, 118
Easy Rice Pudding, 501

F
Fajita Steak, 141

G
Garlic Lime Chicken, 13
Green Beans and Sausage,
214

H
Herby Barbecued Chicken, 67
Honey Garlic Chicken, 19
Honey-Mustard Chicken, 18
Hot Cheddar Mushroom

Spread, 540
Hot Chili Dip, 535
Hot Fruit, 412
Hot Spicy Lemonade Punch,
549

M
Marshmallow Applesauce
Dessert, 505
Matthew's Hot Mulled Cider,
554
Mexican Pot Roast, 93
Mexican Rice and Beans, 251

P
Piquant Chuck Roast, 92
Pork Chops with Mushroom
Sauce, 171
Pork Roast with Sauerkraut,
191

Q
Quick Yummy Peaches, 470

R
Rosemary New Potatoes, 38

S
So-Simple Salsa Chicken, 62
Southwest Cranberries, 518
Spicy Nut and Pretzel Mix,
544
Spicy Pork Chops, 157
Steel-Cut Oats with Bananas,
454

T
Tangy Chicken, 21
Tortellini with Broccoli, 244

W
Wine Tender Roast, 95

Indexes